THE MAGICIANS
ALICE'S STORY

STORY BASED ON THE NOVEL *THE MAGICIANS* BY **LEV GROSSMAN**.

WRITTEN BY
LILAH STURGES

ILLUSTRATED BY
PIUS BAK

COLORED BY
DAN JACKSON

LETTERED BY
MIKE FIORENTINO

Published by
ARCHAIA™

Los Angeles, California

COVER ART BY
STEVE MORRIS

DESIGN BY
SCOTT NEWMAN

ASSOCIATE EDITOR
SOPHIE PHILIPS-ROBERTS

EDITOR
SIERRA HAHN

10TH ANNIVERSARY EDITION
COVER ART AND DESIGN BY **SCOTT NEWMAN**

Ross Richie CEO & Founder
Joy Huffman CFO
Matt Gagnon Editor-in-Chief
Filip Sablik President, Publishing & Marketing
Stephen Christy President, Development
Lance Kreiter Vice President, Licensing & Merchandising
Arune Singh Vice President, Marketing
Bryce Carlson Vice President, Editorial & Creative Strategy
Scott Newman Manager, Production Design
Kate Henning Manager, Operations
Spencer Simpson Manager, Sales
Sierra Hahn Executive Editor
Jeanine Schaefer Executive Editor
Dafna Pleban Senior Editor
Shannon Watters Senior Editor
Eric Harburn Senior Editor
Chris Rosa Editor
Matthew Levine Editor
Sophie Philips-Roberts Associate Editor
Gavin Gronenthal Assistant Editor

Michael Moccio Assistant Editor
Gwen Waller Assistant Editor
Amanda LaFranco Executive Assistant
Jillian Crab Design Coordinator
Michelle Ankley Design Coordinator
Kara Leopard Production Designer
Marie Krupina Production Designer
Grace Park Production Designer
Chelsea Roberts Production Design Assistant
Samantha Knapp Production Design Assistant
José Meza Live Events Lead
Stephanie Hocutt Digital Marketing Lead
Esther Kim Marketing Coordinator
Cat O'Grady Digital Marketing Coordinator
Holly Aitchison Digital Sales Coordinator
Morgan Perry Retail Sales Coordinator
Megan Christopher Operations Coordinator
Rodrigo Hernandez Mailroom Assistant
Zipporah Smith Operations Assistant
Breanna Sarpy Executive Assistant

 **ARCHAIA**™

THE MAGICIANS: ALICE'S STORY, July 2019. Published by Archaia, a division of Boom Entertainment, Inc. The Magicians is ™ & © 2019 Lev Grossman. All rights reserved. Archaia™ and the Archaia logo are trademarks of Boom Entertainment, Inc., registered in various countries and categories. All characters, events, and institutions depicted herein are fictional. Any similarity between any of the names, characters, persons, events, and/or institutions in this publication to actual names, characters, and persons, whether living or dead, events, and/or institutions is unintended and purely coincidental.

BOOM! Studios, 5670 Wilshire Boulevard, Suite 450, Los Angeles, CA 90036-5679. Printed in China. First Printing.

ISBN: 978-1-68415-021-2, eISBN: 978-1-61398-698-1

10th Anniversary Edition
ISBN: 978-1-68415-382-4, eISBN: 978-1-64144-365-4

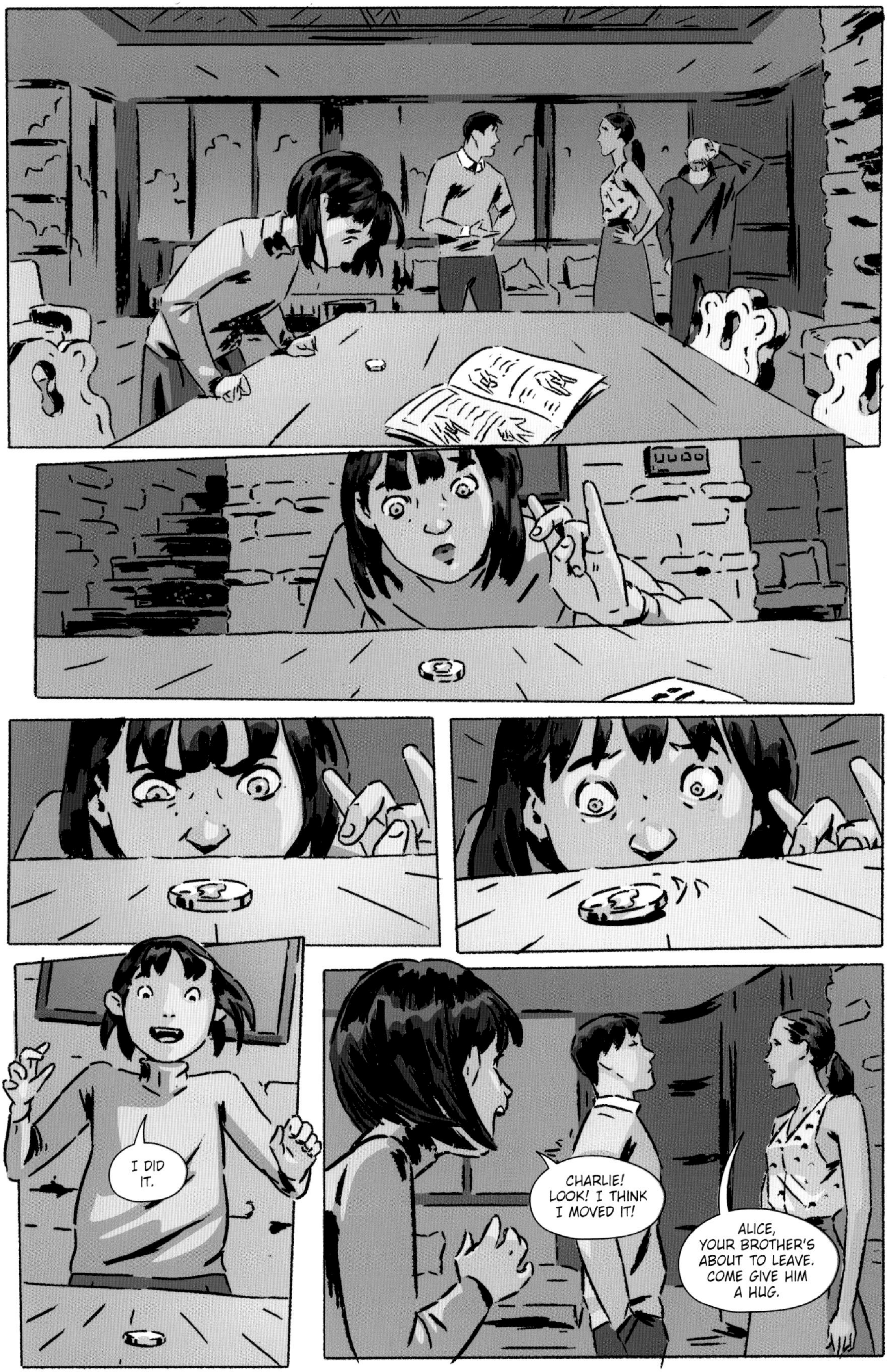
I DID IT.
CHARLIE! LOOK! I THINK I MOVED IT!
ALICE, YOUR BROTHER'S ABOUT TO LEAVE. COME GIVE HIM A HUG.

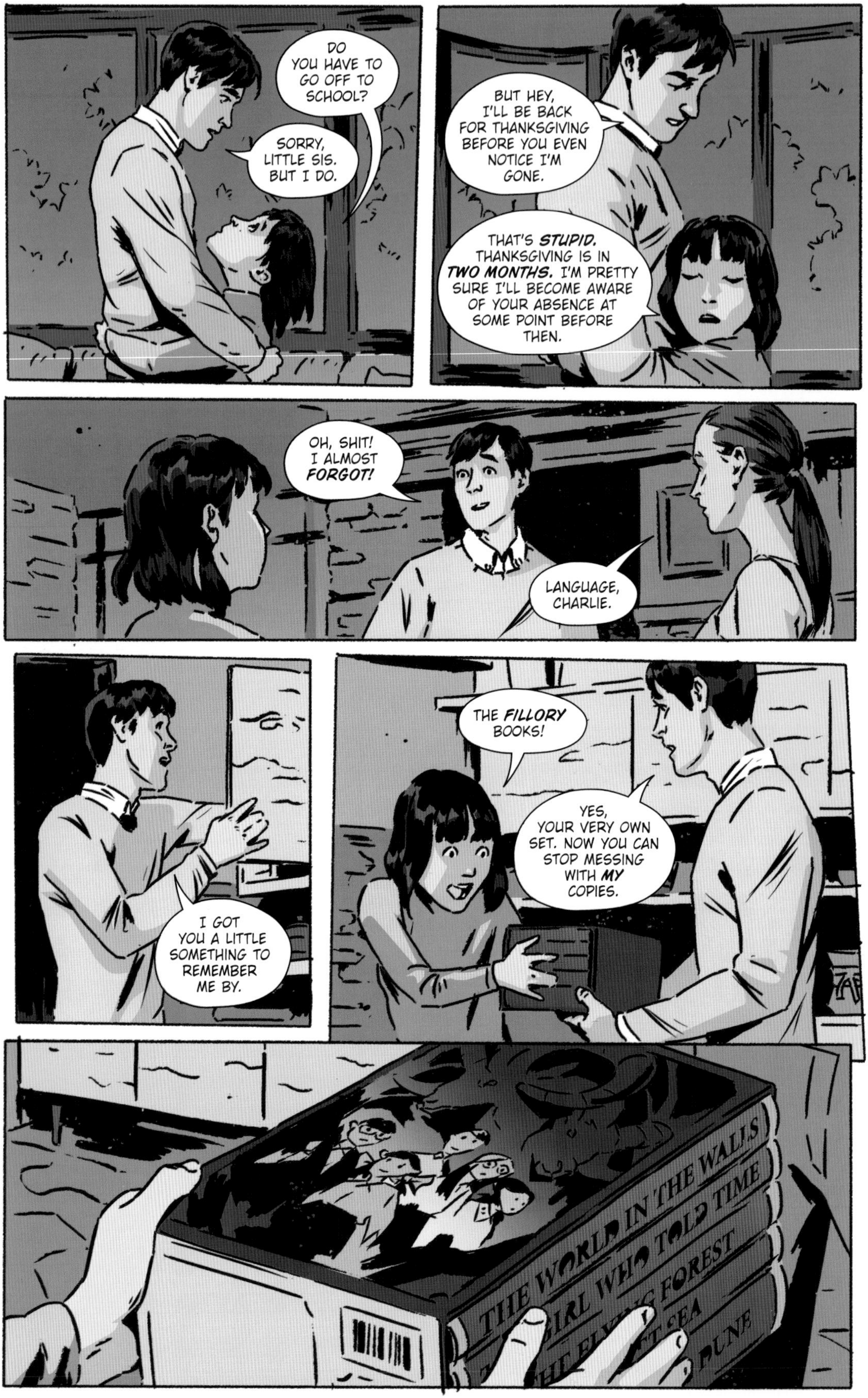
DO YOU HAVE TO GO OFF TO SCHOOL?
SORRY, LITTLE SIS. BUT I DO.
BUT HEY, I'LL BE BACK FOR THANKSGIVING BEFORE YOU EVEN NOTICE I'M GONE.
THAT'S STUPID. THANKSGIVING IS IN TWO MONTHS. I'M PRETTY SURE I'LL BECOME AWARE OF YOUR ABSENCE AT SOME POINT BEFORE THEN.
OH, SHIT! I ALMOST FORGOT!
LANGUAGE, CHARLIE.
I GOT YOU A LITTLE SOMETHING TO REMEMBER ME BY.
THE FILLORY BOOKS!
YES, YOUR VERY OWN SET. NOW YOU CAN STOP MESSING WITH MY COPIES.
THE WORLD IN THE WALLS
GIRL WHO TOLD TIME
THE FLYING FOREST

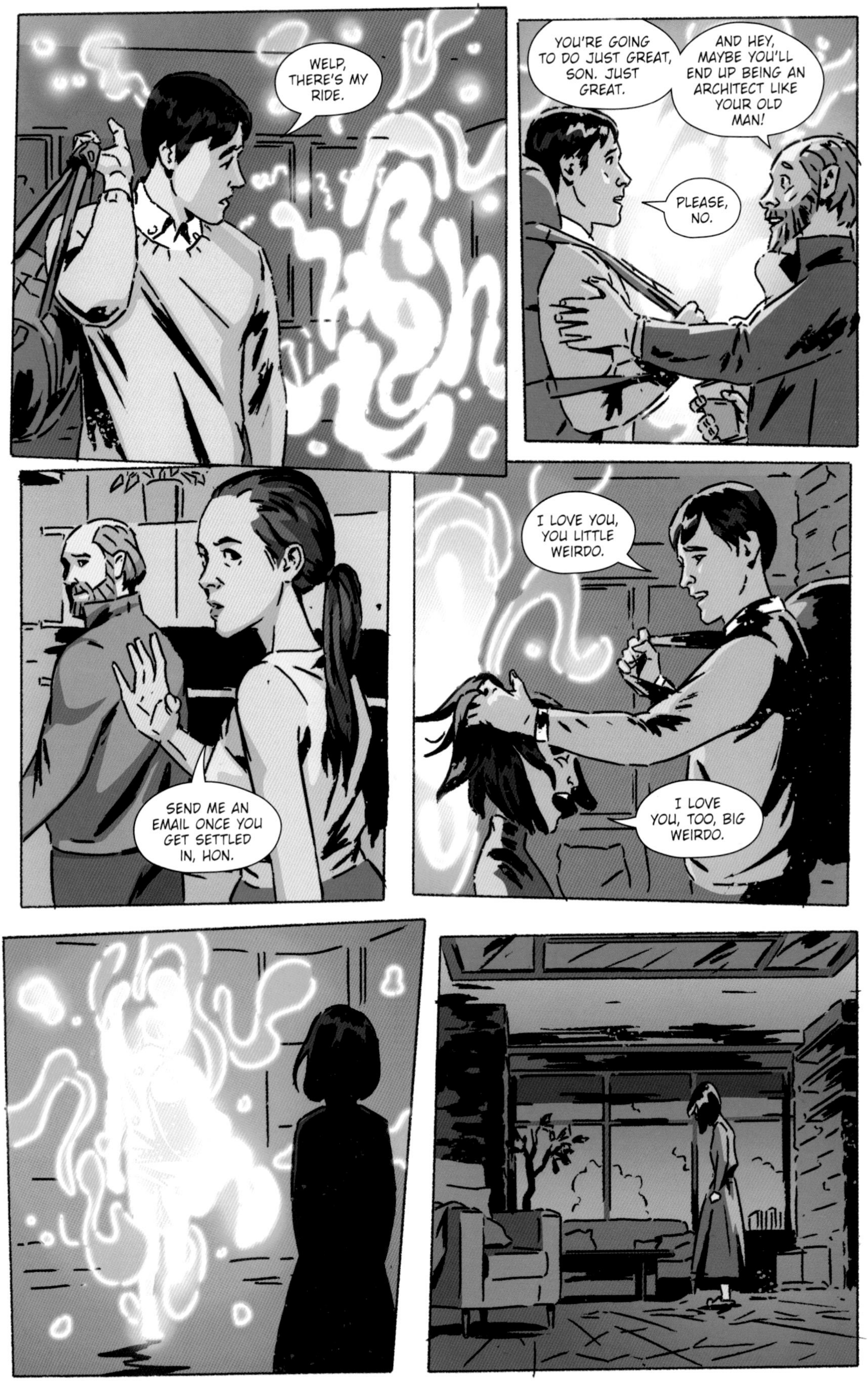
WELP, THERE'S MY RIDE.
YOU'RE GOING TO DO JUST GREAT, SON. JUST GREAT.
AND HEY, MAYBE YOU'LL END UP BEING AN ARCHITECT LIKE YOUR OLD MAN!
PLEASE, NO.
SEND ME AN EMAIL ONCE YOU GET SETTLED IN, HON.
I LOVE YOU, YOU LITTLE WEIRDO.
I LOVE YOU, TOO, BIG WEIRDO.

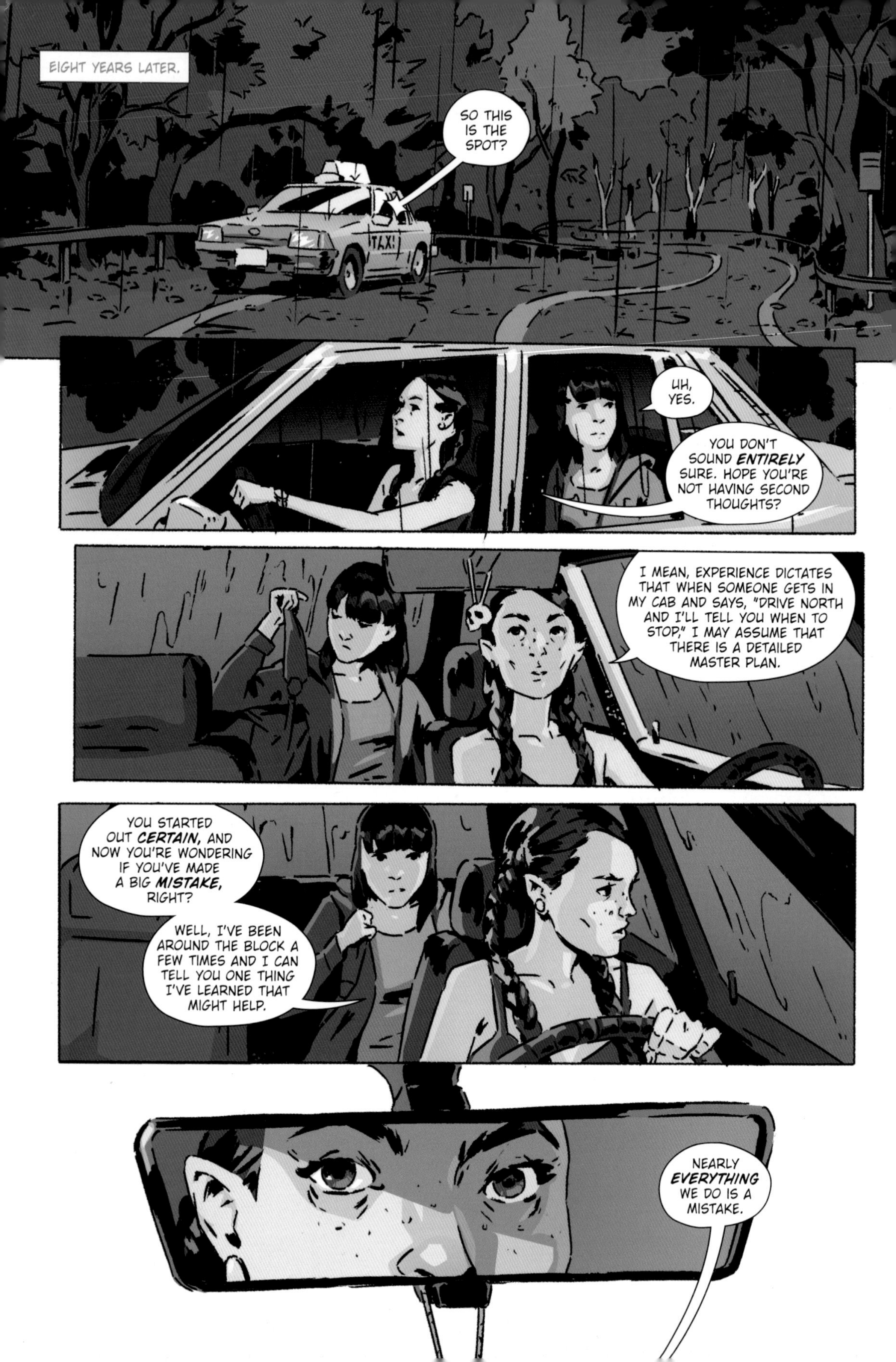
EIGHT YEARS LATER.
SO THIS IS THE SPOT?
UH, YES.
YOU DON'T SOUND ENTIRELY SURE. HOPE YOU'RE NOT HAVING SECOND THOUGHTS?
I MEAN, EXPERIENCE DICTATES THAT WHEN SOMEONE GETS IN MY CAB AND SAYS, "DRIVE NORTH AND I'LL TELL YOU WHEN TO STOP," I MAY ASSUME THAT THERE IS A DETAILED MASTER PLAN.
YOU STARTED OUT CERTAIN, AND NOW YOU'RE WONDERING IF YOU'VE MADE A BIG MISTAKE, RIGHT?
WELL, I'VE BEEN AROUND THE BLOCK A FEW TIMES AND I CAN TELL YOU ONE THING I'VE LEARNED THAT MIGHT HELP.
NEARLY EVERYTHING WE DO IS A MISTAKE.

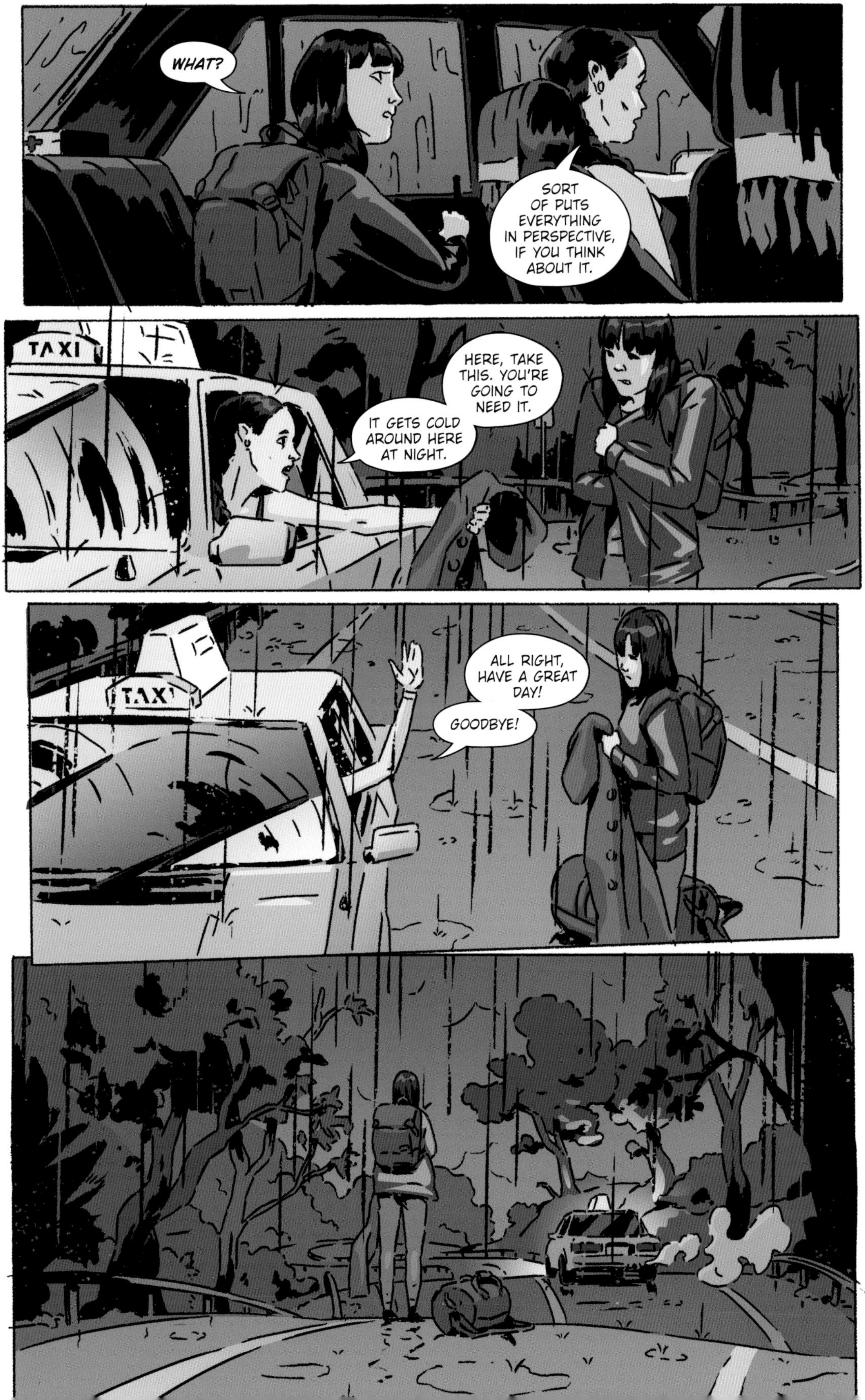
WHAT?
SORT OF PUTS EVERYTHING IN PERSPECTIVE, IF YOU THINK ABOUT IT.
TAXI
HERE, TAKE THIS. YOU'RE GOING TO NEED IT.
IT GETS COLD AROUND HERE AT NIGHT.
ALL RIGHT, HAVE A GREAT DAY!
GOODBYE!

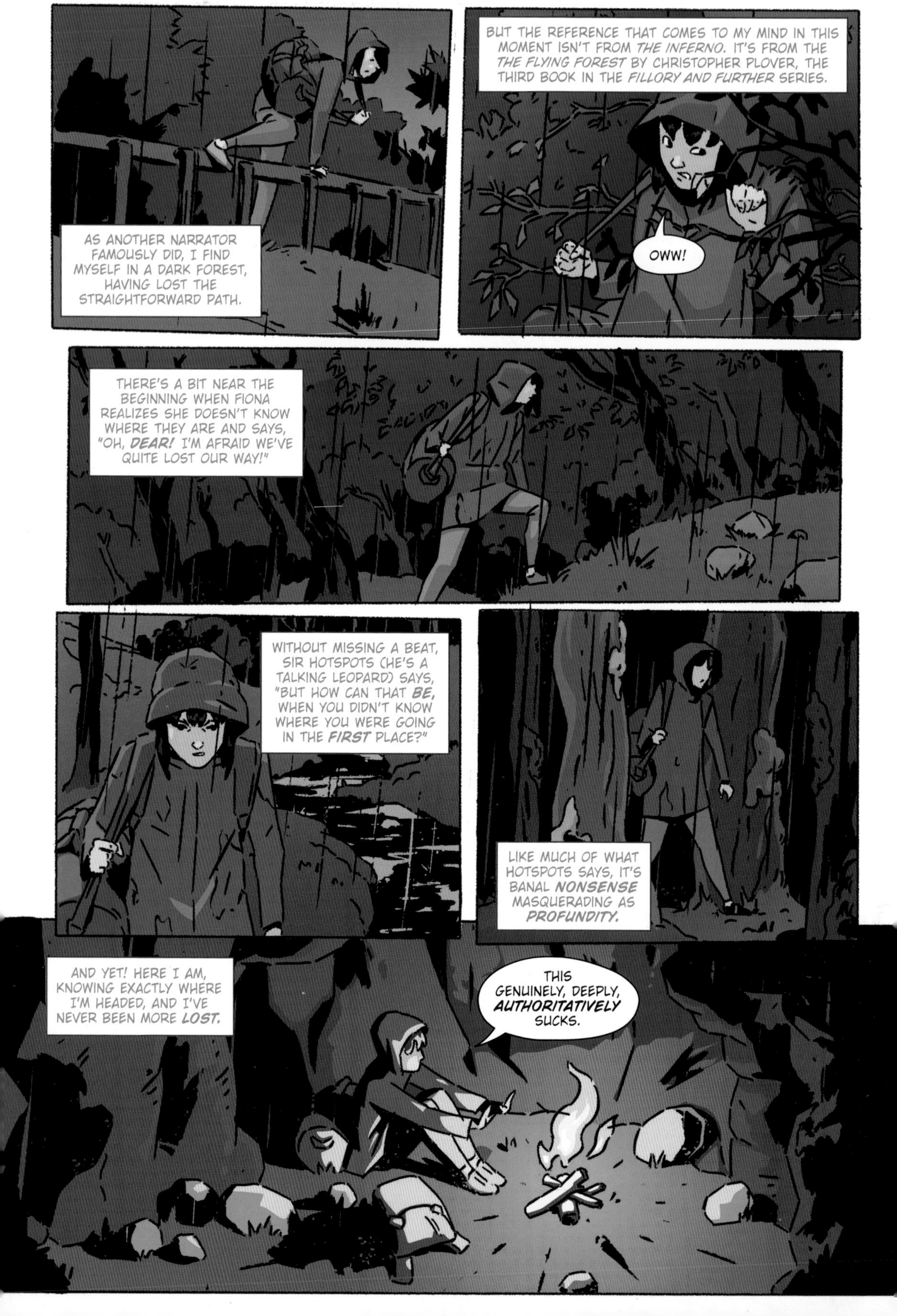
AS ANOTHER NARRATOR FAMOUSLY DID, I FIND MYSELF IN A DARK FOREST, HAVING LOST THE STRAIGHTFORWARD PATH.
BUT THE REFERENCE THAT COMES TO MY MIND IN THIS MOMENT ISN'T FROM *THE INFERNO.* IT'S FROM THE *THE FLYING FOREST* BY CHRISTOPHER PLOVER, THE THIRD BOOK IN THE *FILLORY AND FURTHER* SERIES.
OWW!
THERE'S A BIT NEAR THE BEGINNING WHEN FIONA REALIZES SHE DOESN'T KNOW WHERE THEY ARE AND SAYS, "OH, ***DEAR!*** I'M AFRAID WE'VE QUITE LOST OUR WAY!"
WITHOUT MISSING A BEAT, SIR HOTSPOTS (HE'S A TALKING LEOPARD) SAYS, "BUT HOW CAN THAT ***BE,*** WHEN YOU DIDN'T KNOW WHERE YOU WERE GOING IN THE ***FIRST*** PLACE?"
LIKE MUCH OF WHAT HOTSPOTS SAYS, IT'S BANAL ***NONSENSE*** MASQUERADING AS ***PROFUNDITY.***
AND YET! HERE I AM, KNOWING EXACTLY WHERE I'M HEADED, AND I'VE NEVER BEEN MORE ***LOST.***
THIS GENUINELY, DEEPLY, ***AUTHORITATIVELY*** SUCKS.

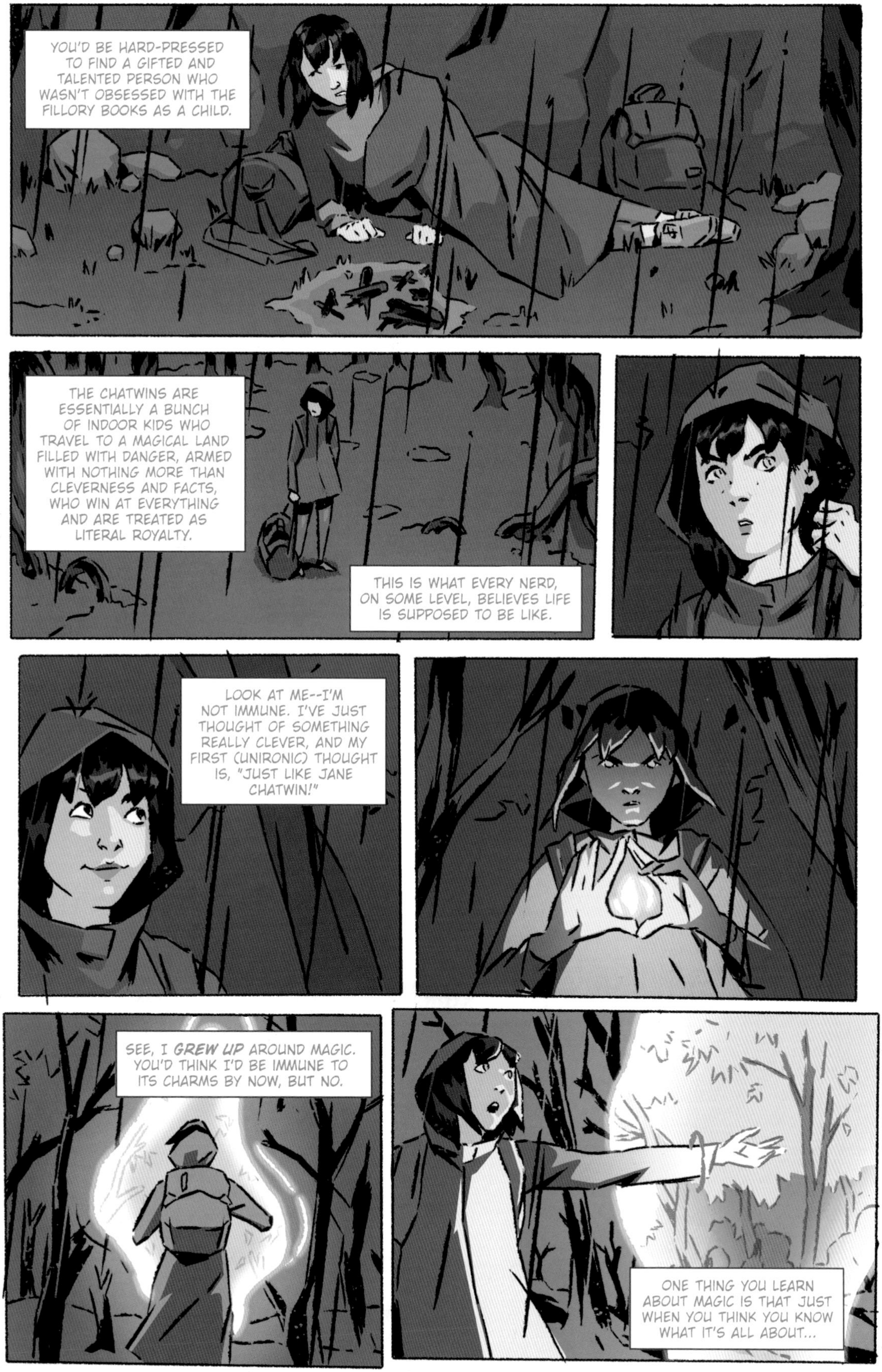
YOU'D BE HARD-PRESSED TO FIND A GIFTED AND TALENTED PERSON WHO WASN'T OBSESSED WITH THE FILLORY BOOKS AS A CHILD.
THE CHATWINS ARE ESSENTIALLY A BUNCH OF INDOOR KIDS WHO TRAVEL TO A MAGICAL LAND FILLED WITH DANGER, ARMED WITH NOTHING MORE THAN CLEVERNESS AND FACTS, WHO WIN AT EVERYTHING AND ARE TREATED AS LITERAL ROYALTY.
THIS IS WHAT EVERY NERD, ON SOME LEVEL, BELIEVES LIFE IS SUPPOSED TO BE LIKE.
LOOK AT ME--I'M NOT IMMUNE. I'VE JUST THOUGHT OF SOMETHING REALLY CLEVER, AND MY FIRST (UNIRONIC) THOUGHT IS, "JUST LIKE JANE CHATWIN!"
SEE, I ***GREW UP*** AROUND MAGIC. YOU'D THINK I'D BE IMMUNE TO ITS CHARMS BY NOW, BUT NO.
ONE THING YOU LEARN ABOUT MAGIC IS THAT JUST WHEN YOU THINK YOU KNOW WHAT IT'S ALL ABOUT...

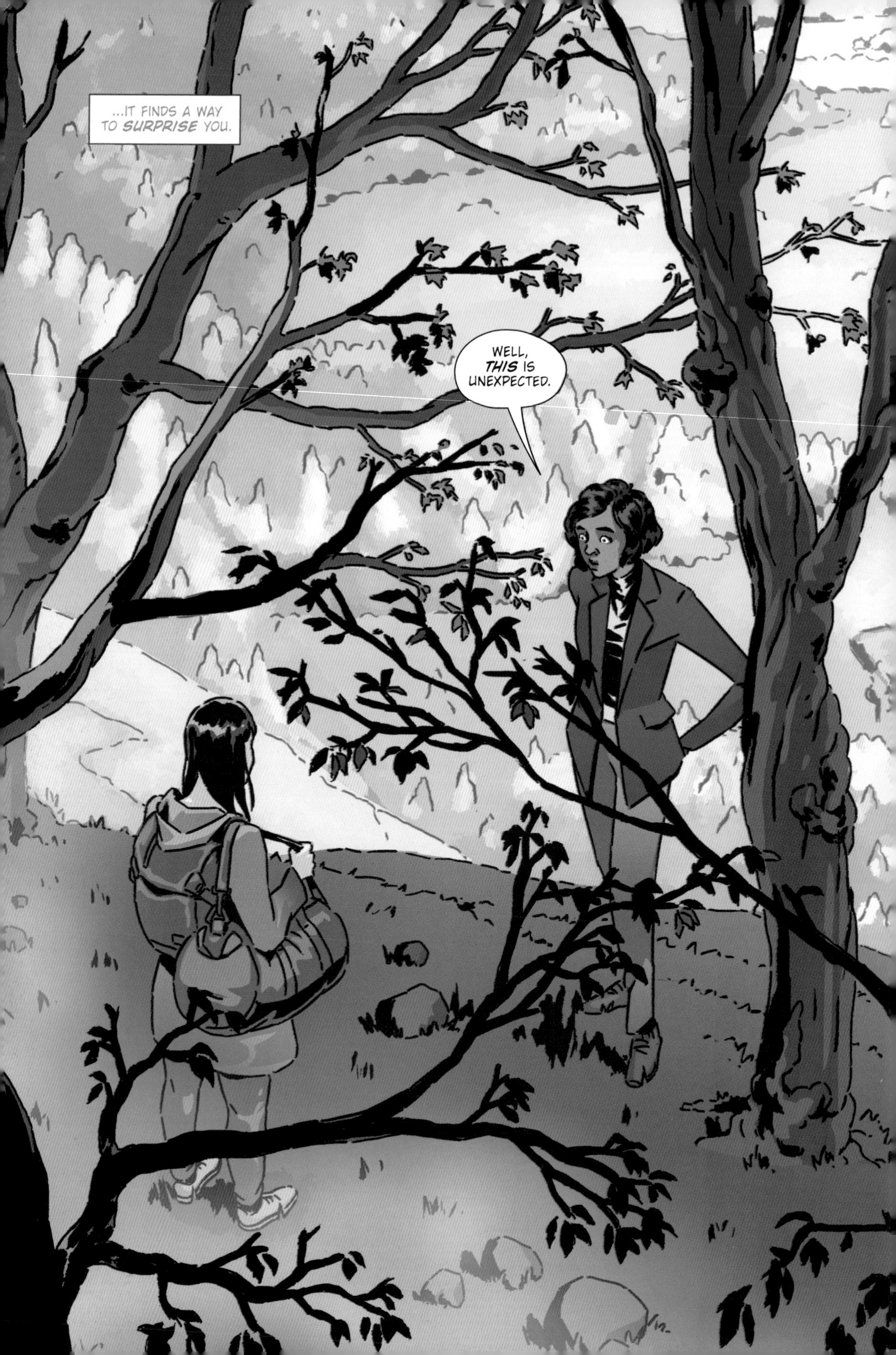
...IT FINDS A WAY TO *SURPRISE* YOU.
WELL, *THIS* IS UNEXPECTED.

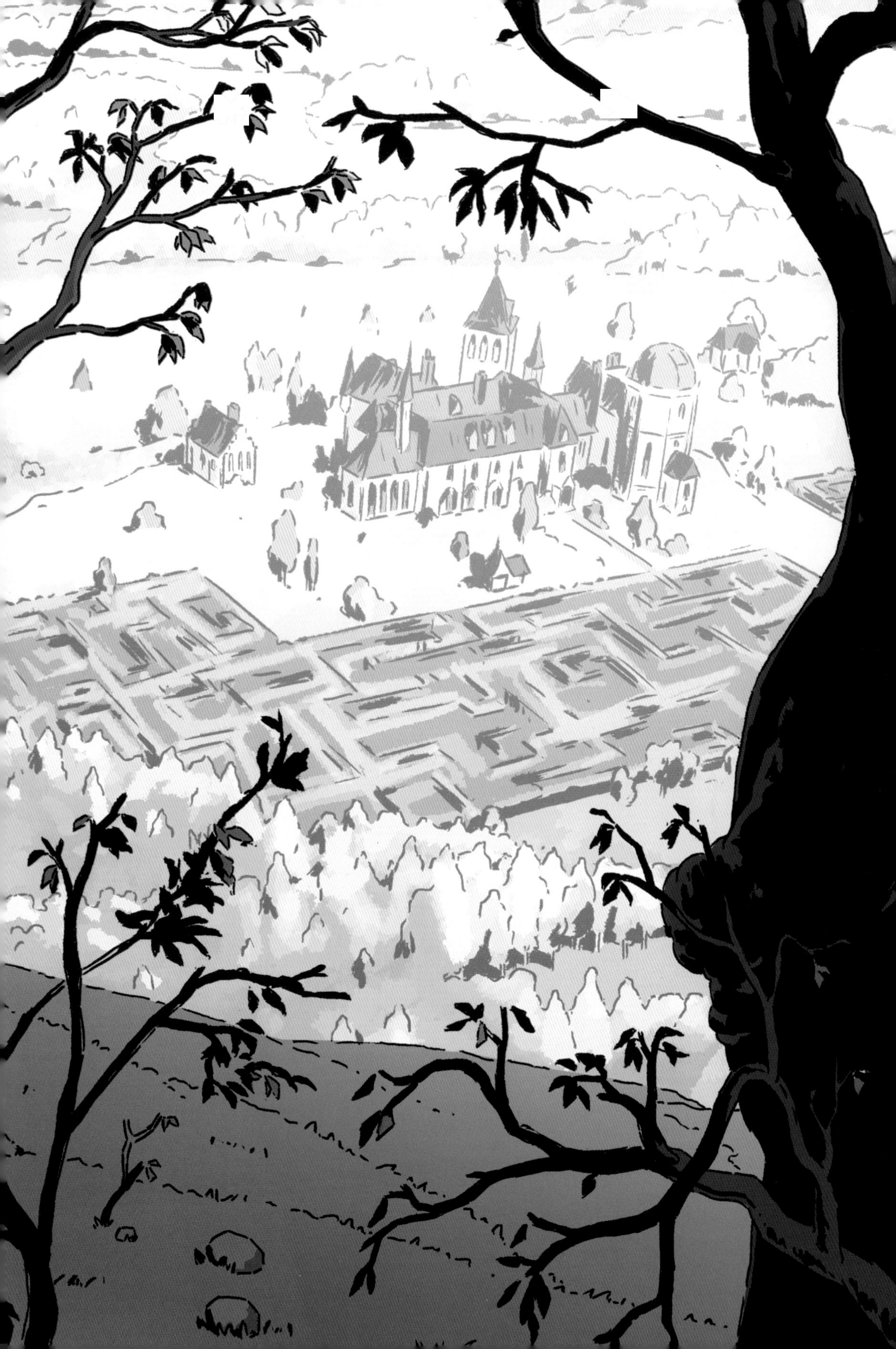

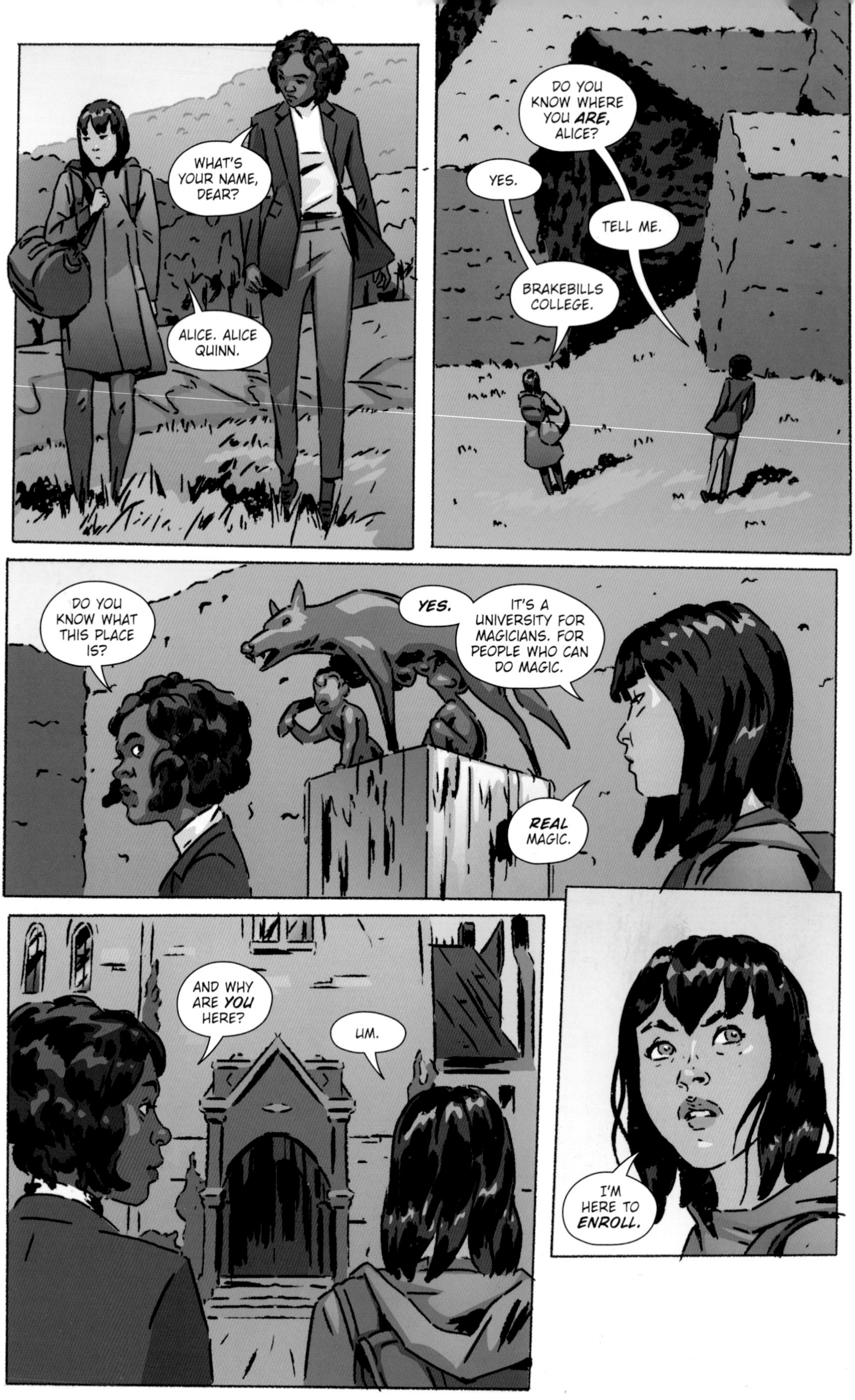
WHAT'S YOUR NAME, DEAR?
ALICE. ALICE QUINN.
DO YOU KNOW WHERE YOU **ARE,** ALICE?
YES.
TELL ME.
BRAKEBILLS COLLEGE.
DO YOU KNOW WHAT THIS PLACE IS?
YES.
IT'S A UNIVERSITY FOR MAGICIANS. FOR PEOPLE WHO CAN DO MAGIC.
REAL MAGIC.
AND WHY ARE ***YOU*** HERE?
UM.
I'M HERE TO ***ENROLL.***

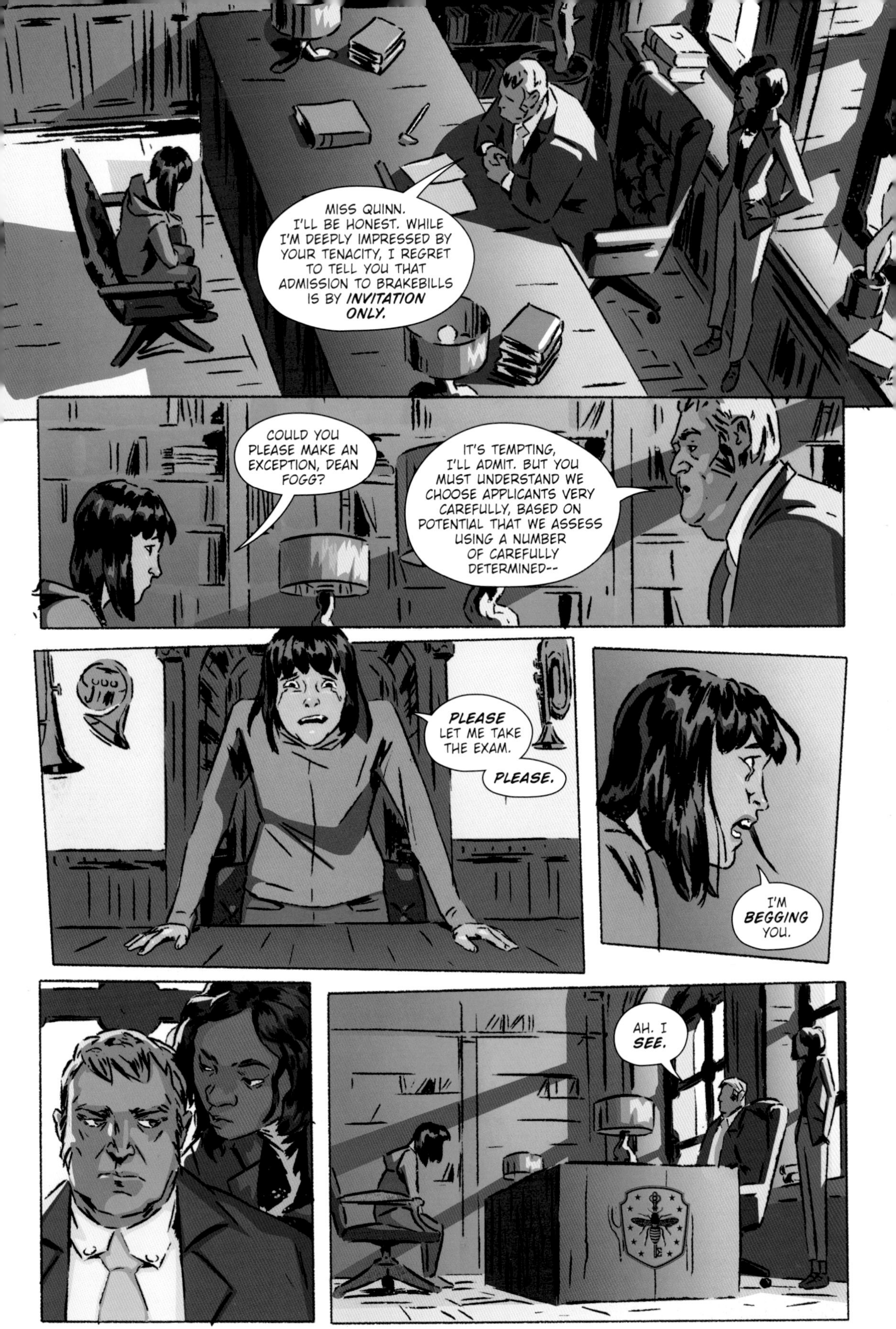

MISS QUINN. I'LL BE HONEST. WHILE I'M DEEPLY IMPRESSED BY YOUR TENACITY, I REGRET TO TELL YOU THAT ADMISSION TO BRAKEBILLS IS BY ***INVITATION ONLY.***
COULD YOU PLEASE MAKE AN EXCEPTION, DEAN FOGG?
IT'S TEMPTING, I'LL ADMIT. BUT YOU MUST UNDERSTAND WE CHOOSE APPLICANTS VERY CAREFULLY, BASED ON POTENTIAL THAT WE ASSESS USING A NUMBER OF CAREFULLY DETERMINED--
PLEASE LET ME TAKE THE EXAM.
PLEASE.
I'M ***BEGGING*** YOU.
AH. I ***SEE.***

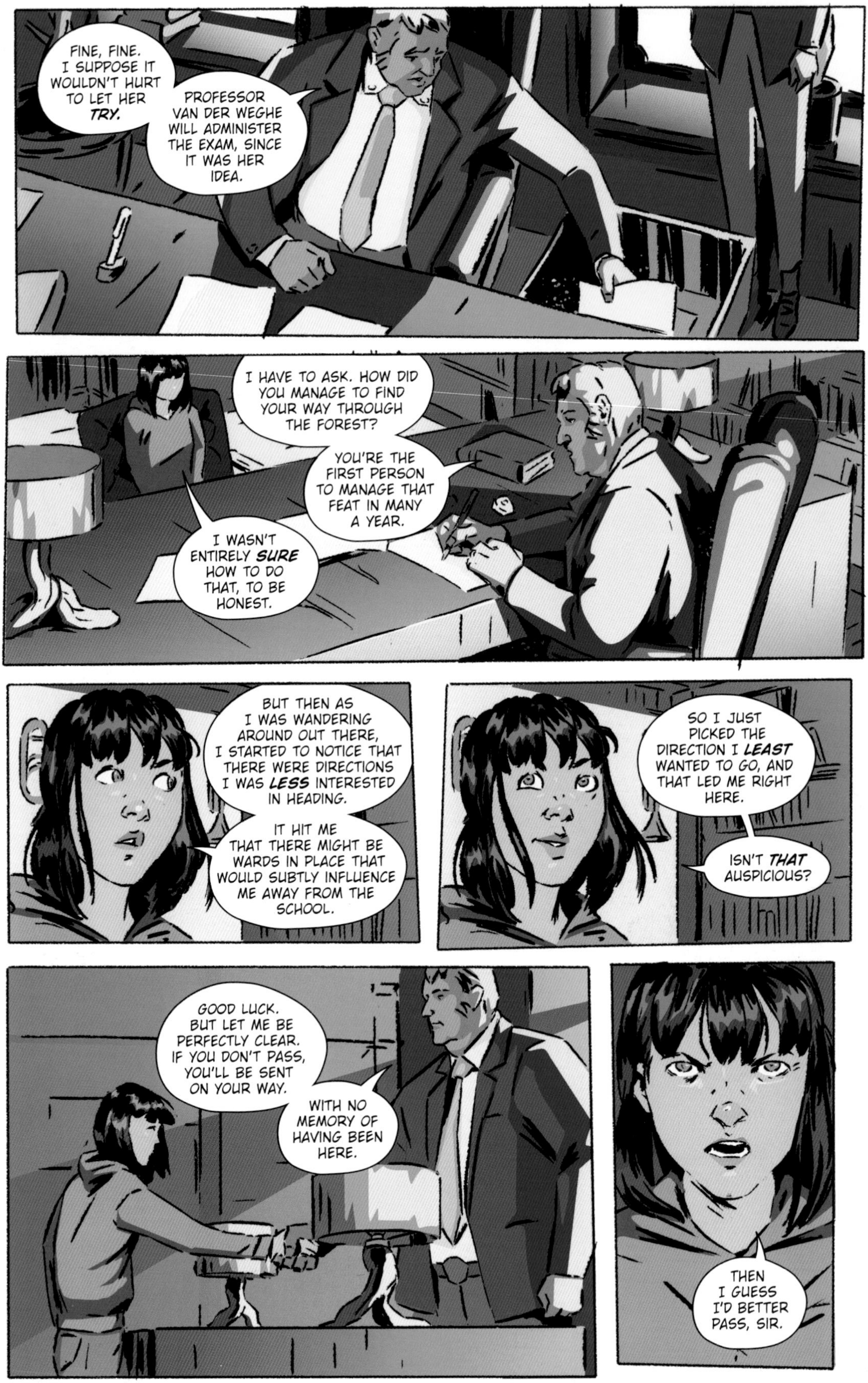
FINE, FINE. I SUPPOSE IT WOULDN'T HURT TO LET HER TRY.
PROFESSOR VAN DER WEGHE WILL ADMINISTER THE EXAM, SINCE IT WAS HER IDEA.
I HAVE TO ASK. HOW DID YOU MANAGE TO FIND YOUR WAY THROUGH THE FOREST?
YOU'RE THE FIRST PERSON TO MANAGE THAT FEAT IN MANY A YEAR.
I WASN'T ENTIRELY SURE HOW TO DO THAT, TO BE HONEST.
BUT THEN AS I WAS WANDERING AROUND OUT THERE, I STARTED TO NOTICE THAT THERE WERE DIRECTIONS I WAS LESS INTERESTED IN HEADING.
IT HIT ME THAT THERE MIGHT BE WARDS IN PLACE THAT WOULD SUBTLY INFLUENCE ME AWAY FROM THE SCHOOL.
SO I JUST PICKED THE DIRECTION I LEAST WANTED TO GO, AND THAT LED ME RIGHT HERE.
ISN'T THAT AUSPICIOUS?
GOOD LUCK. BUT LET ME BE PERFECTLY CLEAR. IF YOU DON'T PASS, YOU'LL BE SENT ON YOUR WAY.
WITH NO MEMORY OF HAVING BEEN HERE.
THEN I GUESS I'D BETTER PASS, SIR.

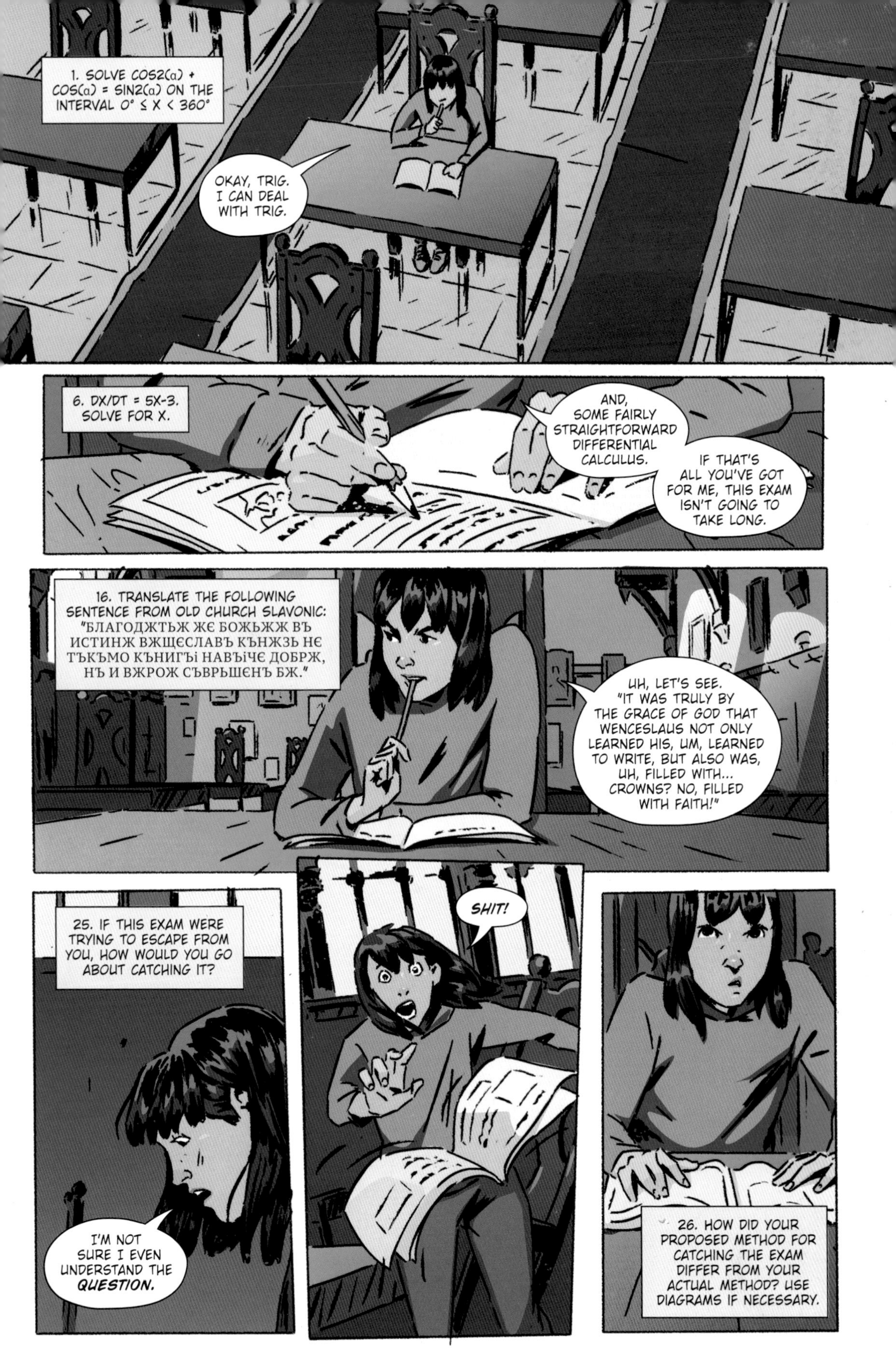

1. SOLVE COS2(a) + COS(a) = SIN2(a) ON THE INTERVAL 0° ≤ X < 360°
OKAY, TRIG. I CAN DEAL WITH TRIG.
6. DX/DT = 5X-3. SOLVE FOR X.
AND, SOME FAIRLY STRAIGHTFORWARD DIFFERENTIAL CALCULUS.
IF THAT'S ALL YOU'VE GOT FOR ME, THIS EXAM ISN'T GOING TO TAKE LONG.
16. TRANSLATE THE FOLLOWING SENTENCE FROM OLD CHURCH SLAVONIC: "БЛАГОДЖТЬЖ ЖЄ БОЖЬЖЖ ВЪ ИСТИНЖ ВЖЩЄСЛАВЪ КЪНЖЗЬ НЄ ТЪКЪМО КЪНИГЪі НАВЪіЧЄ ДОБРЖ, НЪ И ВЖРОЖ СЪВРЬШЄНЪ БЖ."
UH, LET'S SEE. "IT WAS TRULY BY THE GRACE OF GOD THAT WENCESLAUS NOT ONLY LEARNED HIS, UM, LEARNED TO WRITE, BUT ALSO WAS, UH, FILLED WITH... CROWNS? NO, FILLED WITH FAITH!"
25. IF THIS EXAM WERE TRYING TO ESCAPE FROM YOU, HOW WOULD YOU GO ABOUT CATCHING IT?
I'M NOT SURE I EVEN UNDERSTAND THE QUESTION.
SHIT!
26. HOW DID YOUR PROPOSED METHOD FOR CATCHING THE EXAM DIFFER FROM YOUR ACTUAL METHOD? USE DIAGRAMS IF NECESSARY.

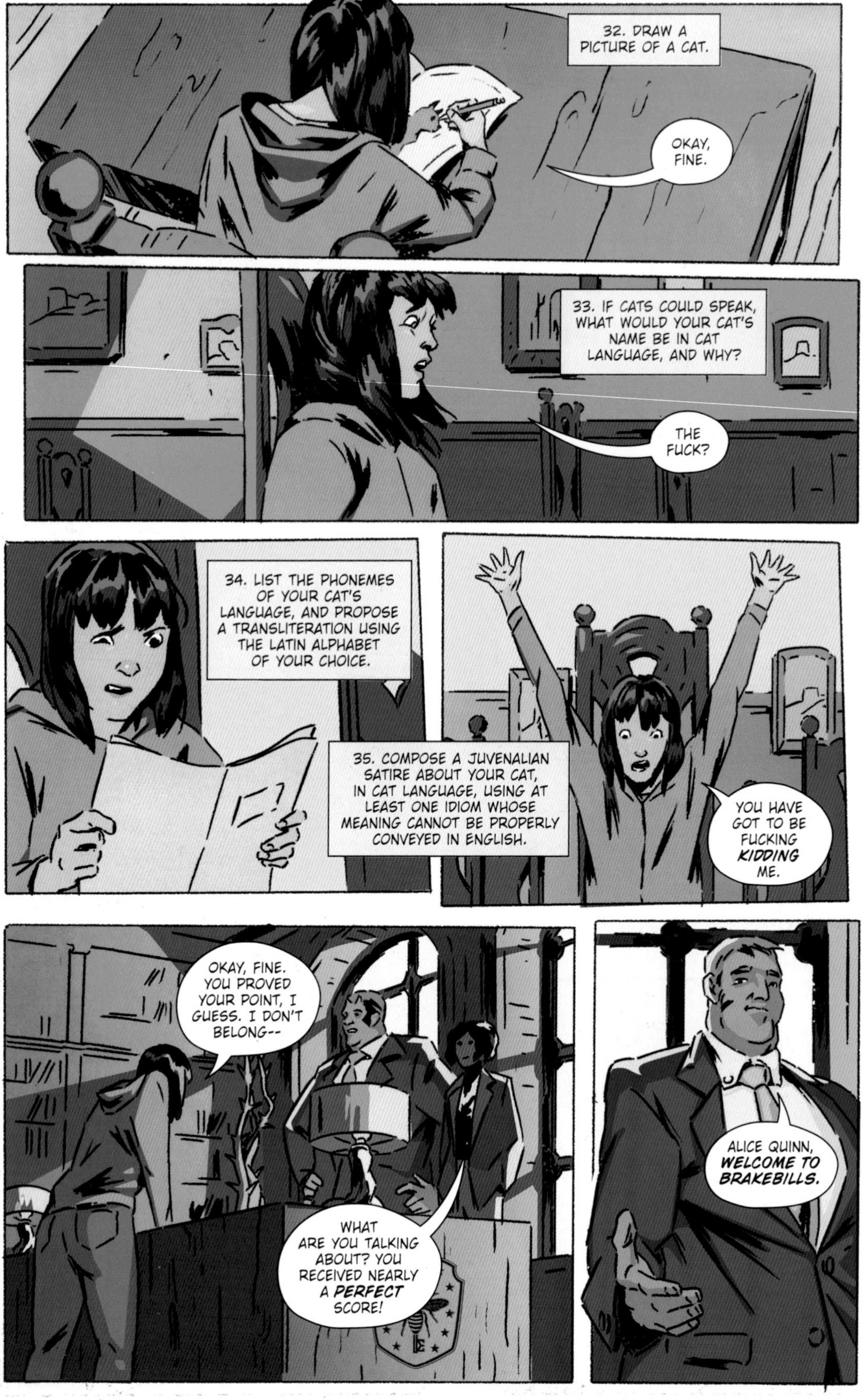
32. DRAW A PICTURE OF A CAT.
OKAY, FINE.
33. IF CATS COULD SPEAK, WHAT WOULD YOUR CAT'S NAME BE IN CAT LANGUAGE, AND WHY?
THE FUCK?
34. LIST THE PHONEMES OF YOUR CAT'S LANGUAGE, AND PROPOSE A TRANSLITERATION USING THE LATIN ALPHABET OF YOUR CHOICE.
35. COMPOSE A JUVENALIAN SATIRE ABOUT YOUR CAT, IN CAT LANGUAGE, USING AT LEAST ONE IDIOM WHOSE MEANING CANNOT BE PROPERLY CONVEYED IN ENGLISH.
YOU HAVE GOT TO BE FUCKING KIDDING ME.
OKAY, FINE. YOU PROVED YOUR POINT, I GUESS. I DON'T BELONG--
WHAT ARE YOU TALKING ABOUT? YOU RECEIVED NEARLY A PERFECT SCORE!
ALICE QUINN, WELCOME TO BRAKEBILLS.

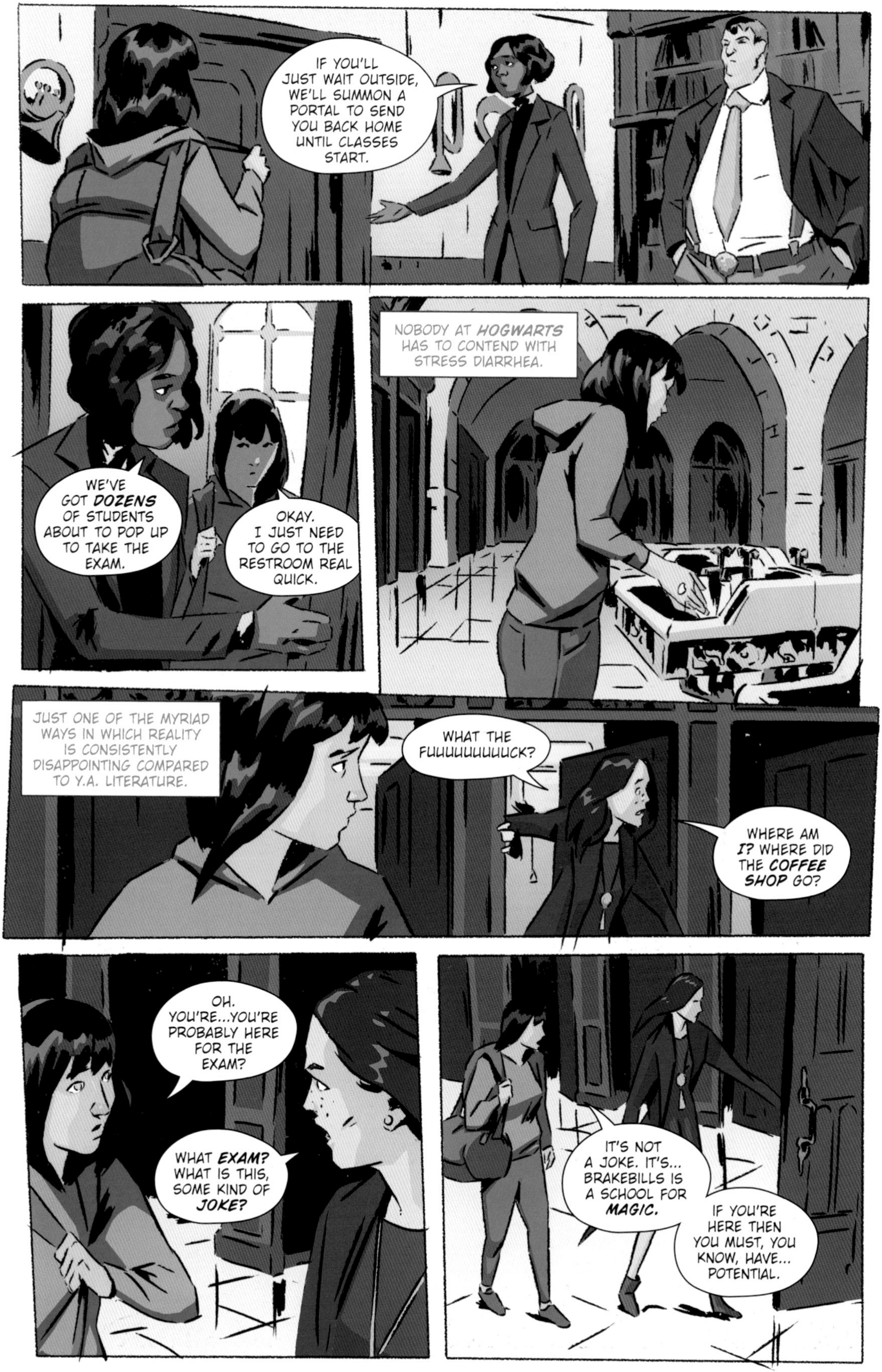
IF YOU'LL JUST WAIT OUTSIDE, WE'LL SUMMON A PORTAL TO SEND YOU BACK HOME UNTIL CLASSES START.
WE'VE GOT DOZENS OF STUDENTS ABOUT TO POP UP TO TAKE THE EXAM.
OKAY. I JUST NEED TO GO TO THE RESTROOM REAL QUICK.
NOBODY AT HOGWARTS HAS TO CONTEND WITH STRESS DIARRHEA.
JUST ONE OF THE MYRIAD WAYS IN WHICH REALITY IS CONSISTENTLY DISAPPOINTING COMPARED TO Y.A. LITERATURE.
WHAT THE FUUUUUUUUUCK?
WHERE AM I? WHERE DID THE COFFEE SHOP GO?
OH. YOU'RE...YOU'RE PROBABLY HERE FOR THE EXAM?
WHAT EXAM? WHAT IS THIS, SOME KIND OF JOKE?
IT'S NOT A JOKE. IT'S... BRAKEBILLS IS A SCHOOL FOR MAGIC.
IF YOU'RE HERE THEN YOU MUST, YOU KNOW, HAVE... POTENTIAL.

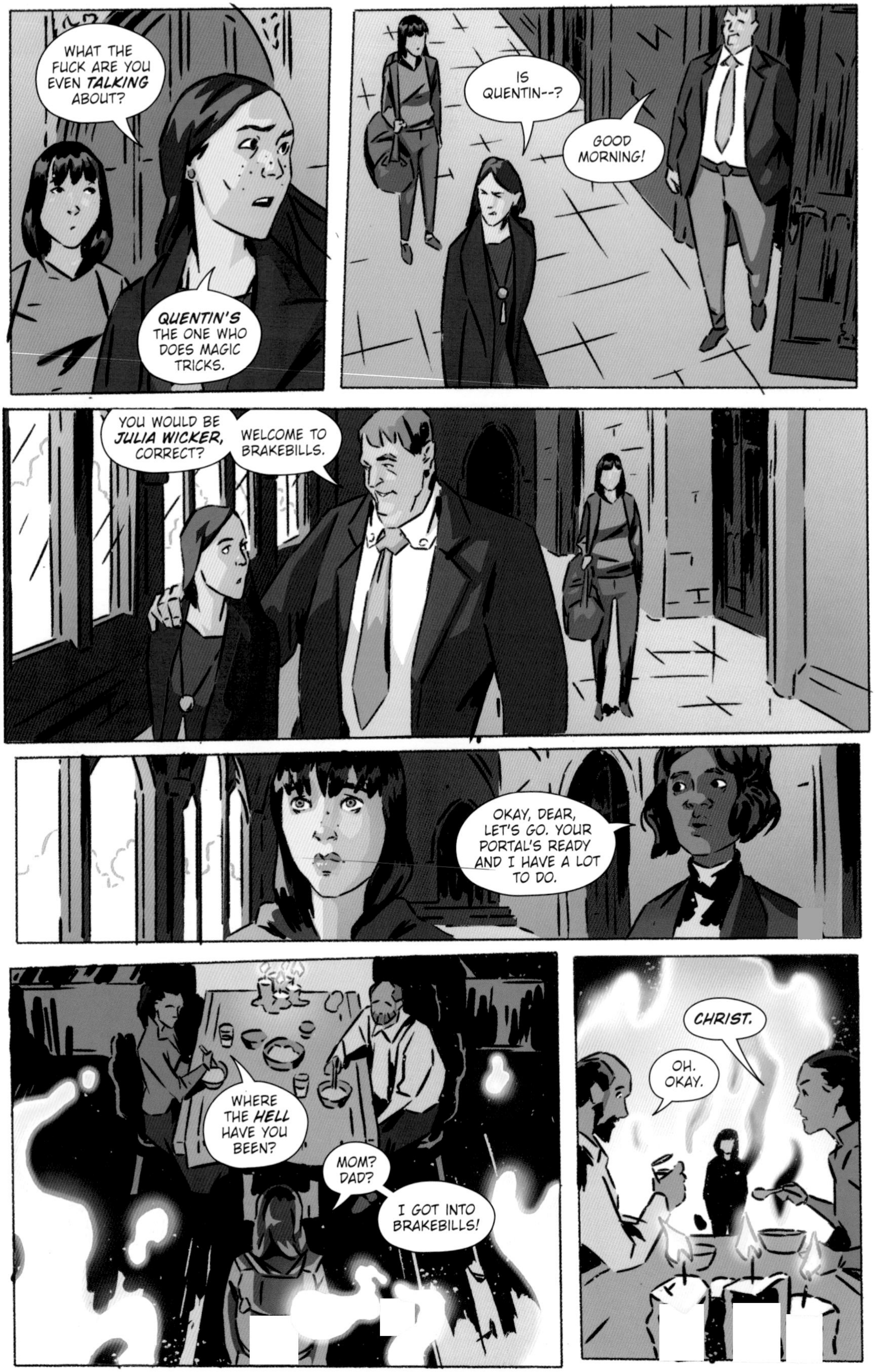
WHAT THE FUCK ARE YOU EVEN TALKING ABOUT?
QUENTIN'S THE ONE WHO DOES MAGIC TRICKS.
IS QUENTIN--?
GOOD MORNING!
YOU WOULD BE JULIA WICKER, CORRECT?
WELCOME TO BRAKEBILLS.
OKAY, DEAR, LET'S GO. YOUR PORTAL'S READY AND I HAVE A LOT TO DO.
WHERE THE HELL HAVE YOU BEEN?
MOM? DAD?
I GOT INTO BRAKEBILLS!
OH. OKAY.
CHRIST.

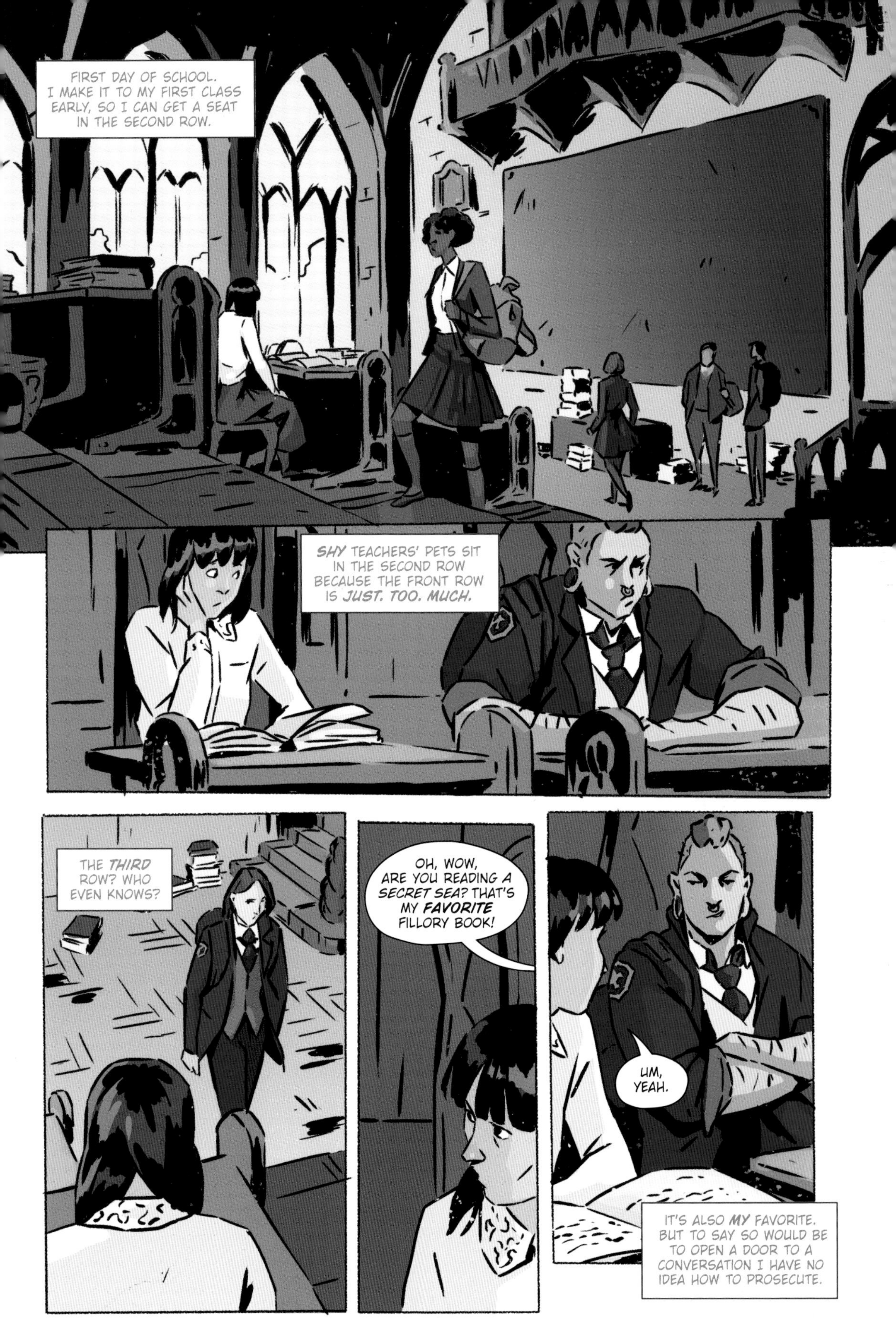
FIRST DAY OF SCHOOL. I MAKE IT TO MY FIRST CLASS EARLY, SO I CAN GET A SEAT IN THE SECOND ROW.
SHY TEACHERS' PETS SIT IN THE SECOND ROW BECAUSE THE FRONT ROW IS JUST. TOO. MUCH.
THE THIRD ROW? WHO EVEN KNOWS?
OH, WOW, ARE YOU READING A SECRET SEA? THAT'S MY FAVORITE FILLORY BOOK!
UM, YEAH.
IT'S ALSO MY FAVORITE. BUT TO SAY SO WOULD BE TO OPEN A DOOR TO A CONVERSATION I HAVE NO IDEA HOW TO PROSECUTE.

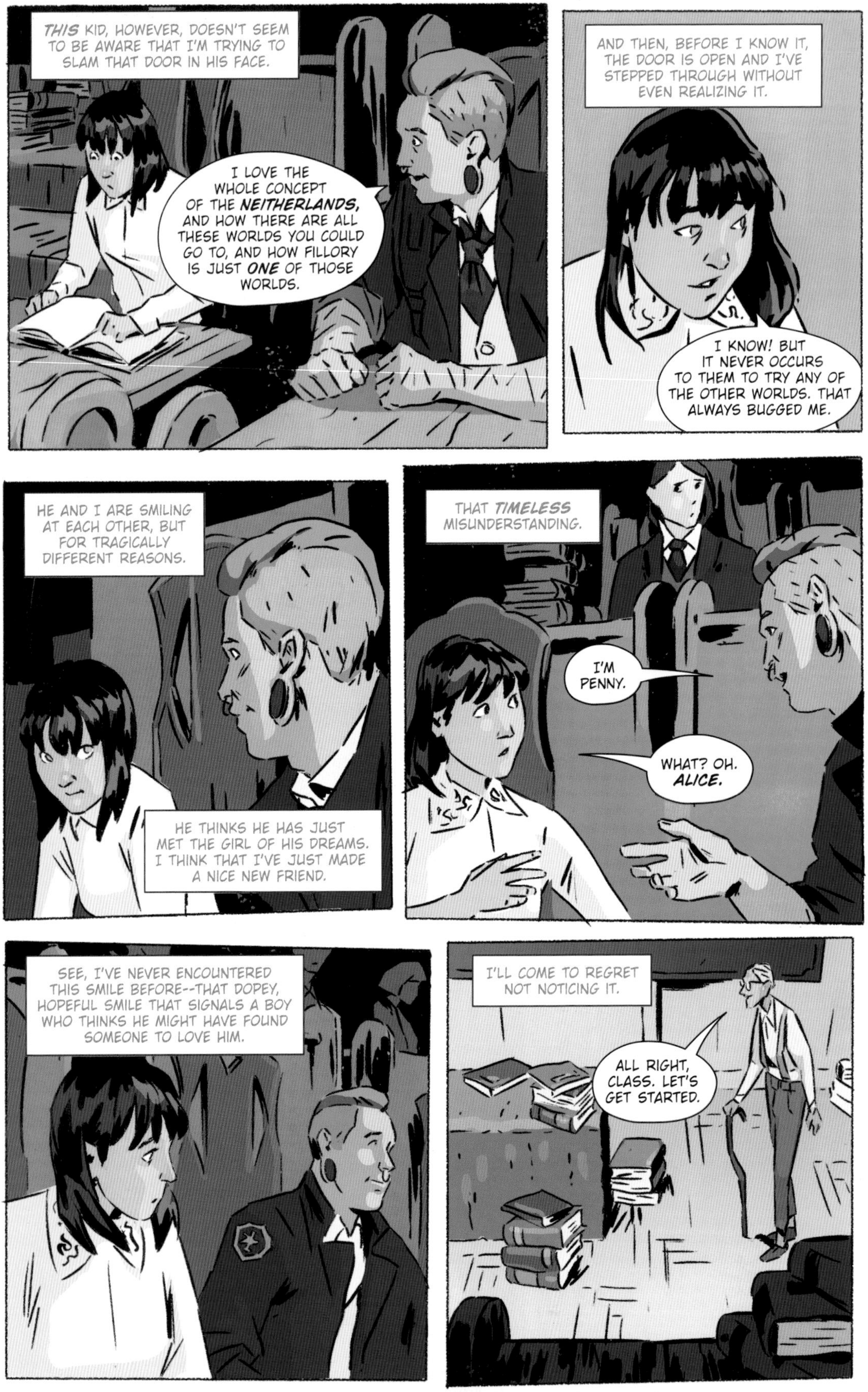
THIS KID, HOWEVER, DOESN'T SEEM TO BE AWARE THAT I'M TRYING TO SLAM THAT DOOR IN HIS FACE.
I LOVE THE WHOLE CONCEPT OF THE NEITHERLANDS, AND HOW THERE ARE ALL THESE WORLDS YOU COULD GO TO, AND HOW FILLORY IS JUST ONE OF THOSE WORLDS.
AND THEN, BEFORE I KNOW IT, THE DOOR IS OPEN AND I'VE STEPPED THROUGH WITHOUT EVEN REALIZING IT.
I KNOW! BUT IT NEVER OCCURS TO THEM TO TRY ANY OF THE OTHER WORLDS. THAT ALWAYS BUGGED ME.
HE AND I ARE SMILING AT EACH OTHER, BUT FOR TRAGICALLY DIFFERENT REASONS.
HE THINKS HE HAS JUST MET THE GIRL OF HIS DREAMS. I THINK THAT I'VE JUST MADE A NICE NEW FRIEND.
THAT TIMELESS MISUNDERSTANDING.
I'M PENNY.
WHAT? OH. ALICE.
SEE, I'VE NEVER ENCOUNTERED THIS SMILE BEFORE--THAT DOPEY, HOPEFUL SMILE THAT SIGNALS A BOY WHO THINKS HE MIGHT HAVE FOUND SOMEONE TO LOVE HIM.
I'LL COME TO REGRET NOT NOTICING IT.
ALL RIGHT, CLASS. LET'S GET STARTED.

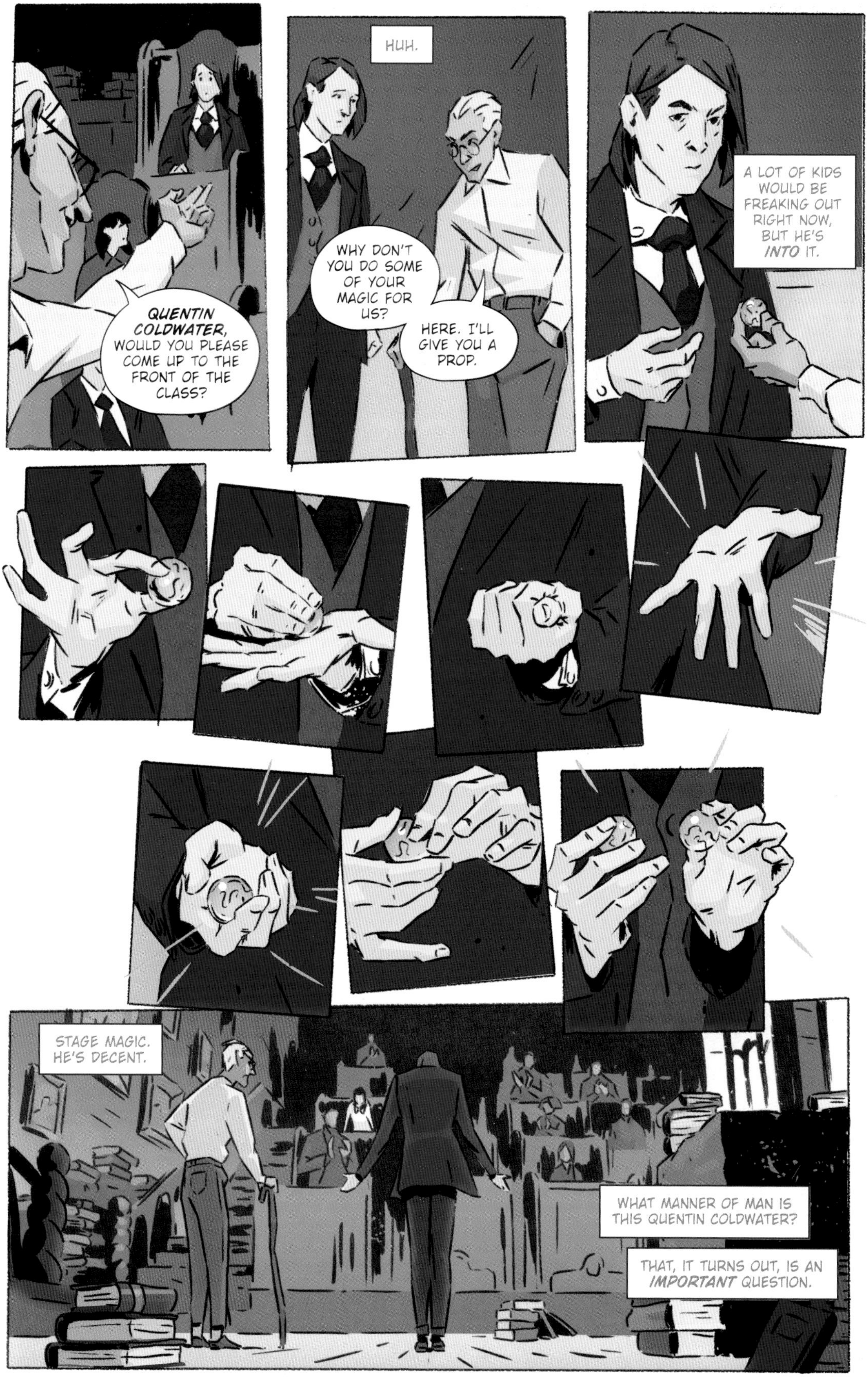
QUENTIN COLDWATER, WOULD YOU PLEASE COME UP TO THE FRONT OF THE CLASS?
HUH.
WHY DON'T YOU DO SOME OF YOUR MAGIC FOR US?
HERE. I'LL GIVE YOU A PROP.
A LOT OF KIDS WOULD BE FREAKING OUT RIGHT NOW, BUT HE'S INTO IT.
STAGE MAGIC. HE'S DECENT.
WHAT MANNER OF MAN IS THIS QUENTIN COLDWATER?
THAT, IT TURNS OUT, IS AN IMPORTANT QUESTION.

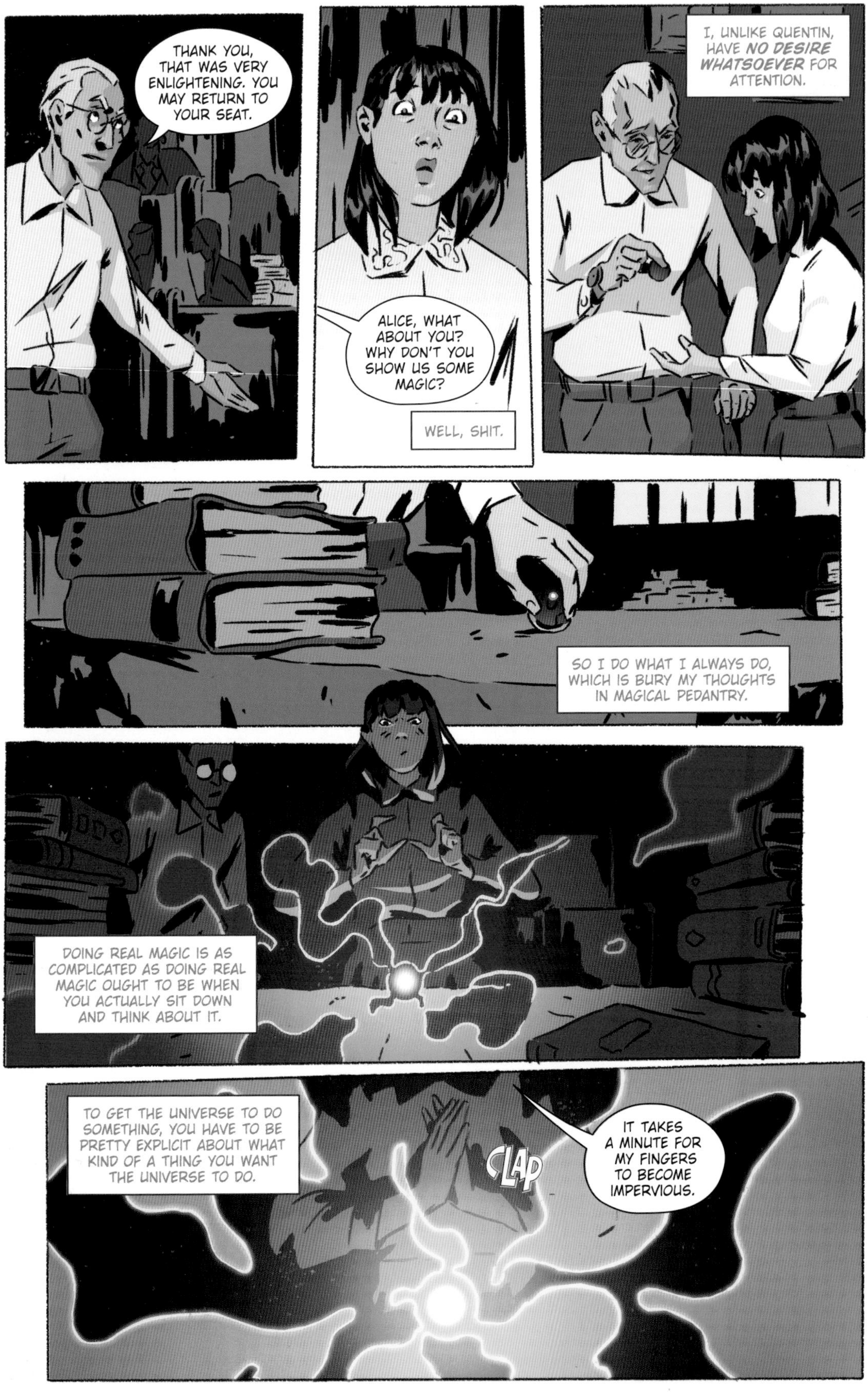
THANK YOU, THAT WAS VERY ENLIGHTENING. YOU MAY RETURN TO YOUR SEAT.
ALICE, WHAT ABOUT YOU? WHY DON'T YOU SHOW US SOME MAGIC?
WELL, SHIT.
I, UNLIKE QUENTIN, HAVE NO DESIRE WHATSOEVER FOR ATTENTION.
SO I DO WHAT I ALWAYS DO, WHICH IS BURY MY THOUGHTS IN MAGICAL PEDANTRY.
DOING REAL MAGIC IS AS COMPLICATED AS DOING REAL MAGIC OUGHT TO BE WHEN YOU ACTUALLY SIT DOWN AND THINK ABOUT IT.
TO GET THE UNIVERSE TO DO SOMETHING, YOU HAVE TO BE PRETTY EXPLICIT ABOUT WHAT KIND OF A THING YOU WANT THE UNIVERSE TO DO.
CLAP
IT TAKES A MINUTE FOR MY FINGERS TO BECOME IMPERVIOUS.

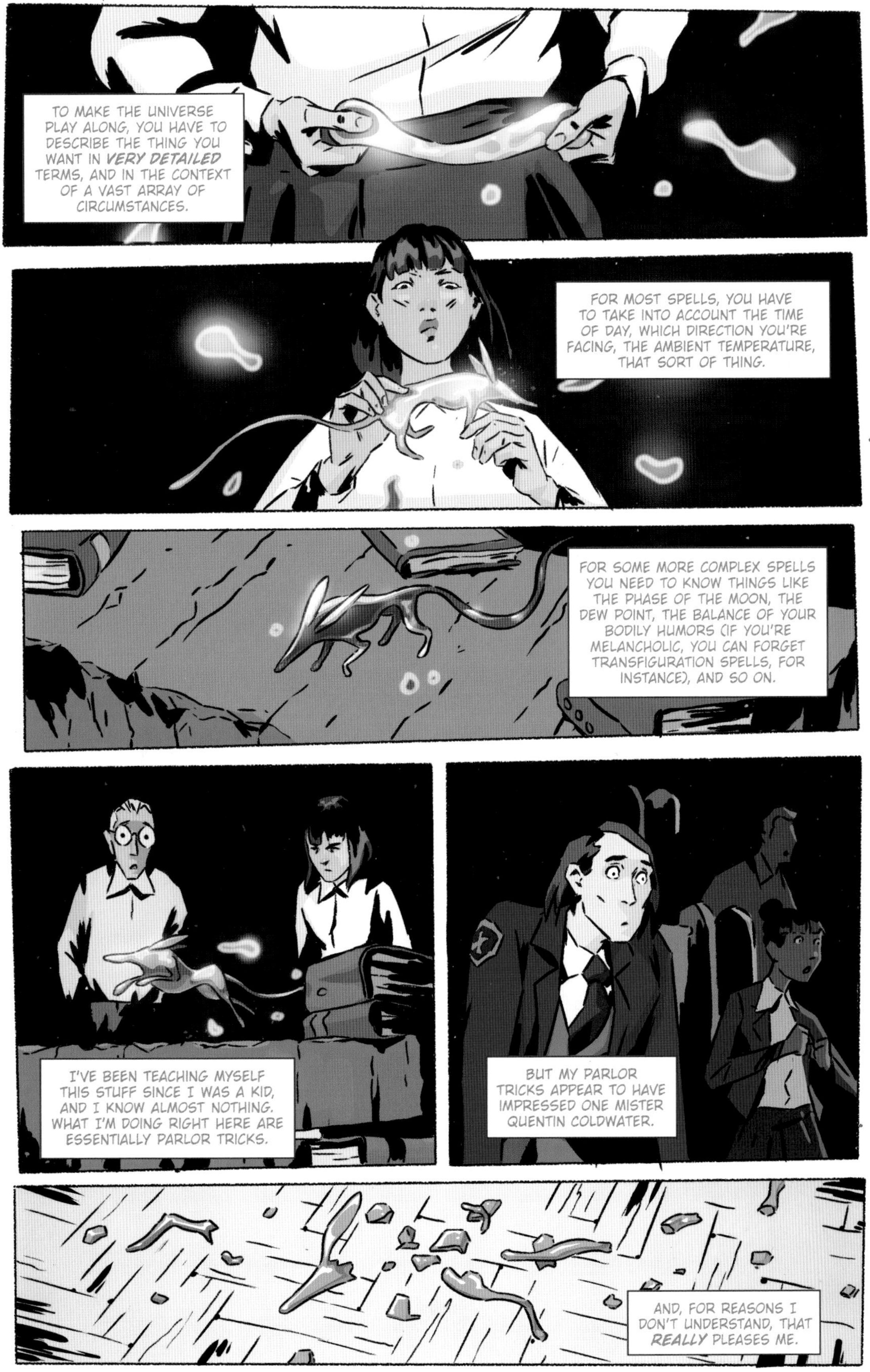
TO MAKE THE UNIVERSE PLAY ALONG, YOU HAVE TO DESCRIBE THE THING YOU WANT IN VERY DETAILED TERMS, AND IN THE CONTEXT OF A VAST ARRAY OF CIRCUMSTANCES.
FOR MOST SPELLS, YOU HAVE TO TAKE INTO ACCOUNT THE TIME OF DAY, WHICH DIRECTION YOU'RE FACING, THE AMBIENT TEMPERATURE, THAT SORT OF THING.
FOR SOME MORE COMPLEX SPELLS YOU NEED TO KNOW THINGS LIKE THE PHASE OF THE MOON, THE DEW POINT, THE BALANCE OF YOUR BODILY HUMORS (IF YOU'RE MELANCHOLIC, YOU CAN FORGET TRANSFIGURATION SPELLS, FOR INSTANCE), AND SO ON.
I'VE BEEN TEACHING MYSELF THIS STUFF SINCE I WAS A KID, AND I KNOW ALMOST NOTHING. WHAT I'M DOING RIGHT HERE ARE ESSENTIALLY PARLOR TRICKS.
BUT MY PARLOR TRICKS APPEAR TO HAVE IMPRESSED ONE MISTER QUENTIN COLDWATER.
AND, FOR REASONS I DON'T UNDERSTAND, THAT REALLY PLEASES ME.

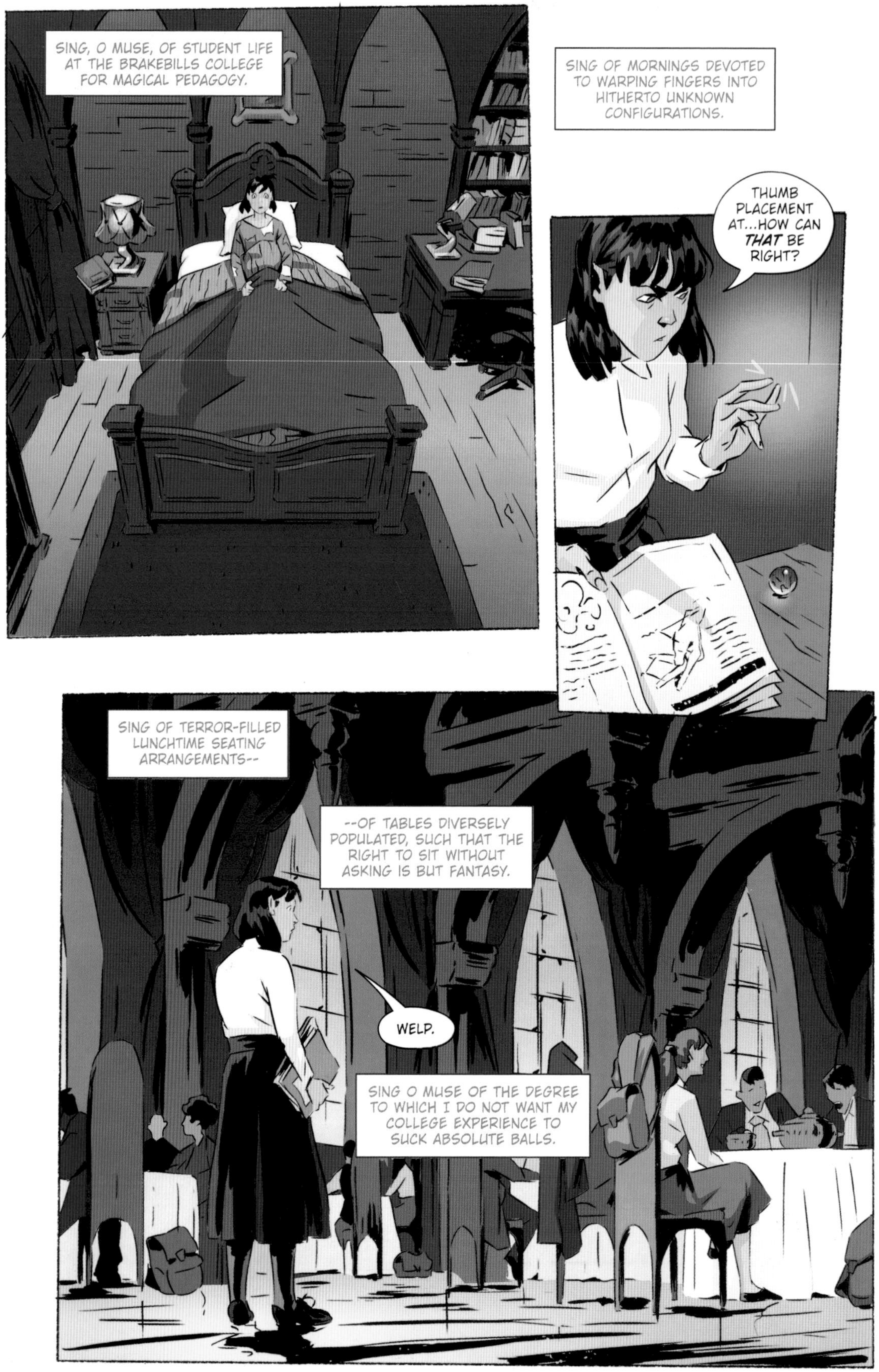
SING, O MUSE, OF STUDENT LIFE AT THE BRAKEBILLS COLLEGE FOR MAGICAL PEDAGOGY.
SING OF MORNINGS DEVOTED TO WARPING FINGERS INTO HITHERTO UNKNOWN CONFIGURATIONS.
THUMB PLACEMENT AT...HOW CAN ***THAT*** BE RIGHT?
SING OF TERROR-FILLED LUNCHTIME SEATING ARRANGEMENTS--
--OF TABLES DIVERSELY POPULATED, SUCH THAT THE RIGHT TO SIT WITHOUT ASKING IS BUT FANTASY.
WELP.
SING O MUSE OF THE DEGREE TO WHICH I DO NOT WANT MY COLLEGE EXPERIENCE TO SUCK ABSOLUTE BALLS.

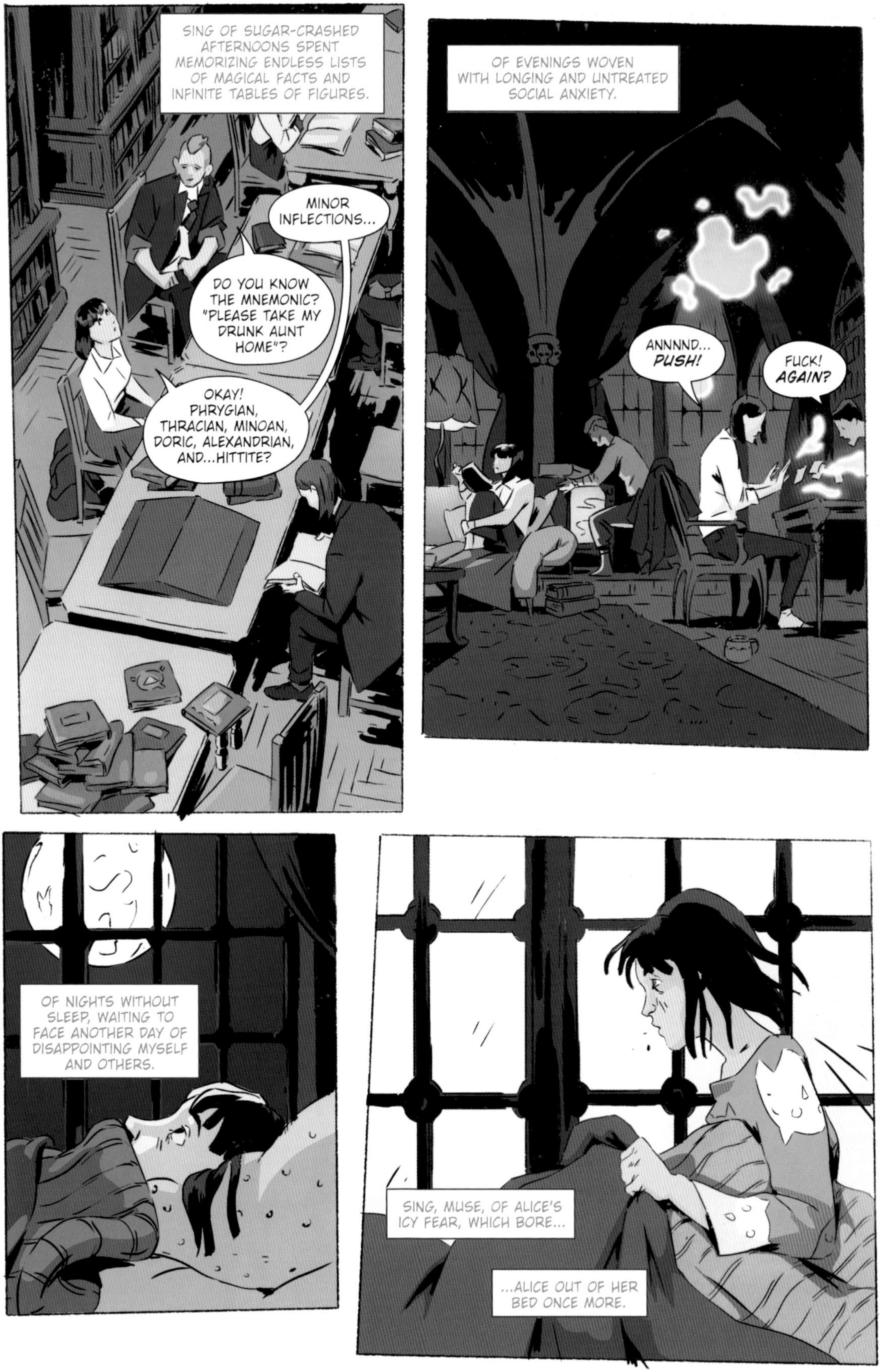
SING OF SUGAR-CRASHED AFTERNOONS SPENT MEMORIZING ENDLESS LISTS OF MAGICAL FACTS AND INFINITE TABLES OF FIGURES.
MINOR INFLECTIONS...
DO YOU KNOW THE MNEMONIC? "PLEASE TAKE MY DRUNK AUNT HOME"?
OKAY! PHRYGIAN, THRACIAN, MINOAN, DORIC, ALEXANDRIAN, AND...HITTITE?
OF EVENINGS WOVEN WITH LONGING AND UNTREATED SOCIAL ANXIETY.
ANNNND... PUSH!
FUCK! AGAIN?
OF NIGHTS WITHOUT SLEEP, WAITING TO FACE ANOTHER DAY OF DISAPPOINTING MYSELF AND OTHERS.
SING, MUSE, OF ALICE'S ICY FEAR, WHICH BORE...
...ALICE OUT OF HER BED ONCE MORE.

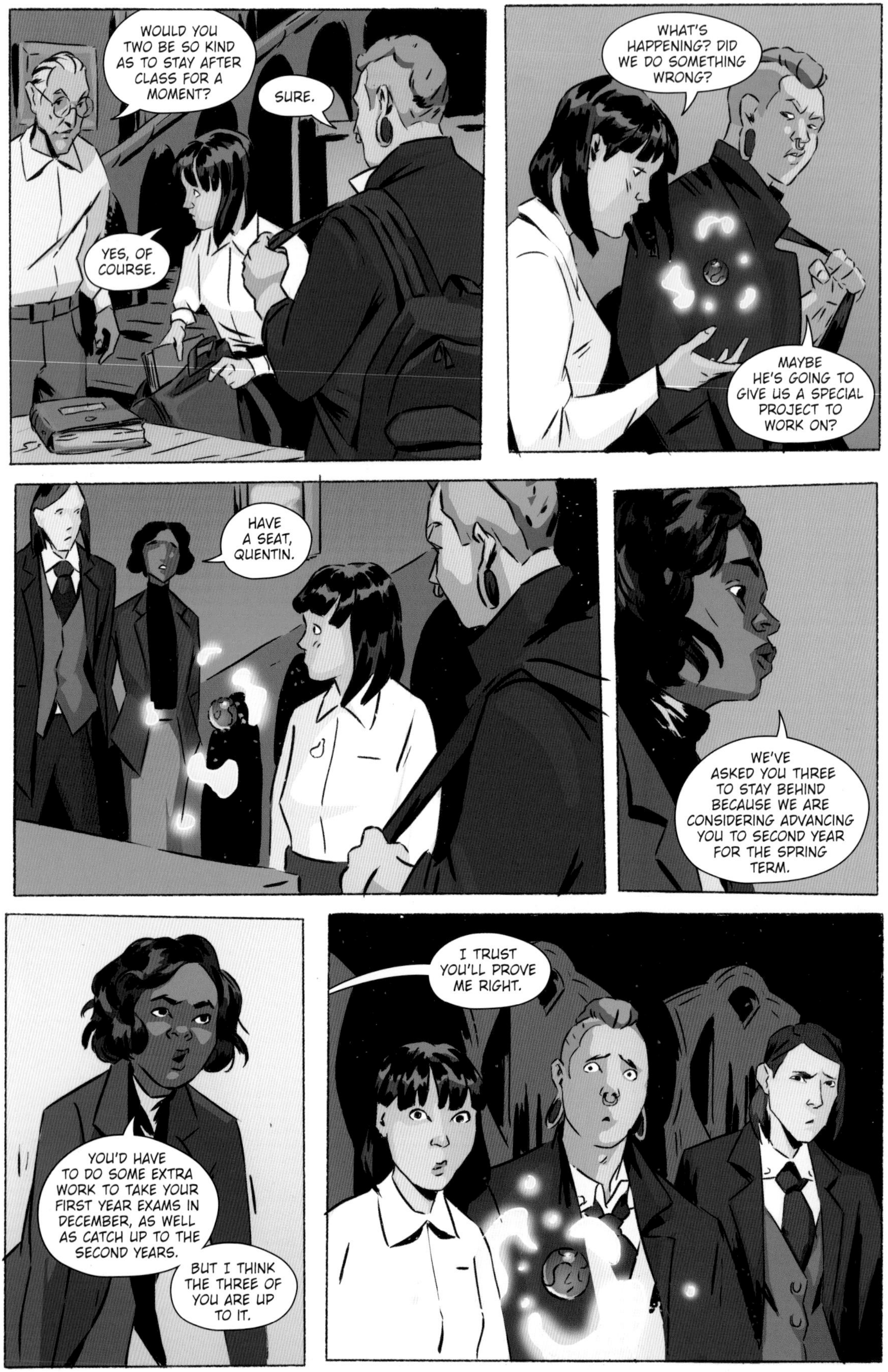
WOULD YOU TWO BE SO KIND AS TO STAY AFTER CLASS FOR A MOMENT?
SURE.
YES, OF COURSE.
WHAT'S HAPPENING? DID WE DO SOMETHING WRONG?
MAYBE HE'S GOING TO GIVE US A SPECIAL PROJECT TO WORK ON?
HAVE A SEAT, QUENTIN.
WE'VE ASKED YOU THREE TO STAY BEHIND BECAUSE WE ARE CONSIDERING ADVANCING YOU TO SECOND YEAR FOR THE SPRING TERM.
YOU'D HAVE TO DO SOME EXTRA WORK TO TAKE YOUR FIRST YEAR EXAMS IN DECEMBER, AS WELL AS CATCH UP TO THE SECOND YEARS.
BUT I THINK THE THREE OF YOU ARE UP TO IT.
I TRUST YOU'LL PROVE ME RIGHT.

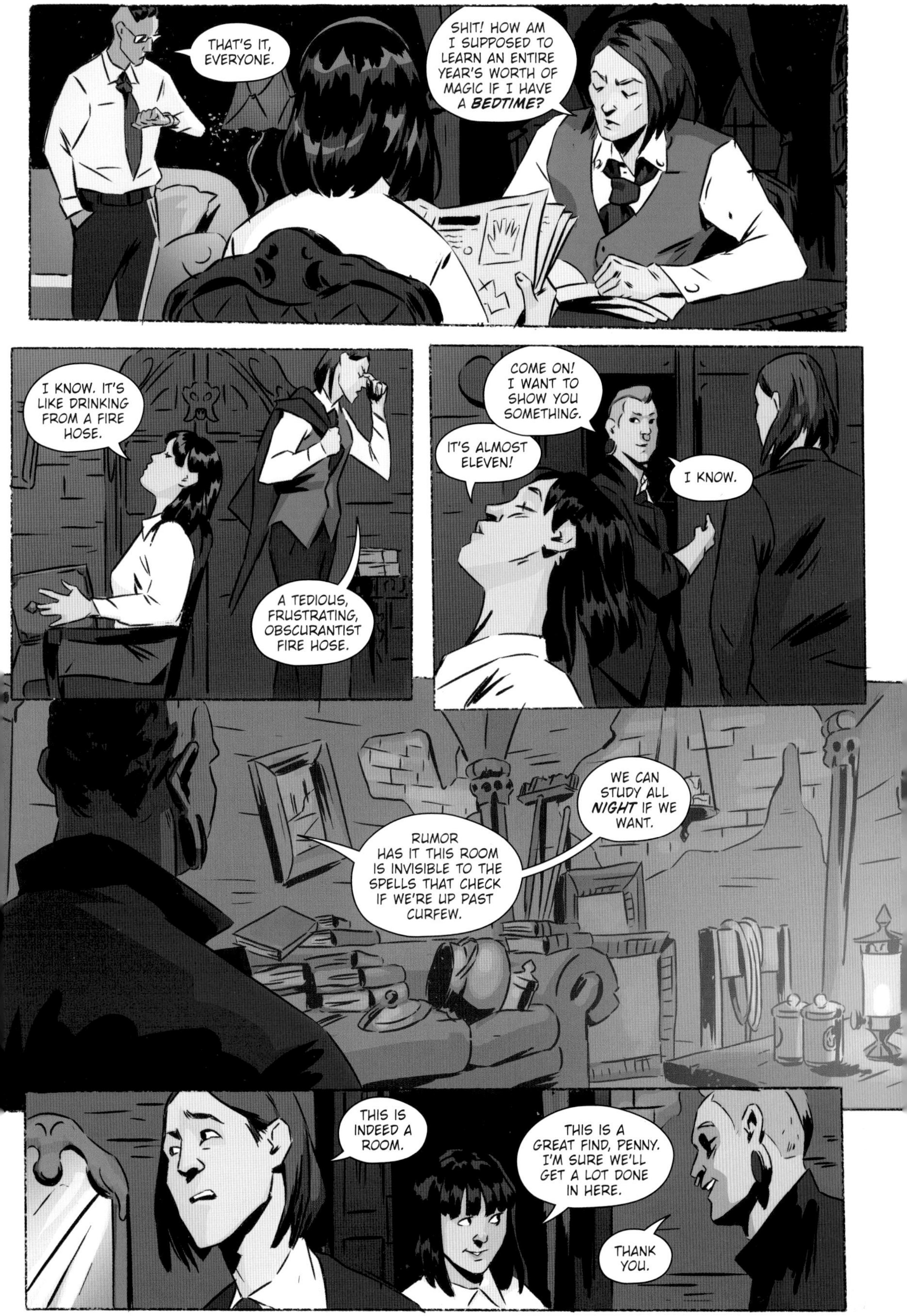
THAT'S IT, EVERYONE.
SHIT! HOW AM I SUPPOSED TO LEARN AN ENTIRE YEAR'S WORTH OF MAGIC IF I HAVE A ***BEDTIME?***
I KNOW. IT'S LIKE DRINKING FROM A FIRE HOSE.
A TEDIOUS, FRUSTRATING, OBSCURANTIST FIRE HOSE.
COME ON! I WANT TO SHOW YOU SOMETHING.
IT'S ALMOST ELEVEN!
I KNOW.
RUMOR HAS IT THIS ROOM IS INVISIBLE TO THE SPELLS THAT CHECK IF WE'RE UP PAST CURFEW.
WE CAN STUDY ALL ***NIGHT*** IF WE WANT.
THIS IS INDEED A ROOM.
THIS IS A GREAT FIND, PENNY. I'M SURE WE'LL GET A LOT DONE IN HERE.
THANK YOU.

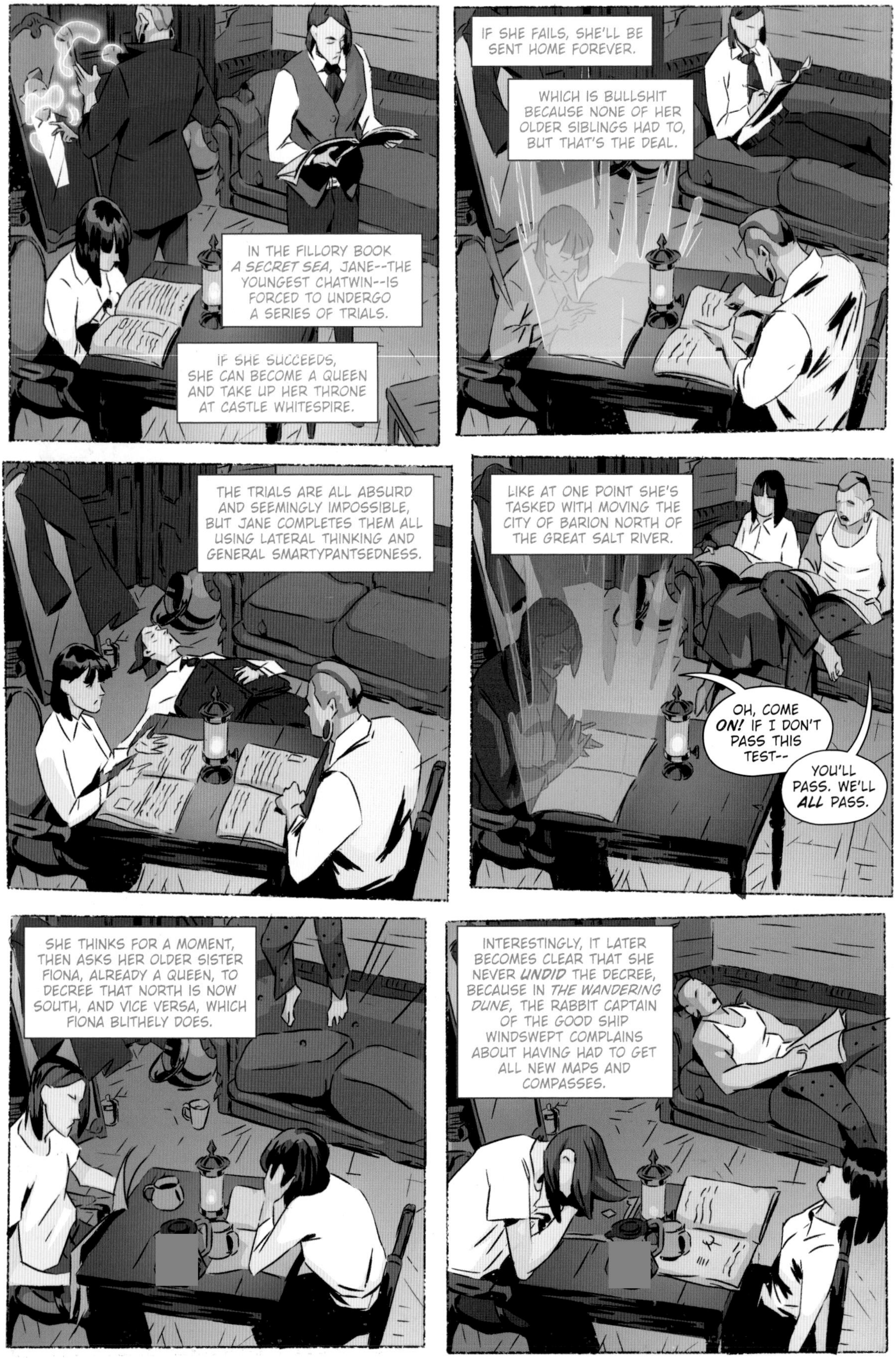
IN THE FILLORY BOOK *A SECRET SEA*, JANE--THE YOUNGEST CHATWIN--IS FORCED TO UNDERGO A SERIES OF TRIALS.
IF SHE SUCCEEDS, SHE CAN BECOME A QUEEN AND TAKE UP HER THRONE AT CASTLE WHITESPIRE.
IF SHE FAILS, SHE'LL BE SENT HOME FOREVER.
WHICH IS BULLSHIT BECAUSE NONE OF HER OLDER SIBLINGS HAD TO, BUT THAT'S THE DEAL.
THE TRIALS ARE ALL ABSURD AND SEEMINGLY IMPOSSIBLE, BUT JANE COMPLETES THEM ALL USING LATERAL THINKING AND GENERAL SMARTYPANTSEDNESS.
LIKE AT ONE POINT SHE'S TASKED WITH MOVING THE CITY OF BARION NORTH OF THE GREAT SALT RIVER.
OH, COME **ON!** IF I DON'T PASS THIS TEST--
YOU'LL PASS. WE'LL ***ALL*** PASS.
SHE THINKS FOR A MOMENT, THEN ASKS HER OLDER SISTER FIONA, ALREADY A QUEEN, TO DECREE THAT NORTH IS NOW SOUTH, AND VICE VERSA, WHICH FIONA BLITHELY DOES.
INTERESTINGLY, IT LATER BECOMES CLEAR THAT SHE NEVER ***UNDID*** THE DECREE, BECAUSE IN *THE WANDERING DUNE*, THE RABBIT CAPTAIN OF THE GOOD SHIP WINDSWEPT COMPLAINS ABOUT HAVING HAD TO GET ALL NEW MAPS AND COMPASSES.

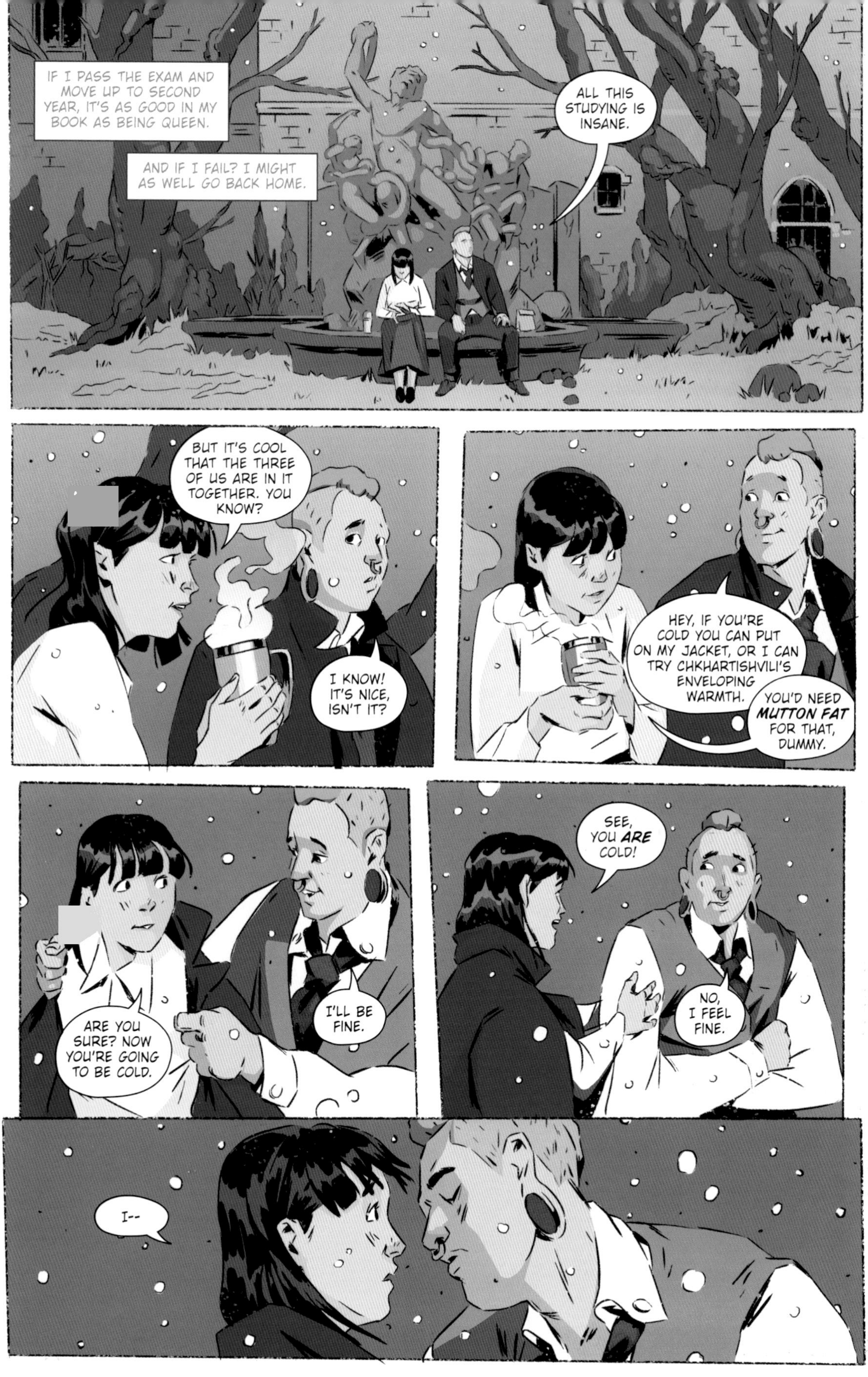
IF I PASS THE EXAM AND MOVE UP TO SECOND YEAR, IT'S AS GOOD IN MY BOOK AS BEING QUEEN.
AND IF I FAIL? I MIGHT AS WELL GO BACK HOME.
ALL THIS STUDYING IS INSANE.
BUT IT'S COOL THAT THE THREE OF US ARE IN IT TOGETHER. YOU KNOW?
I KNOW! IT'S NICE, ISN'T IT?
HEY, IF YOU'RE COLD YOU CAN PUT ON MY JACKET, OR I CAN TRY CHKHARTISHVILI'S ENVELOPING WARMTH.
YOU'D NEED **MUTTON FAT** FOR THAT, DUMMY.
ARE YOU SURE? NOW YOU'RE GOING TO BE COLD.
I'LL BE FINE.
SEE, YOU **ARE** COLD!
NO, I FEEL FINE.
I--

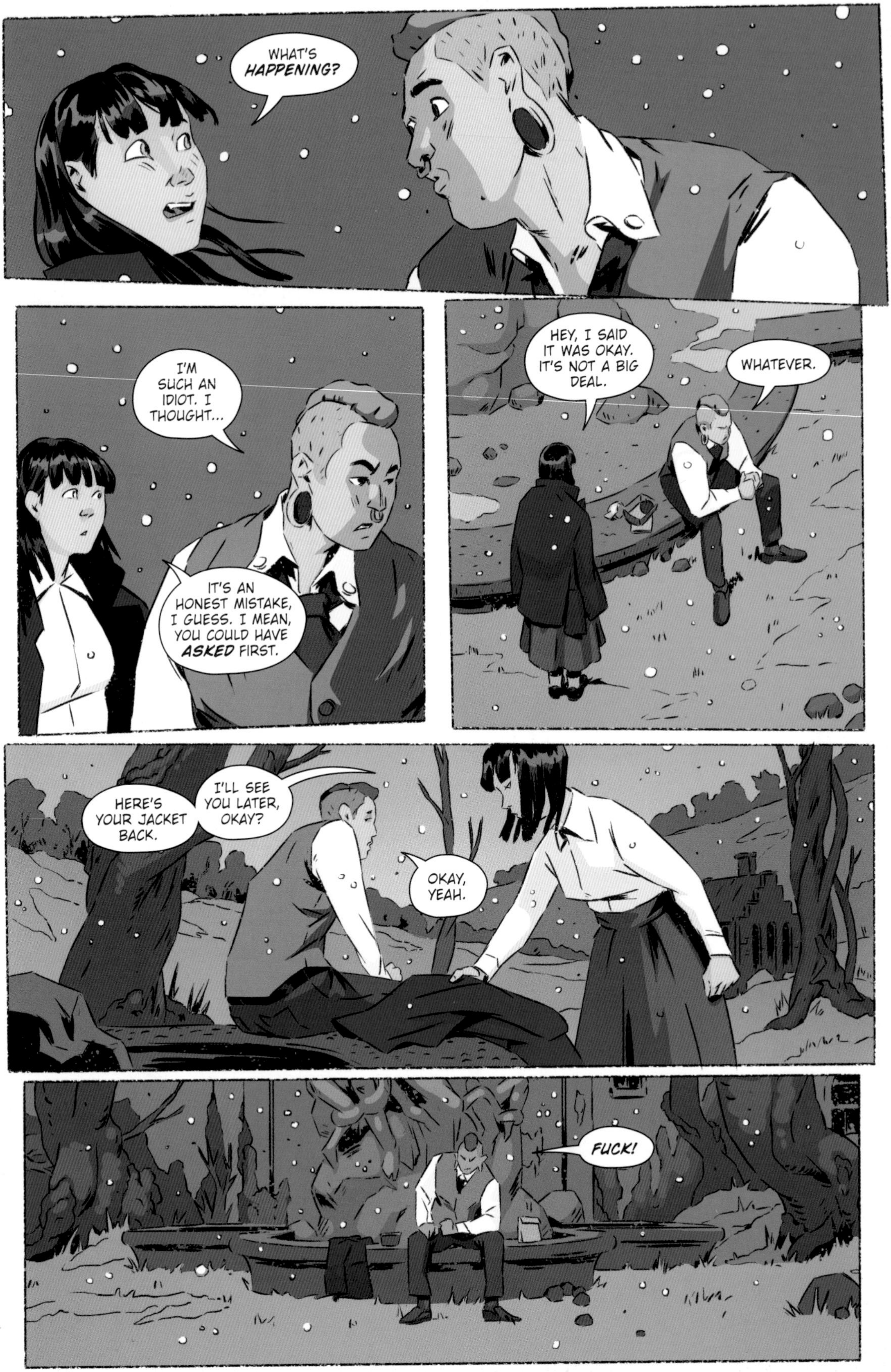
WHAT'S HAPPENING?
I'M SUCH AN IDIOT. I THOUGHT...
IT'S AN HONEST MISTAKE, I GUESS. I MEAN, YOU COULD HAVE ASKED FIRST.
HEY, I SAID IT WAS OKAY. IT'S NOT A BIG DEAL.
WHATEVER.
HERE'S YOUR JACKET BACK.
I'LL SEE YOU LATER, OKAY?
OKAY, YEAH.
FUCK!

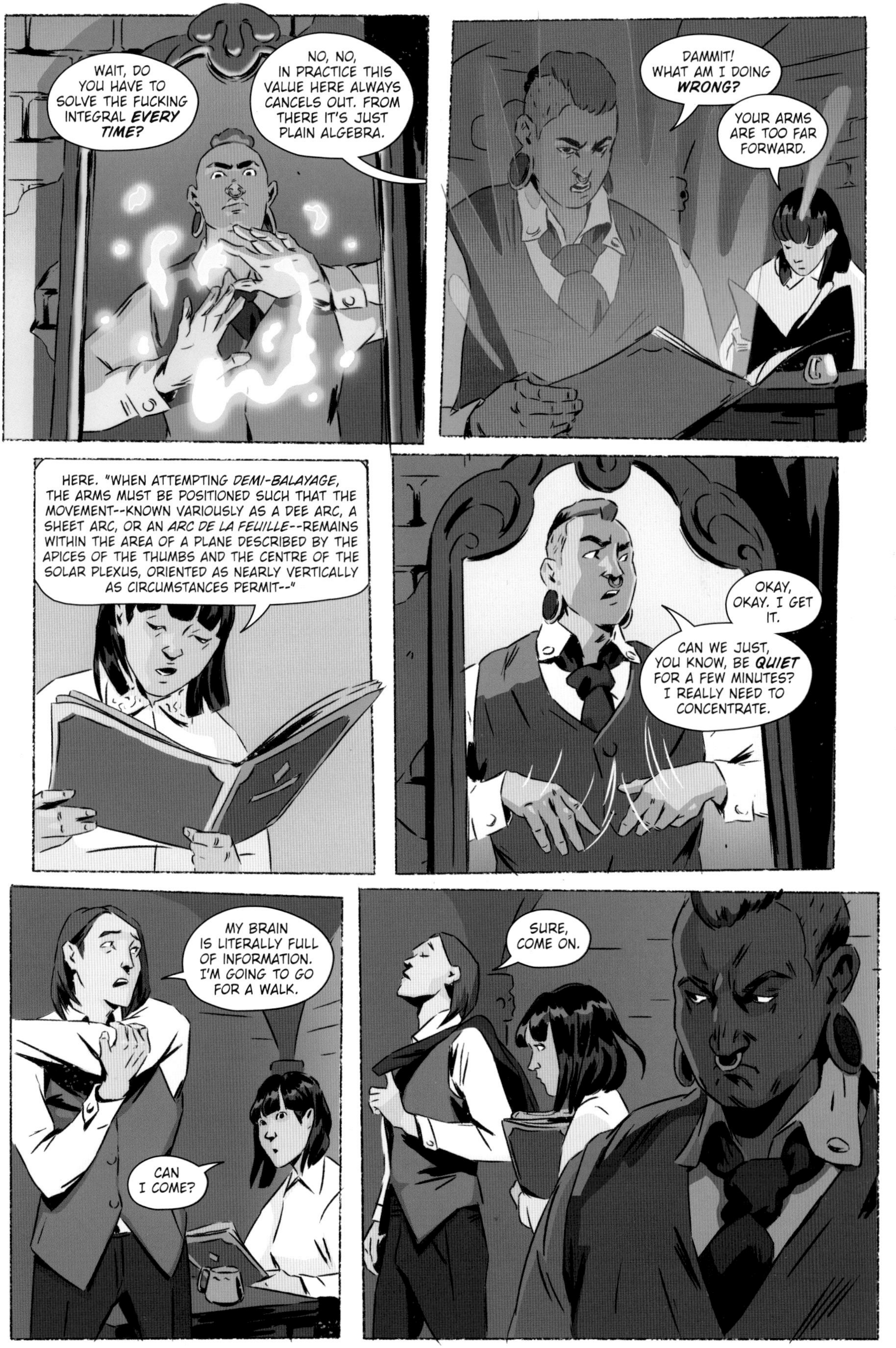
WAIT, DO YOU HAVE TO SOLVE THE FUCKING INTEGRAL **EVERY TIME?**
NO, NO, IN PRACTICE THIS VALUE HERE ALWAYS CANCELS OUT. FROM THERE IT'S JUST PLAIN ALGEBRA.
DAMMIT! WHAT AM I DOING **WRONG?**
YOUR ARMS ARE TOO FAR FORWARD.
HERE. "WHEN ATTEMPTING *DEMI-BALAYAGE*, THE ARMS MUST BE POSITIONED SUCH THAT THE MOVEMENT--KNOWN VARIOUSLY AS A DEE ARC, A SHEET ARC, OR AN *ARC DE LA FEUILLE*--REMAINS WITHIN THE AREA OF A PLANE DESCRIBED BY THE APICES OF THE THUMBS AND THE CENTRE OF THE SOLAR PLEXUS, ORIENTED AS NEARLY VERTICALLY AS CIRCUMSTANCES PERMIT--"
OKAY, OKAY. I GET IT.
CAN WE JUST, YOU KNOW, BE **QUIET** FOR A FEW MINUTES? I REALLY NEED TO CONCENTRATE.
MY BRAIN IS LITERALLY FULL OF INFORMATION. I'M GOING TO GO FOR A WALK.
CAN I COME?
SURE, COME ON.

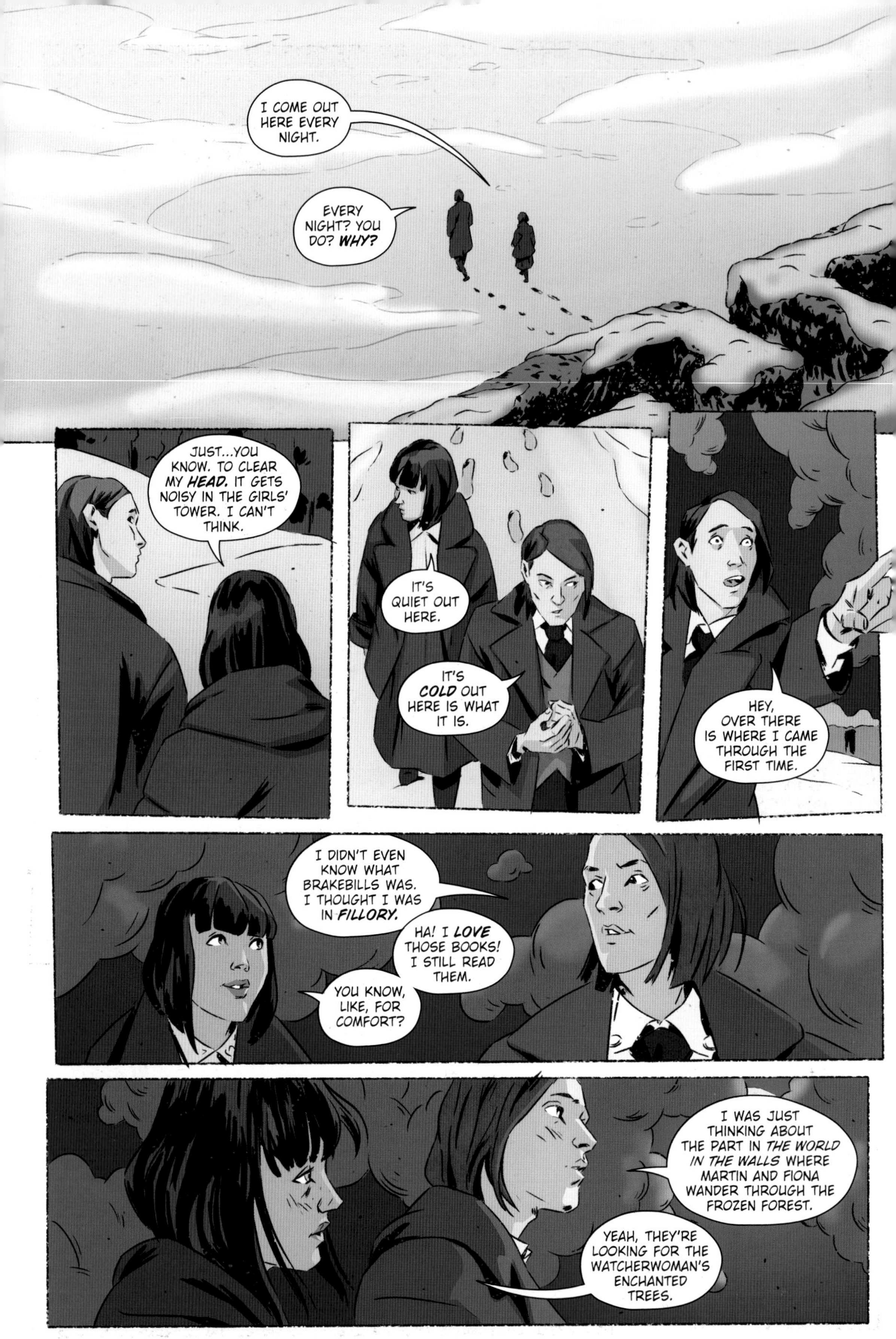
I COME OUT HERE EVERY NIGHT.
EVERY NIGHT? YOU DO? **WHY?**
JUST...YOU KNOW. TO CLEAR MY **HEAD.** IT GETS NOISY IN THE GIRLS' TOWER. I CAN'T THINK.
IT'S QUIET OUT HERE.
IT'S **COLD** OUT HERE IS WHAT IT IS.
HEY, OVER THERE IS WHERE I CAME THROUGH THE FIRST TIME.
I DIDN'T EVEN KNOW WHAT BRAKEBILLS WAS. I THOUGHT I WAS IN **FILLORY.**
HA! I **LOVE** THOSE BOOKS! I STILL READ THEM.
YOU KNOW, LIKE, FOR COMFORT?
I WAS JUST THINKING ABOUT THE PART IN *THE WORLD IN THE WALLS* WHERE MARTIN AND FIONA WANDER THROUGH THE FROZEN FOREST.
YEAH, THEY'RE LOOKING FOR THE WATCHERWOMAN'S ENCHANTED TREES.

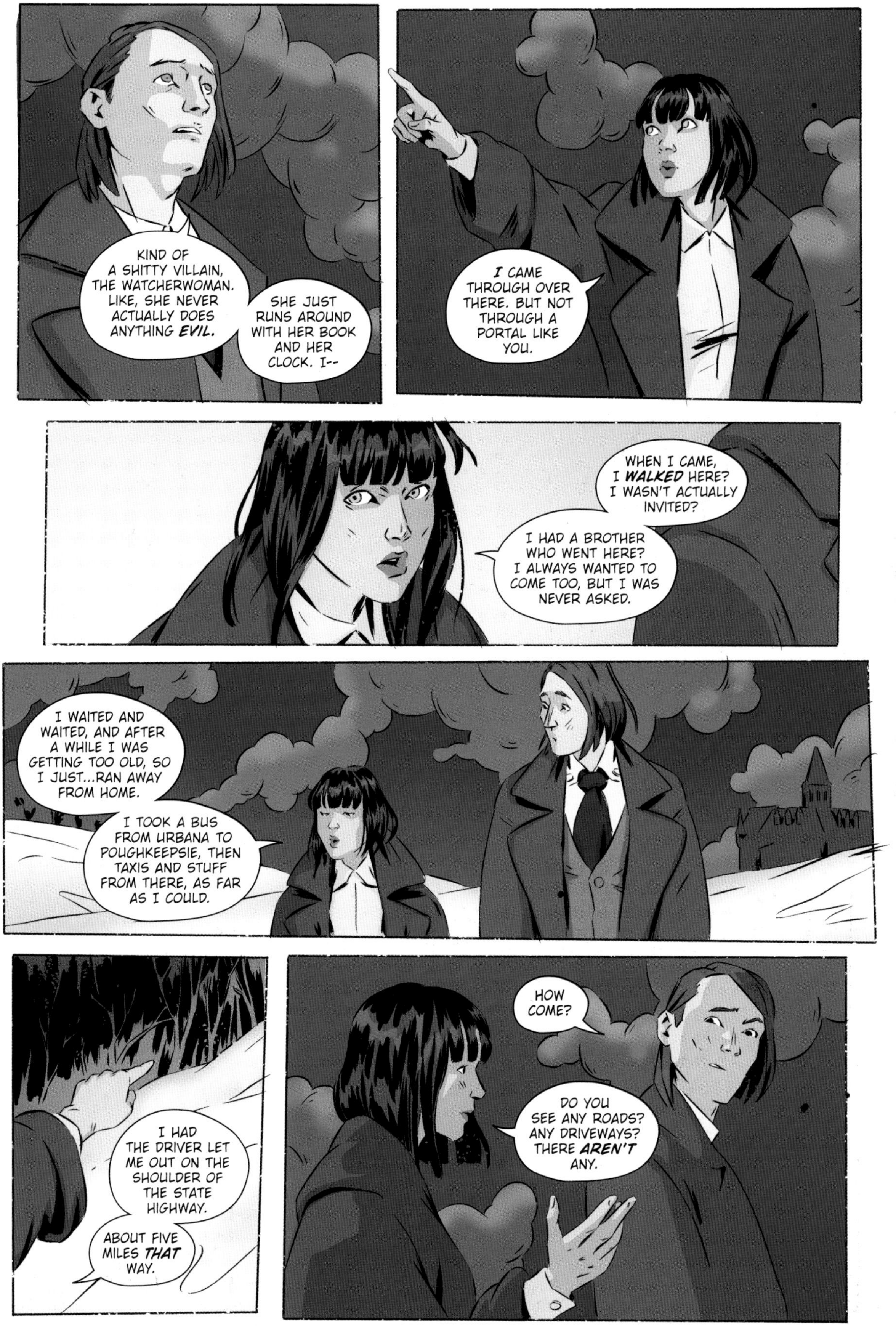
KIND OF A SHITTY VILLAIN, THE WATCHERWOMAN. LIKE, SHE NEVER ACTUALLY DOES ANYTHING **EVIL.**
SHE JUST RUNS AROUND WITH HER BOOK AND HER CLOCK. I--
I CAME THROUGH OVER THERE. BUT NOT THROUGH A PORTAL LIKE YOU.
WHEN I CAME, I **WALKED** HERE? I WASN'T ACTUALLY INVITED?
I HAD A BROTHER WHO WENT HERE? I ALWAYS WANTED TO COME TOO, BUT I WAS NEVER ASKED.
I WAITED AND WAITED, AND AFTER A WHILE I WAS GETTING TOO OLD, SO I JUST...RAN AWAY FROM HOME.
I TOOK A BUS FROM URBANA TO POUGHKEEPSIE, THEN TAXIS AND STUFF FROM THERE, AS FAR AS I COULD.
I HAD THE DRIVER LET ME OUT ON THE SHOULDER OF THE STATE HIGHWAY.
ABOUT FIVE MILES **THAT** WAY.
HOW COME?
DO YOU SEE ANY ROADS? ANY DRIVEWAYS? THERE **AREN'T** ANY.

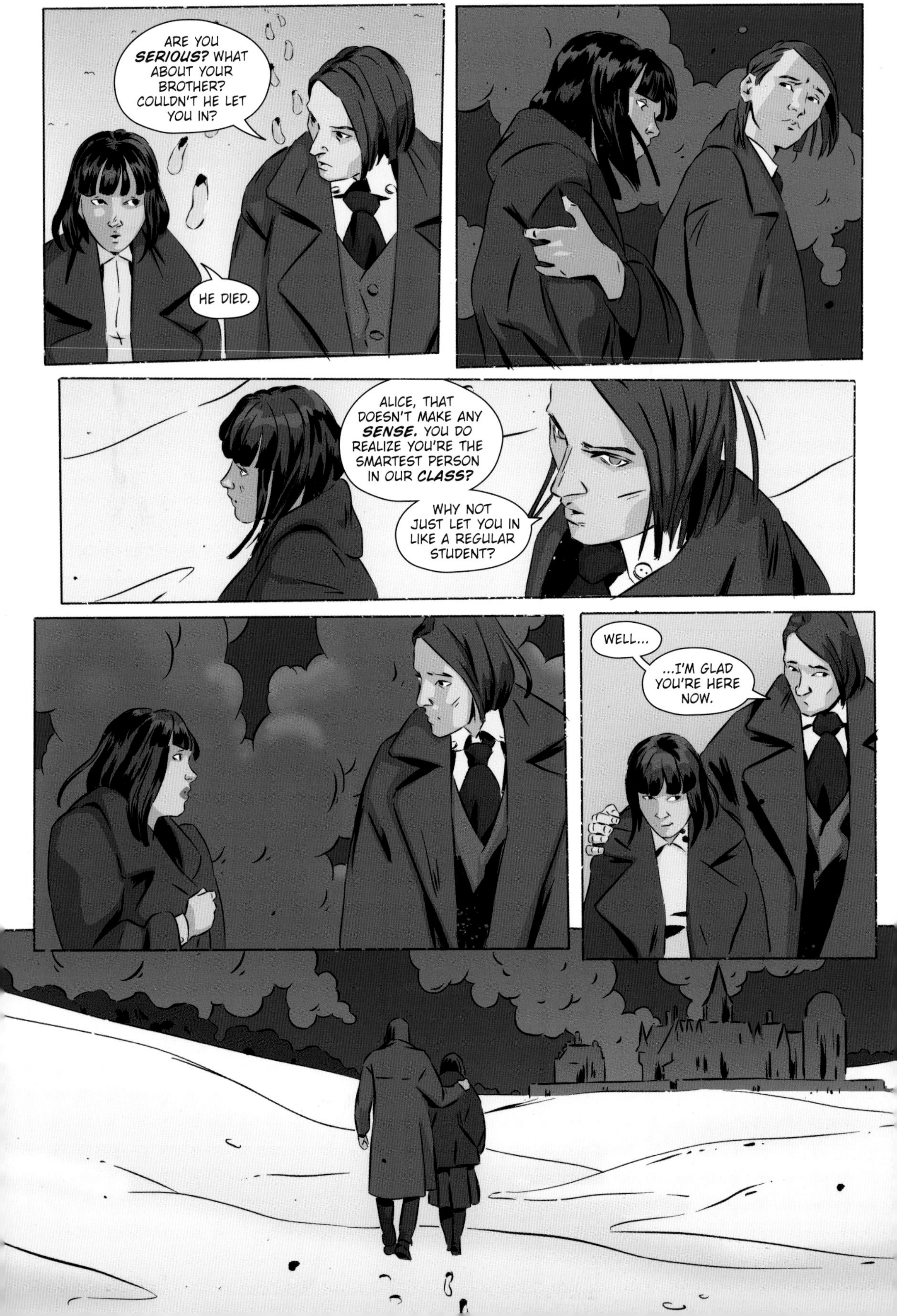
ARE YOU SERIOUS? WHAT ABOUT YOUR BROTHER? COULDN'T HE LET YOU IN?
HE DIED.
ALICE, THAT DOESN'T MAKE ANY SENSE. YOU DO REALIZE YOU'RE THE SMARTEST PERSON IN OUR CLASS?
WHY NOT JUST LET YOU IN LIKE A REGULAR STUDENT?
WELL...
...I'M GLAD YOU'RE HERE NOW.

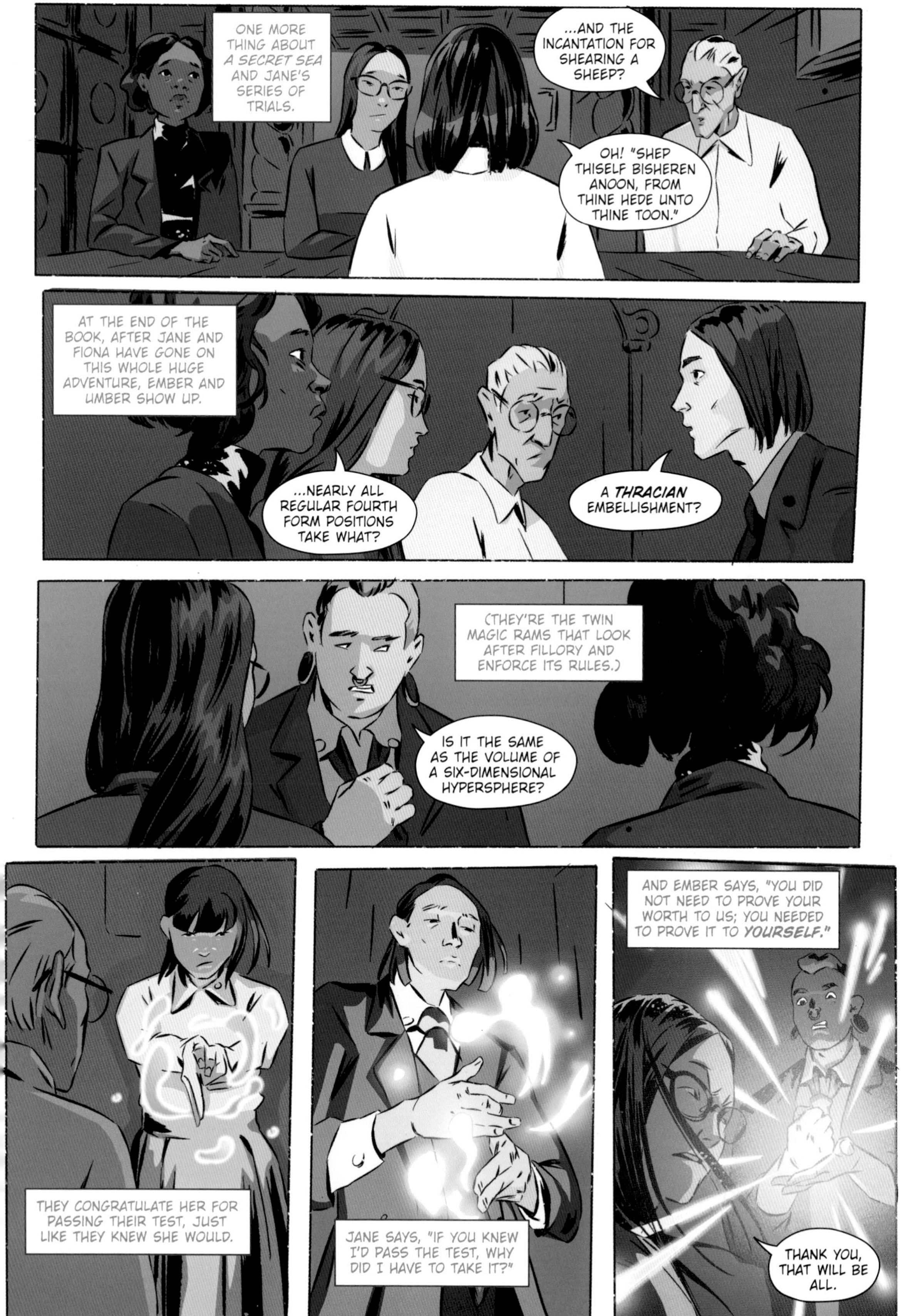
ONE MORE THING ABOUT *A SECRET SEA* AND JANE'S SERIES OF TRIALS.
...AND THE INCANTATION FOR SHEARING A SHEEP?
OH! "SHEP THISELF BISHEREN ANOON, FROM THINE HEDE UNTO THINE TOON."
AT THE END OF THE BOOK, AFTER JANE AND FIONA HAVE GONE ON THIS WHOLE HUGE ADVENTURE, EMBER AND UMBER SHOW UP.
...NEARLY ALL REGULAR FOURTH FORM POSITIONS TAKE WHAT?
A ***THRACIAN*** EMBELLISHMENT?
(THEY'RE THE TWIN MAGIC RAMS THAT LOOK AFTER FILLORY AND ENFORCE ITS RULES.)
IS IT THE SAME AS THE VOLUME OF A SIX-DIMENSIONAL HYPERSPHERE?
THEY CONGRATULATE HER FOR PASSING THEIR TEST, JUST LIKE THEY KNEW SHE WOULD.
JANE SAYS, "IF YOU KNEW I'D PASS THE TEST, WHY DID I HAVE TO TAKE IT?"
AND EMBER SAYS, "YOU DID NOT NEED TO PROVE YOUR WORTH TO US; YOU NEEDED TO PROVE IT TO ***YOURSELF.***"
THANK YOU, THAT WILL BE ALL.

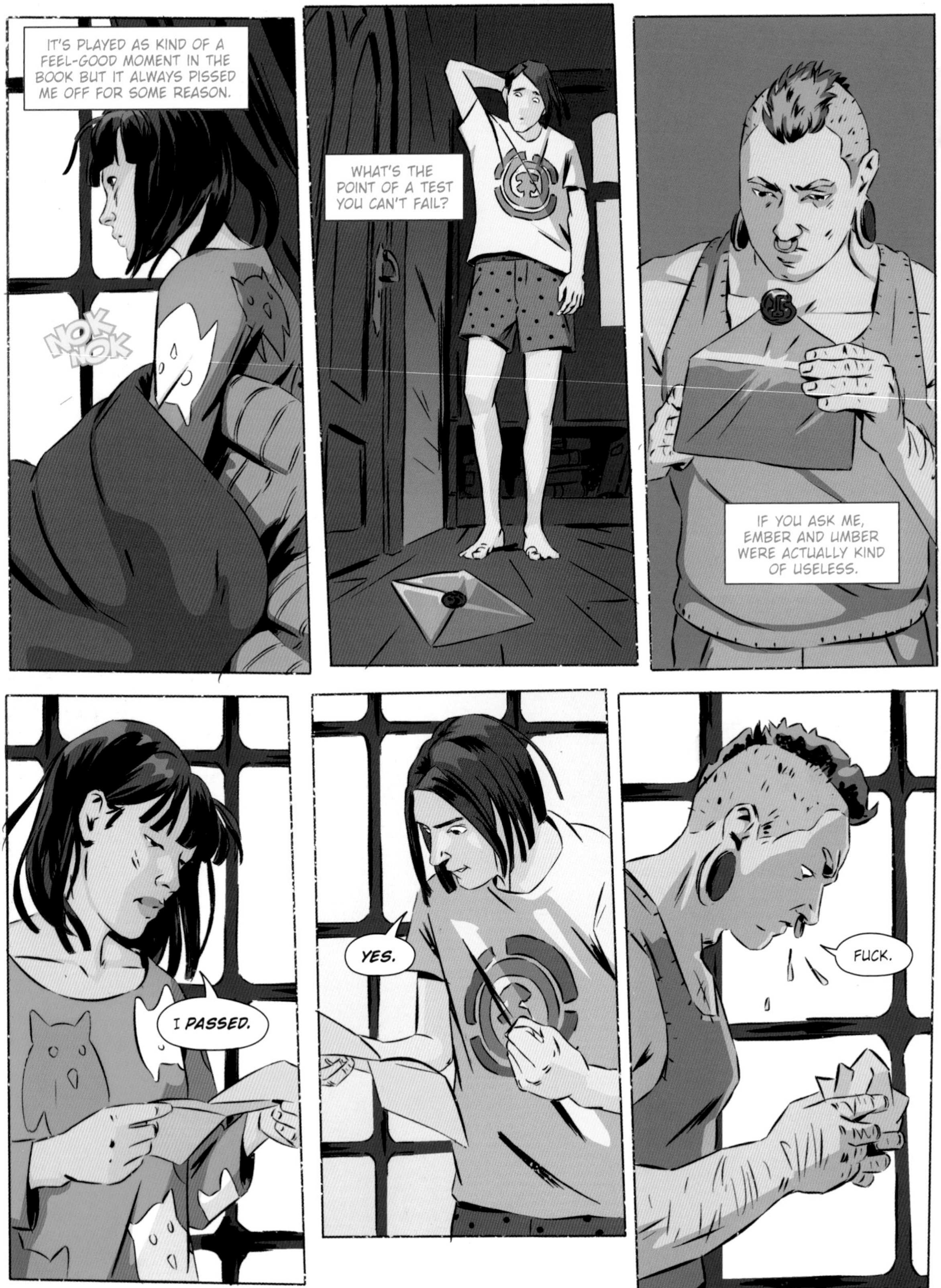
IT'S PLAYED AS KIND OF A FEEL-GOOD MOMENT IN THE BOOK BUT IT ALWAYS PISSED ME OFF FOR SOME REASON.
NOK NOK
WHAT'S THE POINT OF A TEST YOU CAN'T FAIL?
IF YOU ASK ME, EMBER AND UMBER WERE ACTUALLY KIND OF USELESS.
I *PASSED.*
YES.
FUCK.

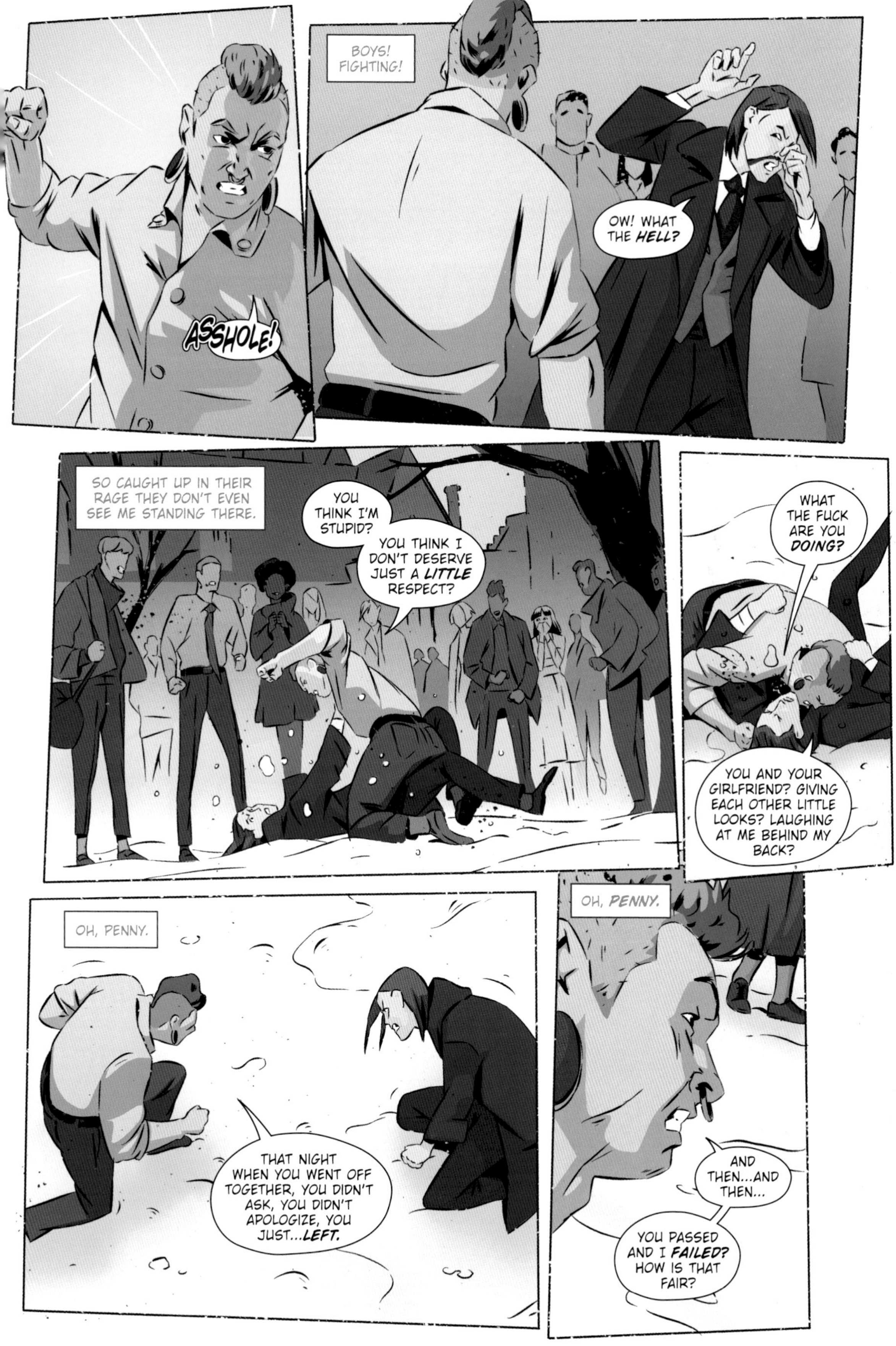
ASSHOLE!
BOYS! FIGHTING!
OW! WHAT THE **HELL?**
SO CAUGHT UP IN THEIR RAGE THEY DON'T EVEN SEE ME STANDING THERE.
YOU THINK I'M STUPID?
YOU THINK I DON'T DESERVE JUST A ***LITTLE*** RESPECT?
WHAT THE FUCK ARE YOU ***DOING?***
YOU AND YOUR GIRLFRIEND? GIVING EACH OTHER LITTLE LOOKS? LAUGHING AT ME BEHIND MY BACK?
OH, PENNY.
THAT NIGHT WHEN YOU WENT OFF TOGETHER, YOU DIDN'T ASK, YOU DIDN'T APOLOGIZE, YOU JUST...***LEFT.***
OH, ***PENNY.***
AND THEN...AND THEN...
YOU PASSED AND I ***FAILED?*** HOW IS THAT FAIR?

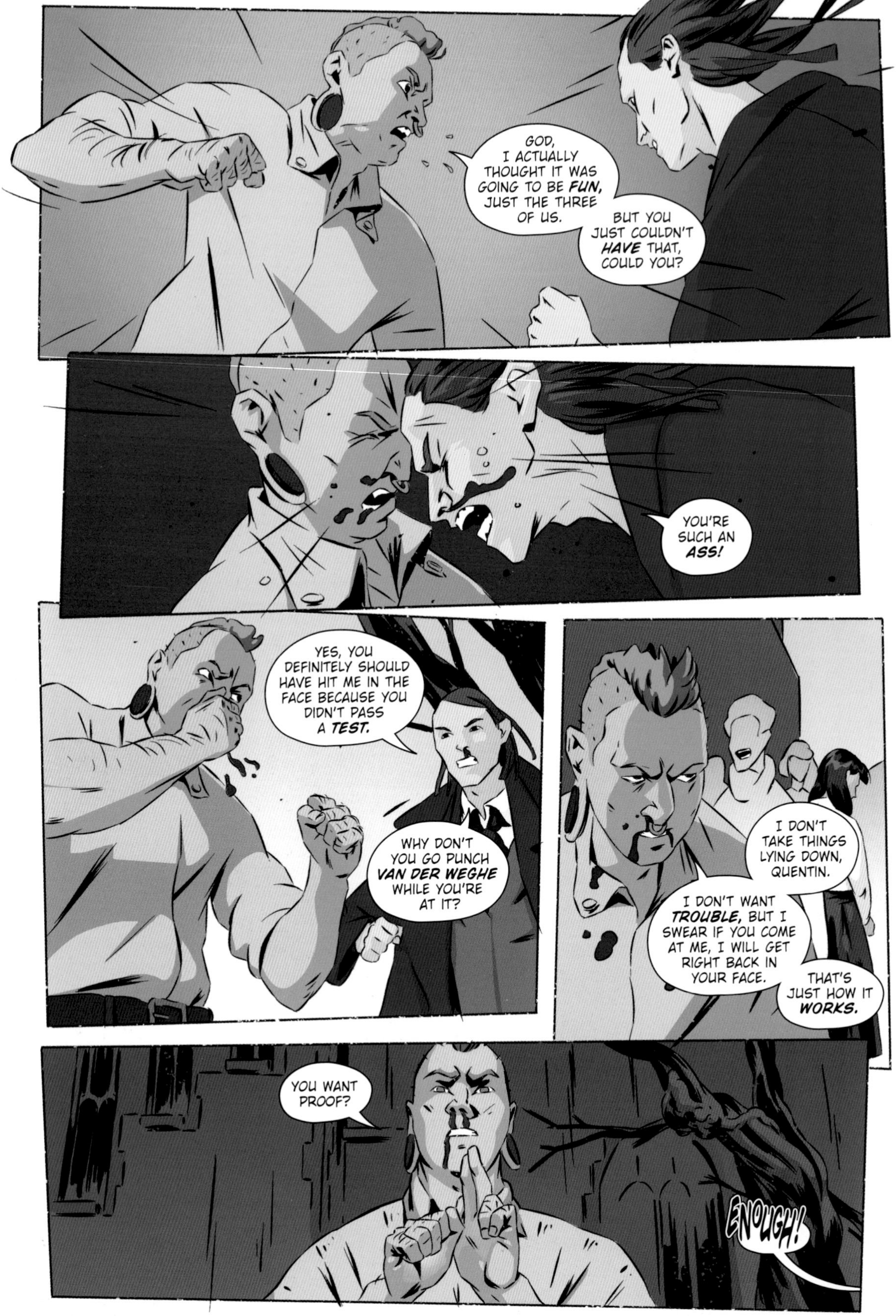
GOD, I ACTUALLY THOUGHT IT WAS GOING TO BE FUN, JUST THE THREE OF US.
BUT YOU JUST COULDN'T HAVE THAT, COULD YOU?
YOU'RE SUCH AN ASS!
YES, YOU DEFINITELY SHOULD HAVE HIT ME IN THE FACE BECAUSE YOU DIDN'T PASS A TEST.
WHY DON'T YOU GO PUNCH VAN DER WEGHE WHILE YOU'RE AT IT?
I DON'T TAKE THINGS LYING DOWN, QUENTIN.
I DON'T WANT TROUBLE, BUT I SWEAR IF YOU COME AT ME, I WILL GET RIGHT BACK IN YOUR FACE.
THAT'S JUST HOW IT WORKS.
YOU WANT PROOF?
ENOUGH!

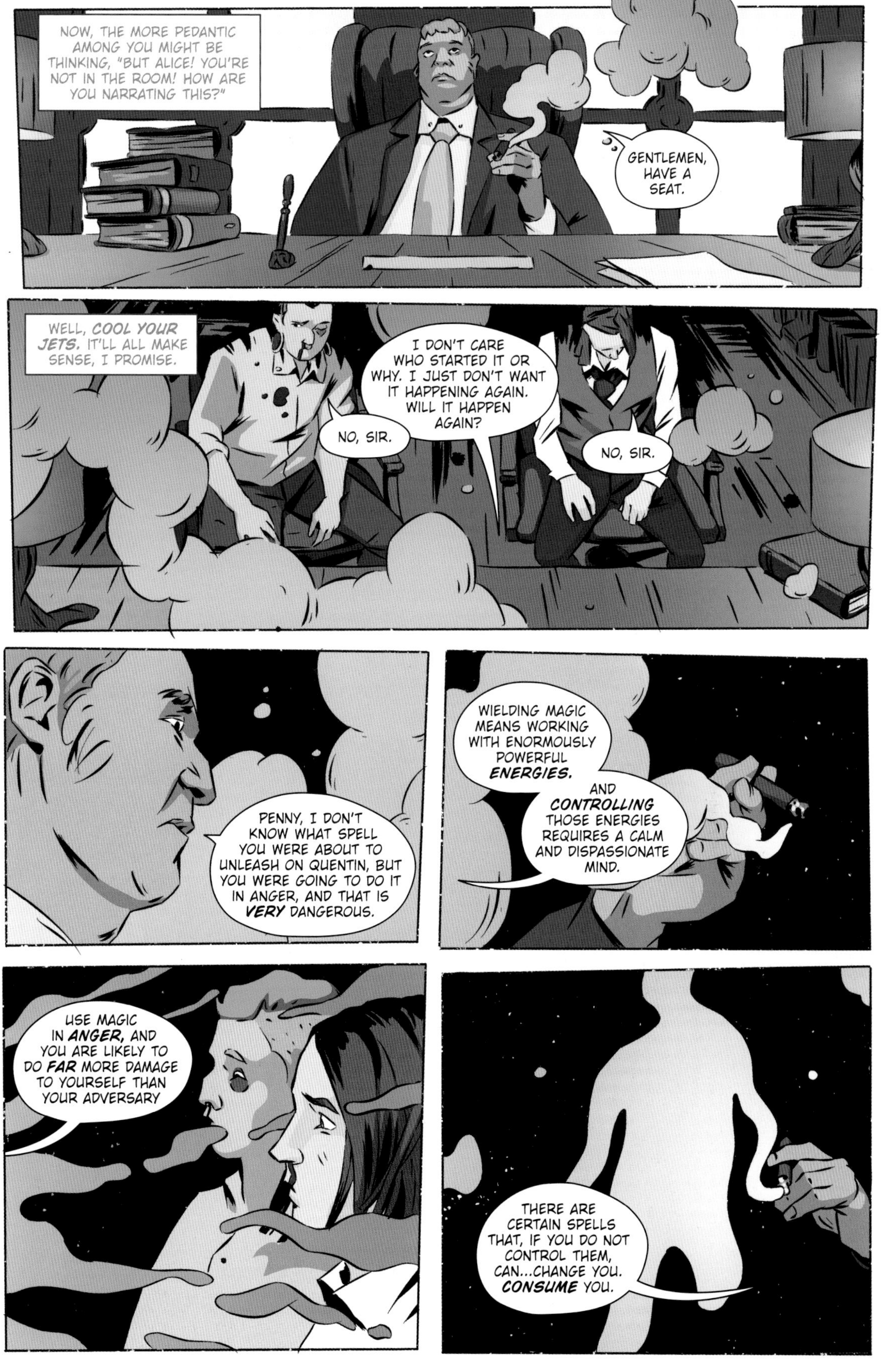
NOW, THE MORE PEDANTIC AMONG YOU MIGHT BE THINKING, "BUT ALICE! YOU'RE NOT IN THE ROOM! HOW ARE YOU NARRATING THIS?"
GENTLEMEN, HAVE A SEAT.
WELL, COOL YOUR JETS. IT'LL ALL MAKE SENSE, I PROMISE.
I DON'T CARE WHO STARTED IT OR WHY. I JUST DON'T WANT IT HAPPENING AGAIN. WILL IT HAPPEN AGAIN?
NO, SIR.
NO, SIR.
PENNY, I DON'T KNOW WHAT SPELL YOU WERE ABOUT TO UNLEASH ON QUENTIN, BUT YOU WERE GOING TO DO IT IN ANGER, AND THAT IS VERY DANGEROUS.
WIELDING MAGIC MEANS WORKING WITH ENORMOUSLY POWERFUL ENERGIES.
AND CONTROLLING THOSE ENERGIES REQUIRES A CALM AND DISPASSIONATE MIND.
USE MAGIC IN ANGER, AND YOU ARE LIKELY TO DO FAR MORE DAMAGE TO YOURSELF THAN YOUR ADVERSARY
THERE ARE CERTAIN SPELLS THAT, IF YOU DO NOT CONTROL THEM, CAN...CHANGE YOU. CONSUME YOU.

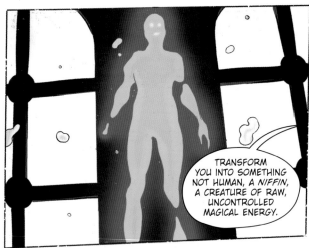

TRANSFORM YOU INTO SOMETHING NOT HUMAN, A *NIFFIN*, A CREATURE OF RAW, UNCONTROLLED MAGICAL ENERGY.

MOST PEOPLE ARE BLIND TO MAGIC, BOYS. THEY MOVE THROUGH A *BLANK* AND *EMPTY* WORLD.

THEY'RE EATEN ALIVE BY LONGING AND THEY'RE *DEAD* BEFORE THEY *DIE.*

BUT *YOU* LIVE IN THE MAGICAL WORLD, AND IF YOU WANT TO GET KILLED AROUND HERE THERE ARE PLENTY OF OPPORTUNITIES WITHOUT KILLING EACH OTHER.

IF IT HAPPENS AGAIN, YOU'RE *BOTH* EXPELLED.

DISMISSED.

WOW, COULD YOU BELIEVE THAT? ABOUT THE *NIFFIN*? ABOUT MAGIC CONSUMING YOU?

FIRST OF ALL, YOUR HAIR IS STUPID.

SECOND, IF YOU EVER DO ANYTHING THAT MIGHT GET ME SENT BACK TO BROOKLYN AGAIN?

I WON'T JUST BREAK YOUR NOSE. I WILL MOTHERFUCKING *KILL* YOU.

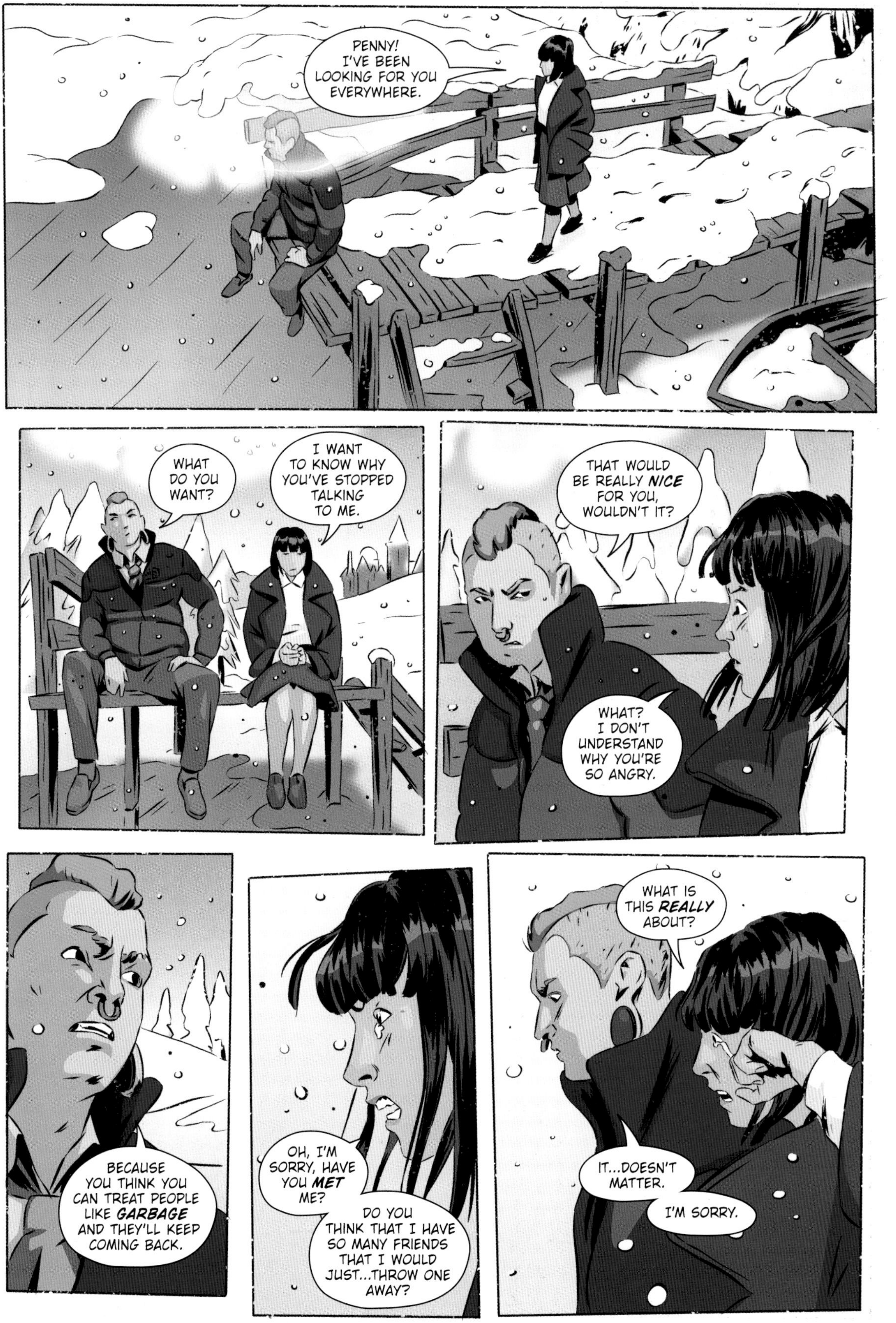
PENNY! I'VE BEEN LOOKING FOR YOU EVERYWHERE.
WHAT DO YOU WANT?
I WANT TO KNOW WHY YOU'VE STOPPED TALKING TO ME.
THAT WOULD BE REALLY NICE FOR YOU, WOULDN'T IT?
WHAT? I DON'T UNDERSTAND WHY YOU'RE SO ANGRY.
BECAUSE YOU THINK YOU CAN TREAT PEOPLE LIKE GARBAGE AND THEY'LL KEEP COMING BACK.
OH, I'M SORRY, HAVE YOU MET ME?
DO YOU THINK THAT I HAVE SO MANY FRIENDS THAT I WOULD JUST...THROW ONE AWAY?
WHAT IS THIS REALLY ABOUT?
IT...DOESN'T MATTER.
I'M SORRY.

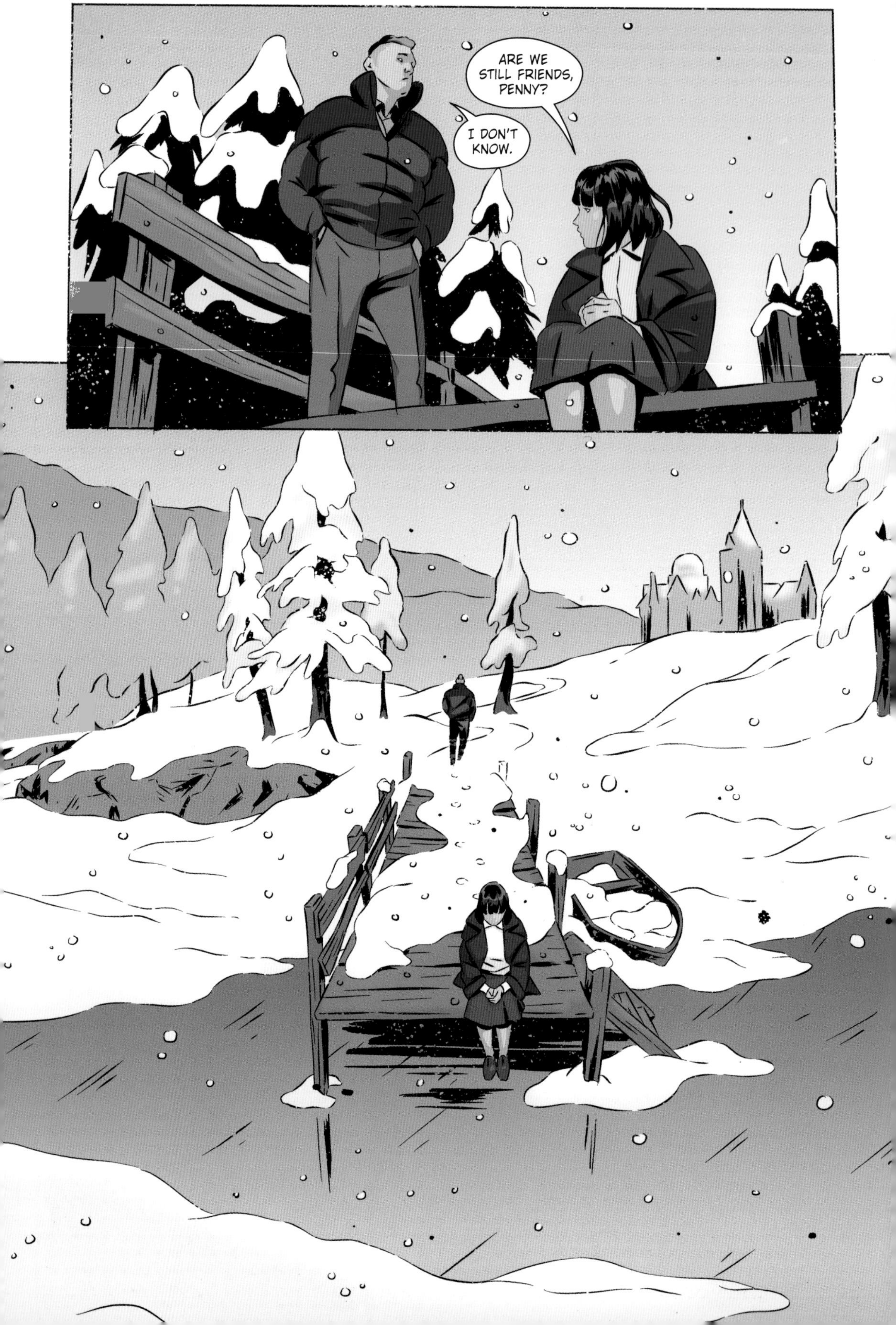
ARE WE STILL FRIENDS, PENNY?
I DON'T KNOW.

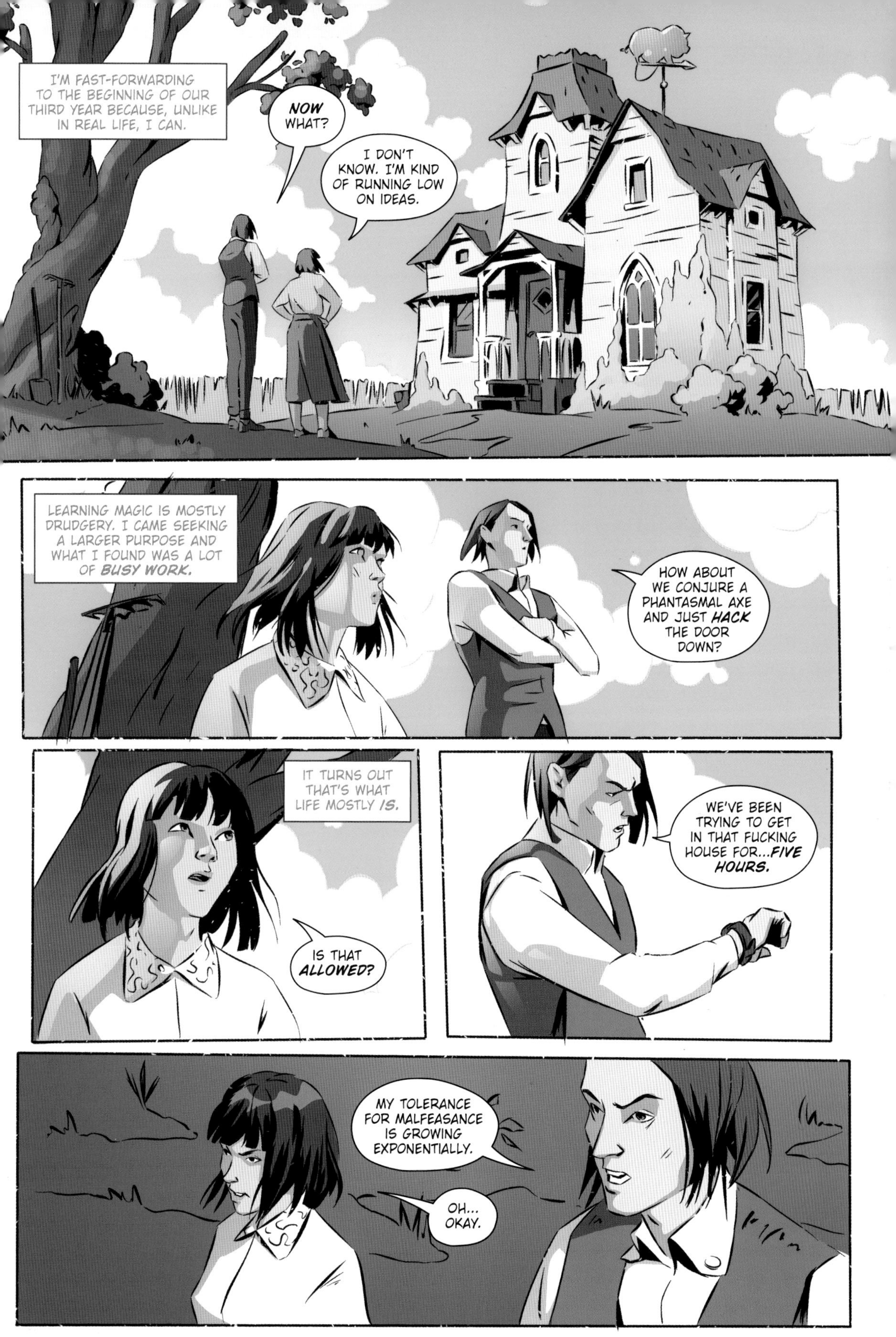
I'M FAST-FORWARDING TO THE BEGINNING OF OUR THIRD YEAR BECAUSE, UNLIKE IN REAL LIFE, I CAN.
NOW WHAT?
I DON'T KNOW. I'M KIND OF RUNNING LOW ON IDEAS.
LEARNING MAGIC IS MOSTLY DRUDGERY. I CAME SEEKING A LARGER PURPOSE AND WHAT I FOUND WAS A LOT OF BUSY WORK.
HOW ABOUT WE CONJURE A PHANTASMAL AXE AND JUST HACK THE DOOR DOWN?
IT TURNS OUT THAT'S WHAT LIFE MOSTLY IS.
IS THAT ALLOWED?
WE'VE BEEN TRYING TO GET IN THAT FUCKING HOUSE FOR...FIVE HOURS.
MY TOLERANCE FOR MALFEASANCE IS GROWING EXPONENTIALLY.
OH... OKAY.

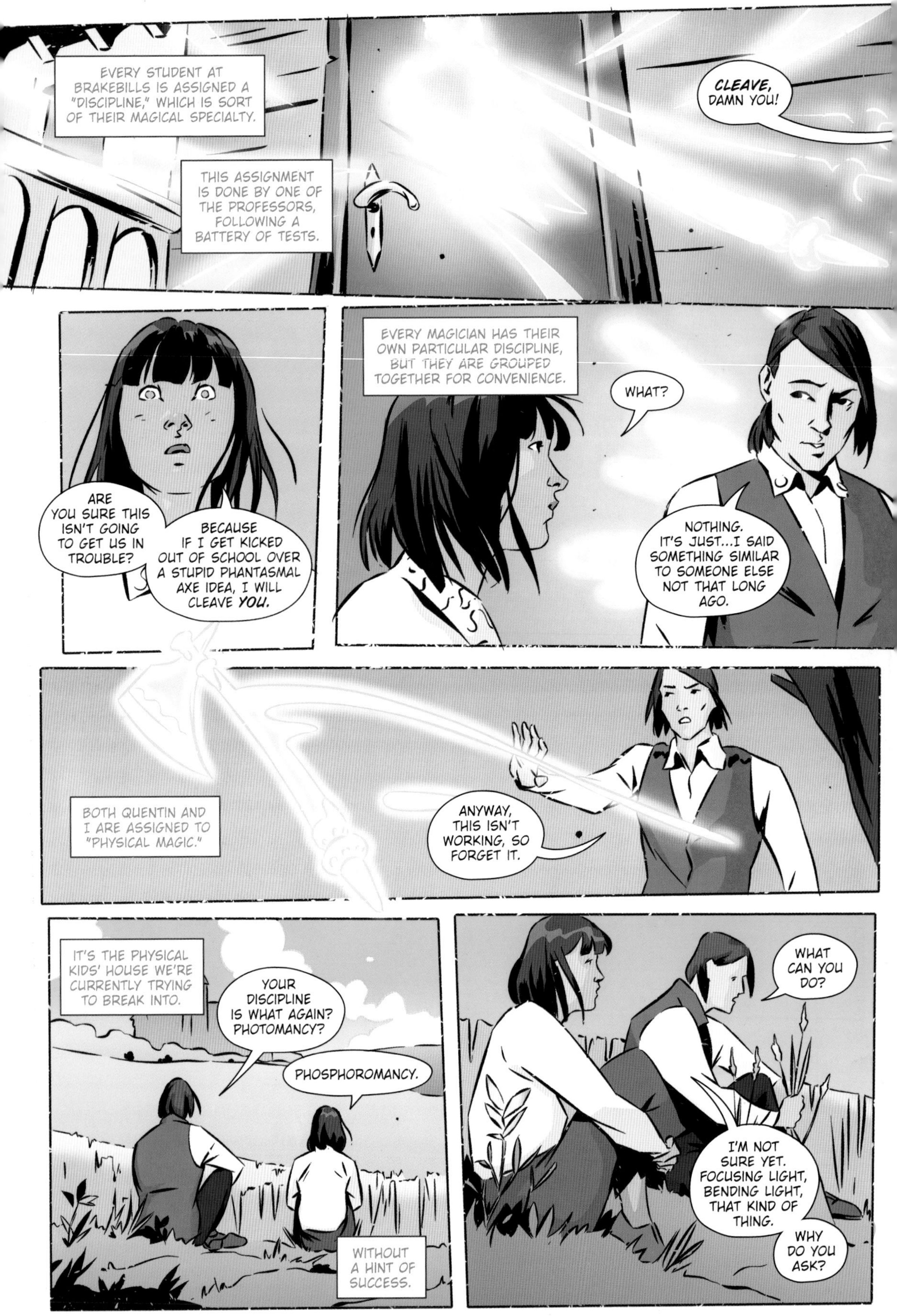
EVERY STUDENT AT BRAKEBILLS IS ASSIGNED A "DISCIPLINE," WHICH IS SORT OF THEIR MAGICAL SPECIALTY.
THIS ASSIGNMENT IS DONE BY ONE OF THE PROFESSORS, FOLLOWING A BATTERY OF TESTS.
CLEAVE, DAMN YOU!
ARE YOU SURE THIS ISN'T GOING TO GET US IN TROUBLE?
BECAUSE IF I GET KICKED OUT OF SCHOOL OVER A STUPID PHANTASMAL AXE IDEA, I WILL CLEAVE YOU.
EVERY MAGICIAN HAS THEIR OWN PARTICULAR DISCIPLINE, BUT THEY ARE GROUPED TOGETHER FOR CONVENIENCE.
WHAT?
NOTHING. IT'S JUST...I SAID SOMETHING SIMILAR TO SOMEONE ELSE NOT THAT LONG AGO.
BOTH QUENTIN AND I ARE ASSIGNED TO "PHYSICAL MAGIC."
ANYWAY, THIS ISN'T WORKING, SO FORGET IT.
IT'S THE PHYSICAL KIDS' HOUSE WE'RE CURRENTLY TRYING TO BREAK INTO.
YOUR DISCIPLINE IS WHAT AGAIN? PHOTOMANCY?
PHOSPHOROMANCY.
WITHOUT A HINT OF SUCCESS.
WHAT CAN YOU DO?
I'M NOT SURE YET. FOCUSING LIGHT, BENDING LIGHT, THAT KIND OF THING.
WHY DO YOU ASK?

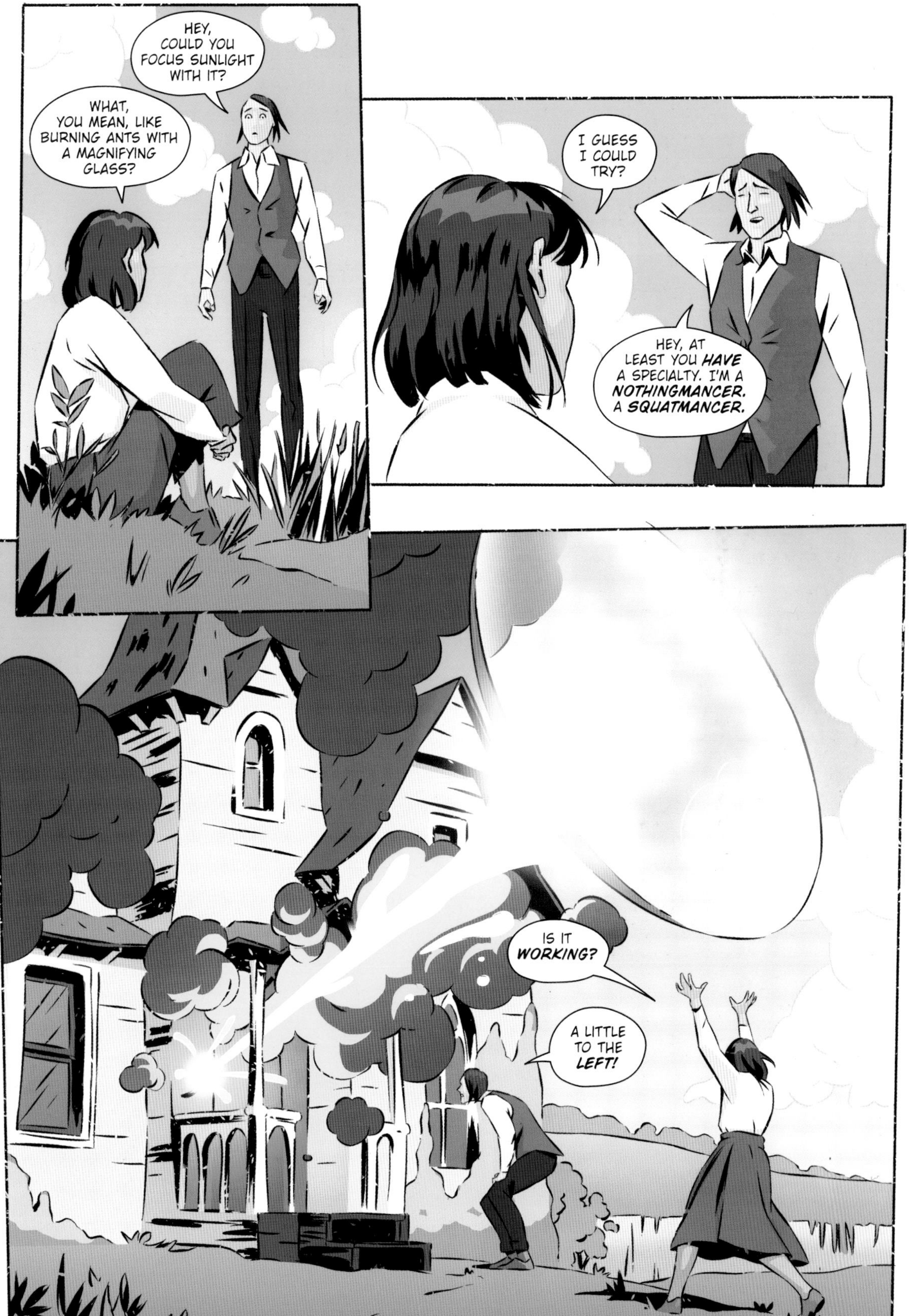
HEY, COULD YOU FOCUS SUNLIGHT WITH IT?
WHAT, YOU MEAN, LIKE BURNING ANTS WITH A MAGNIFYING GLASS?
I GUESS I COULD TRY?
HEY, AT LEAST YOU **HAVE** A SPECIALTY. I'M A ***NOTHINGMANCER.*** A ***SQUATMANCER.***
IS IT ***WORKING?***
A LITTLE TO THE ***LEFT!***

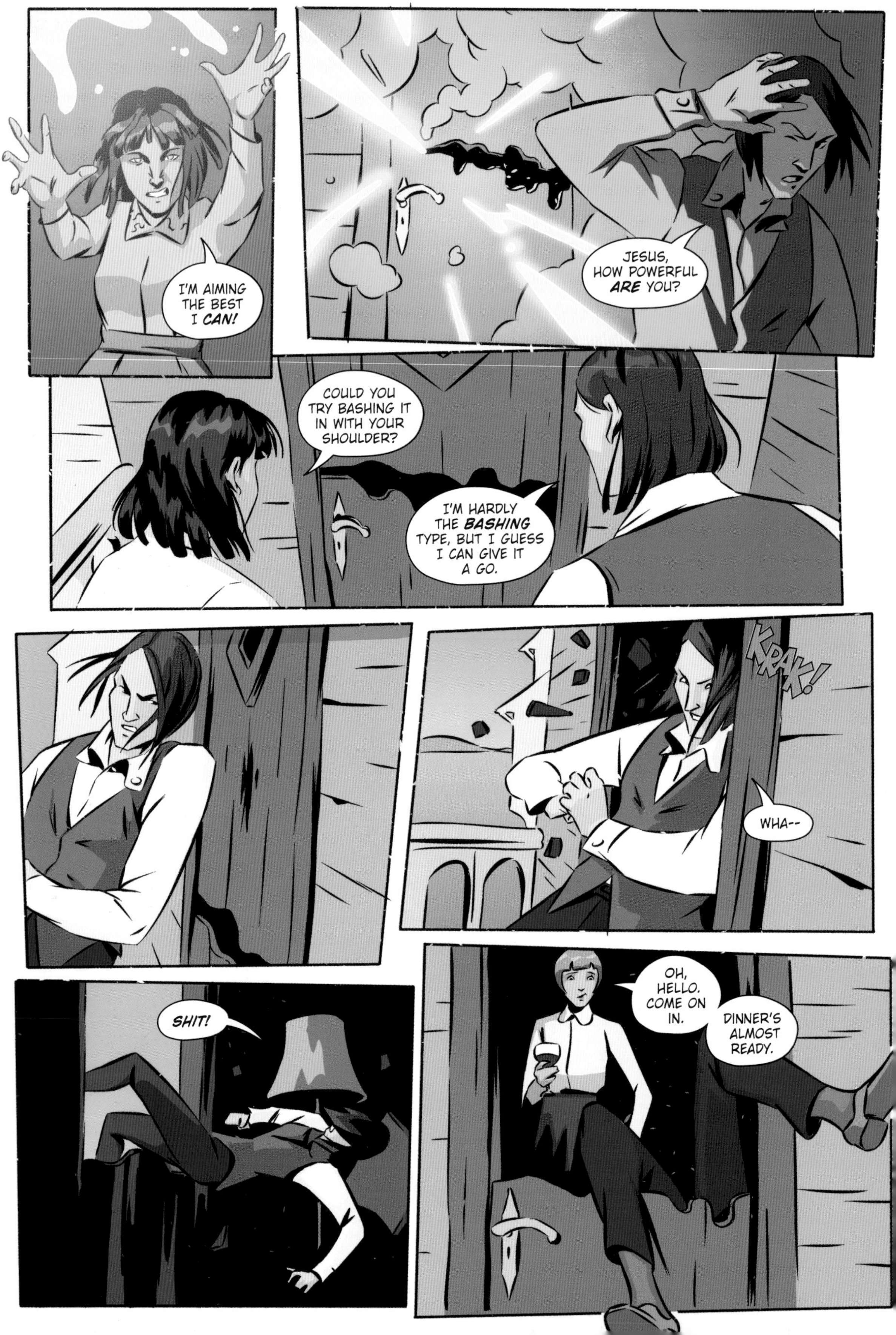
I'M AIMING THE BEST I *CAN!*
JESUS, HOW POWERFUL *ARE* YOU?
COULD YOU TRY BASHING IT IN WITH YOUR SHOULDER?
I'M HARDLY THE *BASHING* TYPE, BUT I GUESS I CAN GIVE IT A GO.
KRAK!
WHA--
SHIT!
OH, HELLO. COME ON IN.
DINNER'S ALMOST READY.

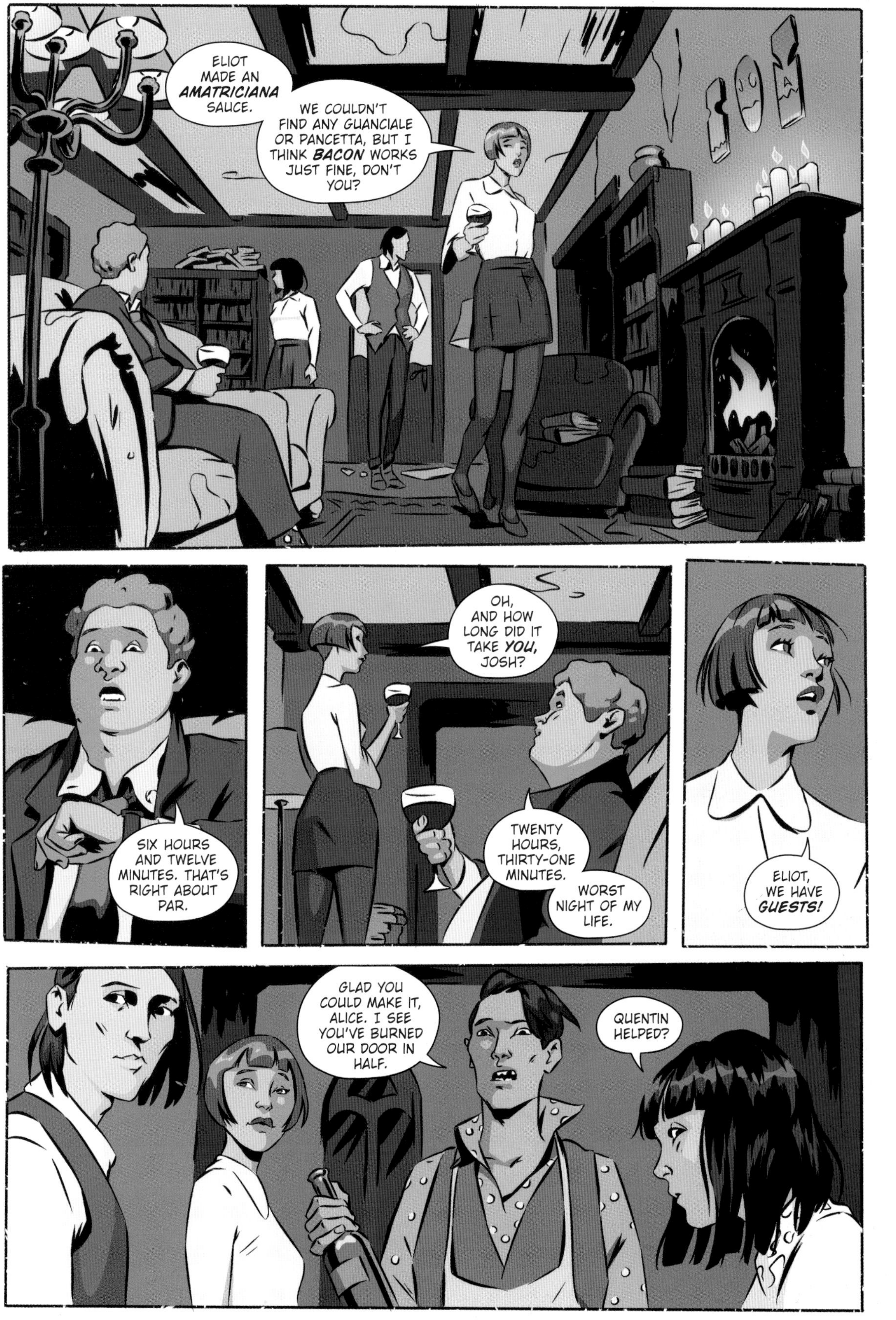
ELIOT MADE AN AMATRICIANA SAUCE.
WE COULDN'T FIND ANY GUANCIALE OR PANCETTA, BUT I THINK BACON WORKS JUST FINE, DON'T YOU?
SIX HOURS AND TWELVE MINUTES. THAT'S RIGHT ABOUT PAR.
OH, AND HOW LONG DID IT TAKE YOU, JOSH?
TWENTY HOURS, THIRTY-ONE MINUTES.
WORST NIGHT OF MY LIFE.
ELIOT, WE HAVE GUESTS!
GLAD YOU COULD MAKE IT, ALICE. I SEE YOU'VE BURNED OUR DOOR IN HALF.
QUENTIN HELPED?

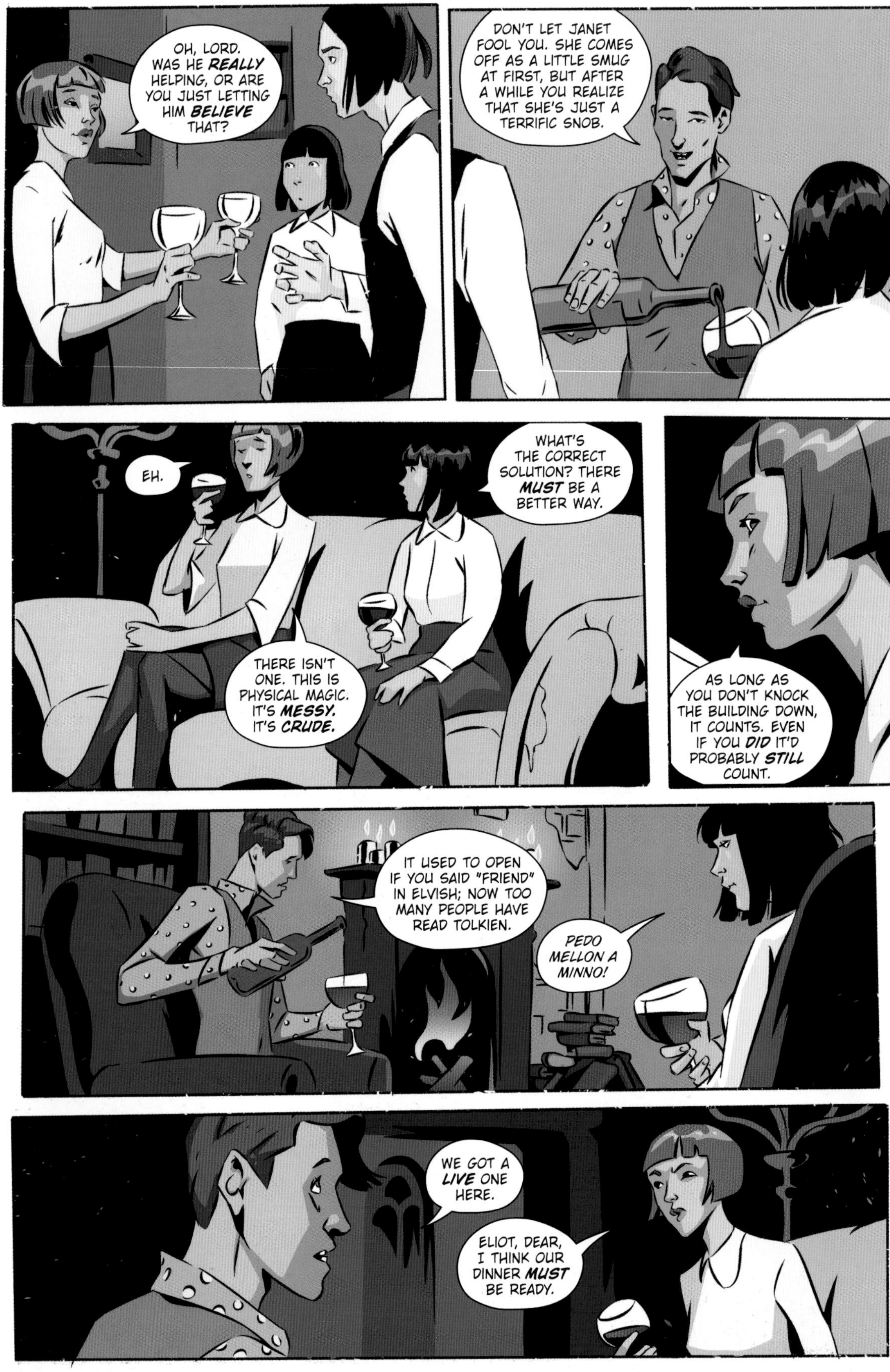
OH, LORD. WAS HE *REALLY* HELPING, OR ARE YOU JUST LETTING HIM *BELIEVE* THAT?
DON'T LET JANET FOOL YOU. SHE COMES OFF AS A LITTLE SMUG AT FIRST, BUT AFTER A WHILE YOU REALIZE THAT SHE'S JUST A TERRIFIC SNOB.
EH.
WHAT'S THE CORRECT SOLUTION? THERE *MUST* BE A BETTER WAY.
THERE ISN'T ONE. THIS IS PHYSICAL MAGIC. IT'S *MESSY.* IT'S *CRUDE.*
AS LONG AS YOU DON'T KNOCK THE BUILDING DOWN, IT COUNTS. EVEN IF YOU *DID* IT'D PROBABLY *STILL* COUNT.
IT USED TO OPEN IF YOU SAID "FRIEND" IN ELVISH; NOW TOO MANY PEOPLE HAVE READ TOLKIEN.
PEDO MELLON A MINNO!
WE GOT A *LIVE* ONE HERE.
ELIOT, DEAR, I THINK OUR DINNER *MUST* BE READY.

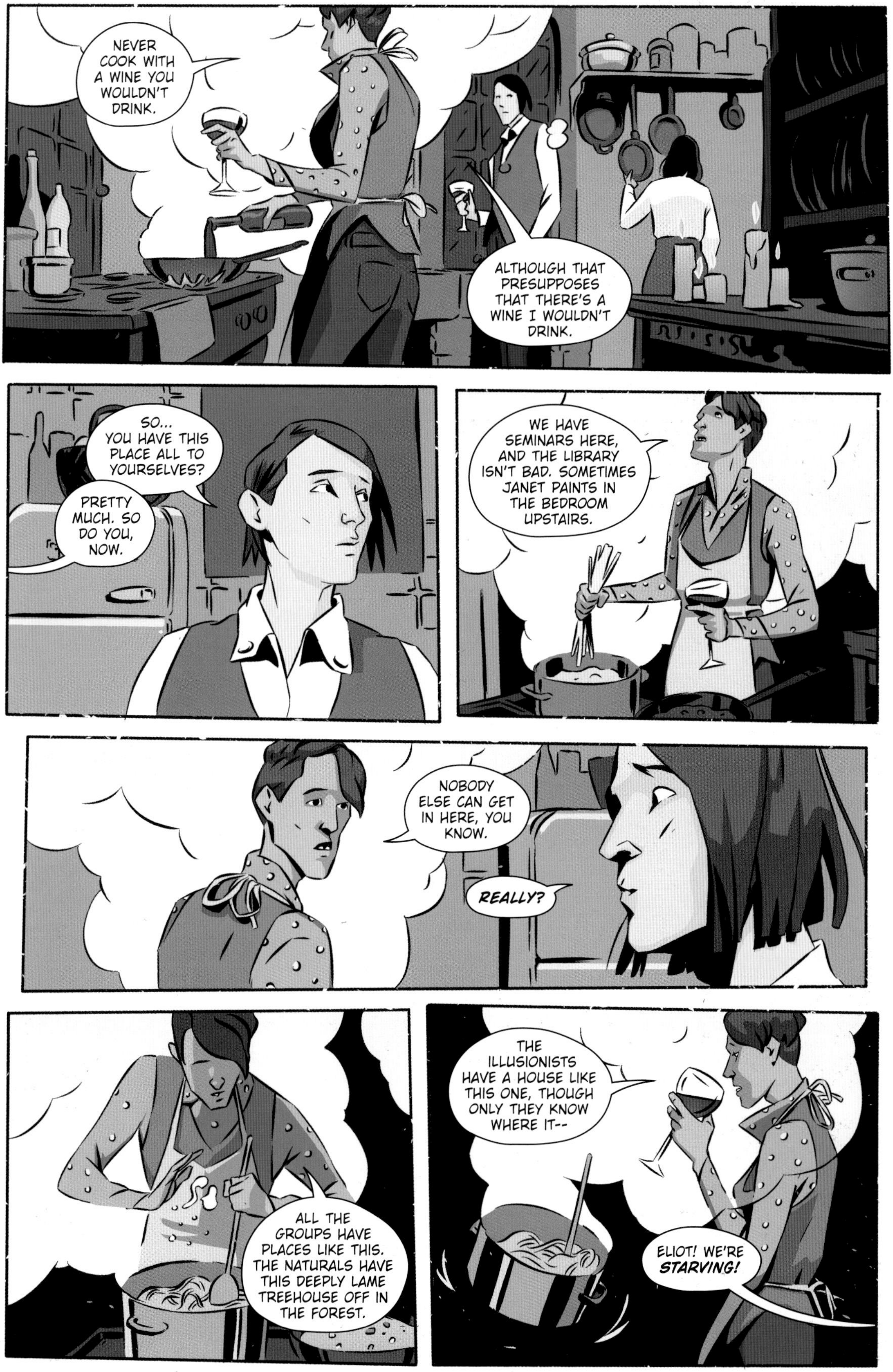
NEVER COOK WITH A WINE YOU WOULDN'T DRINK.
ALTHOUGH THAT PRESUPPOSES THAT THERE'S A WINE I WOULDN'T DRINK.
SO... YOU HAVE THIS PLACE ALL TO YOURSELVES?
PRETTY MUCH. SO DO YOU, NOW.
WE HAVE SEMINARS HERE, AND THE LIBRARY ISN'T BAD. SOMETIMES JANET PAINTS IN THE BEDROOM UPSTAIRS.
NOBODY ELSE CAN GET IN HERE, YOU KNOW.
REALLY?
ALL THE GROUPS HAVE PLACES LIKE THIS. THE NATURALS HAVE THIS DEEPLY LAME TREEHOUSE OFF IN THE FOREST.
THE ILLUSIONISTS HAVE A HOUSE LIKE THIS ONE, THOUGH ONLY THEY KNOW WHERE IT--
ELIOT! WE'RE STARVING!

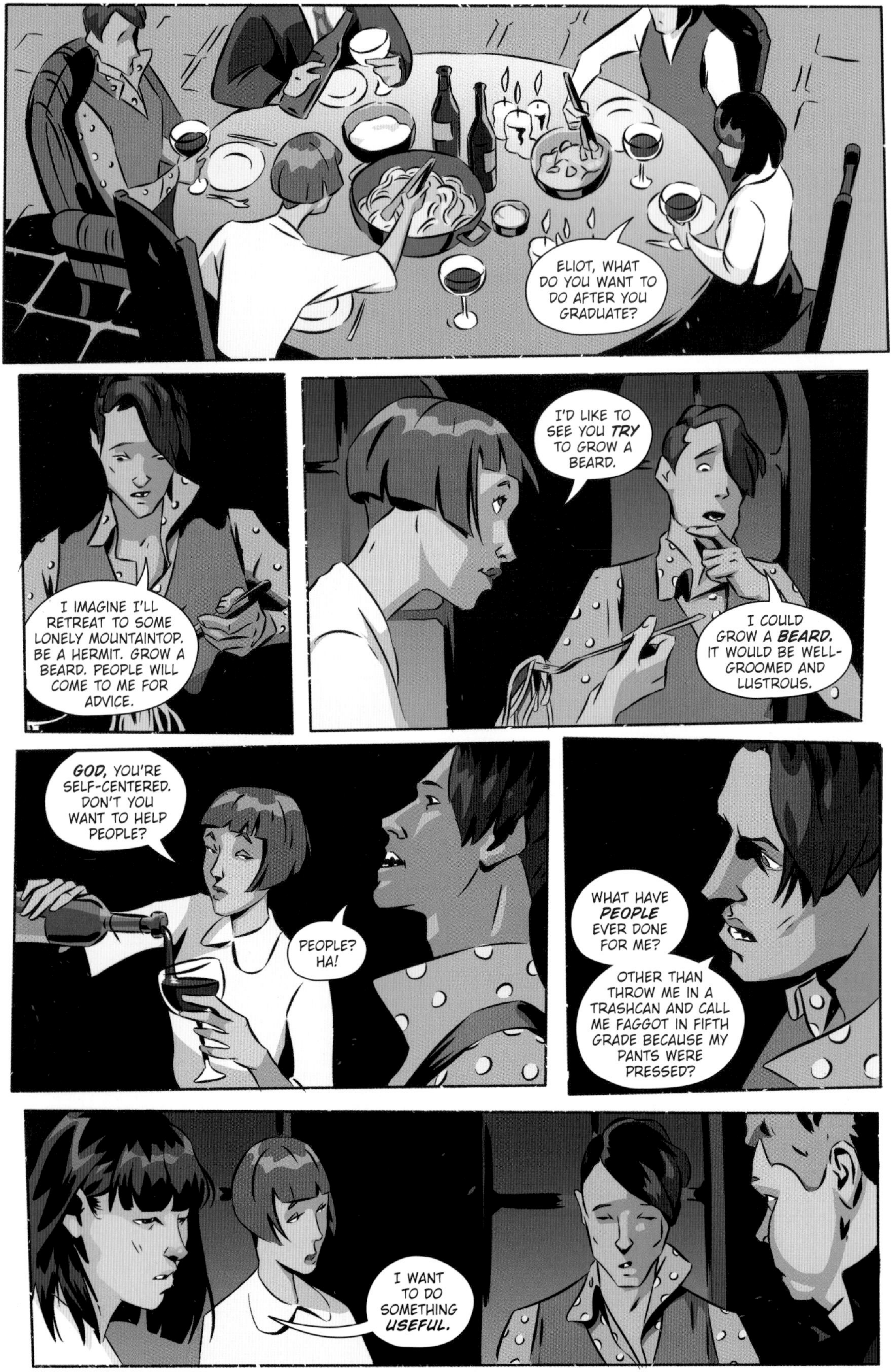
ELIOT, WHAT DO YOU WANT TO DO AFTER YOU GRADUATE?
I IMAGINE I'LL RETREAT TO SOME LONELY MOUNTAINTOP. BE A HERMIT. GROW A BEARD. PEOPLE WILL COME TO ME FOR ADVICE.
I'D LIKE TO SEE YOU TRY TO GROW A BEARD.
I COULD GROW A BEARD. IT WOULD BE WELL-GROOMED AND LUSTROUS.
GOD, YOU'RE SELF-CENTERED. DON'T YOU WANT TO HELP PEOPLE?
PEOPLE? HA!
WHAT HAVE PEOPLE EVER DONE FOR ME?
OTHER THAN THROW ME IN A TRASHCAN AND CALL ME FAGGOT IN FIFTH GRADE BECAUSE MY PANTS WERE PRESSED?
I WANT TO DO SOMETHING USEFUL.

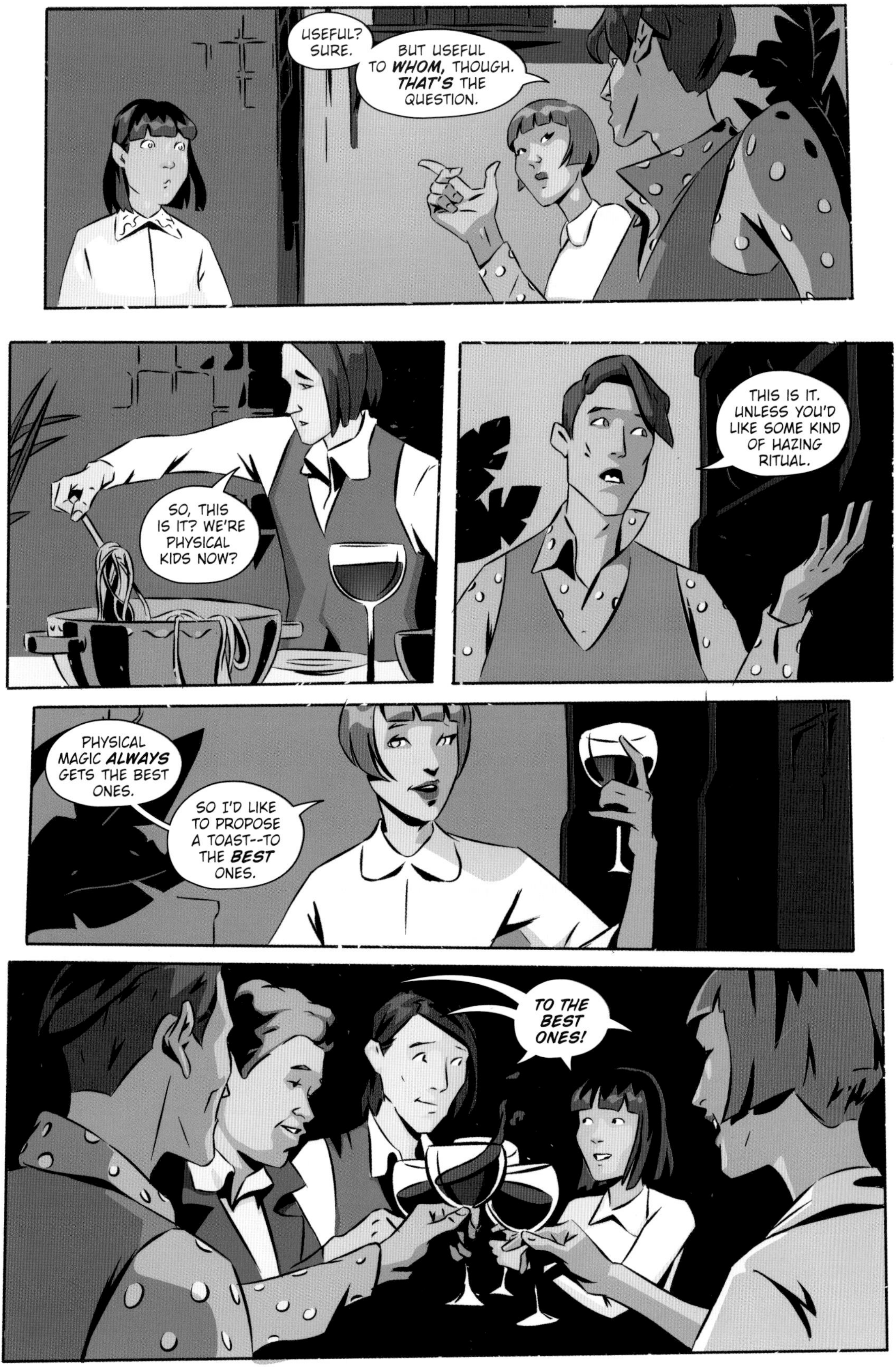
USEFUL? SURE.
BUT USEFUL TO WHOM, THOUGH. THAT'S THE QUESTION.
SO, THIS IS IT? WE'RE PHYSICAL KIDS NOW?
THIS IS IT. UNLESS YOU'D LIKE SOME KIND OF HAZING RITUAL.
PHYSICAL MAGIC ALWAYS GETS THE BEST ONES.
SO I'D LIKE TO PROPOSE A TOAST--TO THE BEST ONES.
TO THE BEST ONES!

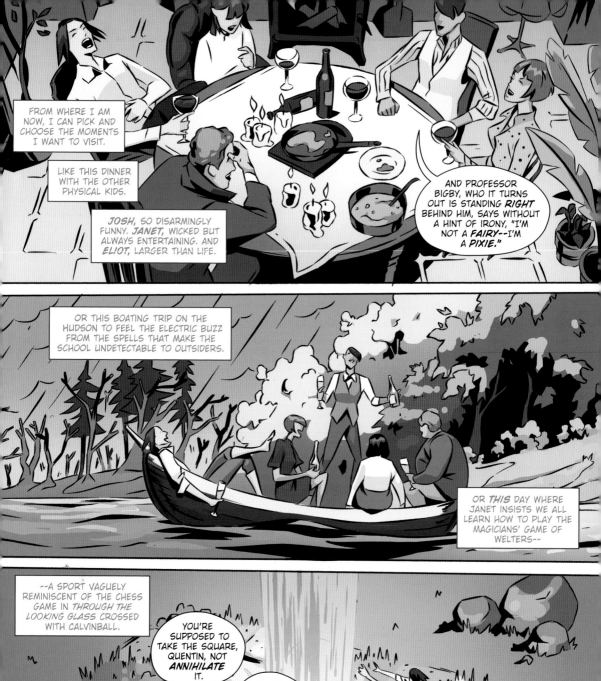

FROM WHERE I AM NOW, I CAN PICK AND CHOOSE THE MOMENTS I WANT TO VISIT.

LIKE THIS DINNER WITH THE OTHER PHYSICAL KIDS.

JOSH, SO DISARMINGLY FUNNY. *JANET*, WICKED BUT ALWAYS ENTERTAINING. AND *ELIOT*, LARGER THAN LIFE.

AND PROFESSOR BIGBY, WHO IT TURNS OUT IS STANDING *RIGHT* BEHIND HIM, SAYS WITHOUT A HINT OF IRONY, "I'M NOT A *FAIRY*--I'M A *PIXIE*."

OR THIS BOATING TRIP ON THE HUDSON TO FEEL THE ELECTRIC BUZZ FROM THE SPELLS THAT MAKE THE SCHOOL UNDETECTABLE TO OUTSIDERS.

OR *THIS* DAY WHERE JANET INSISTS WE ALL LEARN HOW TO PLAY THE MAGICIANS' GAME OF WELTERS--

--A SPORT VAGUELY REMINISCENT OF THE CHESS GAME IN *THROUGH THE LOOKING GLASS* CROSSED WITH CALVINBALL.

YOU'RE SUPPOSED TO TAKE THE SQUARE, QUENTIN, NOT *ANNIHILATE* IT.

THAT IS *CLEARLY* A VIOLATION OF THE OFFSIDES LINE-FOUL RULE!

THAT'S MADE UP. YOU JUST MADE THAT RULE UP.

YOU CAN'T PROVE THAT.

(SERIOUSLY, WELTERS IS BONKERS.)

TELLING A STORY IS LIKE DIPPING A TOE INTO THE PAST, BUT WITHOUT THE ABILITY TO DO ANYTHING ABOUT IT.

LIKE *MEMORY.*

IN THE SECOND FILLORY BOOK, *THE GIRL WHO TOLD TIME,* RUPERT AND HELEN CHATWIN ARE BROUGHT TO FILLORY AT A TIME JUST BEFORE THE BEGINNING OF THE FIRST BOOK.

BRAKEBILLS
UNIVERSITY

FIRST YEAR

RUPERT AND HELEN THEN FOLLOW JUST BEHIND MARTIN AND THE EARLIER VERSION OF HELEN, HELPING THEM OUT, OFFERING THEM CLUES, ETC.

FIR

TOP ROW: Charles Quinn, M
SECOND ROW h Hubert
THIRD ROW. Le a, Su
BOTTOM RO an Brittan

I USED TO WONDER HOW WEIRD THAT MUST HAVE BEEN FOR HELEN, WATCHING HERSELF RELIVE HER LIFE LIKE THAT.

UNI ITY

NOW I'M LEARNING.

FOURTH YEAR

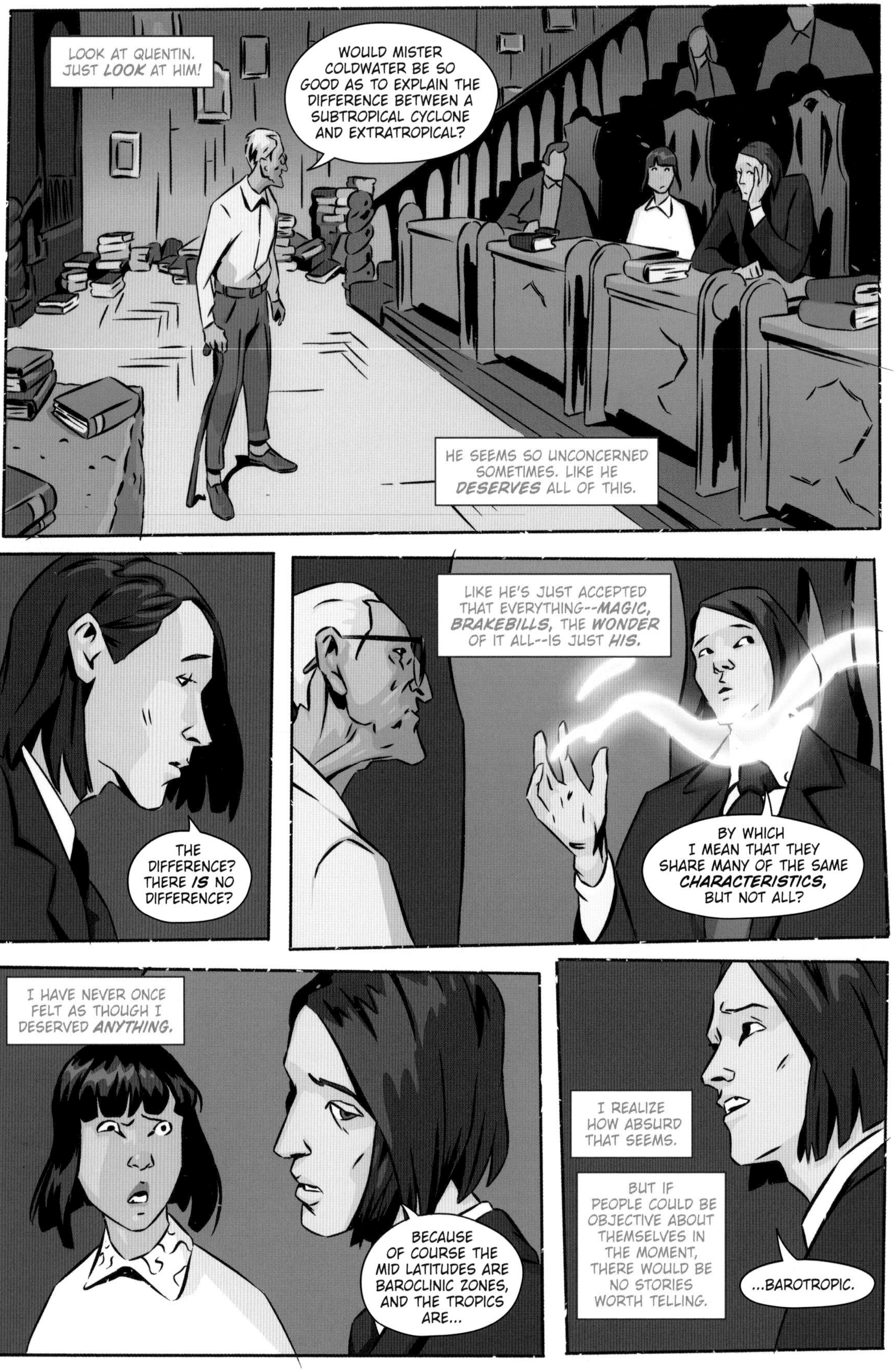
LOOK AT QUENTIN. JUST LOOK AT HIM!
WOULD MISTER COLDWATER BE SO GOOD AS TO EXPLAIN THE DIFFERENCE BETWEEN A SUBTROPICAL CYCLONE AND EXTRATROPICAL?
HE SEEMS SO UNCONCERNED SOMETIMES. LIKE HE DESERVES ALL OF THIS.
THE DIFFERENCE? THERE IS NO DIFFERENCE?
LIKE HE'S JUST ACCEPTED THAT EVERYTHING--MAGIC, BRAKEBILLS, THE WONDER OF IT ALL--IS JUST HIS.
BY WHICH I MEAN THAT THEY SHARE MANY OF THE SAME CHARACTERISTICS, BUT NOT ALL?
I HAVE NEVER ONCE FELT AS THOUGH I DESERVED ANYTHING.
BECAUSE OF COURSE THE MID LATITUDES ARE BAROCLINIC ZONES, AND THE TROPICS ARE...
I REALIZE HOW ABSURD THAT SEEMS.
BUT IF PEOPLE COULD BE OBJECTIVE ABOUT THEMSELVES IN THE MOMENT, THERE WOULD BE NO STORIES WORTH TELLING.
...BAROTROPIC.

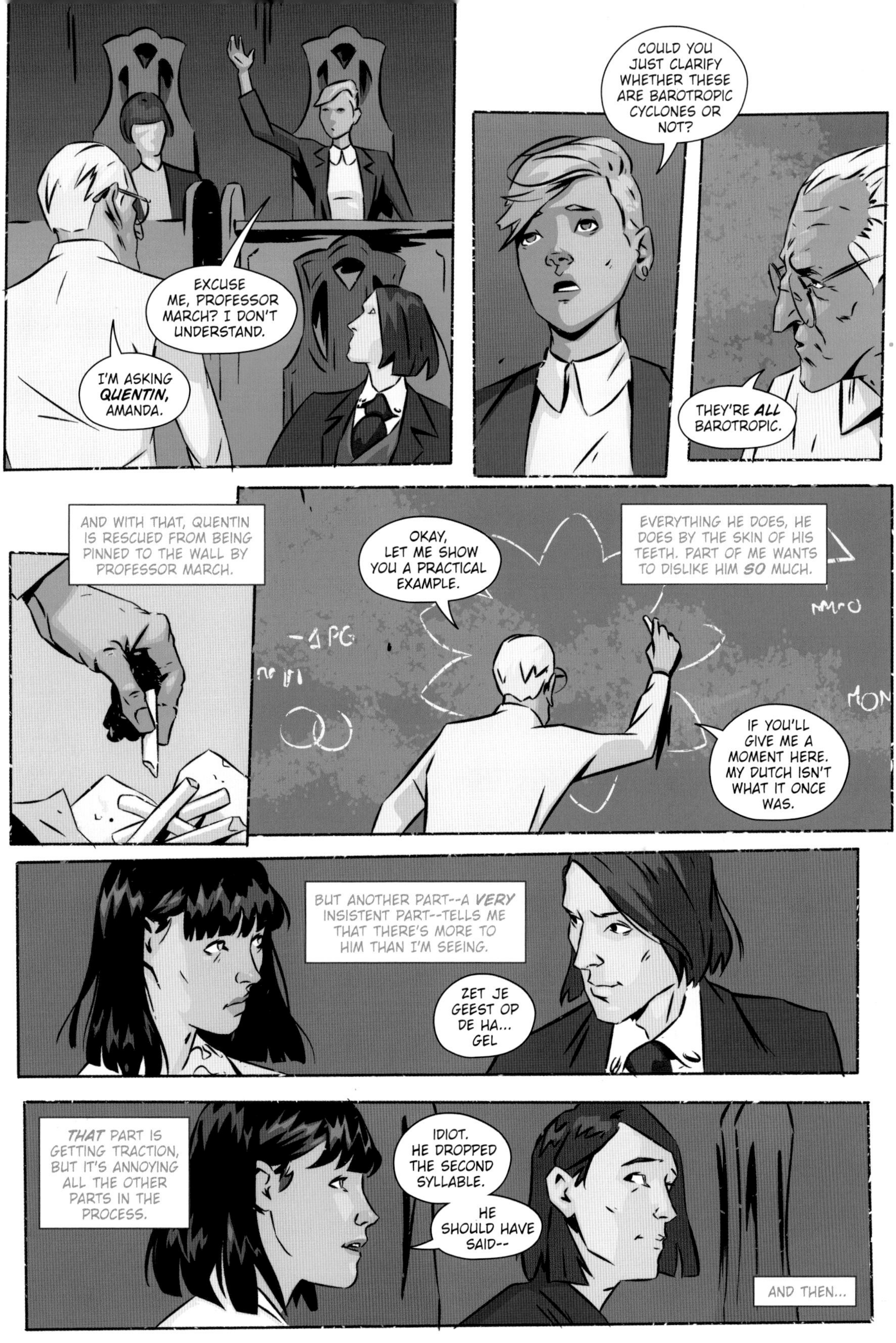
EXCUSE ME, PROFESSOR MARCH? I DON'T UNDERSTAND.
I'M ASKING *QUENTIN*, AMANDA.
COULD YOU JUST CLARIFY WHETHER THESE ARE BAROTROPIC CYCLONES OR NOT?
THEY'RE *ALL* BAROTROPIC.
AND WITH THAT, QUENTIN IS RESCUED FROM BEING PINNED TO THE WALL BY PROFESSOR MARCH.
OKAY, LET ME SHOW YOU A PRACTICAL EXAMPLE.
EVERYTHING HE DOES, HE DOES BY THE SKIN OF HIS TEETH. PART OF ME WANTS TO DISLIKE HIM *SO* MUCH.
IF YOU'LL GIVE ME A MOMENT HERE. MY DUTCH ISN'T WHAT IT ONCE WAS.
BUT ANOTHER PART--A *VERY* INSISTENT PART--TELLS ME THAT THERE'S MORE TO HIM THAN I'M SEEING.
ZET JE GEEST OP DE HA... GEL
THAT PART IS GETTING TRACTION, BUT IT'S ANNOYING ALL THE OTHER PARTS IN THE PROCESS.
IDIOT. HE DROPPED THE SECOND SYLLABLE.
HE SHOULD HAVE SAID--
AND THEN...

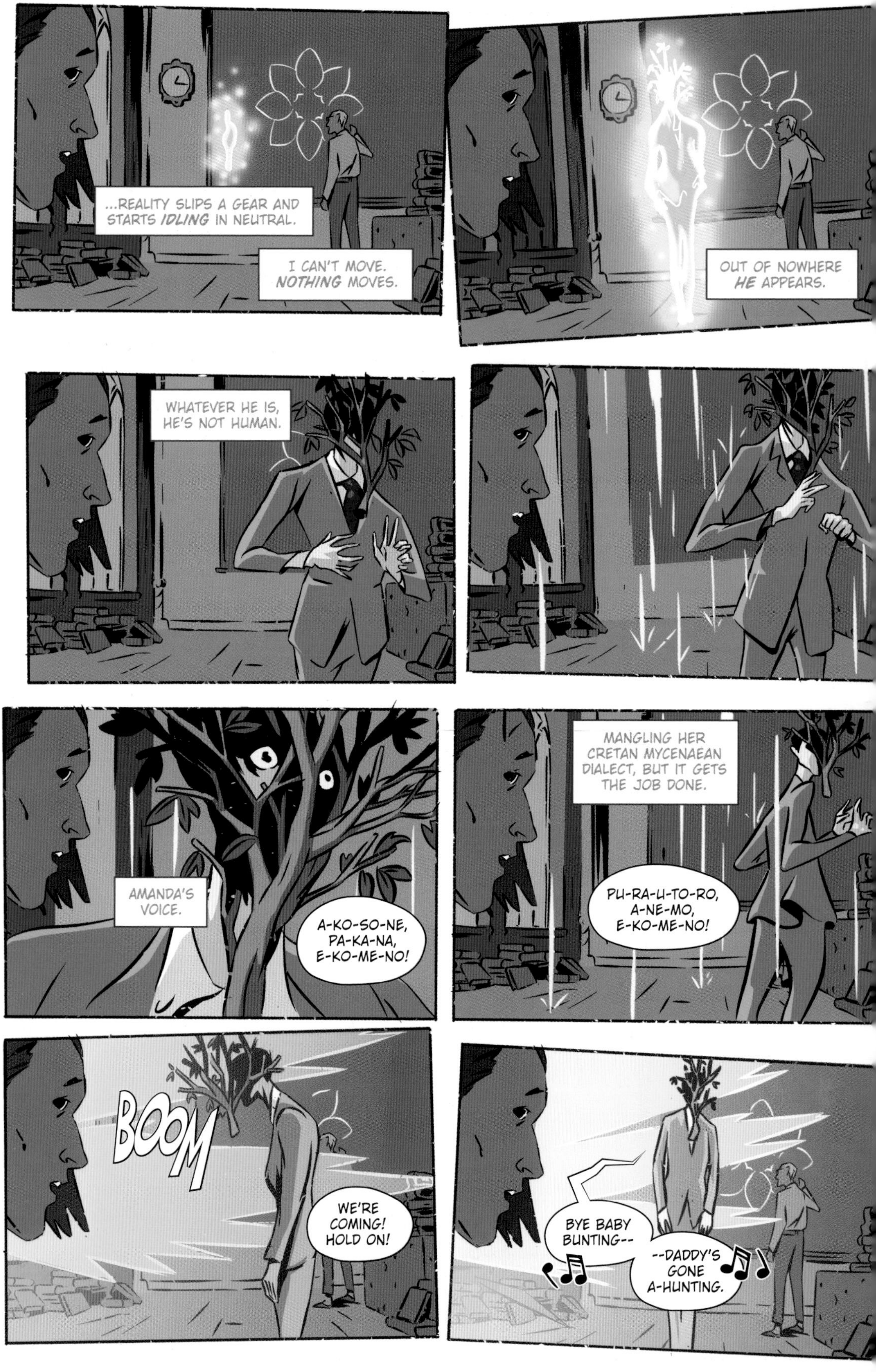
...REALITY SLIPS A GEAR AND STARTS IDLING IN NEUTRAL.
I CAN'T MOVE. NOTHING MOVES.
OUT OF NOWHERE HE APPEARS.
WHATEVER HE IS, HE'S NOT HUMAN.
AMANDA'S VOICE.
A-KO-SO-NE, PA-KA-NA, E-KO-ME-NO!
MANGLING HER CRETAN MYCENAEAN DIALECT, BUT IT GETS THE JOB DONE.
PU-RA-U-TO-RO, A-NE-MO, E-KO-ME-NO!
BOOM
WE'RE COMING! HOLD ON!
BYE BABY BUNTING--
--DADDY'S GONE A-HUNTING.

NO FANFARE. ONE MOMENT NOT THERE, THE NEXT MOMENT THERE.

HE IS IN NO RUSH. TIME PASSES.

HOW MUCH TIME I CAN'T SAY. I WILL LEARN LATER THAT IT'S HOURS.

OR, PERHAPS, NOT HUMAN ANYMORE.

A-KO-SO-NE, PA-KA-NA, E-KO-- >HLK<

MORE TIME PASSES. BUT HOW TO COUNT TIME WHEN YOUR GAZE DOESN'T CHANGE?

GONE TO GET A RABBIT SKIN--

--TO WRAP HIS BABY BUNTING IN. ♪♪

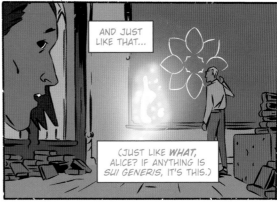

AND JUST LIKE THAT...

(JUST LIKE *WHAT*, ALICE? IF ANYTHING IS *SUI GENERIS*, IT'S THIS.)

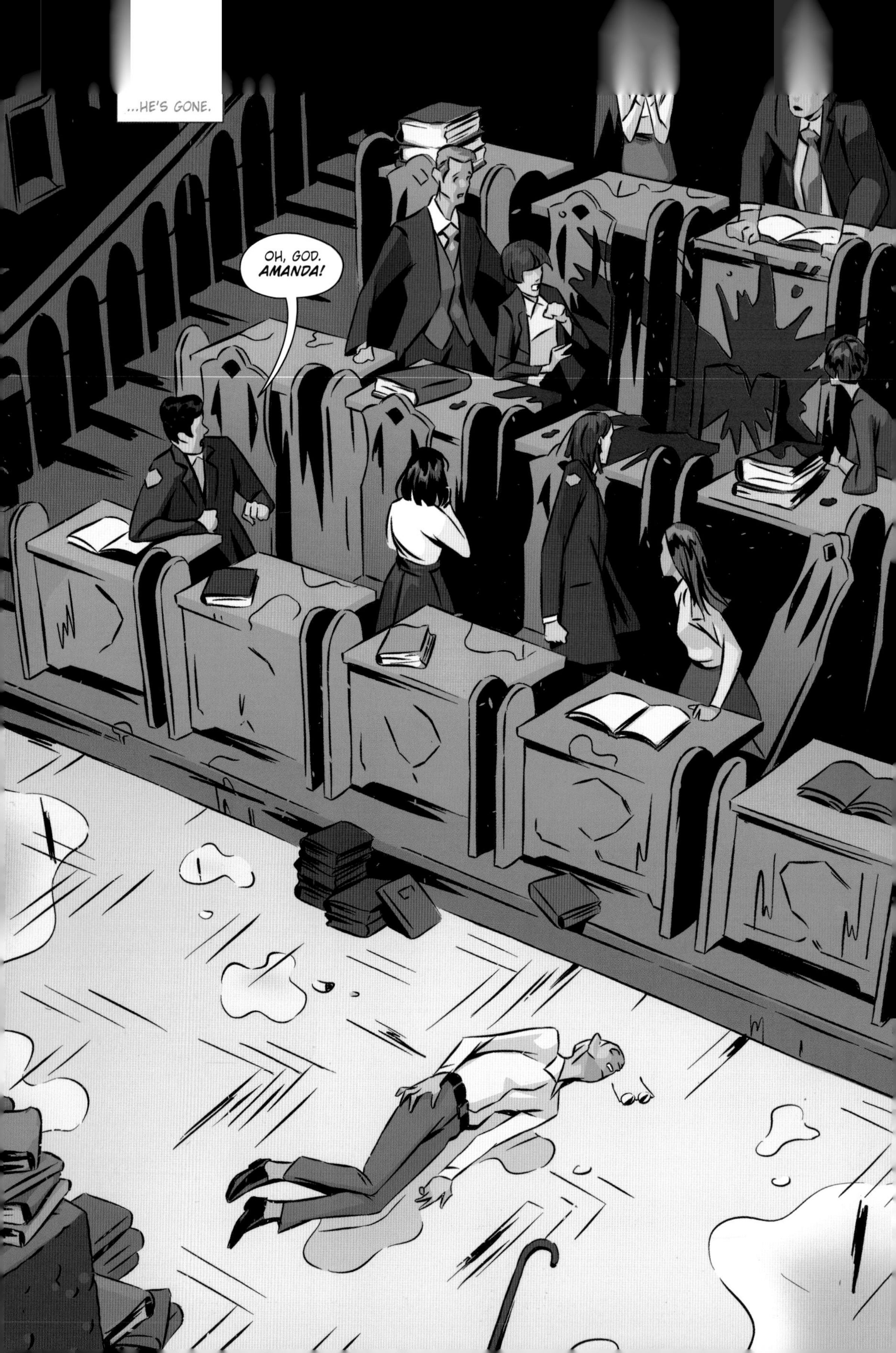
...HE'S GONE.
OH, GOD. AMANDA!

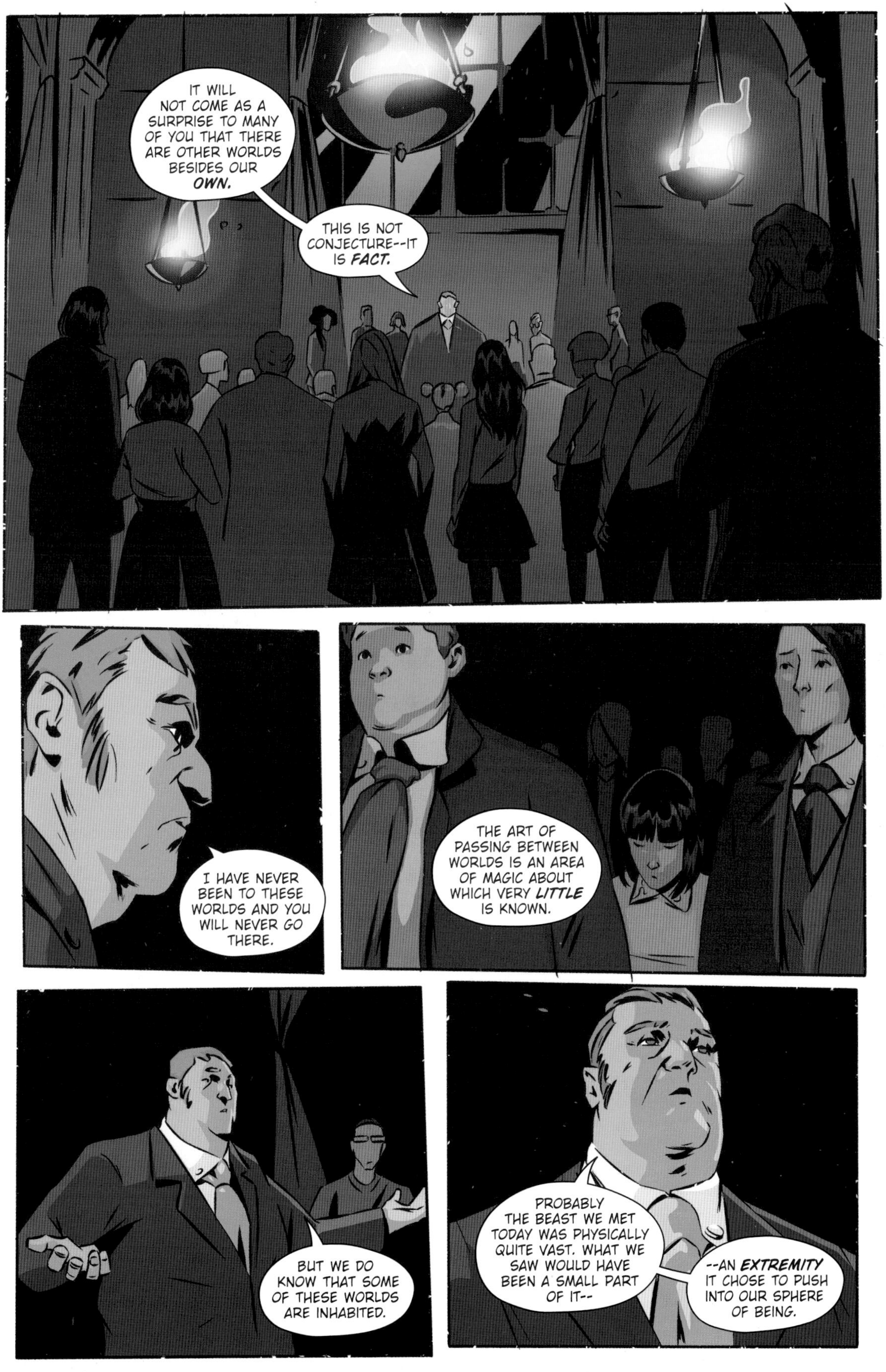
IT WILL NOT COME AS A SURPRISE TO MANY OF YOU THAT THERE ARE OTHER WORLDS BESIDES OUR **OWN.**
THIS IS NOT CONJECTURE--IT IS **FACT.**
I HAVE NEVER BEEN TO THESE WORLDS AND YOU WILL NEVER GO THERE.
THE ART OF PASSING BETWEEN WORLDS IS AN AREA OF MAGIC ABOUT WHICH VERY ***LITTLE*** IS KNOWN.
BUT WE DO KNOW THAT SOME OF THESE WORLDS ARE INHABITED.
PROBABLY THE BEAST WE MET TODAY WAS PHYSICALLY QUITE VAST. WHAT WE SAW WOULD HAVE BEEN A SMALL PART OF IT--
--AN ***EXTREMITY*** IT CHOSE TO PUSH INTO OUR SPHERE OF BEING.

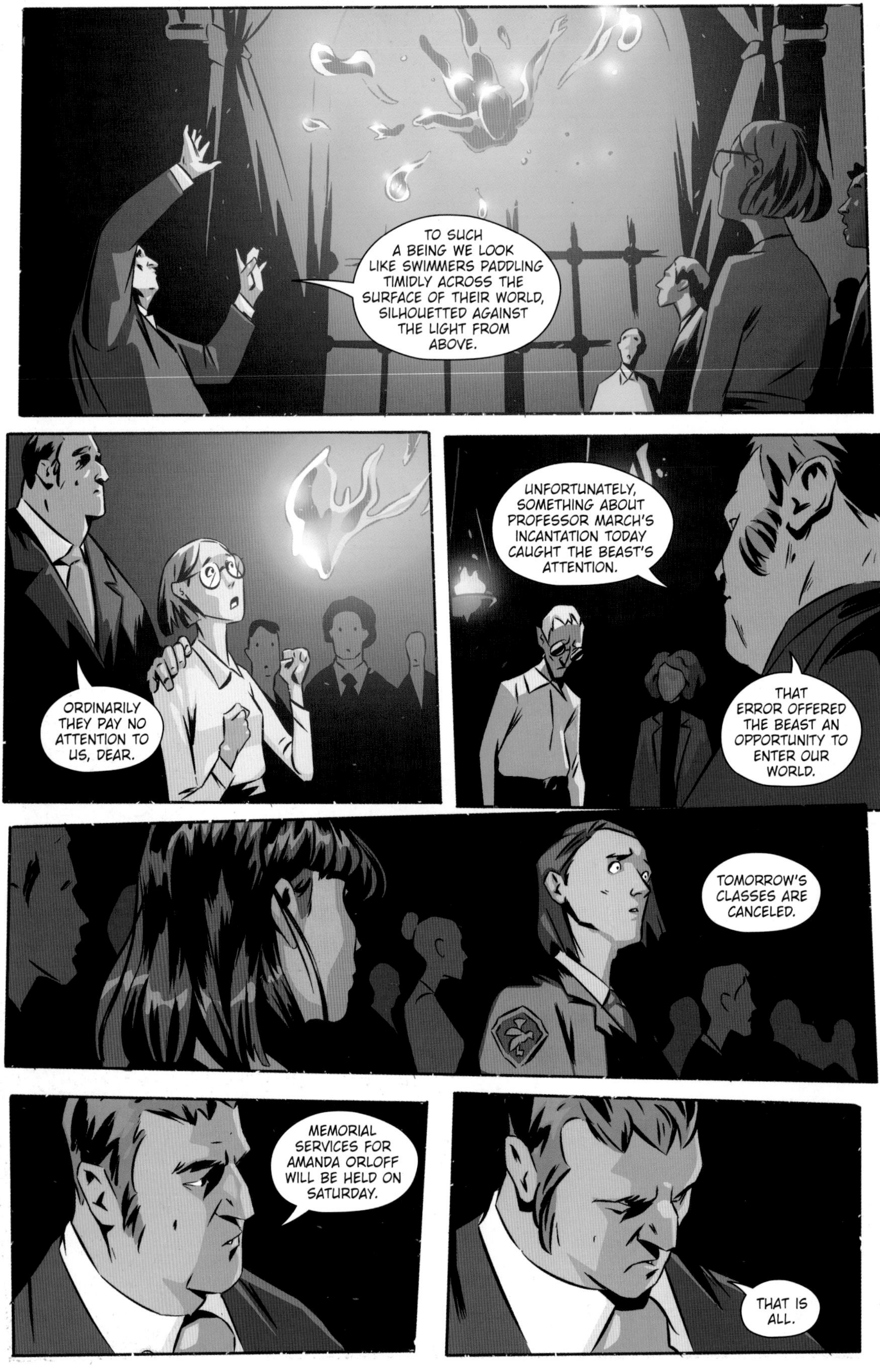
TO SUCH A BEING WE LOOK LIKE SWIMMERS PADDLING TIMIDLY ACROSS THE SURFACE OF THEIR WORLD, SILHOUETTED AGAINST THE LIGHT FROM ABOVE.
ORDINARILY THEY PAY NO ATTENTION TO US, DEAR.
UNFORTUNATELY, SOMETHING ABOUT PROFESSOR MARCH'S INCANTATION TODAY CAUGHT THE BEAST'S ATTENTION.
THAT ERROR OFFERED THE BEAST AN OPPORTUNITY TO ENTER OUR WORLD.
TOMORROW'S CLASSES ARE CANCELED.
MEMORIAL SERVICES FOR AMANDA ORLOFF WILL BE HELD ON SATURDAY.
THAT IS ALL.

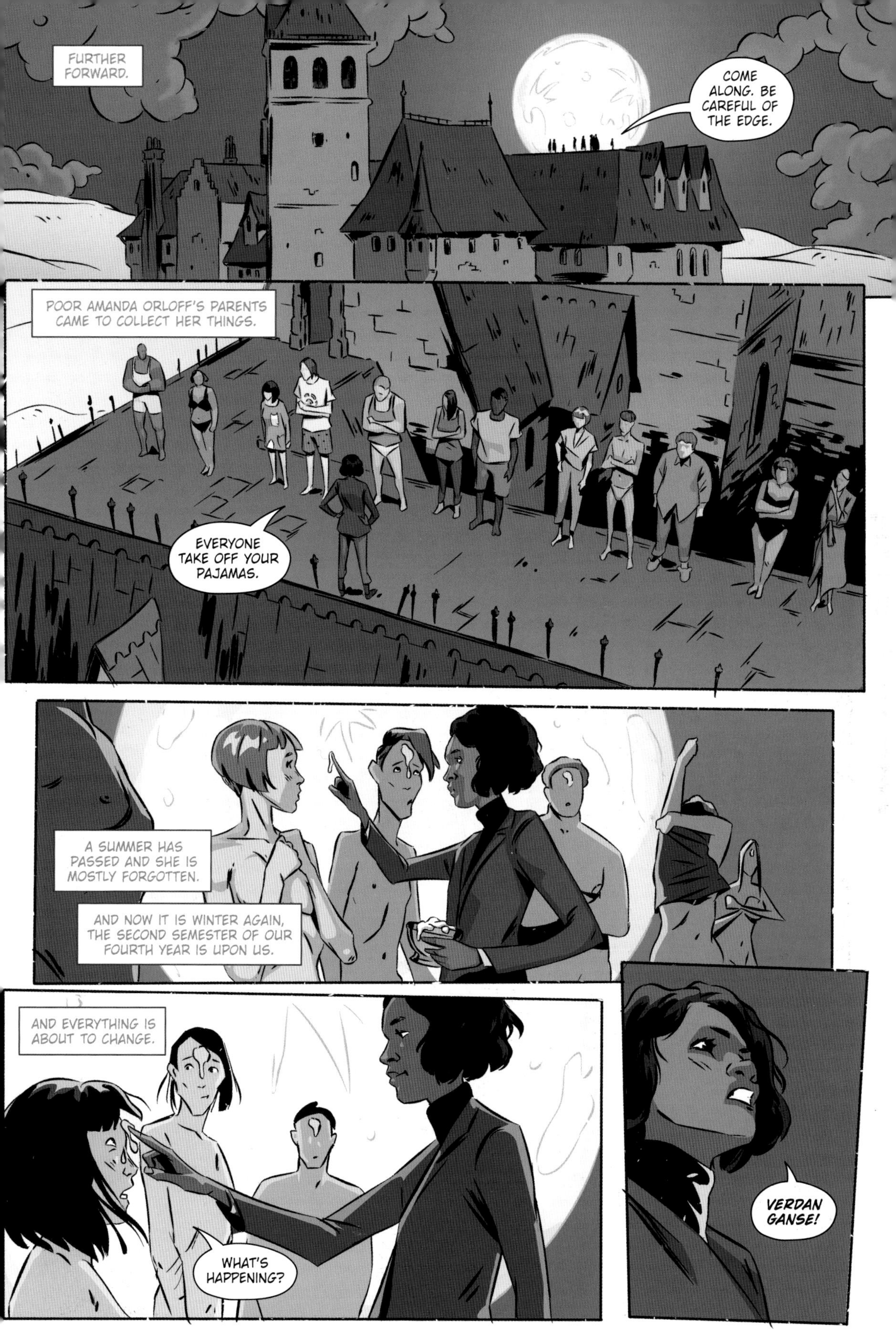
FURTHER FORWARD.
COME ALONG. BE CAREFUL OF THE EDGE.
POOR AMANDA ORLOFF'S PARENTS CAME TO COLLECT HER THINGS.
EVERYONE TAKE OFF YOUR PAJAMAS.
A SUMMER HAS PASSED AND SHE IS MOSTLY FORGOTTEN.
AND NOW IT IS WINTER AGAIN, THE SECOND SEMESTER OF OUR FOURTH YEAR IS UPON US.
AND EVERYTHING IS ABOUT TO CHANGE.
WHAT'S HAPPENING?
VERDAN GANSE!

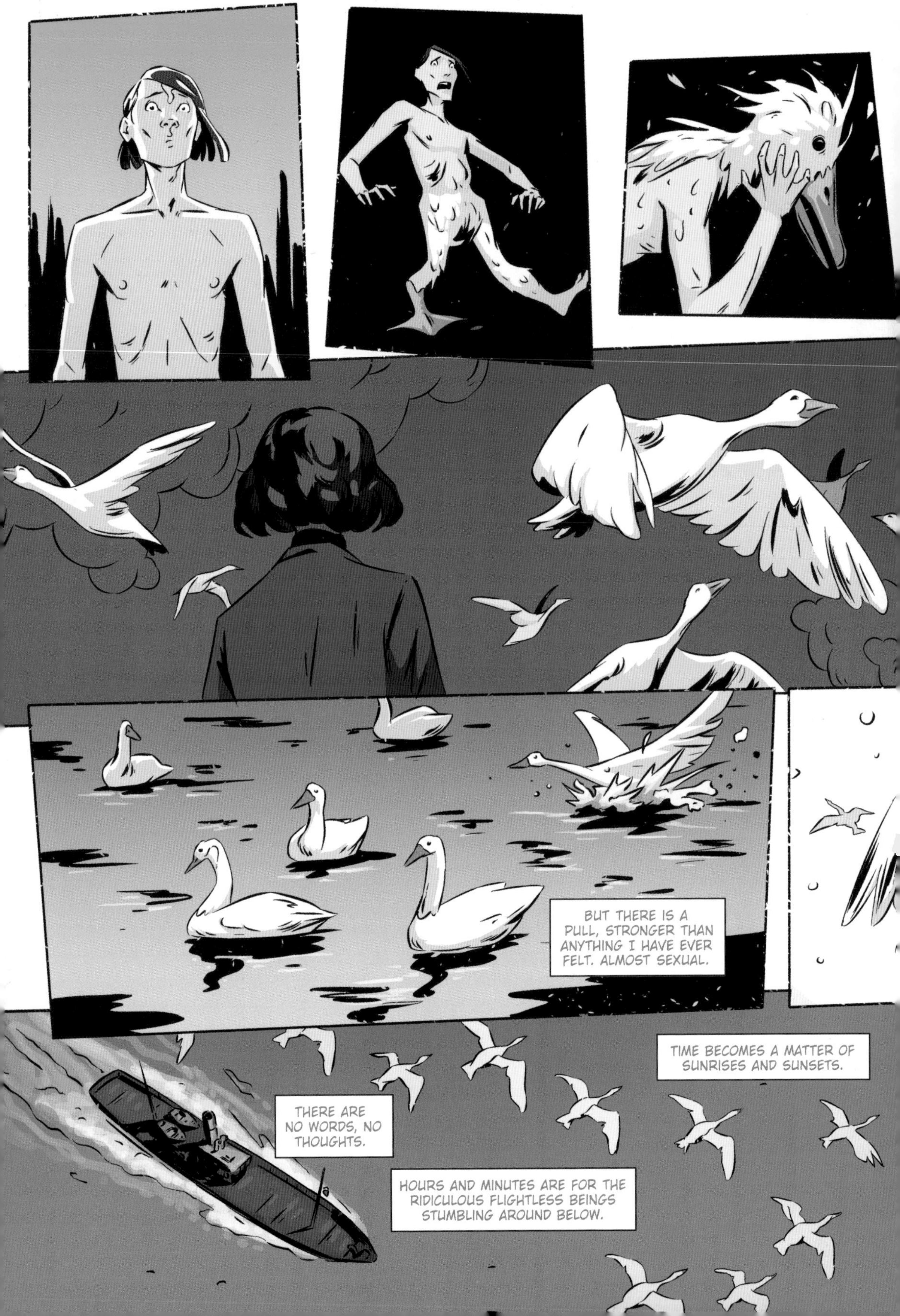
BUT THERE IS A PULL, STRONGER THAN ANYTHING I HAVE EVER FELT. ALMOST SEXUAL.
TIME BECOMES A MATTER OF SUNRISES AND SUNSETS.
THERE ARE NO WORDS, NO THOUGHTS.
HOURS AND MINUTES ARE FOR THE RIDICULOUS FLIGHTLESS BEINGS STUMBLING AROUND BELOW.

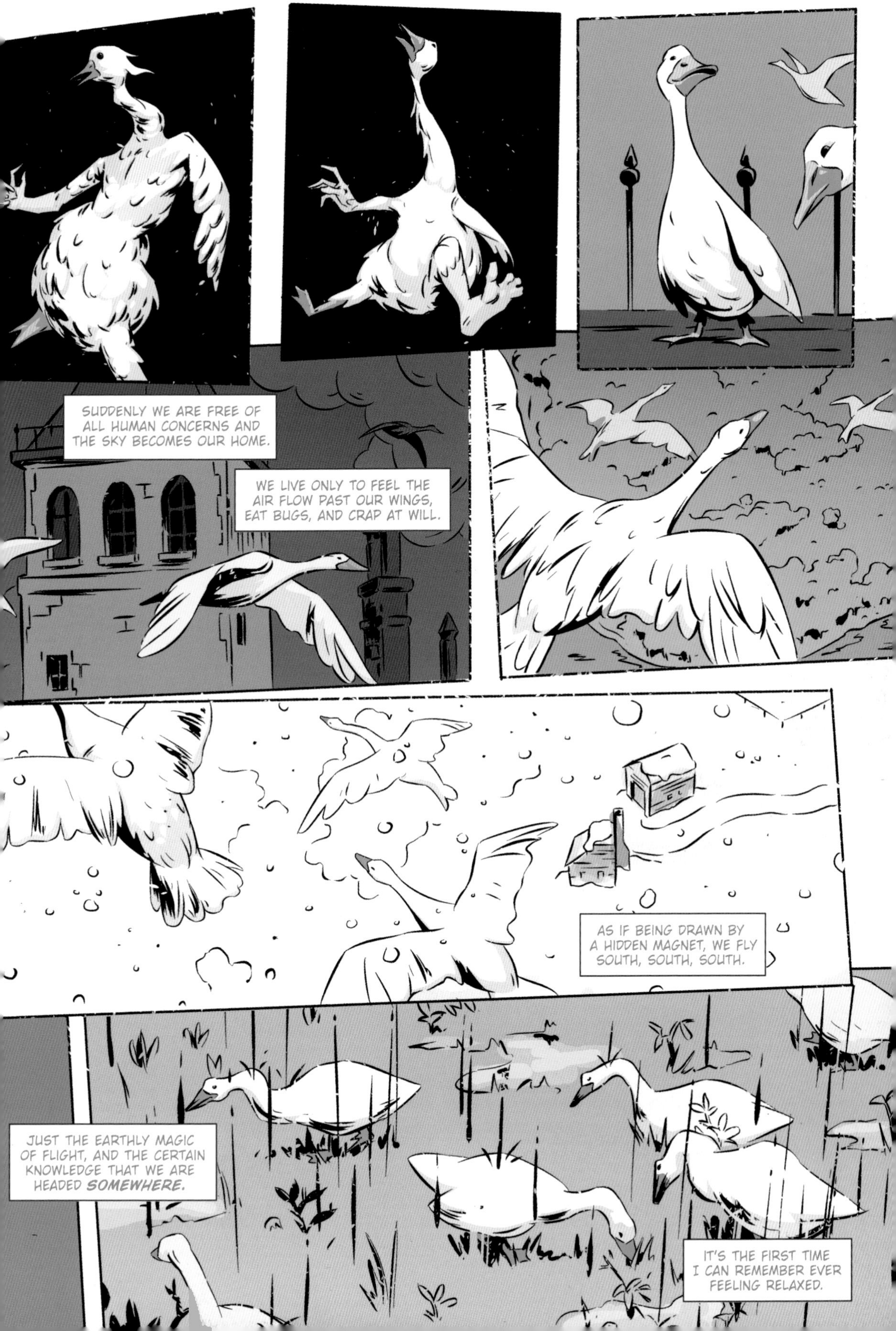
SUDDENLY WE ARE FREE OF ALL HUMAN CONCERNS AND THE SKY BECOMES OUR HOME.
WE LIVE ONLY TO FEEL THE AIR FLOW PAST OUR WINGS, EAT BUGS, AND CRAP AT WILL.
AS IF BEING DRAWN BY A HIDDEN MAGNET, WE FLY SOUTH, SOUTH, SOUTH.
JUST THE EARTHLY MAGIC OF FLIGHT, AND THE CERTAIN KNOWLEDGE THAT WE ARE HEADED ***SOMEWHERE.***
IT'S THE FIRST TIME I CAN REMEMBER EVER FEELING RELAXED.

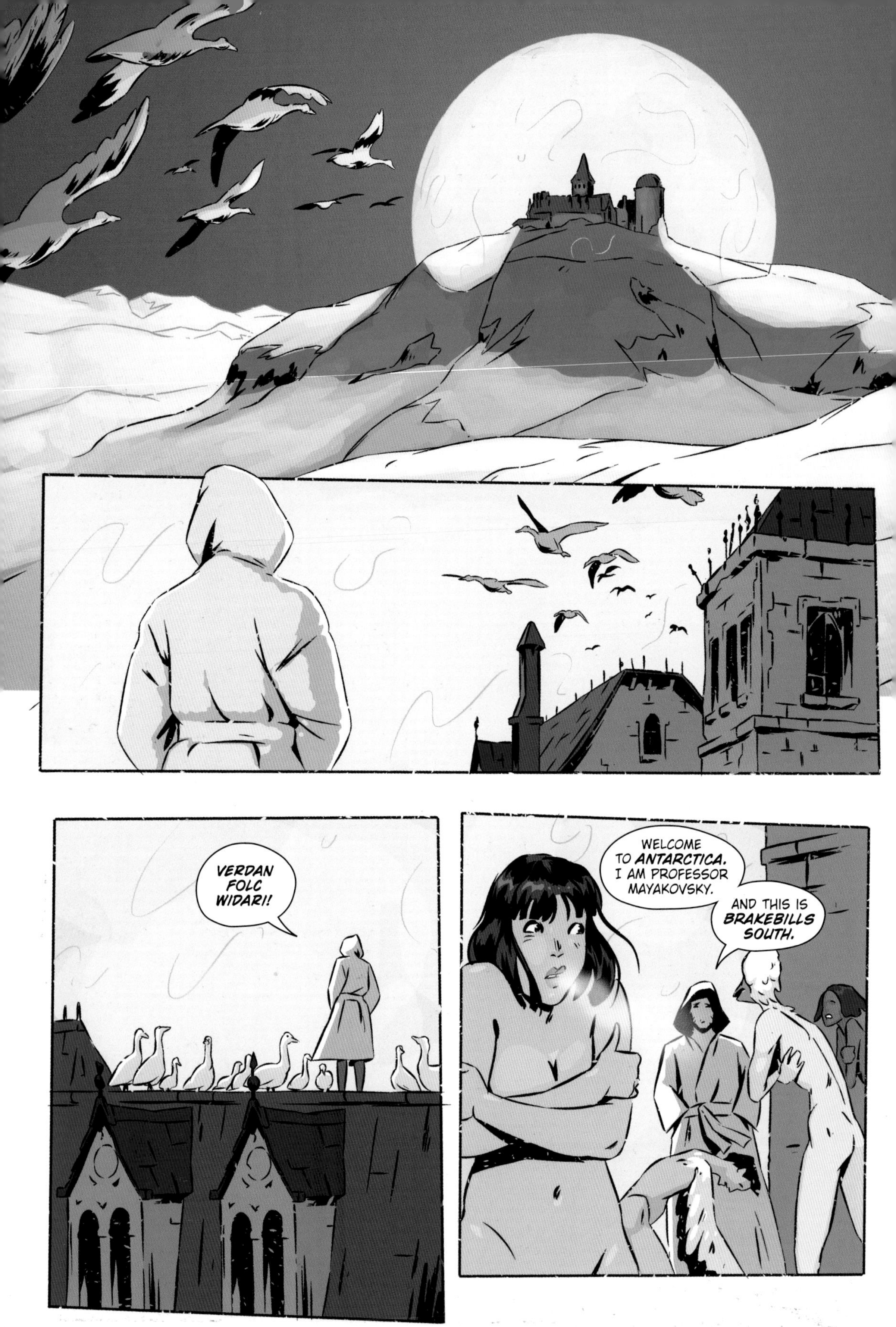
VERDAN FOLC WIDARI!
WELCOME TO ANTARCTICA. I AM PROFESSOR MAYAKOVSKY.
AND THIS IS BRAKEBILLS SOUTH.

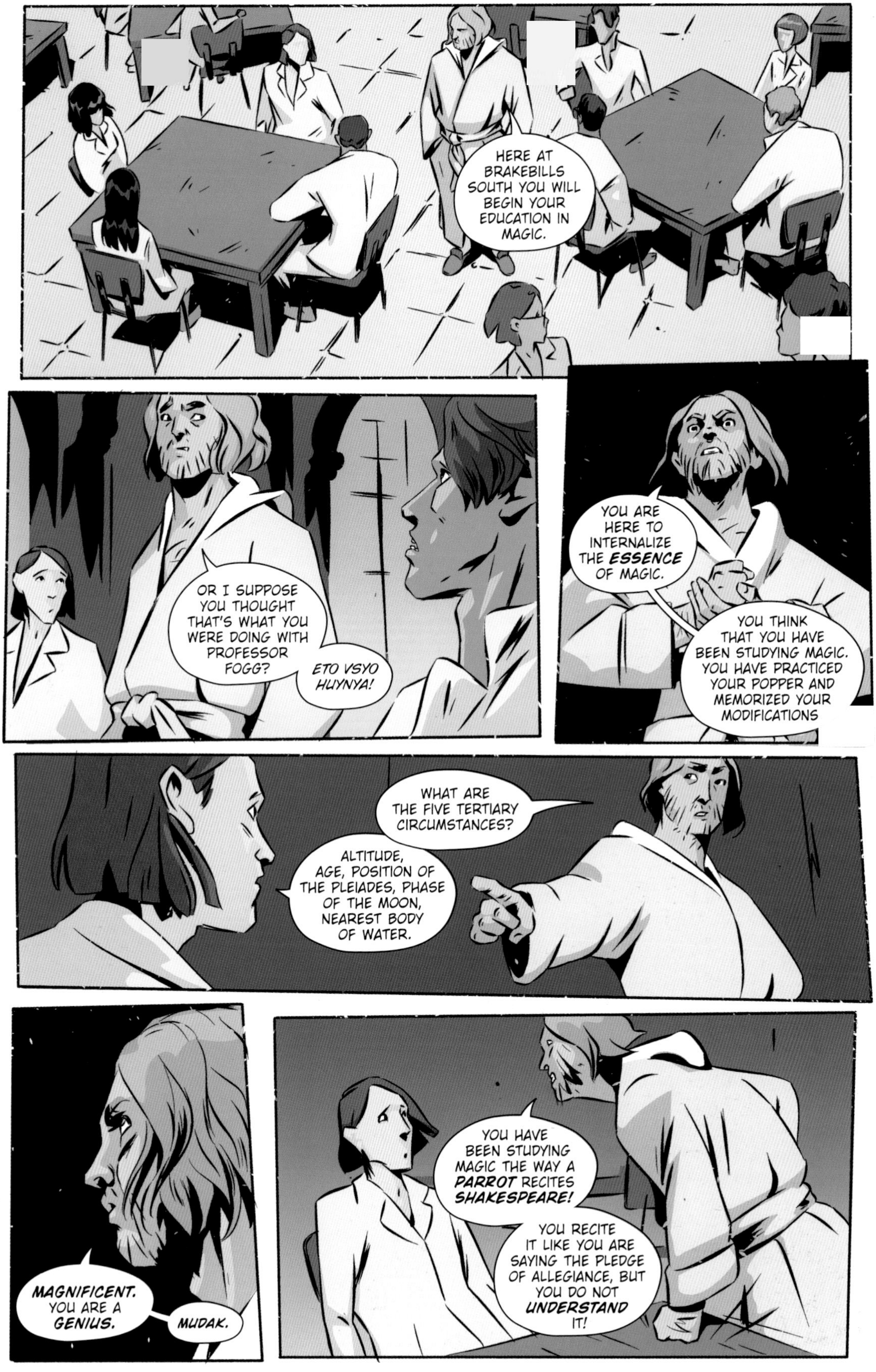
HERE AT BRAKEBILLS SOUTH YOU WILL BEGIN YOUR EDUCATION IN MAGIC.
OR I SUPPOSE YOU THOUGHT THAT'S WHAT YOU WERE DOING WITH PROFESSOR FOGG?
ETO VSYO HUYNYA!
YOU ARE HERE TO INTERNALIZE THE ESSENCE OF MAGIC.
YOU THINK THAT YOU HAVE BEEN STUDYING MAGIC. YOU HAVE PRACTICED YOUR POPPER AND MEMORIZED YOUR MODIFICATIONS
WHAT ARE THE FIVE TERTIARY CIRCUMSTANCES?
ALTITUDE, AGE, POSITION OF THE PLEIADES, PHASE OF THE MOON, NEAREST BODY OF WATER.
MAGNIFICENT. YOU ARE A GENIUS.
MUDAK.
YOU HAVE BEEN STUDYING MAGIC THE WAY A PARROT RECITES SHAKESPEARE!
YOU RECITE IT LIKE YOU ARE SAYING THE PLEDGE OF ALLEGIANCE, BUT YOU DO NOT UNDERSTAND IT!

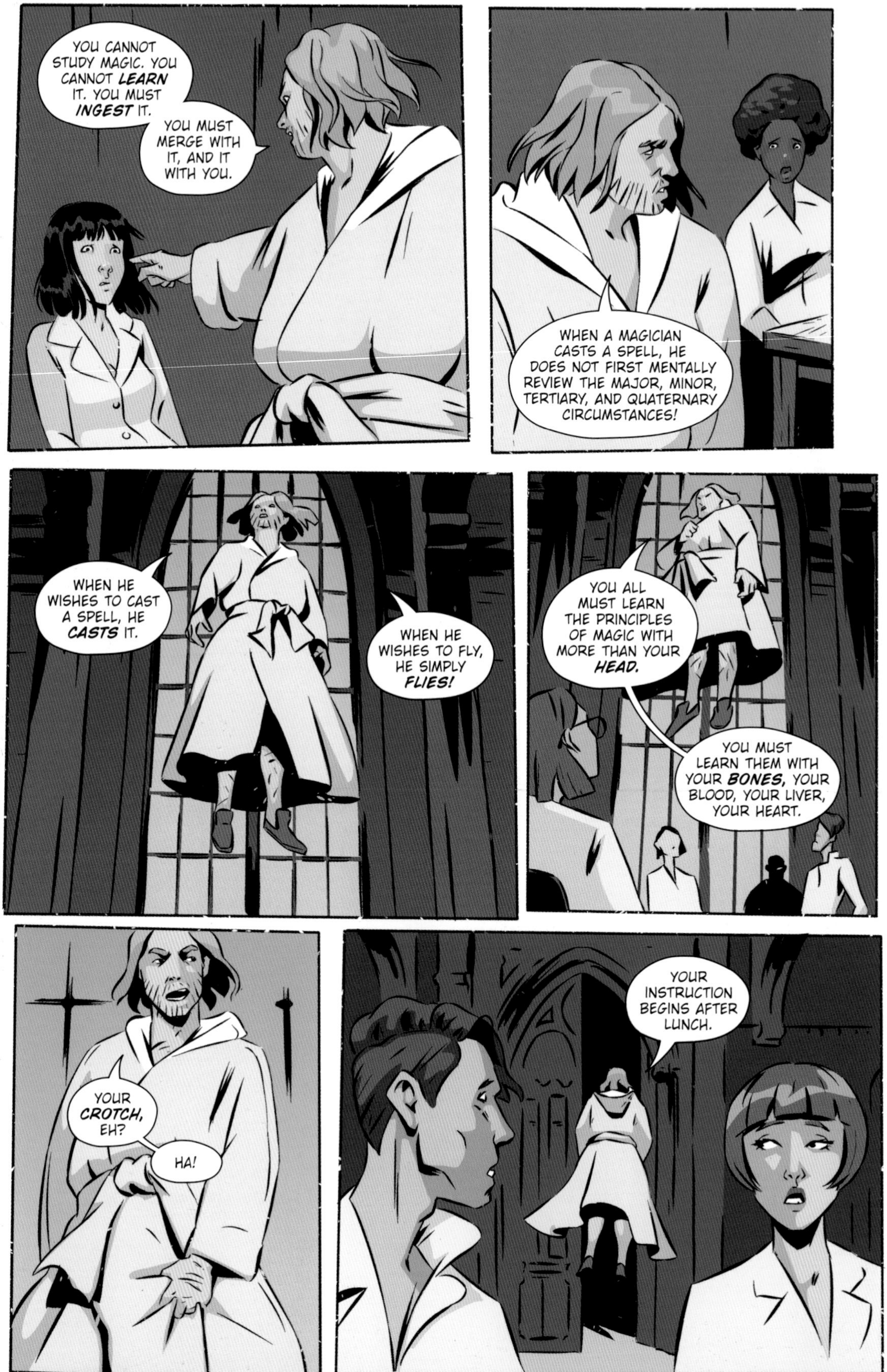
YOU CANNOT STUDY MAGIC. YOU CANNOT LEARN IT. YOU MUST INGEST IT.
YOU MUST MERGE WITH IT, AND IT WITH YOU.
WHEN A MAGICIAN CASTS A SPELL, HE DOES NOT FIRST MENTALLY REVIEW THE MAJOR, MINOR, TERTIARY, AND QUATERNARY CIRCUMSTANCES!
WHEN HE WISHES TO CAST A SPELL, HE CASTS IT.
WHEN HE WISHES TO FLY, HE SIMPLY FLIES!
YOU ALL MUST LEARN THE PRINCIPLES OF MAGIC WITH MORE THAN YOUR HEAD.
YOU MUST LEARN THEM WITH YOUR BONES, YOUR BLOOD, YOUR LIVER, YOUR HEART.
YOUR CROTCH, EH?
HA!
YOUR INSTRUCTION BEGINS AFTER LUNCH.

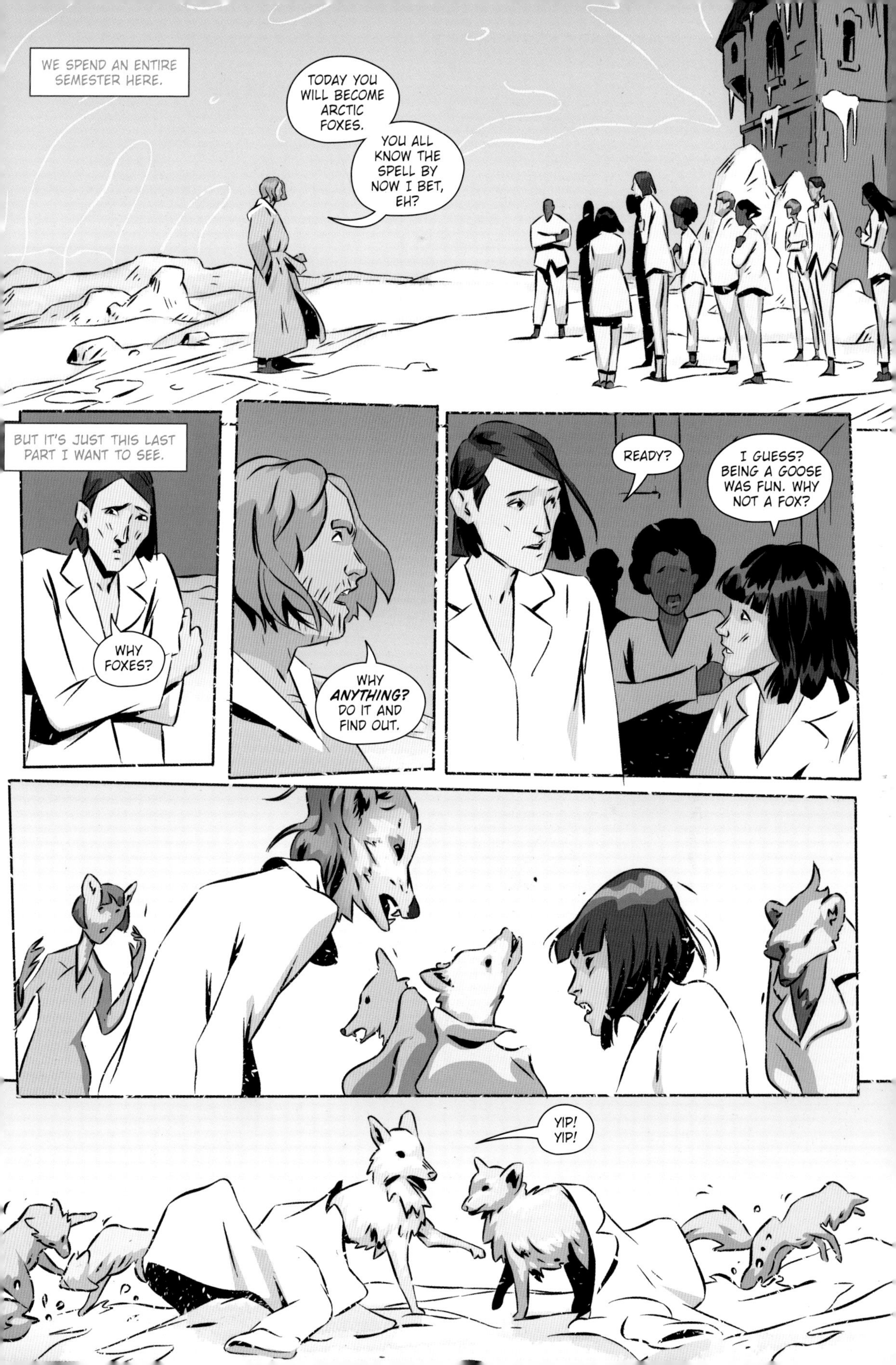
WE SPEND AN ENTIRE SEMESTER HERE.
TODAY YOU WILL BECOME ARCTIC FOXES.
YOU ALL KNOW THE SPELL BY NOW I BET, EH?
BUT IT'S JUST THIS LAST PART I WANT TO SEE.
WHY FOXES?
WHY *ANYTHING?* DO IT AND FIND OUT.
READY?
I GUESS? BEING A GOOSE WAS FUN. WHY NOT A FOX?
YIP! YIP!

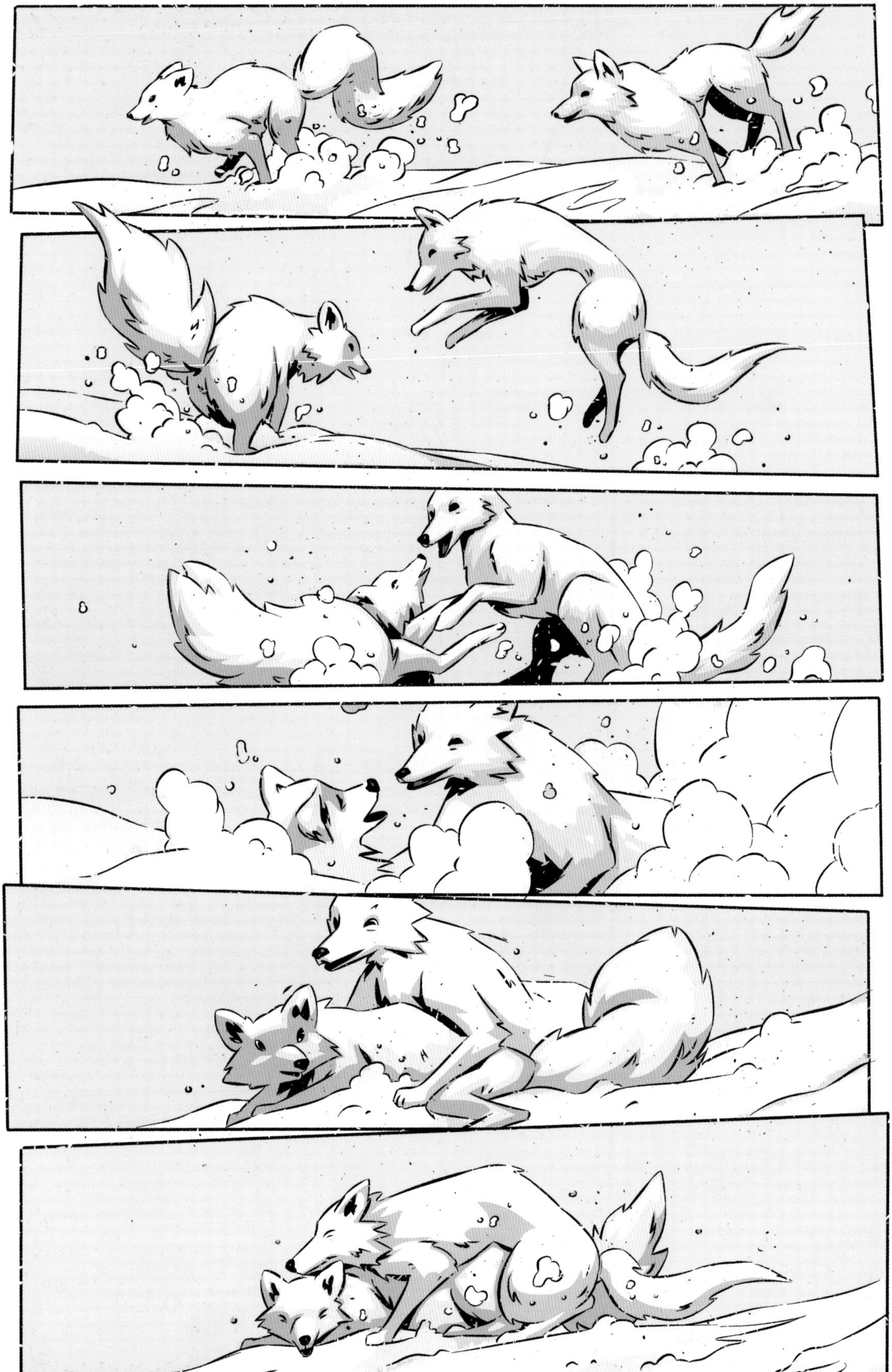

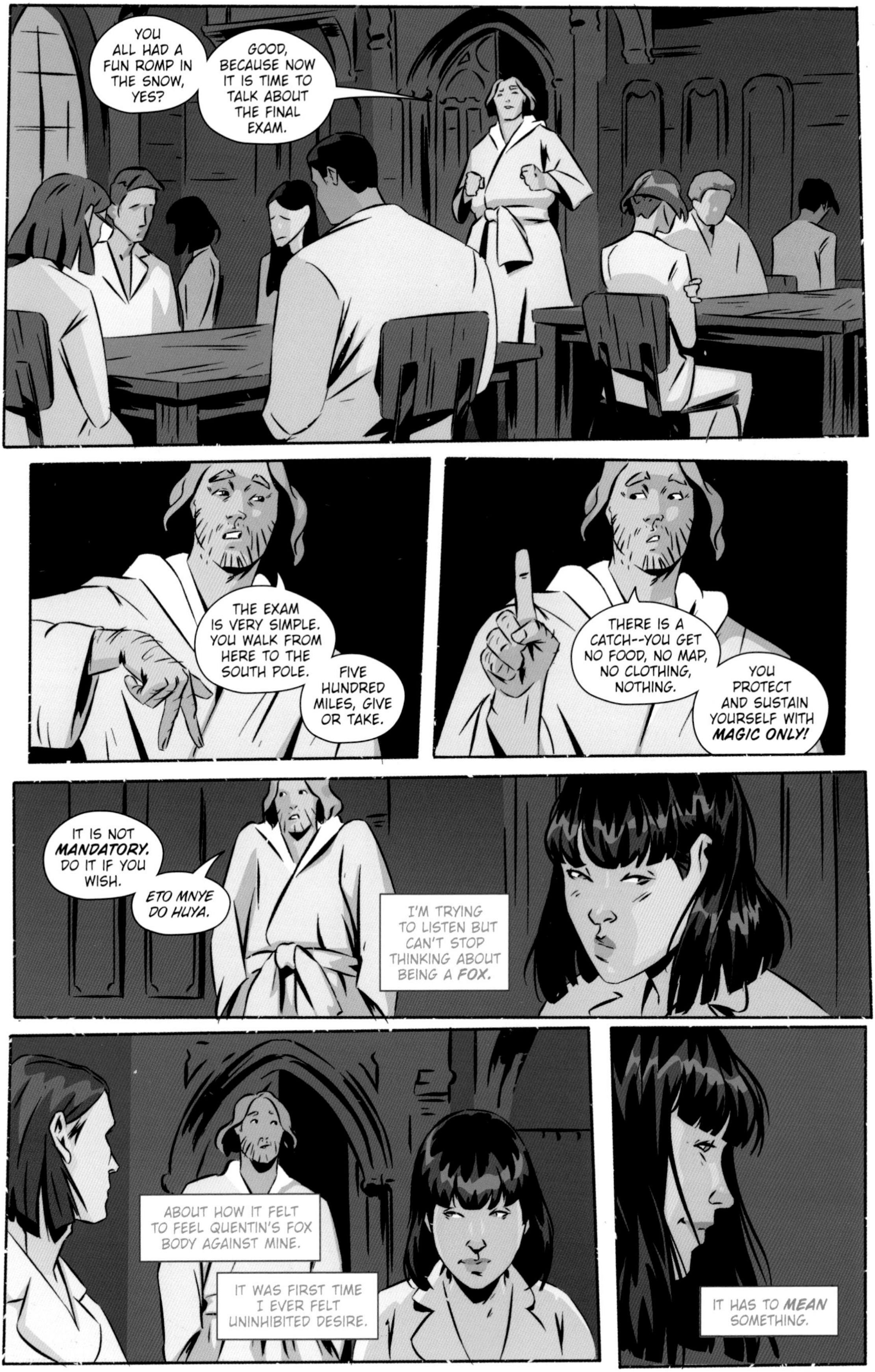
YOU ALL HAD A FUN ROMP IN THE SNOW, YES?
GOOD, BECAUSE NOW IT IS TIME TO TALK ABOUT THE FINAL EXAM.
THE EXAM IS VERY SIMPLE. YOU WALK FROM HERE TO THE SOUTH POLE.
FIVE HUNDRED MILES, GIVE OR TAKE.
THERE IS A CATCH--YOU GET NO FOOD, NO MAP, NO CLOTHING, NOTHING.
YOU PROTECT AND SUSTAIN YOURSELF WITH *MAGIC ONLY!*
IT IS NOT *MANDATORY.* DO IT IF YOU WISH.
ETO MNYE DO HUYA.
I'M TRYING TO LISTEN BUT CAN'T STOP THINKING ABOUT BEING A *FOX.*
ABOUT HOW IT FELT TO FEEL QUENTIN'S FOX BODY AGAINST MINE.
IT WAS FIRST TIME I EVER FELT UNINHIBITED DESIRE.
IT HAS TO *MEAN* SOMETHING.

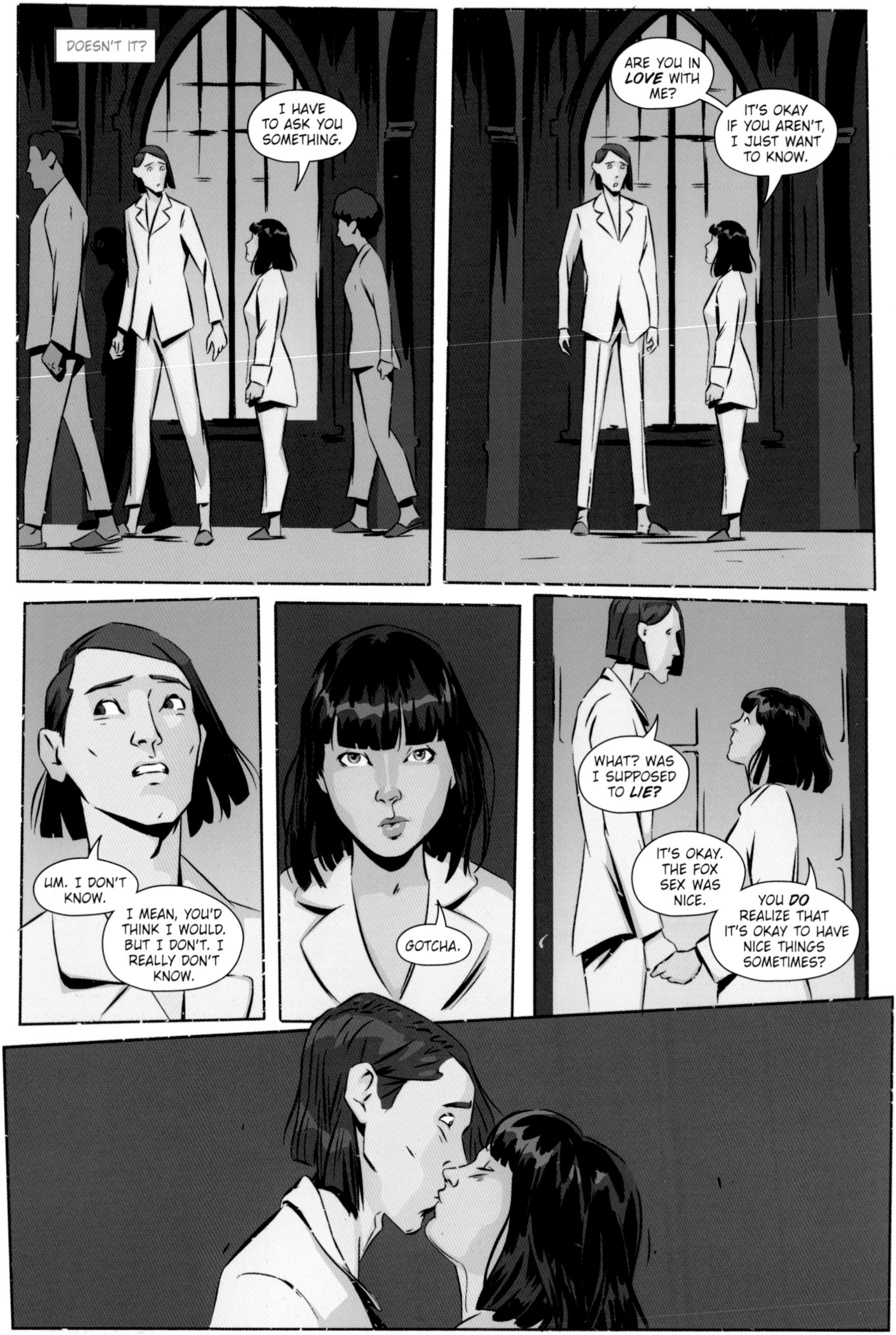
DOESN'T IT?
I HAVE TO ASK YOU SOMETHING.
ARE YOU IN LOVE WITH ME?
IT'S OKAY IF YOU AREN'T, I JUST WANT TO KNOW.
UM. I DON'T KNOW.
I MEAN, YOU'D THINK I WOULD. BUT I DON'T. I REALLY DON'T KNOW.
GOTCHA.
WHAT? WAS I SUPPOSED TO LIE?
IT'S OKAY. THE FOX SEX WAS NICE.
YOU DO REALIZE THAT IT'S OKAY TO HAVE NICE THINGS SOMETIMES?

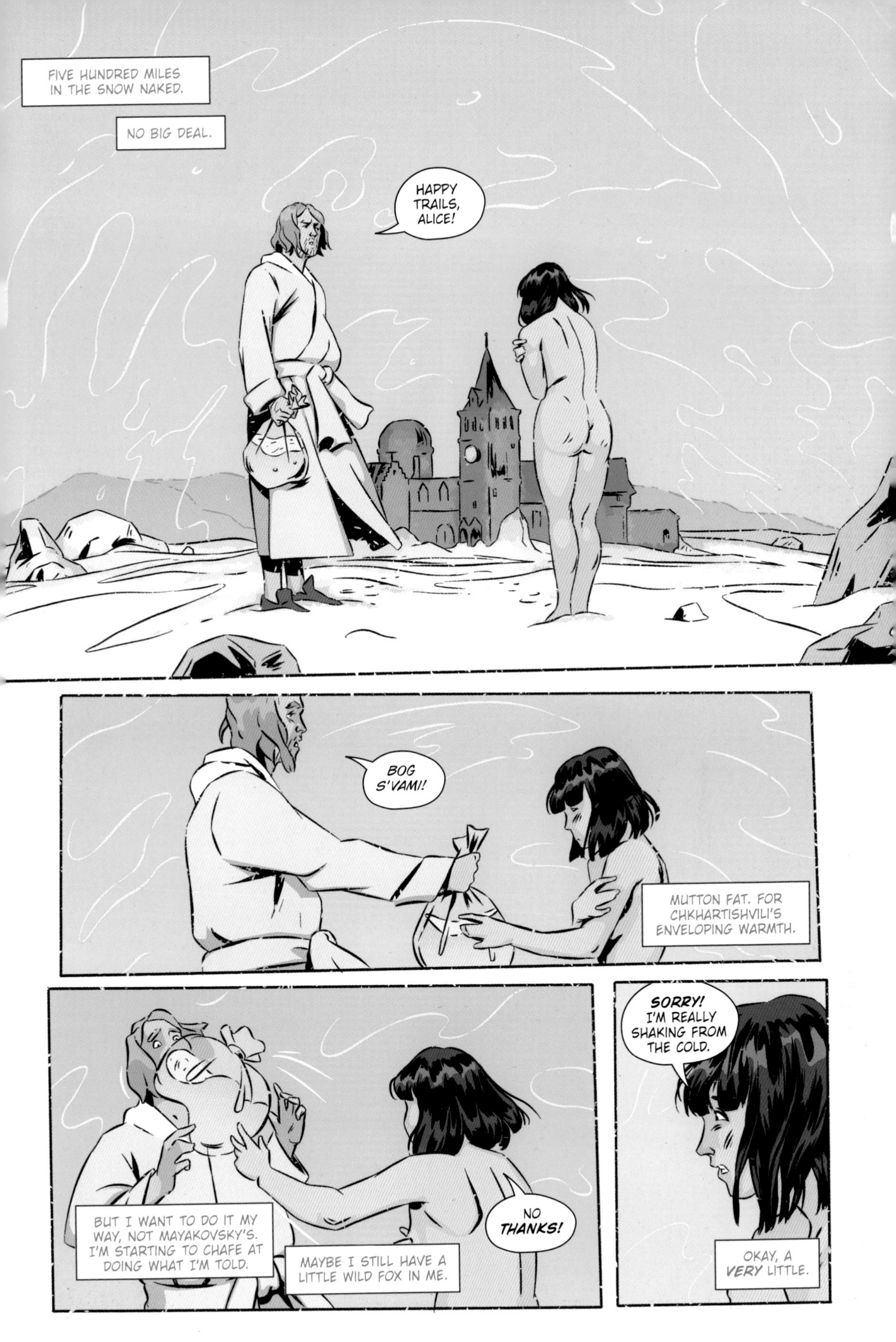
FIVE HUNDRED MILES IN THE SNOW NAKED.
NO BIG DEAL.
HAPPY TRAILS, ALICE!
BOG S'VAMI!
MUTTON FAT. FOR CHKHARTISHVILI'S ENVELOPING WARMTH.
BUT I WANT TO DO IT MY WAY, NOT MAYAKOVSKY'S. I'M STARTING TO CHAFE AT DOING WHAT I'M TOLD.
MAYBE I STILL HAVE A LITTLE WILD FOX IN ME.
NO THANKS!
SORRY! I'M REALLY SHAKING FROM THE COLD.
OKAY, A VERY LITTLE.

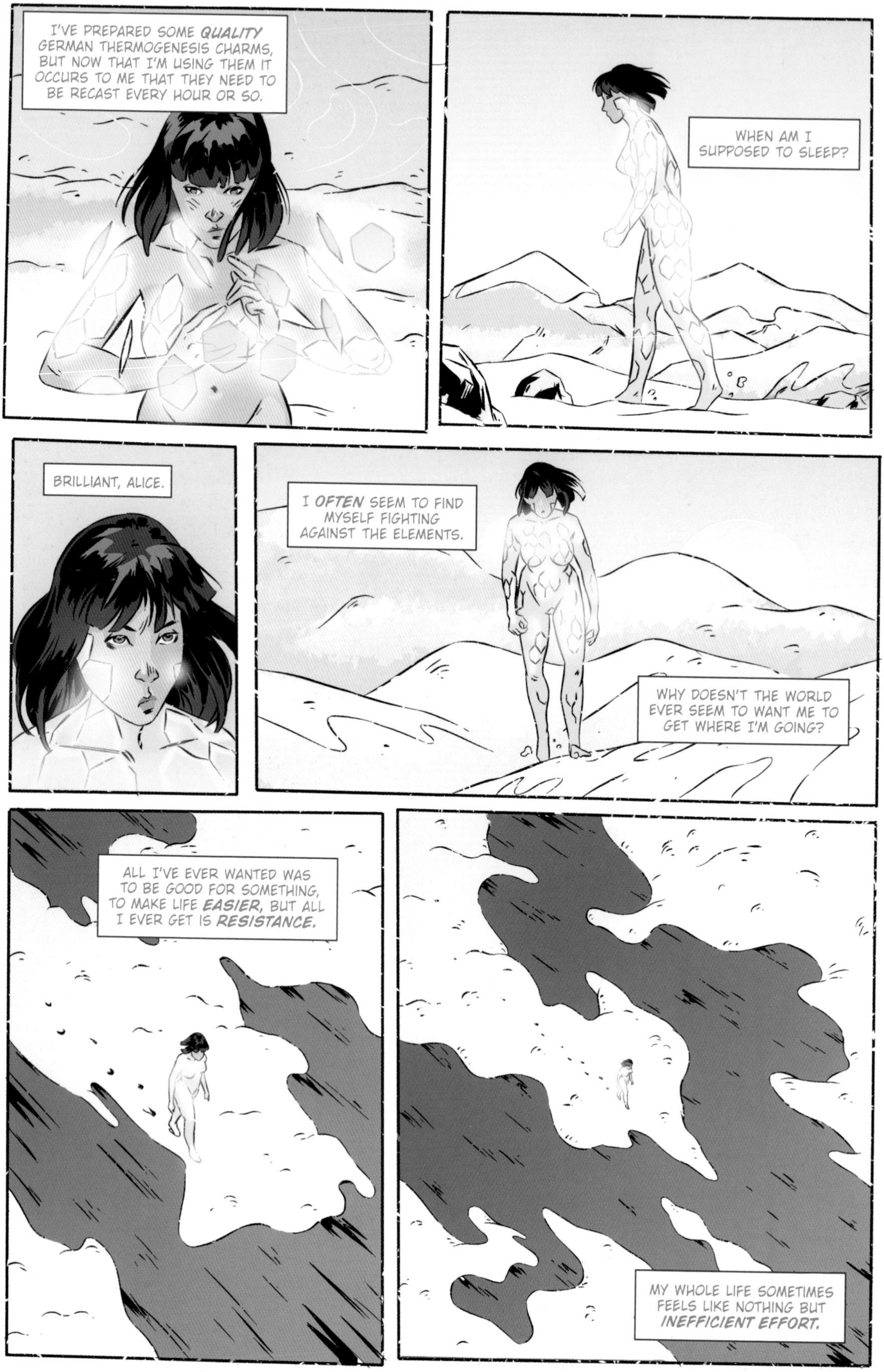
I'VE PREPARED SOME QUALITY GERMAN THERMOGENESIS CHARMS, BUT NOW THAT I'M USING THEM IT OCCURS TO ME THAT THEY NEED TO BE RECAST EVERY HOUR OR SO.
WHEN AM I SUPPOSED TO SLEEP?
BRILLIANT, ALICE.
I OFTEN SEEM TO FIND MYSELF FIGHTING AGAINST THE ELEMENTS.
WHY DOESN'T THE WORLD EVER SEEM TO WANT ME TO GET WHERE I'M GOING?
ALL I'VE EVER WANTED WAS TO BE GOOD FOR SOMETHING, TO MAKE LIFE EASIER, BUT ALL I EVER GET IS RESISTANCE.
MY WHOLE LIFE SOMETIMES FEELS LIKE NOTHING BUT INEFFICIENT EFFORT.

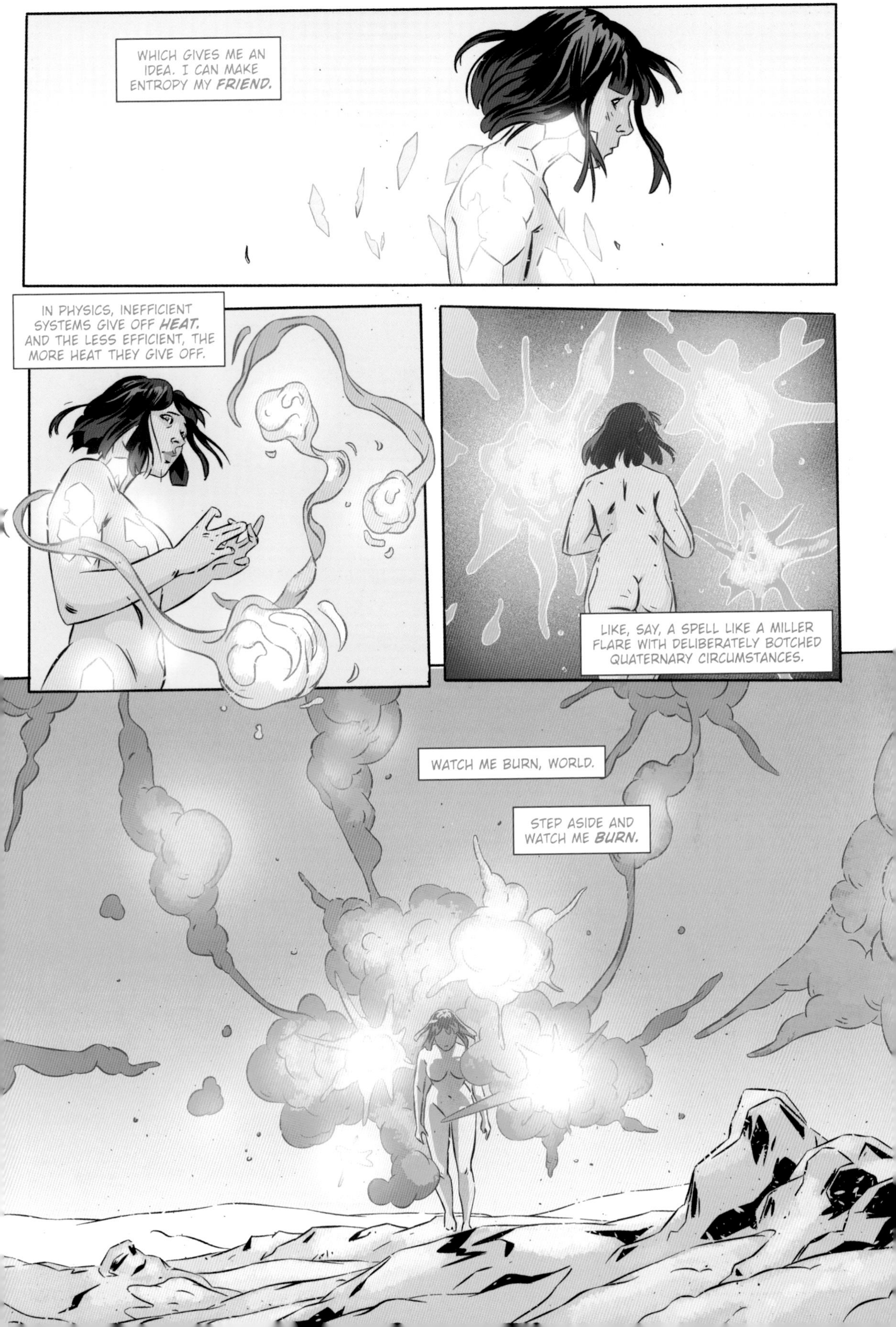
WHICH GIVES ME AN IDEA. I CAN MAKE ENTROPY MY FRIEND.
IN PHYSICS, INEFFICIENT SYSTEMS GIVE OFF HEAT. AND THE LESS EFFICIENT, THE MORE HEAT THEY GIVE OFF.
LIKE, SAY, A SPELL LIKE A MILLER FLARE WITH DELIBERATELY BOTCHED QUATERNARY CIRCUMSTANCES.
WATCH ME BURN, WORLD.
STEP ASIDE AND WATCH ME BURN.

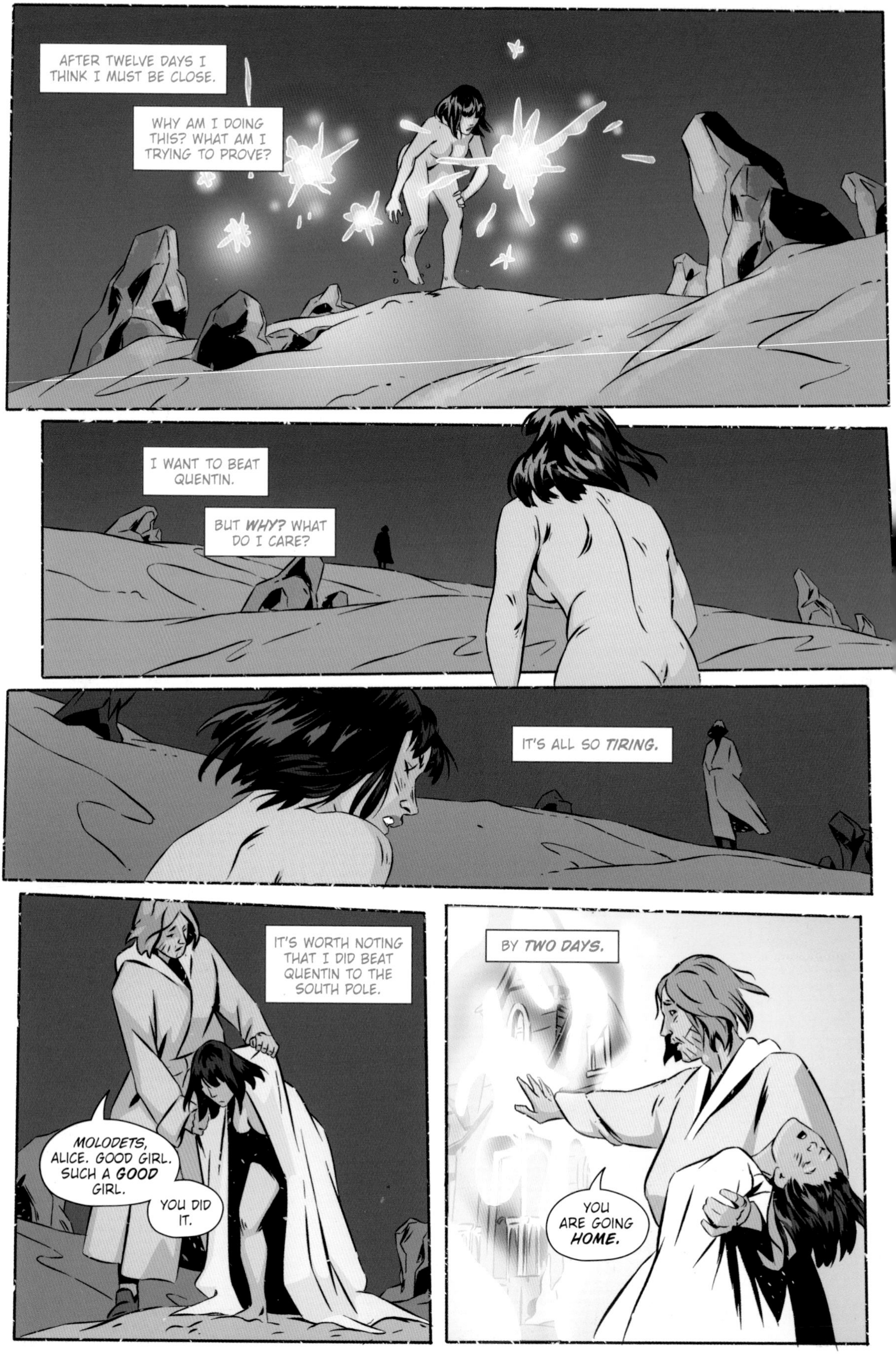
AFTER TWELVE DAYS I THINK I MUST BE CLOSE.
WHY AM I DOING THIS? WHAT AM I TRYING TO PROVE?
I WANT TO BEAT QUENTIN.
BUT *WHY?* WHAT DO I CARE?
IT'S ALL SO *TIRING.*
IT'S WORTH NOTING THAT I DID BEAT QUENTIN TO THE SOUTH POLE.
MOLODETS, ALICE. GOOD GIRL. SUCH A ***GOOD*** GIRL.
YOU DID IT.
BY *TWO DAYS.*
YOU ARE GOING ***HOME.***

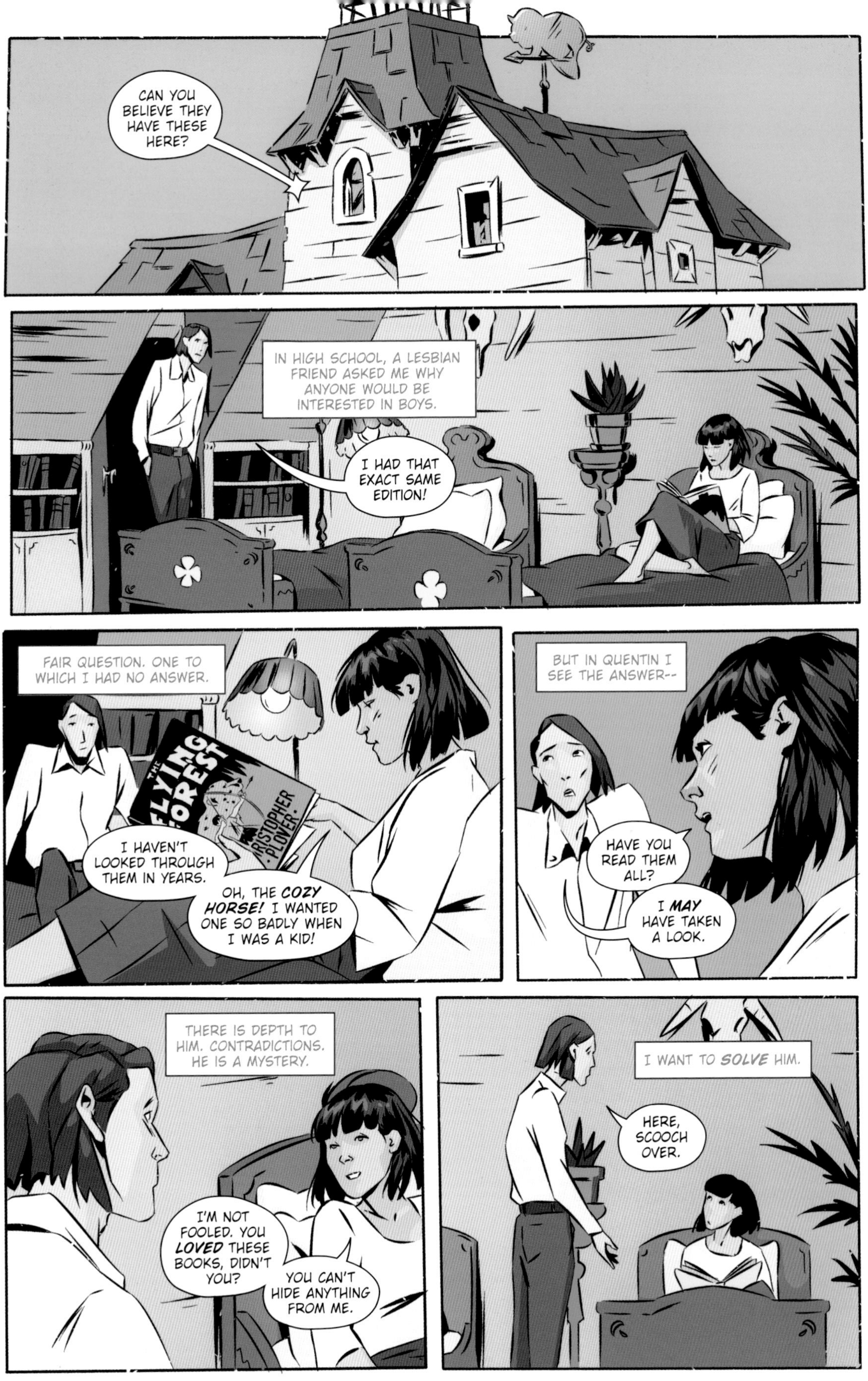
CAN YOU BELIEVE THEY HAVE THESE HERE?
IN HIGH SCHOOL, A LESBIAN FRIEND ASKED ME WHY ANYONE WOULD BE INTERESTED IN BOYS.
I HAD THAT EXACT SAME EDITION!
FAIR QUESTION. ONE TO WHICH I HAD NO ANSWER.
THE LYING OREST
RISTOPHER PLOVER
I HAVEN'T LOOKED THROUGH THEM IN YEARS.
OH, THE **COZY HORSE!** I WANTED ONE SO BADLY WHEN I WAS A KID!
BUT IN QUENTIN I SEE THE ANSWER--
HAVE YOU READ THEM ALL?
I **MAY** HAVE TAKEN A LOOK.
THERE IS DEPTH TO HIM. CONTRADICTIONS. HE IS A MYSTERY.
I'M NOT FOOLED. YOU **LOVED** THESE BOOKS, DIDN'T YOU?
YOU CAN'T HIDE ANYTHING FROM ME.
I WANT TO **SOLVE** HIM.
HERE, SCOOCH OVER.

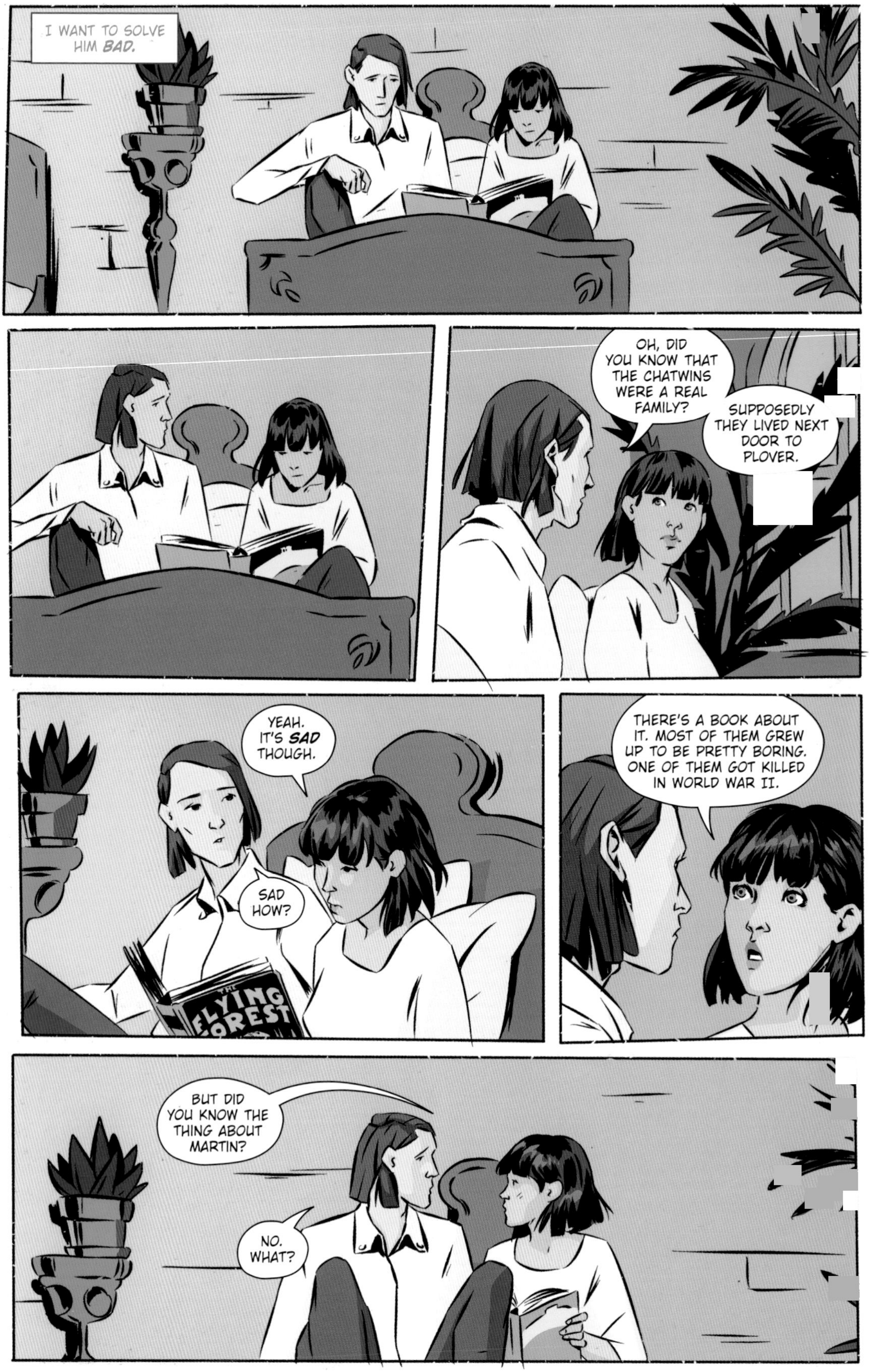
I WANT TO SOLVE HIM BAD.
OH, DID YOU KNOW THAT THE CHATWINS WERE A REAL FAMILY?
SUPPOSEDLY THEY LIVED NEXT DOOR TO PLOVER.
YEAH. IT'S SAD THOUGH.
SAD HOW?
THE FLYING FOREST
THERE'S A BOOK ABOUT IT. MOST OF THEM GREW UP TO BE PRETTY BORING. ONE OF THEM GOT KILLED IN WORLD WAR II.
BUT DID YOU KNOW THE THING ABOUT MARTIN?
NO. WHAT?

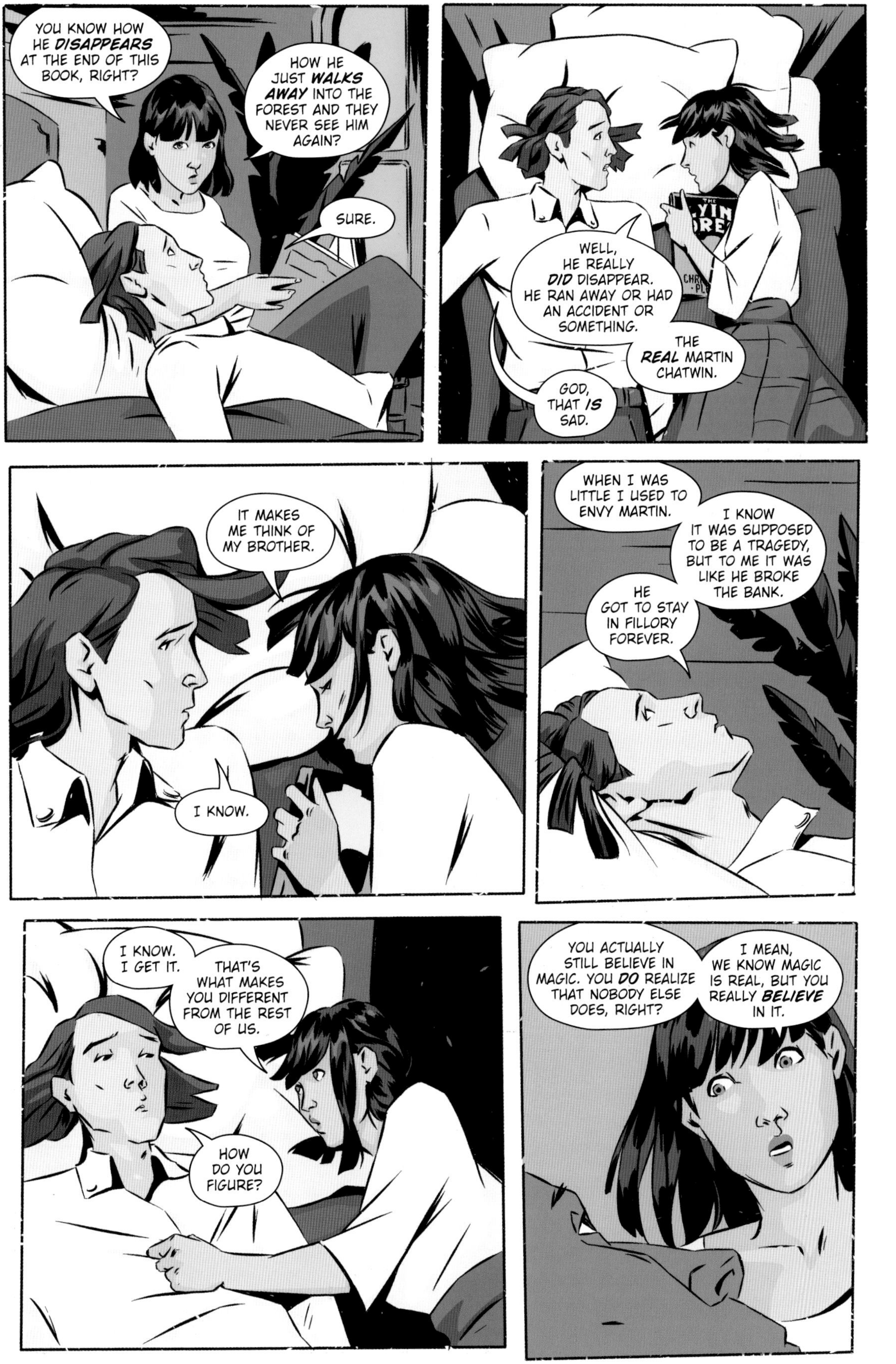
YOU KNOW HOW HE DISAPPEARS AT THE END OF THIS BOOK, RIGHT?
HOW HE JUST WALKS AWAY INTO THE FOREST AND THEY NEVER SEE HIM AGAIN?
SURE.
WELL, HE REALLY DID DISAPPEAR. HE RAN AWAY OR HAD AN ACCIDENT OR SOMETHING.
THE REAL MARTIN CHATWIN.
GOD, THAT IS SAD.
IT MAKES ME THINK OF MY BROTHER.
I KNOW.
WHEN I WAS LITTLE I USED TO ENVY MARTIN.
I KNOW IT WAS SUPPOSED TO BE A TRAGEDY, BUT TO ME IT WAS LIKE HE BROKE THE BANK.
HE GOT TO STAY IN FILLORY FOREVER.
I KNOW. I GET IT.
THAT'S WHAT MAKES YOU DIFFERENT FROM THE REST OF US.
HOW DO YOU FIGURE?
YOU ACTUALLY STILL BELIEVE IN MAGIC. YOU DO REALIZE THAT NOBODY ELSE DOES, RIGHT?
I MEAN, WE KNOW MAGIC IS REAL, BUT YOU REALLY BELIEVE IN IT.

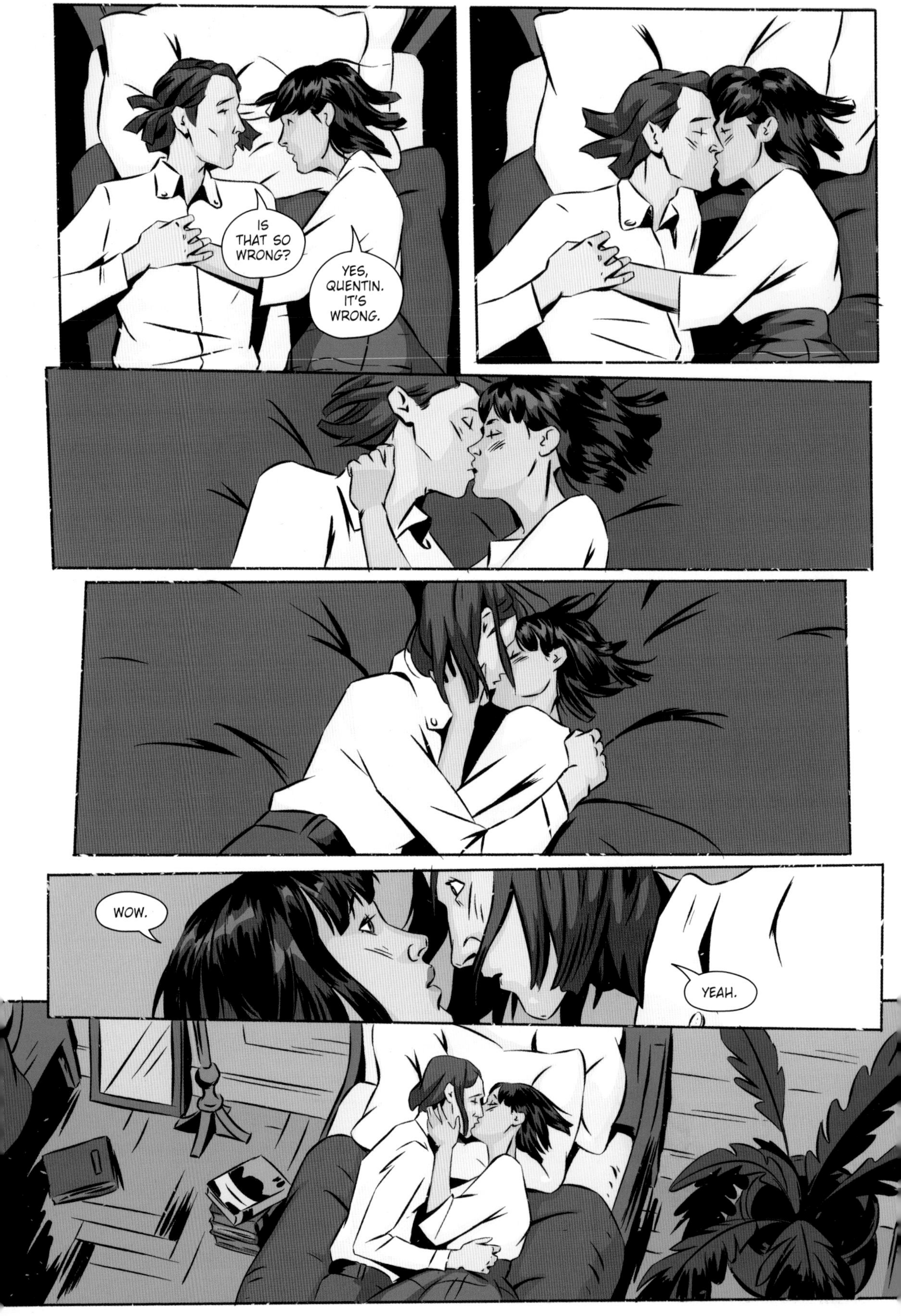
IS THAT SO WRONG?
YES, QUENTIN. IT'S WRONG.
WOW.
YEAH.

WHAT HAVE *YOU TWO* BEEN UP TO?

READING.

UH-HUH.

BE CAREFUL OF BRAKEBILLS ROMANCES, ALICE. YOU DON'T WANT TO END UP LIKE EMILY GREENSTREET.

WHO'S EMILY GREENSTREET?

YOU DON'T KNOW? EMILY GREENSTREET IS THE ONLY PERSON TO LEAVE BRAKEBILLS VOLUNTARILY IN THE LAST HUNDRED AND FIFTY YEARS.

WHAT HAPPENED TO HER?

I'LL TELL YOU.

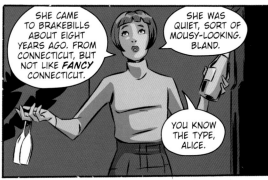

SHE CAME TO BRAKEBILLS ABOUT EIGHT YEARS AGO. FROM CONNECTICUT, BUT NOT LIKE *FANCY* CONNECTICUT.

SHE WAS QUIET, SORT OF MOUSY-LOOKING. BLAND.

YOU KNOW THE TYPE, ALICE.

HOW DO YOU KNOW SHE WAS MOUSY-LOOKING?

IT'S MY STORY AND IF I SAY SHE WAS MOUSY-LOOKING, THEN SHE WAS.

ALSO--SPOILERS--IT'S IMPORTANT TO THE STORY.

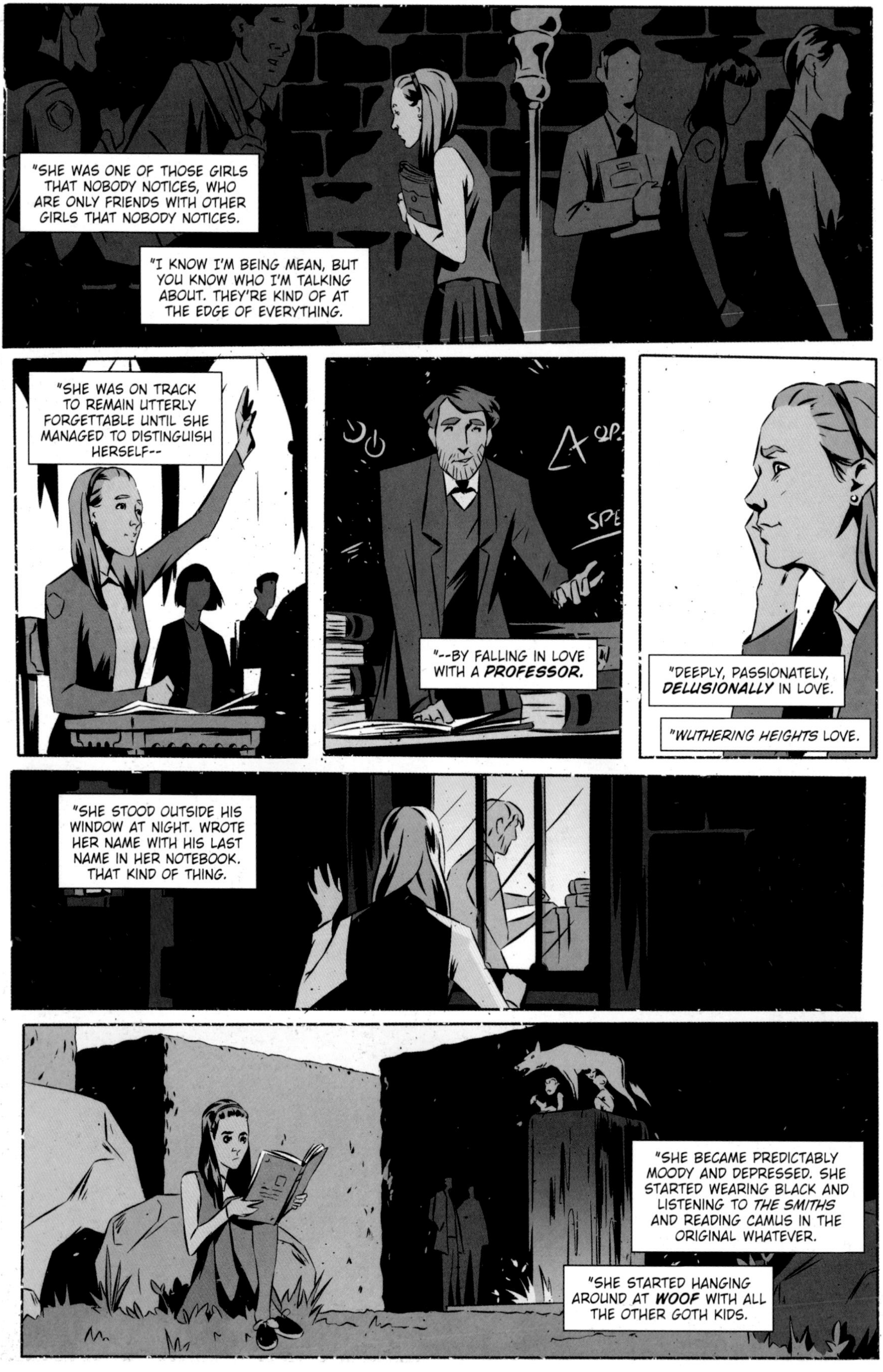
"SHE WAS ONE OF THOSE GIRLS THAT NOBODY NOTICES, WHO ARE ONLY FRIENDS WITH OTHER GIRLS THAT NOBODY NOTICES.
"I KNOW I'M BEING MEAN, BUT YOU KNOW WHO I'M TALKING ABOUT. THEY'RE KIND OF AT THE EDGE OF EVERYTHING.
"SHE WAS ON TRACK TO REMAIN UTTERLY FORGETTABLE UNTIL SHE MANAGED TO DISTINGUISH HERSELF--
"--BY FALLING IN LOVE WITH A ***PROFESSOR.***
"DEEPLY, PASSIONATELY, ***DELUSIONALLY*** IN LOVE.
"*WUTHERING HEIGHTS* LOVE.
"SHE STOOD OUTSIDE HIS WINDOW AT NIGHT. WROTE HER NAME WITH HIS LAST NAME IN HER NOTEBOOK. THAT KIND OF THING.
"SHE BECAME PREDICTABLY MOODY AND DEPRESSED. SHE STARTED WEARING BLACK AND LISTENING TO *THE SMITHS* AND READING CAMUS IN THE ORIGINAL WHATEVER.
"SHE STARTED HANGING AROUND AT ***WOOF*** WITH ALL THE OTHER GOTH KIDS.

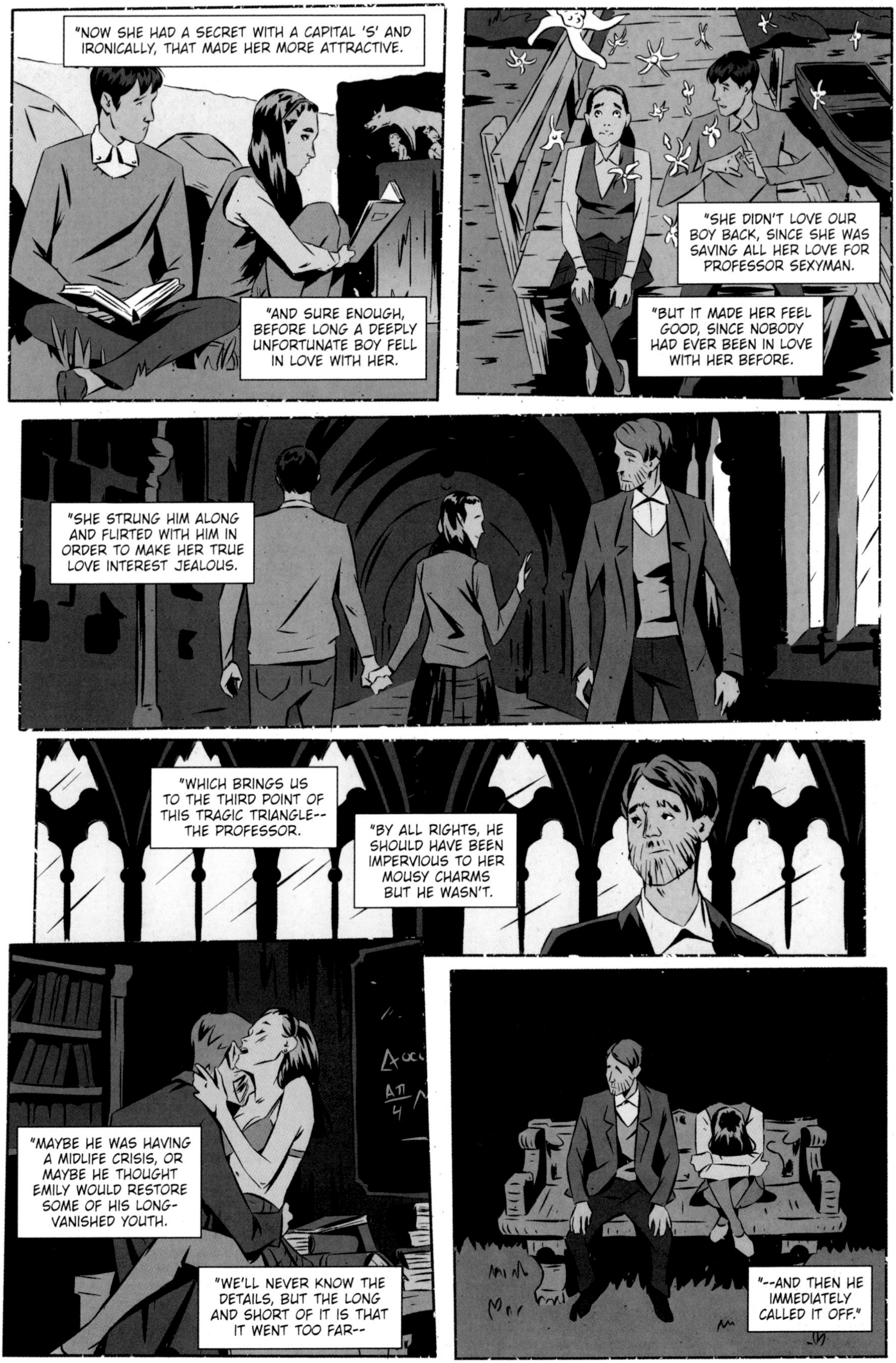
"NOW SHE HAD A SECRET WITH A CAPITAL 'S' AND IRONICALLY, THAT MADE HER MORE ATTRACTIVE.
"AND SURE ENOUGH, BEFORE LONG A DEEPLY UNFORTUNATE BOY FELL IN LOVE WITH HER.
"SHE DIDN'T LOVE OUR BOY BACK, SINCE SHE WAS SAVING ALL HER LOVE FOR PROFESSOR SEXYMAN.
"BUT IT MADE HER FEEL GOOD, SINCE NOBODY HAD EVER BEEN IN LOVE WITH HER BEFORE.
"SHE STRUNG HIM ALONG AND FLIRTED WITH HIM IN ORDER TO MAKE HER TRUE LOVE INTEREST JEALOUS.
"WHICH BRINGS US TO THE THIRD POINT OF THIS TRAGIC TRIANGLE--THE PROFESSOR.
"BY ALL RIGHTS, HE SHOULD HAVE BEEN IMPERVIOUS TO HER MOUSY CHARMS BUT HE WASN'T.
"MAYBE HE WAS HAVING A MIDLIFE CRISIS, OR MAYBE HE THOUGHT EMILY WOULD RESTORE SOME OF HIS LONG-VANISHED YOUTH.
"WE'LL NEVER KNOW THE DETAILS, BUT THE LONG AND SHORT OF IT IS THAT IT WENT TOO FAR--
"--AND THEN HE IMMEDIATELY CALLED IT OFF."

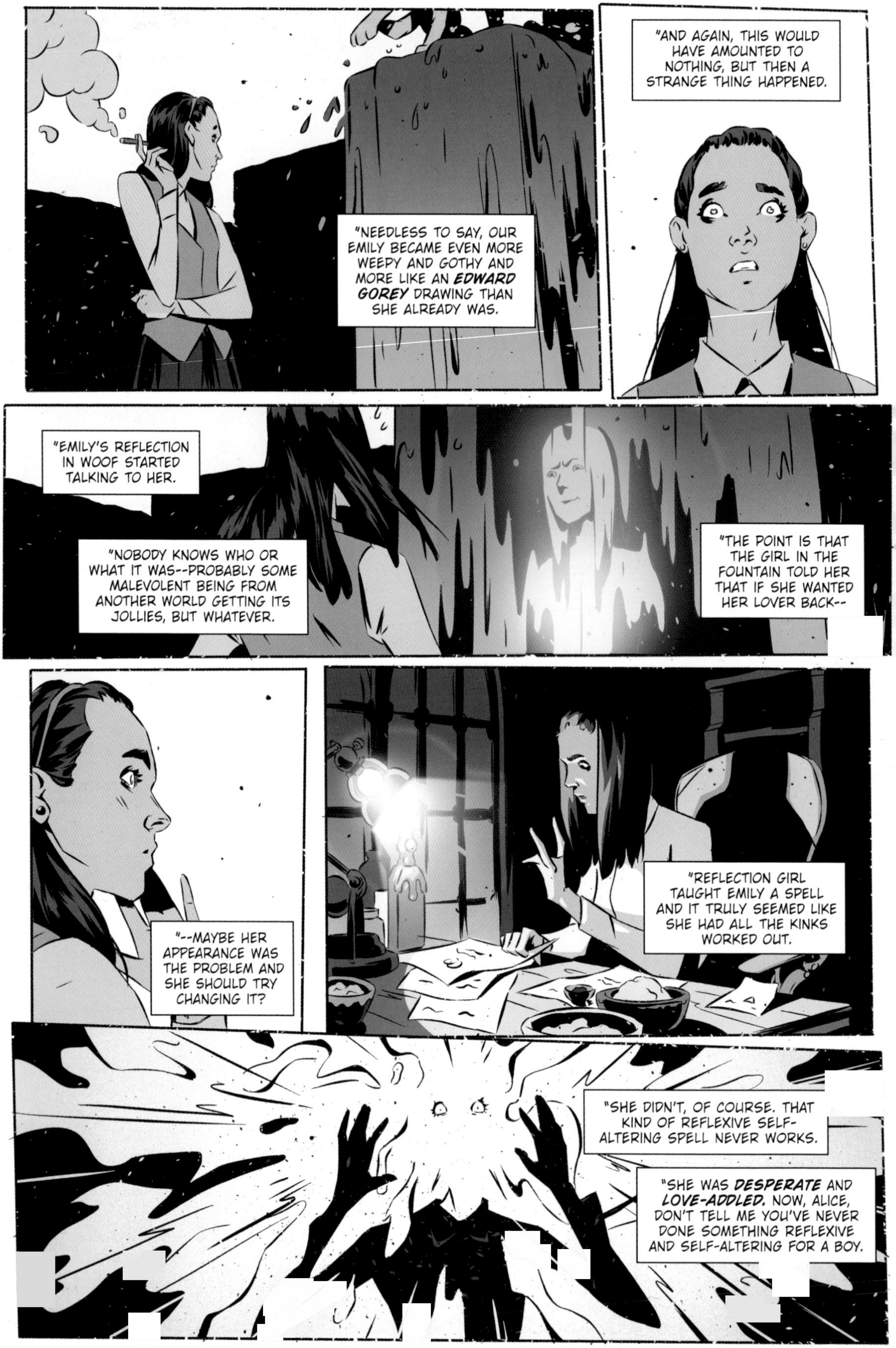
"NEEDLESS TO SAY, OUR EMILY BECAME EVEN MORE WEEPY AND GOTHY AND MORE LIKE AN **EDWARD GOREY** DRAWING THAN SHE ALREADY WAS.
"AND AGAIN, THIS WOULD HAVE AMOUNTED TO NOTHING, BUT THEN A STRANGE THING HAPPENED.
"EMILY'S REFLECTION IN WOOF STARTED TALKING TO HER.
"NOBODY KNOWS WHO OR WHAT IT WAS--PROBABLY SOME MALEVOLENT BEING FROM ANOTHER WORLD GETTING ITS JOLLIES, BUT WHATEVER.
"THE POINT IS THAT THE GIRL IN THE FOUNTAIN TOLD HER THAT IF SHE WANTED HER LOVER BACK--
"--MAYBE HER APPEARANCE WAS THE PROBLEM AND SHE SHOULD TRY CHANGING IT?
"REFLECTION GIRL TAUGHT EMILY A SPELL AND IT TRULY SEEMED LIKE SHE HAD ALL THE KINKS WORKED OUT.
"SHE DIDN'T, OF COURSE. THAT KIND OF REFLEXIVE SELF-ALTERING SPELL NEVER WORKS.
"SHE WAS **DESPERATE** AND **LOVE-ADDLED.** NOW, ALICE, DON'T TELL ME YOU'VE NEVER DONE SOMETHING REFLEXIVE AND SELF-ALTERING FOR A BOY.

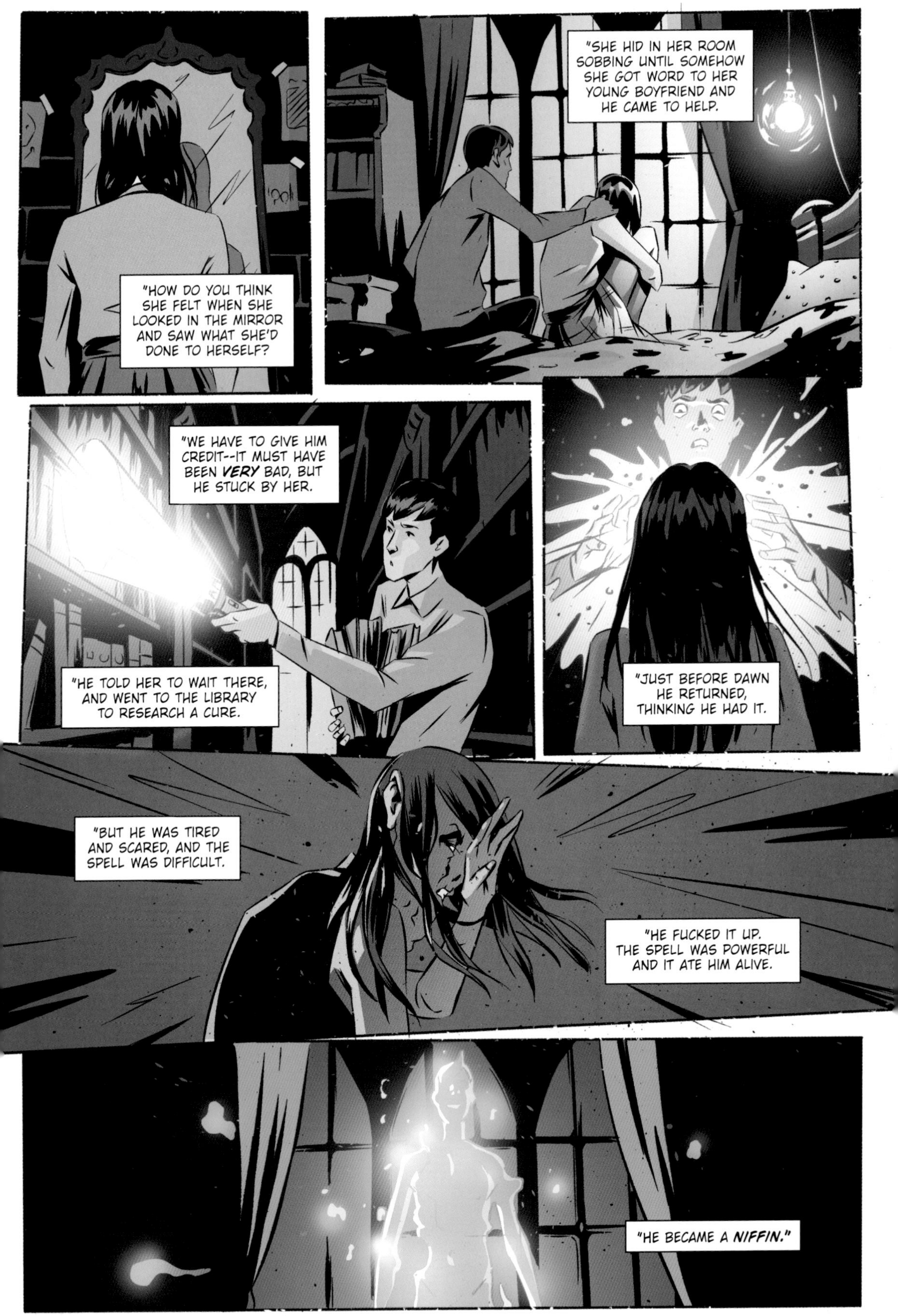
"HOW DO YOU THINK SHE FELT WHEN SHE LOOKED IN THE MIRROR AND SAW WHAT SHE'D DONE TO HERSELF?
"SHE HID IN HER ROOM SOBBING UNTIL SOMEHOW SHE GOT WORD TO HER YOUNG BOYFRIEND AND HE CAME TO HELP.
"WE HAVE TO GIVE HIM CREDIT--IT MUST HAVE BEEN ***VERY*** BAD, BUT HE STUCK BY HER.
"HE TOLD HER TO WAIT THERE, AND WENT TO THE LIBRARY TO RESEARCH A CURE.
"JUST BEFORE DAWN HE RETURNED, THINKING HE HAD IT.
"BUT HE WAS TIRED AND SCARED, AND THE SPELL WAS DIFFICULT.
"HE FUCKED IT UP. THE SPELL WAS POWERFUL AND IT ATE HIM ALIVE.
"HE BECAME A ***NIFFIN.***"

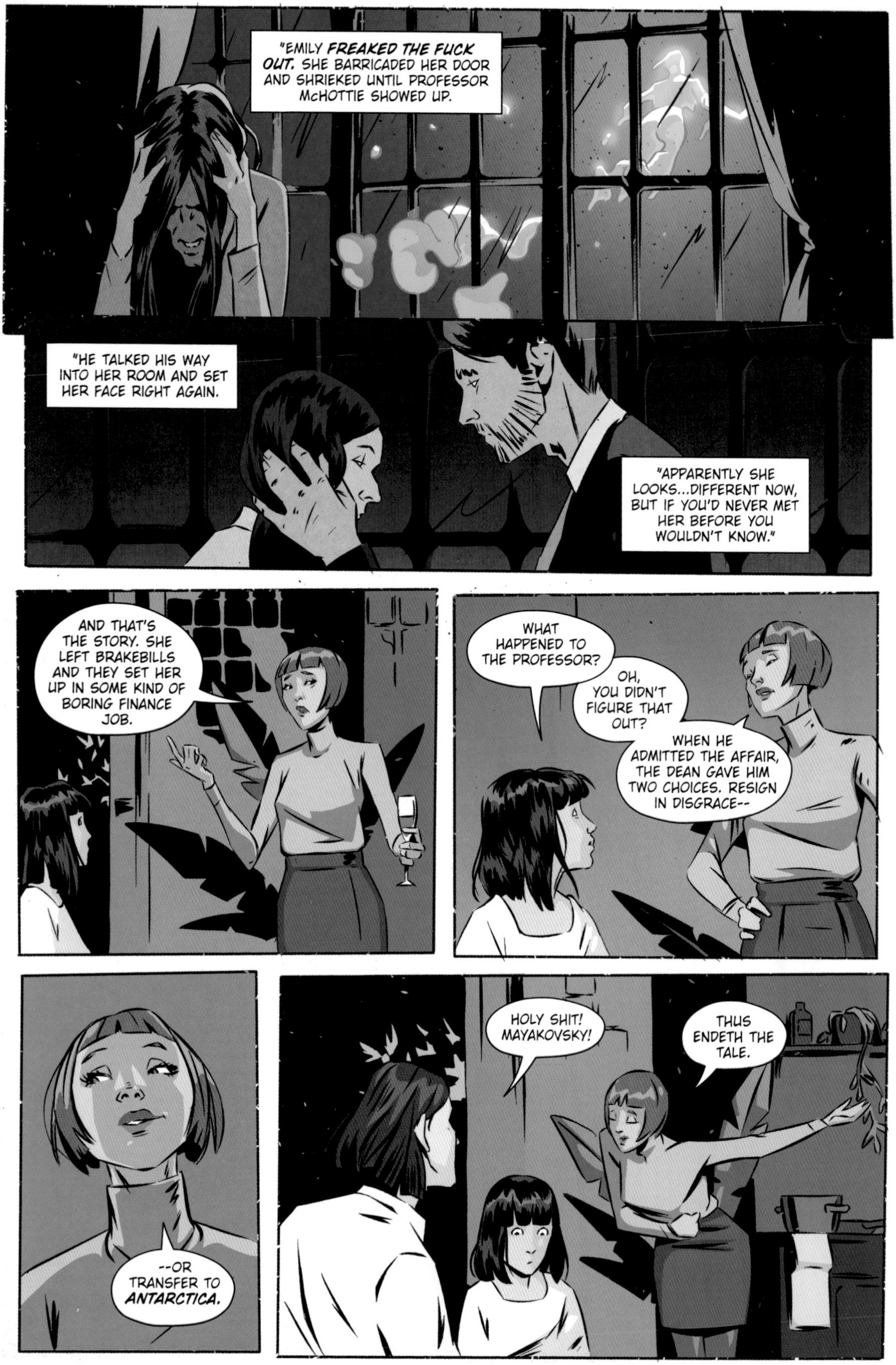
"EMILY **FREAKED THE FUCK OUT.** SHE BARRICADED HER DOOR AND SHRIEKED UNTIL PROFESSOR McHOTTIE SHOWED UP.
"HE TALKED HIS WAY INTO HER ROOM AND SET HER FACE RIGHT AGAIN.
"APPARENTLY SHE LOOKS...DIFFERENT NOW, BUT IF YOU'D NEVER MET HER BEFORE YOU WOULDN'T KNOW."
AND THAT'S THE STORY. SHE LEFT BRAKEBILLS AND THEY SET HER UP IN SOME KIND OF BORING FINANCE JOB.
WHAT HAPPENED TO THE PROFESSOR?
OH, YOU DIDN'T FIGURE THAT OUT?
WHEN HE ADMITTED THE AFFAIR, THE DEAN GAVE HIM TWO CHOICES. RESIGN IN DISGRACE--
--OR TRANSFER TO ***ANTARCTICA.***
HOLY SHIT! MAYAKOVSKY!
THUS ENDETH THE TALE.

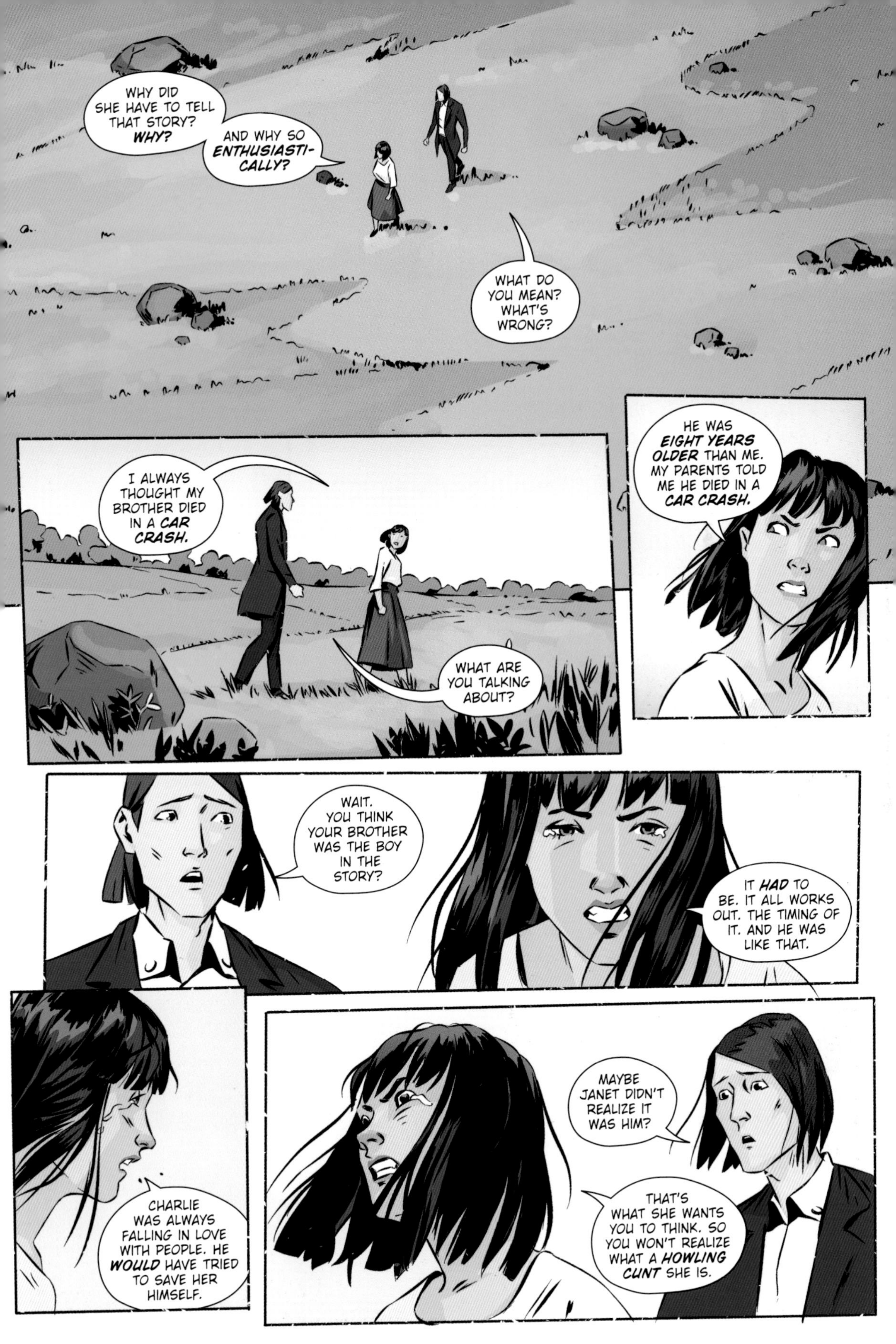
WHY DID SHE HAVE TO TELL THAT STORY? *WHY?*
AND WHY SO *ENTHUSIASTI-CALLY?*
WHAT DO YOU MEAN? WHAT'S WRONG?
I ALWAYS THOUGHT MY BROTHER DIED IN A *CAR CRASH.*
WHAT ARE YOU TALKING ABOUT?
HE WAS *EIGHT YEARS OLDER* THAN ME. MY PARENTS TOLD ME HE DIED IN A *CAR CRASH.*
WAIT. YOU THINK YOUR BROTHER WAS THE BOY IN THE STORY?
IT *HAD* TO BE. IT ALL WORKS OUT. THE TIMING OF IT. AND HE WAS LIKE THAT.
CHARLIE WAS ALWAYS FALLING IN LOVE WITH PEOPLE. HE *WOULD* HAVE TRIED TO SAVE HER HIMSELF.
MAYBE JANET DIDN'T REALIZE IT WAS HIM?
THAT'S WHAT SHE WANTS YOU TO THINK. SO YOU WON'T REALIZE WHAT A *HOWLING CUNT* SHE IS.

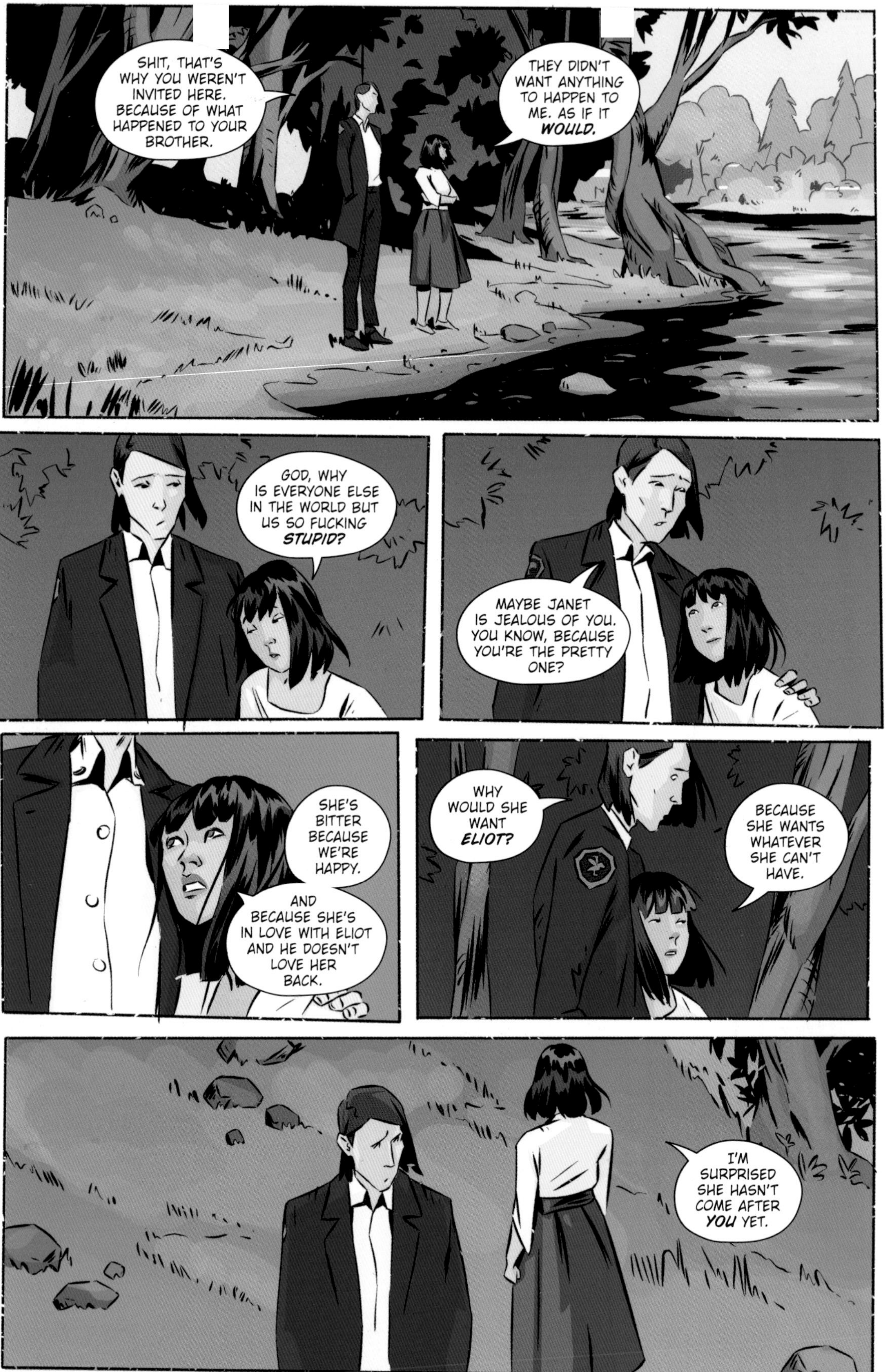
SHIT, THAT'S WHY YOU WEREN'T INVITED HERE. BECAUSE OF WHAT HAPPENED TO YOUR BROTHER.
THEY DIDN'T WANT ANYTHING TO HAPPEN TO ME. AS IF IT *WOULD.*
GOD, WHY IS EVERYONE ELSE IN THE WORLD BUT US SO FUCKING *STUPID?*
MAYBE JANET IS JEALOUS OF YOU. YOU KNOW, BECAUSE YOU'RE THE PRETTY ONE?
SHE'S BITTER BECAUSE WE'RE HAPPY.
AND BECAUSE SHE'S IN LOVE WITH ELIOT AND HE DOESN'T LOVE HER BACK.
WHY WOULD SHE WANT *ELIOT?*
BECAUSE SHE WANTS WHATEVER SHE CAN'T HAVE.
I'M SURPRISED SHE HASN'T COME AFTER *YOU* YET.

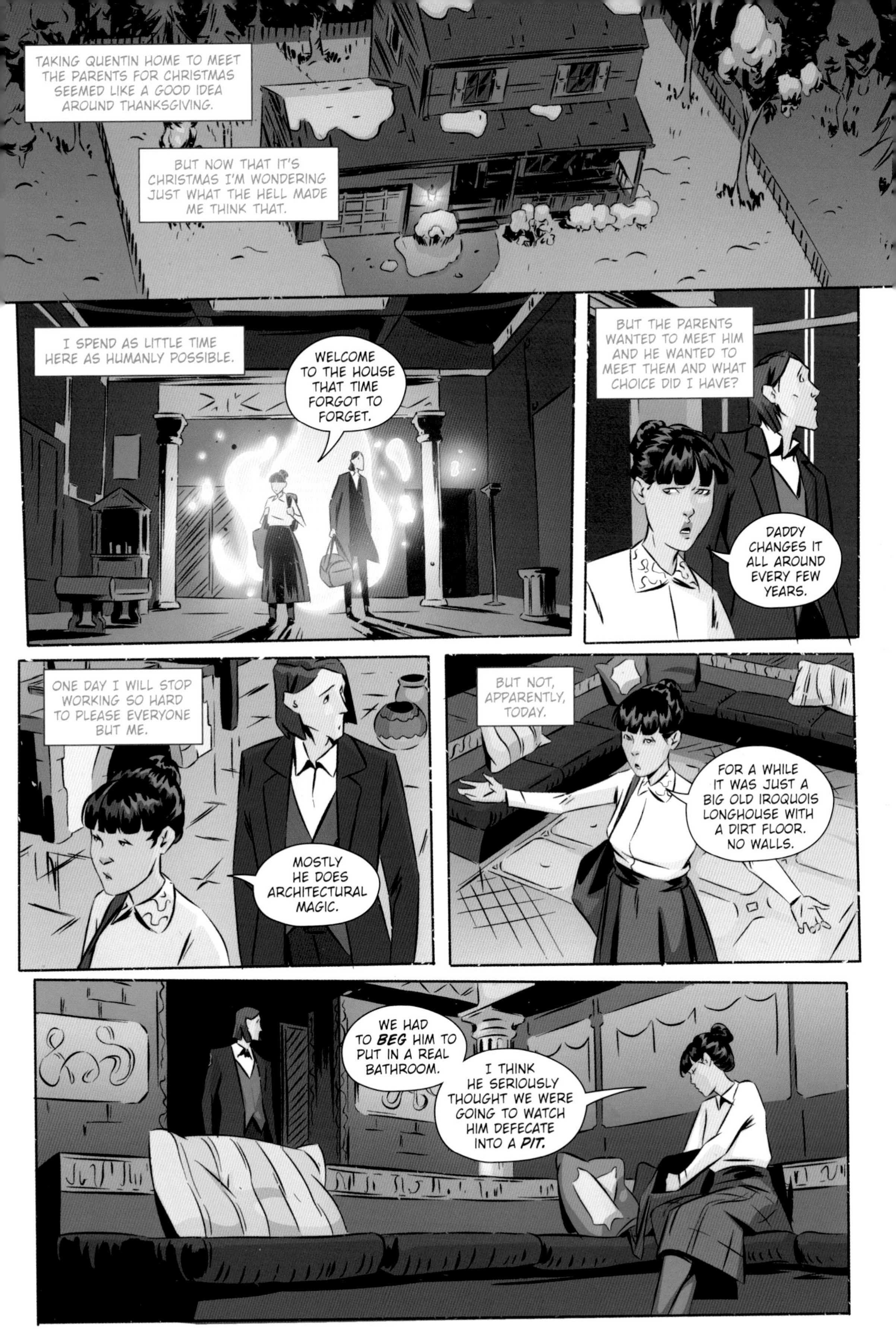
TAKING QUENTIN HOME TO MEET THE PARENTS FOR CHRISTMAS SEEMED LIKE A GOOD IDEA AROUND THANKSGIVING.
BUT NOW THAT IT'S CHRISTMAS I'M WONDERING JUST WHAT THE HELL MADE ME THINK THAT.
I SPEND AS LITTLE TIME HERE AS HUMANLY POSSIBLE.
WELCOME TO THE HOUSE THAT TIME FORGOT TO FORGET.
BUT THE PARENTS WANTED TO MEET HIM AND HE WANTED TO MEET THEM AND WHAT CHOICE DID I HAVE?
DADDY CHANGES IT ALL AROUND EVERY FEW YEARS.
ONE DAY I WILL STOP WORKING SO HARD TO PLEASE EVERYONE BUT ME.
MOSTLY HE DOES ARCHITECTURAL MAGIC.
BUT NOT, APPARENTLY, TODAY.
FOR A WHILE IT WAS JUST A BIG OLD IROQUOIS LONGHOUSE WITH A DIRT FLOOR. NO WALLS.
WE HAD TO ***BEG*** HIM TO PUT IN A REAL BATHROOM.
I THINK HE SERIOUSLY THOUGHT WE WERE GOING TO WATCH HIM DEFECATE INTO A ***PIT.***

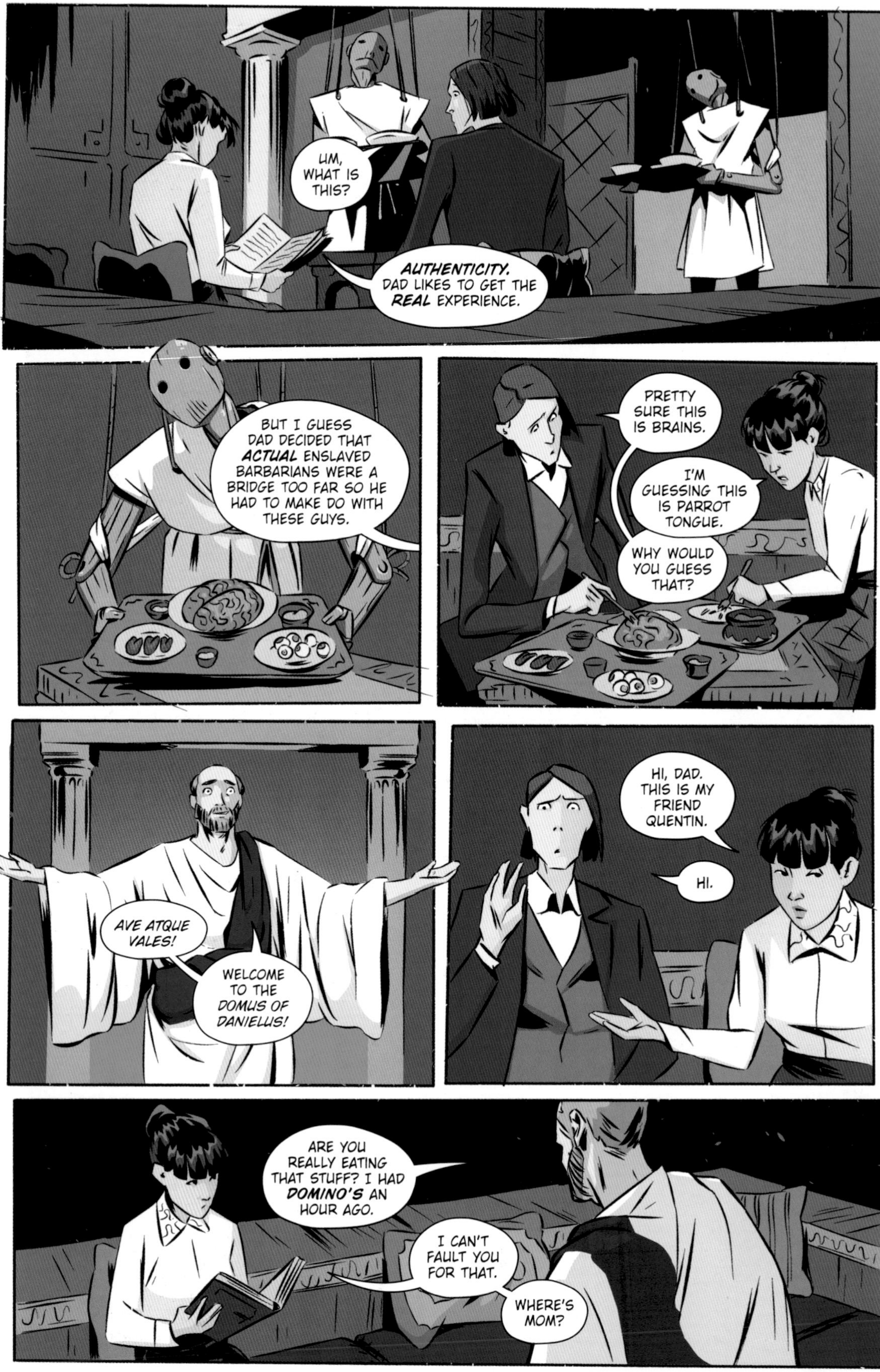
UM, WHAT IS THIS?
AUTHENTICITY. DAD LIKES TO GET THE REAL EXPERIENCE.
BUT I GUESS DAD DECIDED THAT ACTUAL ENSLAVED BARBARIANS WERE A BRIDGE TOO FAR SO HE HAD TO MAKE DO WITH THESE GUYS.
PRETTY SURE THIS IS BRAINS.
I'M GUESSING THIS IS PARROT TONGUE.
WHY WOULD YOU GUESS THAT?
AVE ATQUE VALES!
WELCOME TO THE DOMUS OF DANIELUS!
HI, DAD. THIS IS MY FRIEND QUENTIN.
HI.
ARE YOU REALLY EATING THAT STUFF? I HAD DOMINO'S AN HOUR AGO.
I CAN'T FAULT YOU FOR THAT.
WHERE'S MOM?

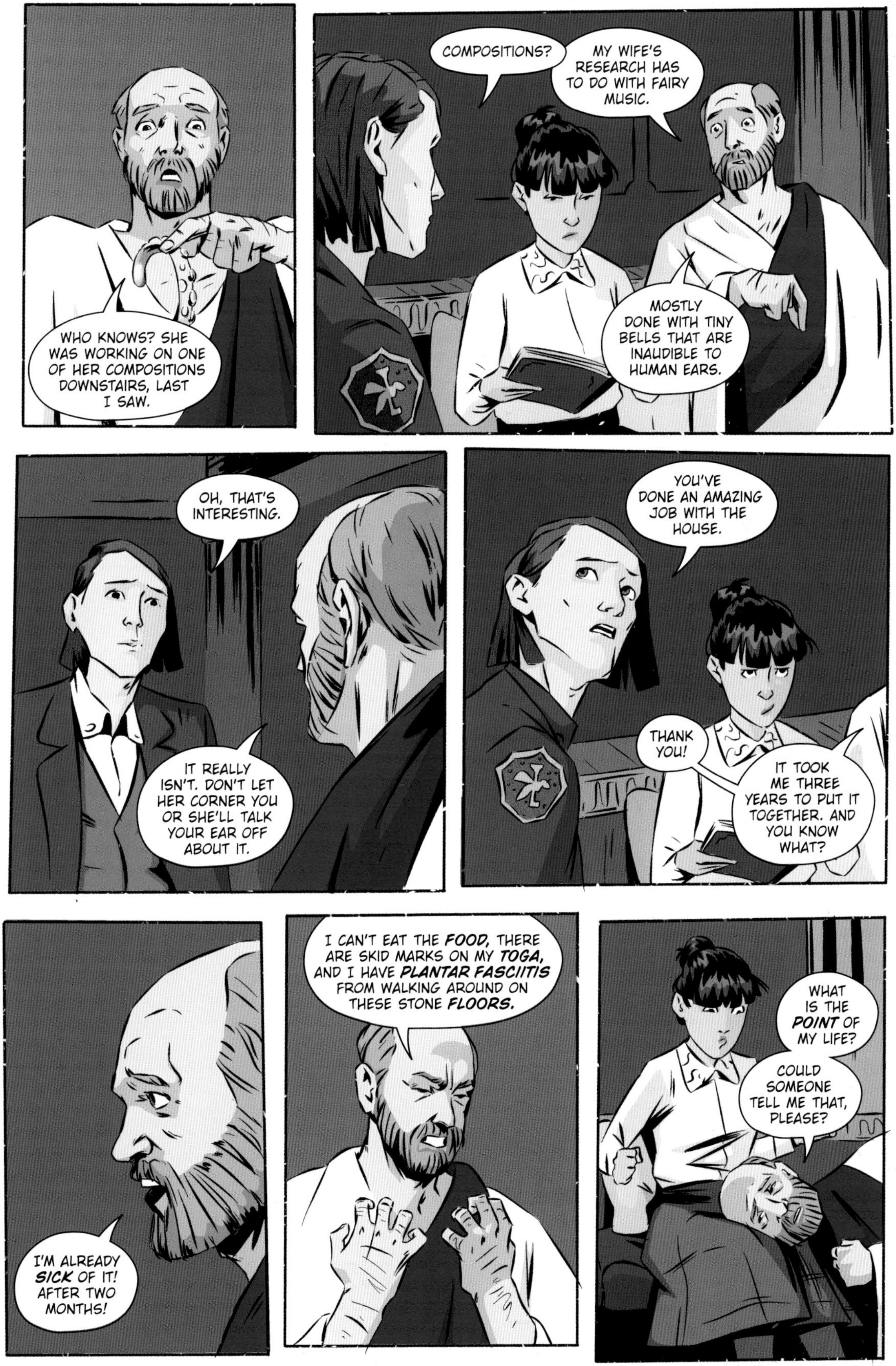
WHO KNOWS? SHE WAS WORKING ON ONE OF HER COMPOSITIONS DOWNSTAIRS, LAST I SAW.
COMPOSITIONS?
MY WIFE'S RESEARCH HAS TO DO WITH FAIRY MUSIC.
MOSTLY DONE WITH TINY BELLS THAT ARE INAUDIBLE TO HUMAN EARS.
OH, THAT'S INTERESTING.
IT REALLY ISN'T. DON'T LET HER CORNER YOU OR SHE'LL TALK YOUR EAR OFF ABOUT IT.
YOU'VE DONE AN AMAZING JOB WITH THE HOUSE.
THANK YOU!
IT TOOK ME THREE YEARS TO PUT IT TOGETHER. AND YOU KNOW WHAT?
I'M ALREADY *SICK* OF IT! AFTER TWO MONTHS!
I CAN'T EAT THE *FOOD,* THERE ARE SKID MARKS ON MY *TOGA,* AND I HAVE *PLANTAR FASCIITIS* FROM WALKING AROUND ON THESE STONE *FLOORS.*
WHAT IS THE *POINT* OF MY LIFE?
COULD SOMEONE TELL ME THAT, PLEASE?

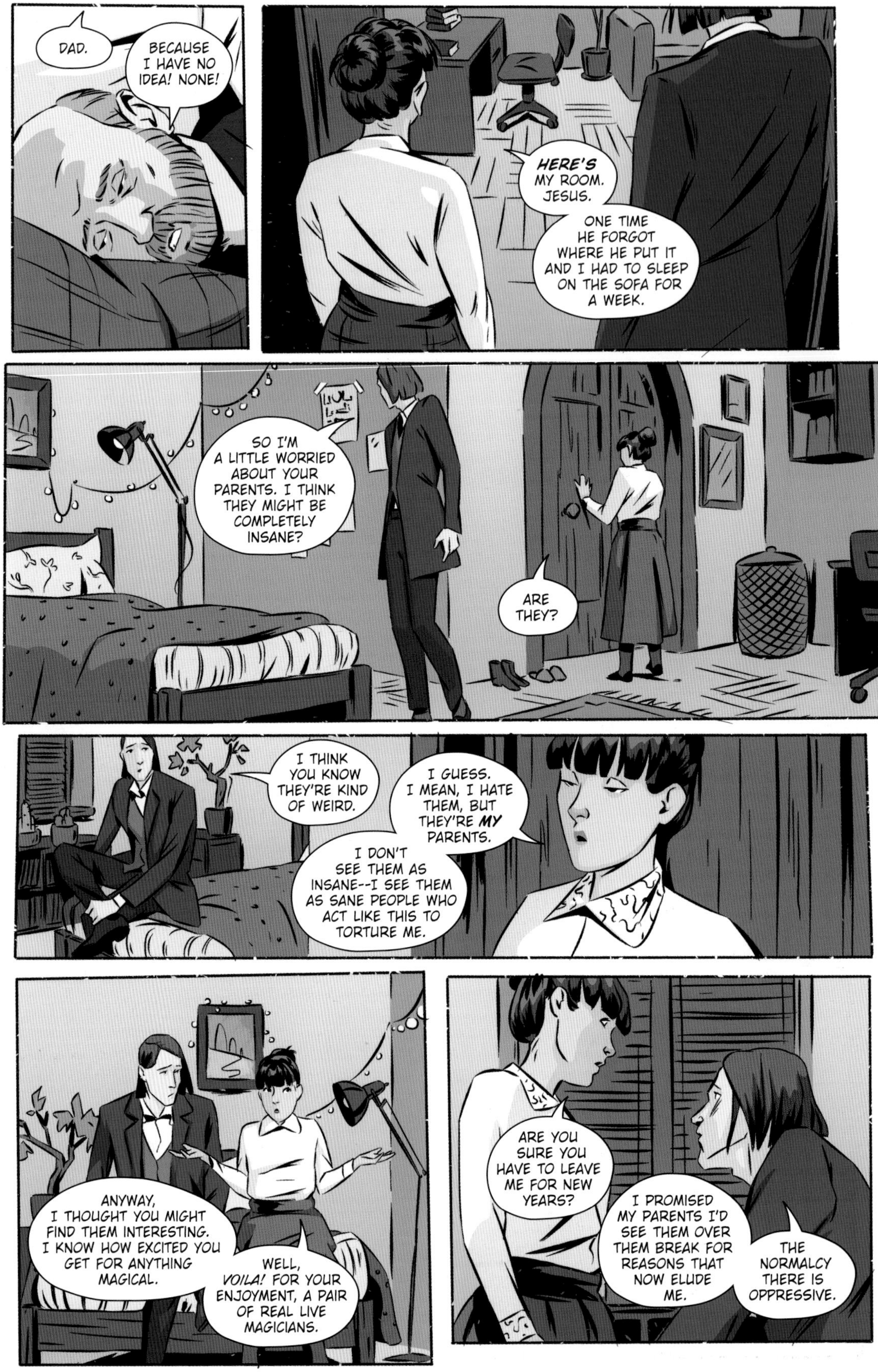
DAD.
BECAUSE I HAVE NO IDEA! NONE!
HERE'S MY ROOM. JESUS.
ONE TIME HE FORGOT WHERE HE PUT IT AND I HAD TO SLEEP ON THE SOFA FOR A WEEK.
SO I'M A LITTLE WORRIED ABOUT YOUR PARENTS. I THINK THEY MIGHT BE COMPLETELY INSANE?
ARE THEY?
I THINK YOU KNOW THEY'RE KIND OF WEIRD.
I GUESS. I MEAN, I HATE THEM, BUT THEY'RE MY PARENTS.
I DON'T SEE THEM AS INSANE--I SEE THEM AS SANE PEOPLE WHO ACT LIKE THIS TO TORTURE ME.
ANYWAY, I THOUGHT YOU MIGHT FIND THEM INTERESTING. I KNOW HOW EXCITED YOU GET FOR ANYTHING MAGICAL.
WELL, VOILA! FOR YOUR ENJOYMENT, A PAIR OF REAL LIVE MAGICIANS.
ARE YOU SURE YOU HAVE TO LEAVE ME FOR NEW YEARS?
I PROMISED MY PARENTS I'D SEE THEM OVER THEM BREAK FOR REASONS THAT NOW ELUDE ME.
THE NORMALCY THERE IS OPPRESSIVE.

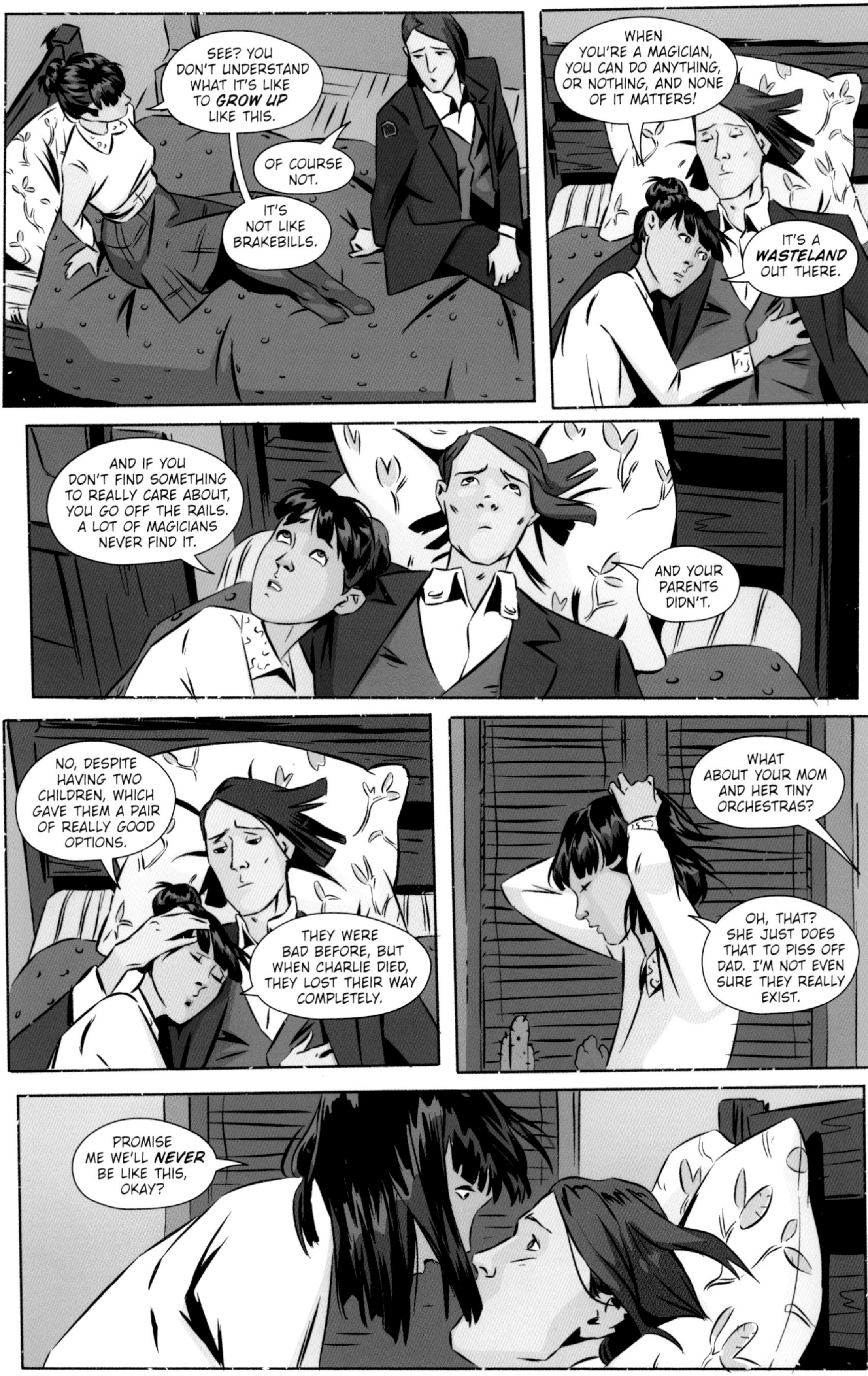
SEE? YOU DON'T UNDERSTAND WHAT IT'S LIKE TO **GROW UP** LIKE THIS.
OF COURSE NOT.
IT'S NOT LIKE BRAKEBILLS.
WHEN YOU'RE A MAGICIAN, YOU CAN DO ANYTHING, OR NOTHING, AND NONE OF IT MATTERS!
IT'S A **WASTELAND** OUT THERE.
AND IF YOU DON'T FIND SOMETHING TO REALLY CARE ABOUT, YOU GO OFF THE RAILS. A LOT OF MAGICIANS NEVER FIND IT.
AND YOUR PARENTS DIDN'T.
NO, DESPITE HAVING TWO CHILDREN, WHICH GAVE THEM A PAIR OF REALLY GOOD OPTIONS.
THEY WERE BAD BEFORE, BUT WHEN CHARLIE DIED, THEY LOST THEIR WAY COMPLETELY.
WHAT ABOUT YOUR MOM AND HER TINY ORCHESTRAS?
OH, THAT? SHE JUST DOES THAT TO PISS OFF DAD. I'M NOT EVEN SURE THEY REALLY EXIST.
PROMISE ME WE'LL **NEVER** BE LIKE THIS, OKAY?

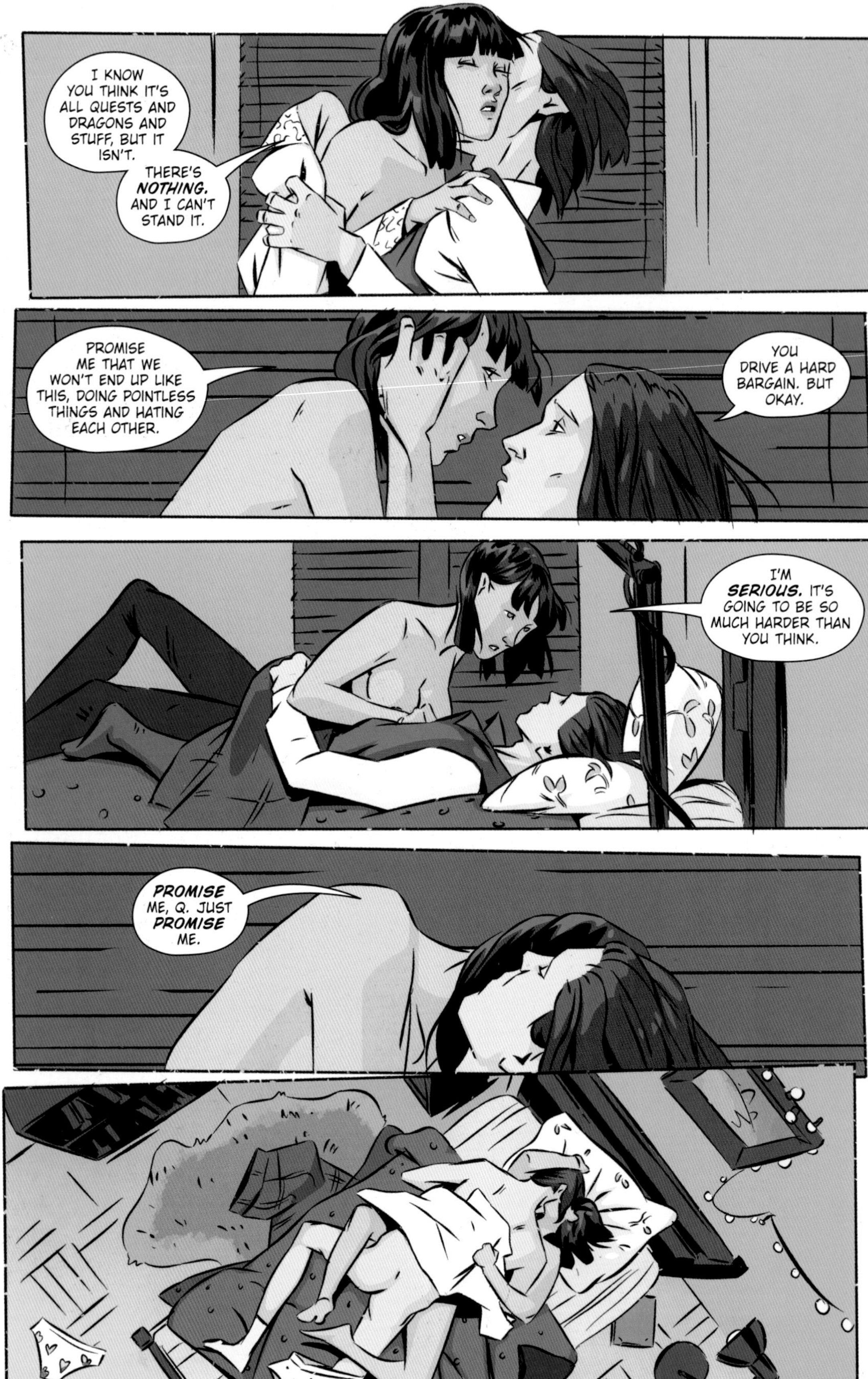
I KNOW YOU THINK IT'S ALL QUESTS AND DRAGONS AND STUFF, BUT IT ISN'T.
THERE'S NOTHING. AND I CAN'T STAND IT.
PROMISE ME THAT WE WON'T END UP LIKE THIS, DOING POINTLESS THINGS AND HATING EACH OTHER.
YOU DRIVE A HARD BARGAIN. BUT OKAY.
I'M SERIOUS. IT'S GOING TO BE SO MUCH HARDER THAN YOU THINK.
PROMISE ME, Q. JUST PROMISE ME.

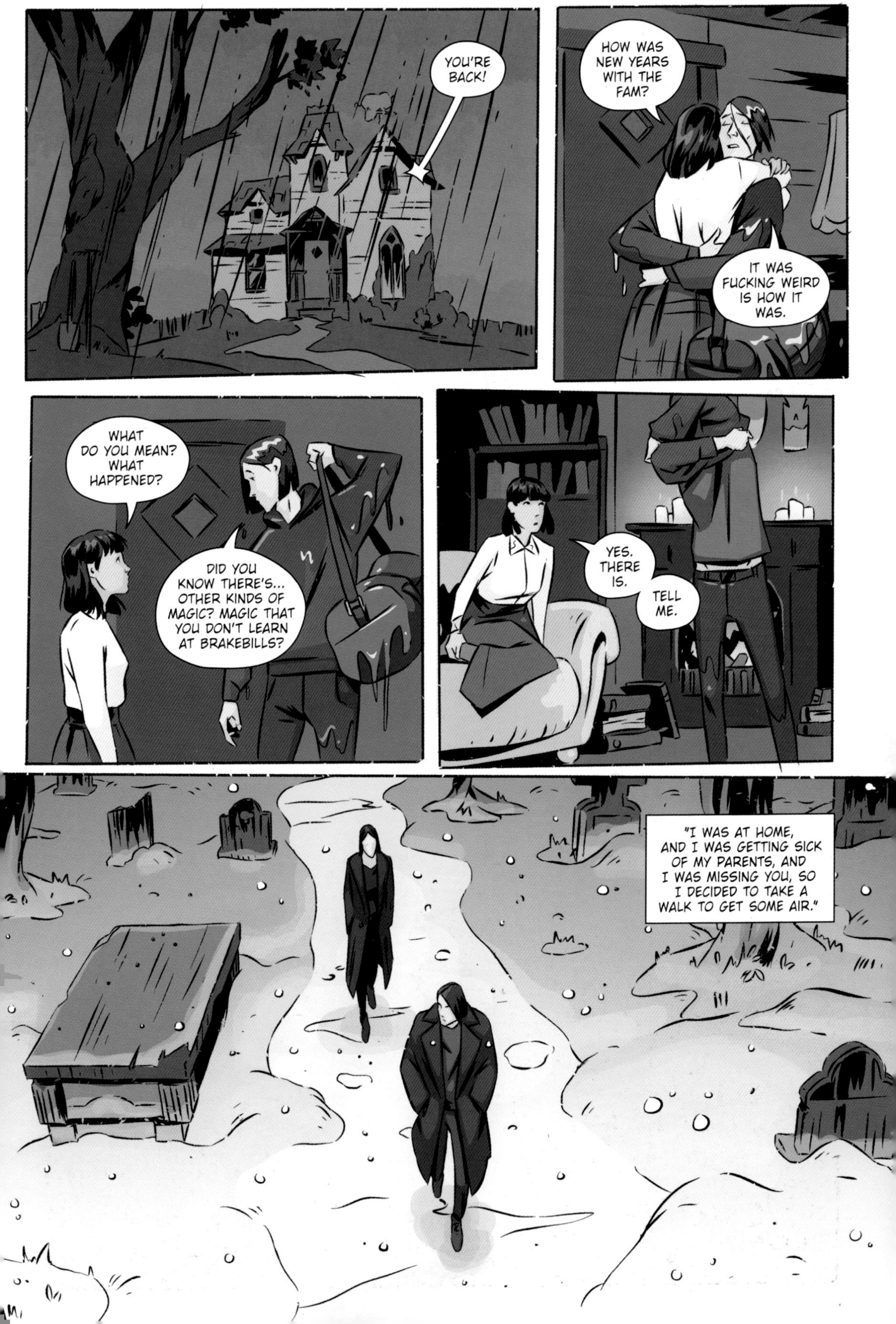
YOU'RE BACK!
HOW WAS NEW YEARS WITH THE FAM?
IT WAS FUCKING WEIRD IS HOW IT WAS.
WHAT DO YOU MEAN? WHAT HAPPENED?
DID YOU KNOW THERE'S... OTHER KINDS OF MAGIC? MAGIC THAT YOU DON'T LEARN AT BRAKEBILLS?
YES. THERE IS.
TELL ME.
"I WAS AT HOME, AND I WAS GETTING SICK OF MY PARENTS, AND I WAS MISSING YOU, SO I DECIDED TO TAKE A WALK TO GET SOME AIR."

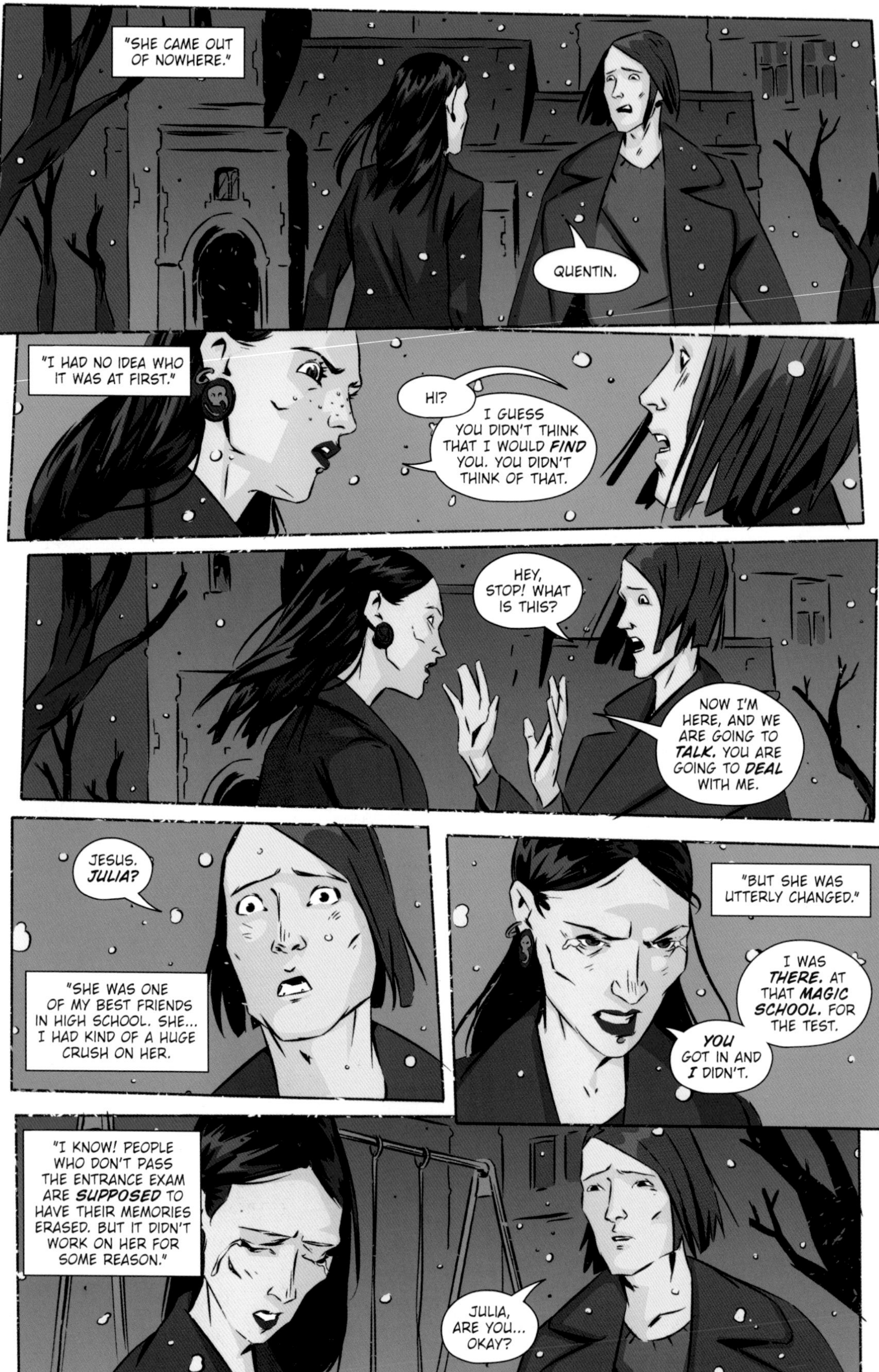
"SHE CAME OUT OF NOWHERE."
QUENTIN.
"I HAD NO IDEA WHO IT WAS AT FIRST."
HI?
I GUESS YOU DIDN'T THINK THAT I WOULD FIND YOU. YOU DIDN'T THINK OF THAT.
HEY, STOP! WHAT IS THIS?
NOW I'M HERE, AND WE ARE GOING TO TALK. YOU ARE GOING TO DEAL WITH ME.
JESUS. JULIA?
"SHE WAS ONE OF MY BEST FRIENDS IN HIGH SCHOOL. SHE... I HAD KIND OF A HUGE CRUSH ON HER.
"BUT SHE WAS UTTERLY CHANGED."
I WAS THERE. AT THAT MAGIC SCHOOL. FOR THE TEST.
YOU GOT IN AND I DIDN'T.
"I KNOW! PEOPLE WHO DON'T PASS THE ENTRANCE EXAM ARE SUPPOSED TO HAVE THEIR MEMORIES ERASED. BUT IT DIDN'T WORK ON HER FOR SOME REASON."
JULIA, ARE YOU... OKAY?

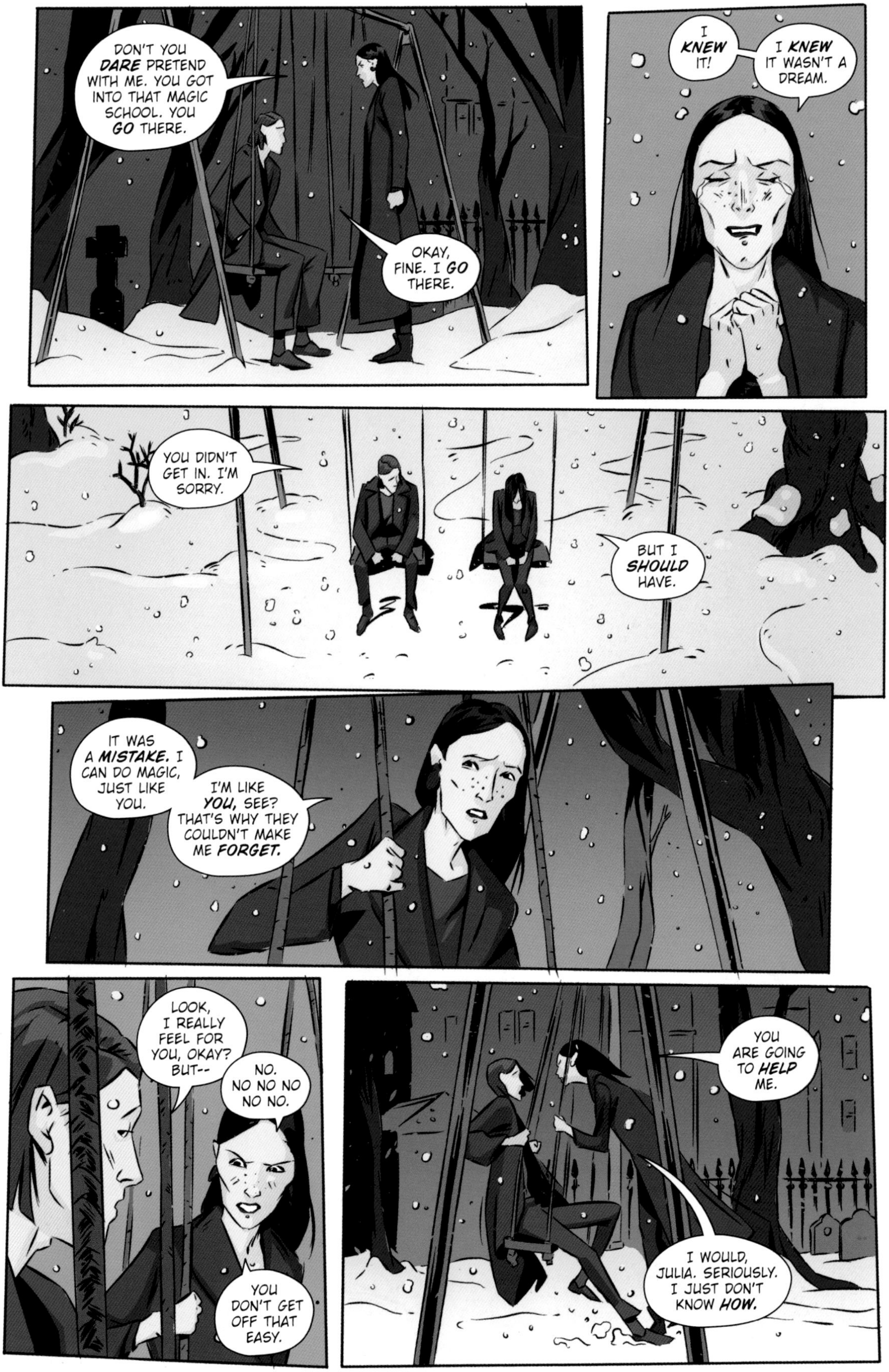

DON'T YOU **DARE** PRETEND WITH ME. YOU GOT INTO THAT MAGIC SCHOOL. YOU **GO** THERE.
OKAY, FINE. I **GO** THERE.
I **KNEW** IT!
I **KNEW** IT WASN'T A DREAM.
YOU DIDN'T GET IN. I'M SORRY.
BUT I **SHOULD** HAVE.
IT WAS A **MISTAKE.** I CAN DO MAGIC, JUST LIKE YOU.
I'M LIKE **YOU,** SEE? THAT'S WHY THEY COULDN'T MAKE ME **FORGET.**
LOOK, I REALLY FEEL FOR YOU, OKAY? BUT--
NO. NO NO NO NO NO.
YOU DON'T GET OFF THAT EASY.
YOU ARE GOING TO **HELP** ME.
I WOULD, JULIA. SERIOUSLY. I JUST DON'T KNOW **HOW.**

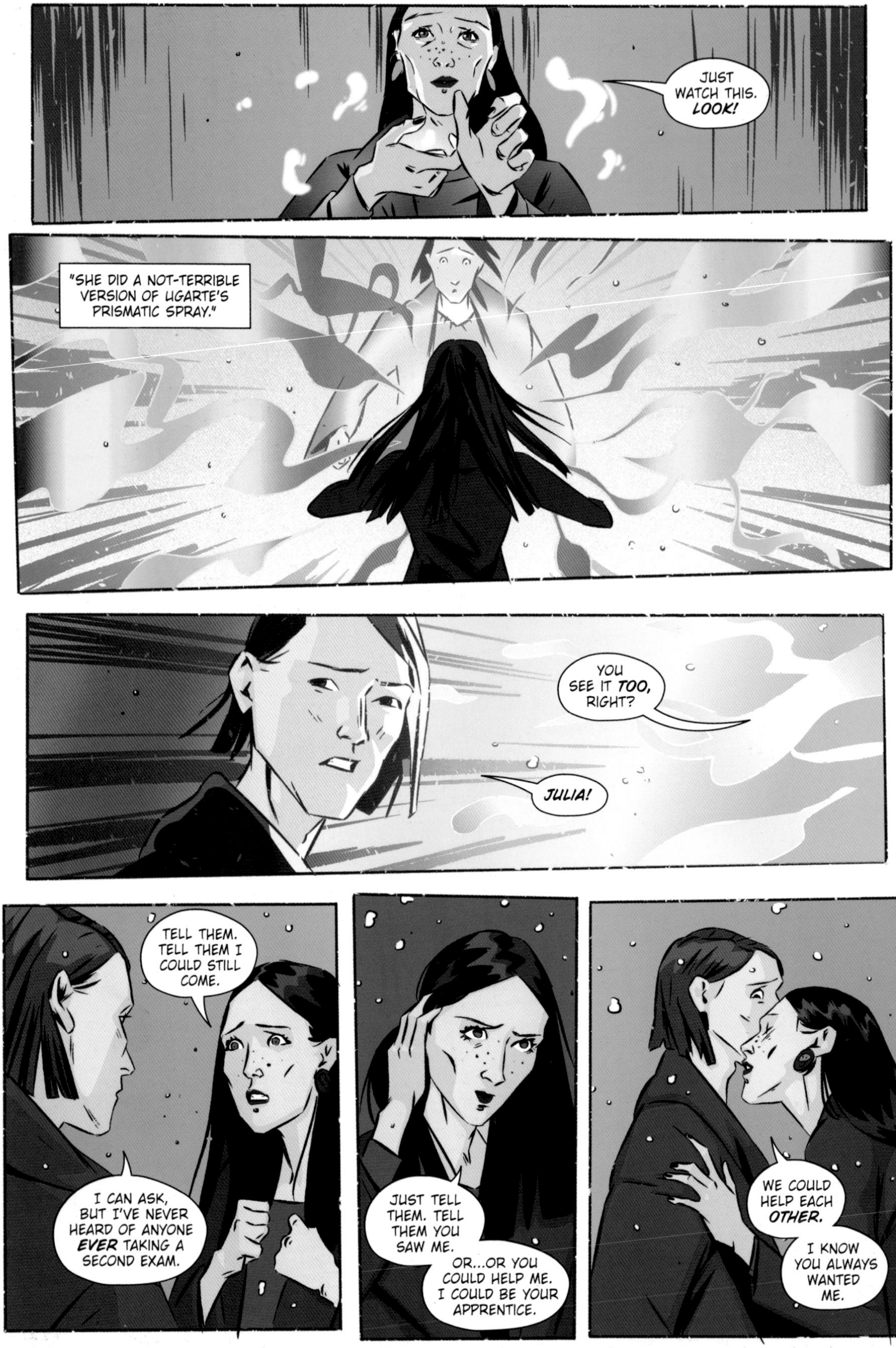
JUST WATCH THIS. LOOK!
"SHE DID A NOT-TERRIBLE VERSION OF UGARTE'S PRISMATIC SPRAY."
YOU SEE IT TOO, RIGHT?
JULIA!
TELL THEM. TELL THEM I COULD STILL COME.
I CAN ASK, BUT I'VE NEVER HEARD OF ANYONE EVER TAKING A SECOND EXAM.
JUST TELL THEM. TELL THEM YOU SAW ME.
OR...OR YOU COULD HELP ME. I COULD BE YOUR APPRENTICE.
WE COULD HELP EACH OTHER.
I KNOW YOU ALWAYS WANTED ME.

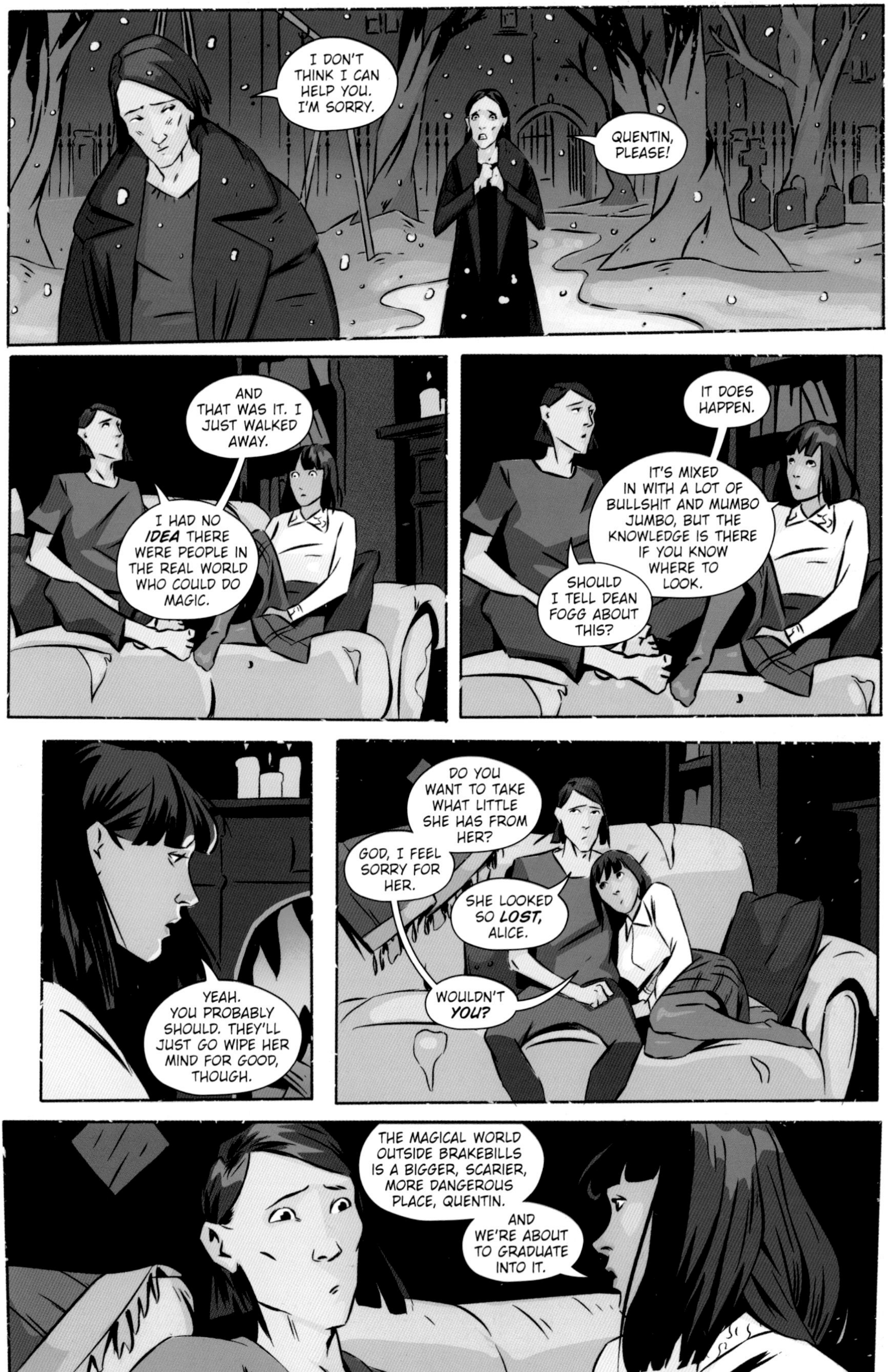

I DON'T THINK I CAN HELP YOU. I'M SORRY.
QUENTIN, PLEASE!
AND THAT WAS IT. I JUST WALKED AWAY.
I HAD NO *IDEA* THERE WERE PEOPLE IN THE REAL WORLD WHO COULD DO MAGIC.
IT DOES HAPPEN.
IT'S MIXED IN WITH A LOT OF BULLSHIT AND MUMBO JUMBO, BUT THE KNOWLEDGE IS THERE IF YOU KNOW WHERE TO LOOK.
SHOULD I TELL DEAN FOGG ABOUT THIS?
YEAH. YOU PROBABLY SHOULD. THEY'LL JUST GO WIPE HER MIND FOR GOOD, THOUGH.
DO YOU WANT TO TAKE WHAT LITTLE SHE HAS FROM HER?
GOD, I FEEL SORRY FOR HER.
SHE LOOKED SO *LOST,* ALICE.
WOULDN'T *YOU?*
THE MAGICAL WORLD OUTSIDE BRAKEBILLS IS A BIGGER, SCARIER, MORE DANGEROUS PLACE, QUENTIN.
AND WE'RE ABOUT TO GRADUATE INTO IT.

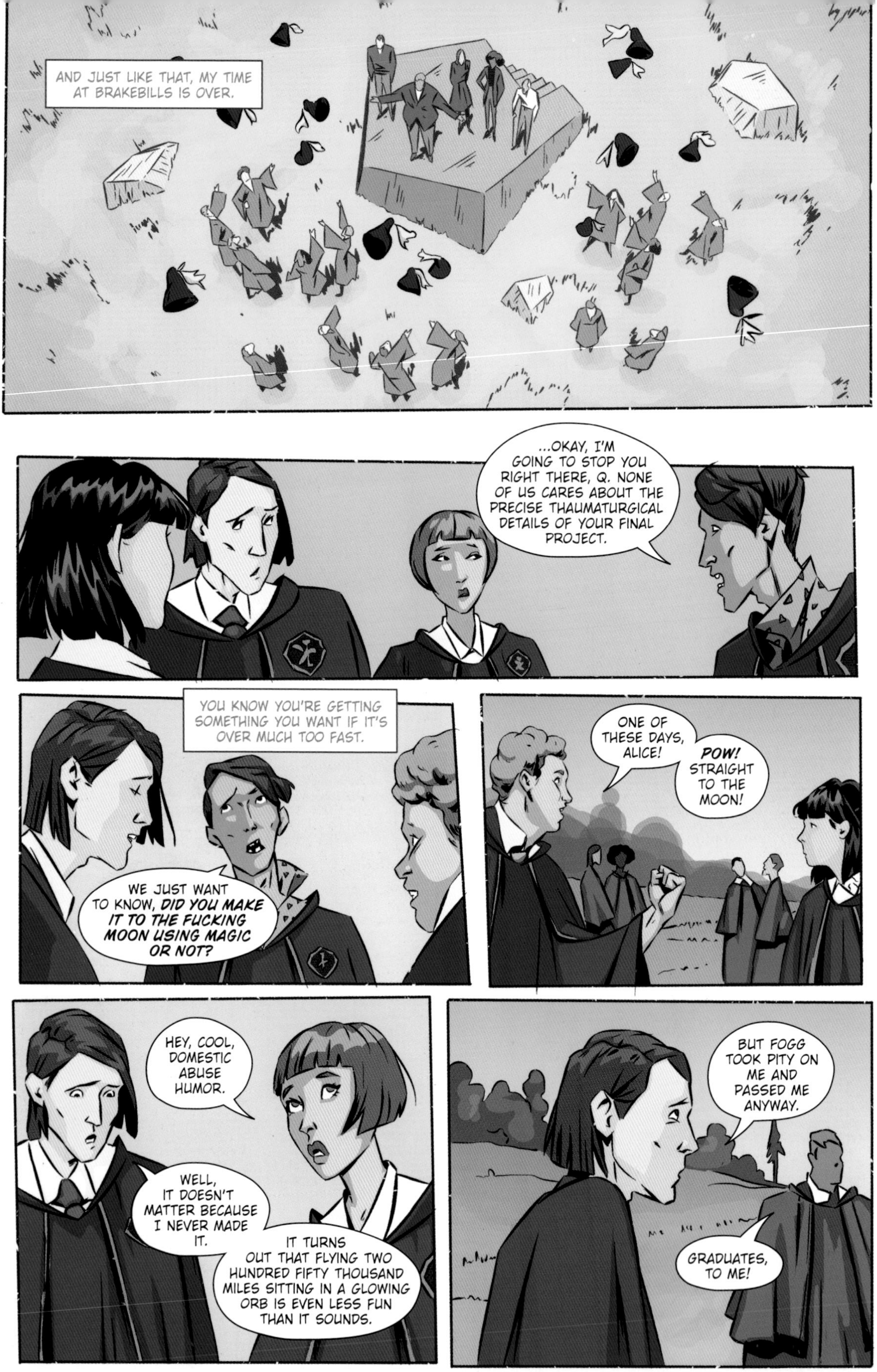
AND JUST LIKE THAT, MY TIME AT BRAKEBILLS IS OVER.
...OKAY, I'M GOING TO STOP YOU RIGHT THERE, Q. NONE OF US CARES ABOUT THE PRECISE THAUMATURGICAL DETAILS OF YOUR FINAL PROJECT.
YOU KNOW YOU'RE GETTING SOMETHING YOU WANT IF IT'S OVER MUCH TOO FAST.
WE JUST WANT TO KNOW, ***DID YOU MAKE IT TO THE FUCKING MOON USING MAGIC OR NOT?***
ONE OF THESE DAYS, ALICE!
POW! STRAIGHT TO THE MOON!
HEY, COOL, DOMESTIC ABUSE HUMOR.
WELL, IT DOESN'T MATTER BECAUSE I NEVER MADE IT.
IT TURNS OUT THAT FLYING TWO HUNDRED FIFTY THOUSAND MILES SITTING IN A GLOWING ORB IS EVEN LESS FUN THAN IT SOUNDS.
BUT FOGG TOOK PITY ON ME AND PASSED ME ANYWAY.
GRADUATES, TO ME!

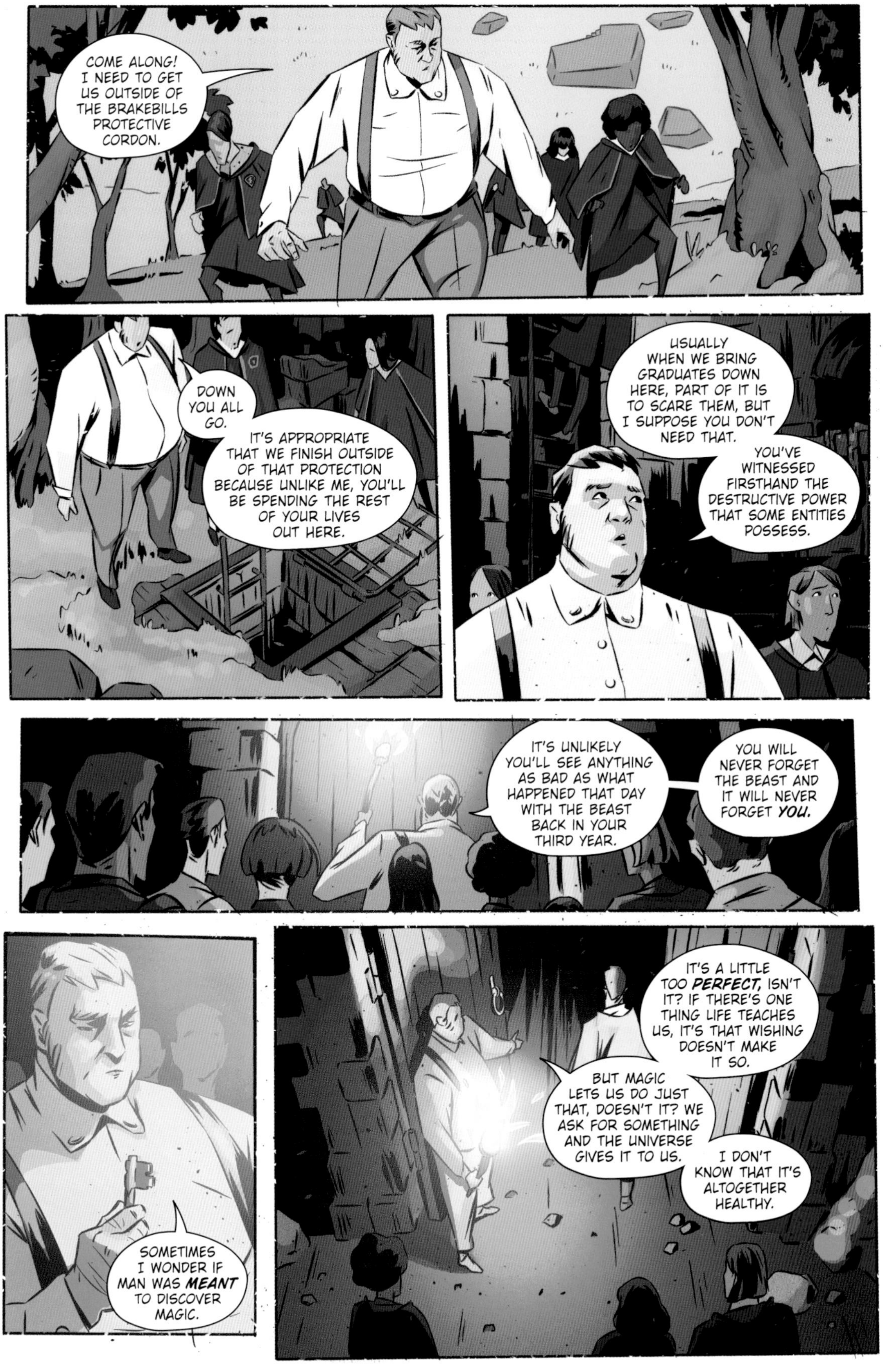
COME ALONG! I NEED TO GET US OUTSIDE OF THE BRAKEBILLS PROTECTIVE CORDON.
DOWN YOU ALL GO.
IT'S APPROPRIATE THAT WE FINISH OUTSIDE OF THAT PROTECTION BECAUSE UNLIKE ME, YOU'LL BE SPENDING THE REST OF YOUR LIVES OUT HERE.
USUALLY WHEN WE BRING GRADUATES DOWN HERE, PART OF IT IS TO SCARE THEM, BUT I SUPPOSE YOU DON'T NEED THAT.
YOU'VE WITNESSED FIRSTHAND THE DESTRUCTIVE POWER THAT SOME ENTITIES POSSESS.
IT'S UNLIKELY YOU'LL SEE ANYTHING AS BAD AS WHAT HAPPENED THAT DAY WITH THE BEAST BACK IN YOUR THIRD YEAR.
YOU WILL NEVER FORGET THE BEAST AND IT WILL NEVER FORGET ***YOU.***
SOMETIMES I WONDER IF MAN WAS ***MEANT*** TO DISCOVER MAGIC.
IT'S A LITTLE TOO ***PERFECT,*** ISN'T IT? IF THERE'S ONE THING LIFE TEACHES US, IT'S THAT WISHING DOESN'T MAKE IT SO.
BUT MAGIC LETS US DO JUST THAT, DOESN'T IT? WE ASK FOR SOMETHING AND THE UNIVERSE GIVES IT TO US.
I DON'T KNOW THAT IT'S ALTOGETHER HEALTHY.

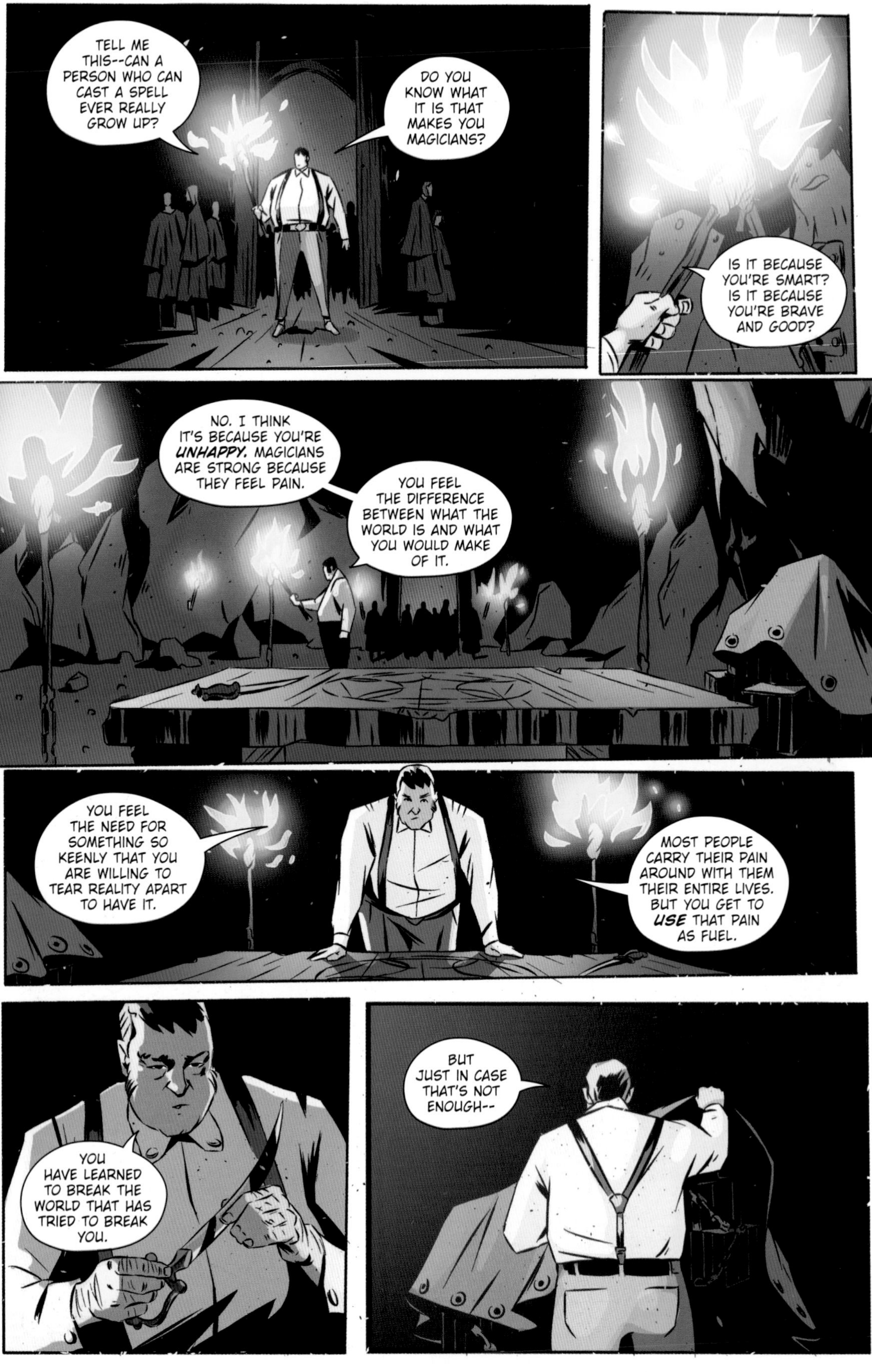
TELL ME THIS--CAN A PERSON WHO CAN CAST A SPELL EVER REALLY GROW UP?
DO YOU KNOW WHAT IT IS THAT MAKES YOU MAGICIANS?
IS IT BECAUSE YOU'RE SMART? IS IT BECAUSE YOU'RE BRAVE AND GOOD?
NO. I THINK IT'S BECAUSE YOU'RE UNHAPPY. MAGICIANS ARE STRONG BECAUSE THEY FEEL PAIN.
YOU FEEL THE DIFFERENCE BETWEEN WHAT THE WORLD IS AND WHAT YOU WOULD MAKE OF IT.
YOU FEEL THE NEED FOR SOMETHING SO KEENLY THAT YOU ARE WILLING TO TEAR REALITY APART TO HAVE IT.
MOST PEOPLE CARRY THEIR PAIN AROUND WITH THEM THEIR ENTIRE LIVES. BUT YOU GET TO USE THAT PAIN AS FUEL.
YOU HAVE LEARNED TO BREAK THE WORLD THAT HAS TRIED TO BREAK YOU.
BUT JUST IN CASE THAT'S NOT ENOUGH--

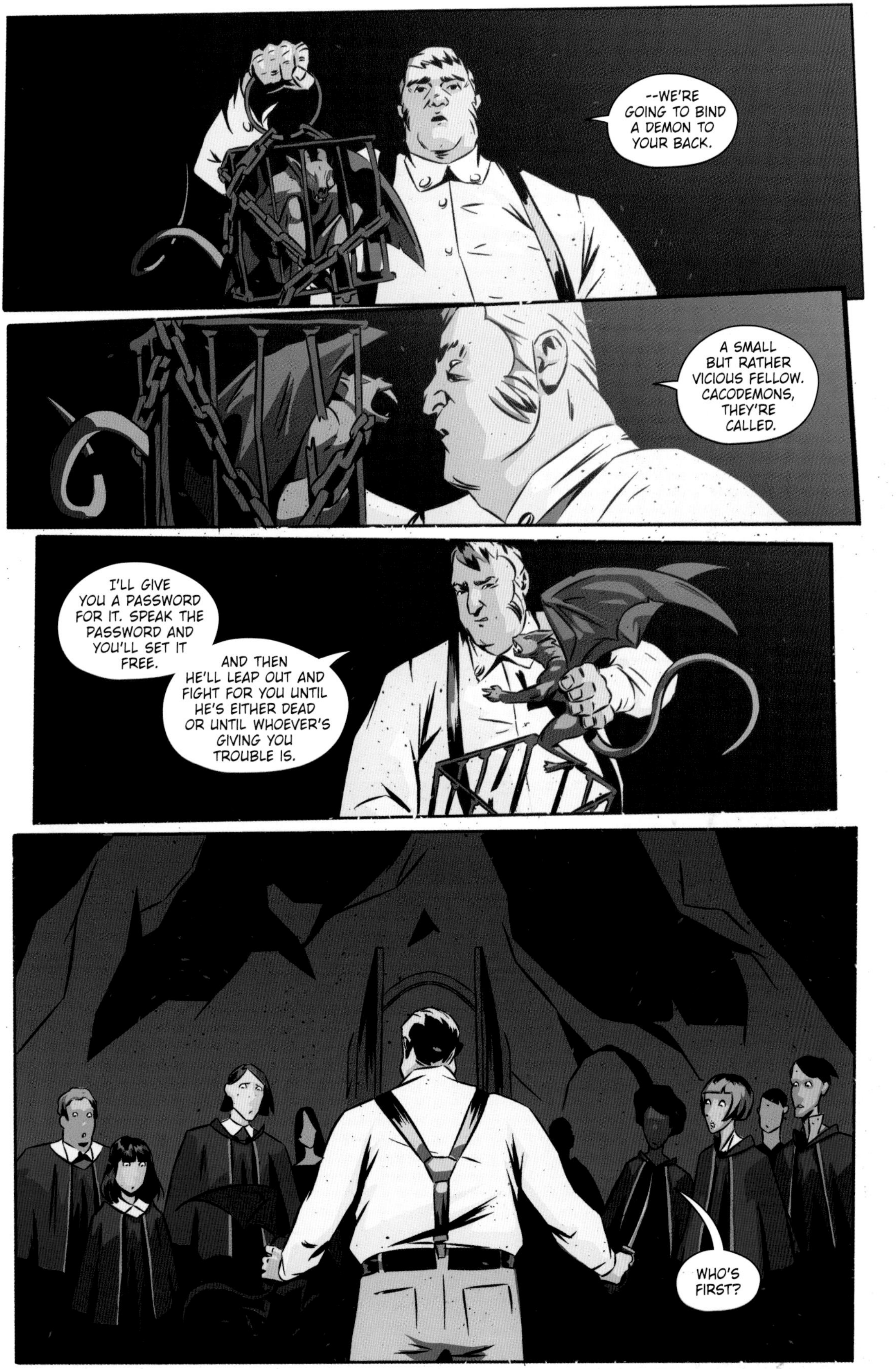
--WE'RE GOING TO BIND A DEMON TO YOUR BACK.
A SMALL BUT RATHER VICIOUS FELLOW. CACODEMONS, THEY'RE CALLED.
I'LL GIVE YOU A PASSWORD FOR IT. SPEAK THE PASSWORD AND YOU'LL SET IT FREE.
AND THEN HE'LL LEAP OUT AND FIGHT FOR YOU UNTIL HE'S EITHER DEAD OR UNTIL WHOEVER'S GIVING YOU TROUBLE IS.
WHO'S FIRST?

FOURTH FORM

As with regular second form spells, the fourth form in most cases requires precise off-hand thumb placement at 3-gemini, 4-libra, or 4/5-leo. Note that during equinoxes, solstices, and during the first intercalary month of the Metonic cycle, nearly all regular fourth form positions take an appropriate Thracian embellishment (for exceptions, see page 480).

1. *Novilunium*

2. *Luna Falcata crescens*

3. *Luna Dividua crescens*

4. *Luna Gibba crescens*

5. *Plenilunium*

6. *Luna Gibba decrescens*

7. *Luna Dividua decrescens*

8. *Luna Falcata decrescens*

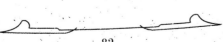

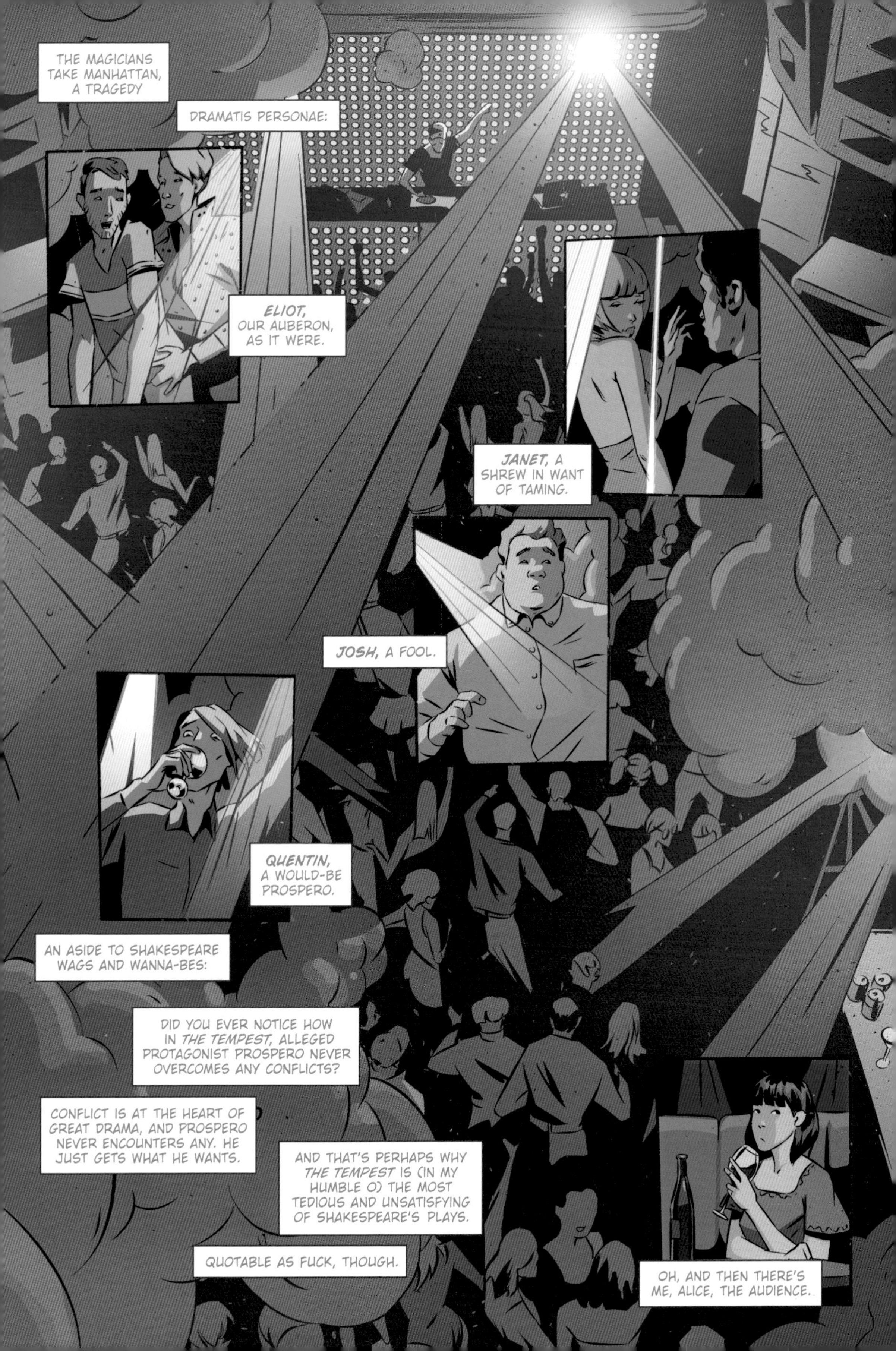
THE MAGICIANS TAKE MANHATTAN, A TRAGEDY
DRAMATIS PERSONAE:
ELIOT, OUR AUBERON, AS IT WERE.
JANET, A SHREW IN WANT OF TAMING.
JOSH, A FOOL.
QUENTIN, A WOULD-BE PROSPERO.
AN ASIDE TO SHAKESPEARE WAGS AND WANNA-BES:
DID YOU EVER NOTICE HOW IN *THE TEMPEST,* ALLEGED PROTAGONIST PROSPERO NEVER OVERCOMES ANY CONFLICTS?
CONFLICT IS AT THE HEART OF GREAT DRAMA, AND PROSPERO NEVER ENCOUNTERS ANY. HE JUST GETS WHAT HE WANTS.
AND THAT'S PERHAPS WHY *THE TEMPEST* IS (IN MY HUMBLE O) THE MOST TEDIOUS AND UNSATISFYING OF SHAKESPEARE'S PLAYS.
QUOTABLE AS FUCK, THOUGH.
OH, AND THEN THERE'S ME, ALICE, THE AUDIENCE.

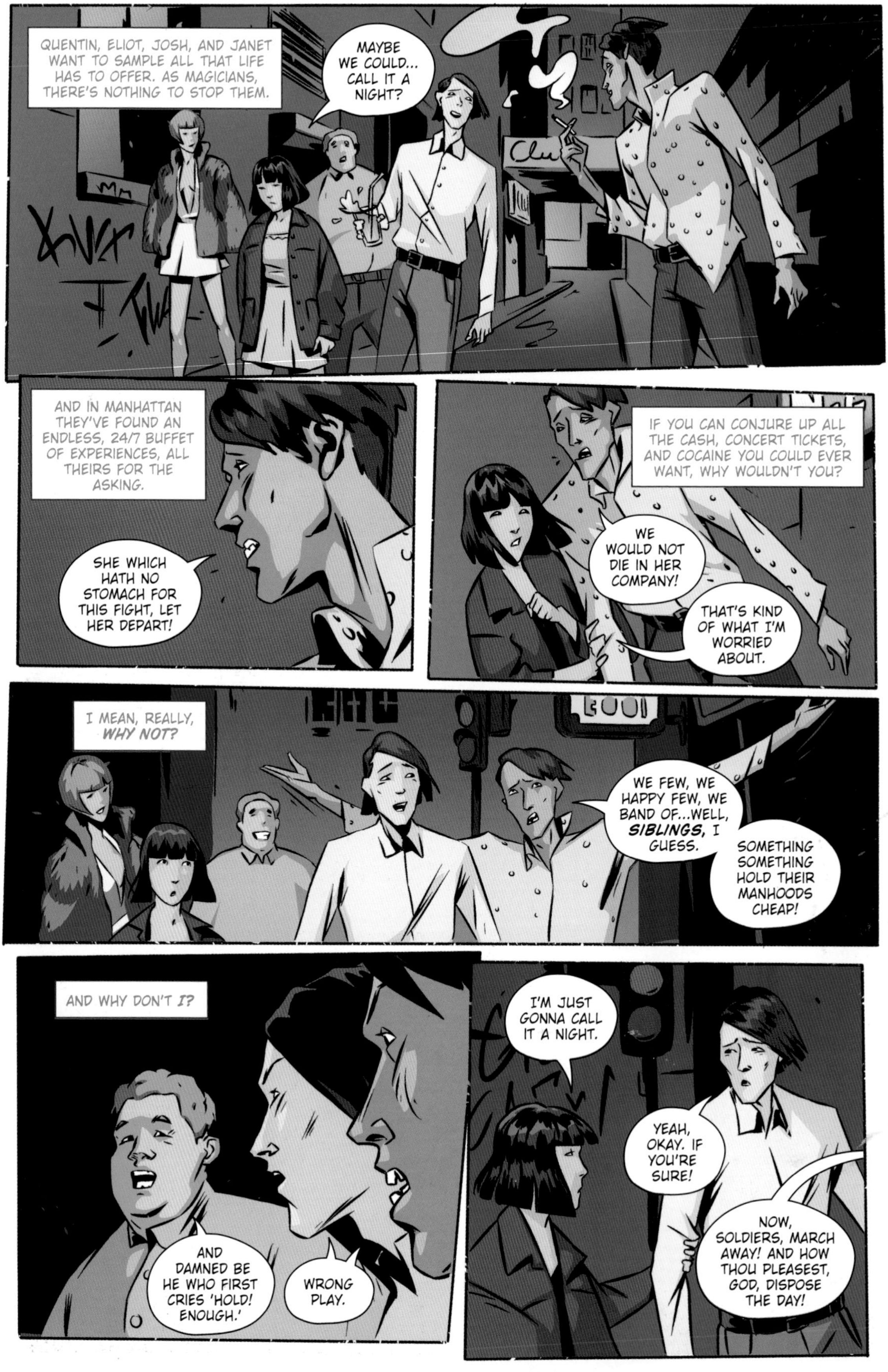
QUENTIN, ELIOT, JOSH, AND JANET WANT TO SAMPLE ALL THAT LIFE HAS TO OFFER. AS MAGICIANS, THERE'S NOTHING TO STOP THEM.
MAYBE WE COULD... CALL IT A NIGHT?
AND IN MANHATTAN THEY'VE FOUND AN ENDLESS, 24/7 BUFFET OF EXPERIENCES, ALL THEIRS FOR THE ASKING.
SHE WHICH HATH NO STOMACH FOR THIS FIGHT, LET HER DEPART!
IF YOU CAN CONJURE UP ALL THE CASH, CONCERT TICKETS, AND COCAINE YOU COULD EVER WANT, WHY WOULDN'T YOU?
WE WOULD NOT DIE IN HER COMPANY!
THAT'S KIND OF WHAT I'M WORRIED ABOUT.
I MEAN, REALLY, *WHY NOT?*
WE FEW, WE HAPPY FEW, WE BAND OF...WELL, ***SIBLINGS,*** I GUESS.
SOMETHING SOMETHING HOLD THEIR MANHOODS CHEAP!
AND WHY DON'T *I?*
AND DAMNED BE HE WHO FIRST CRIES 'HOLD! ENOUGH.'
WRONG PLAY.
I'M JUST GONNA CALL IT A NIGHT.
YEAH, OKAY. IF YOU'RE SURE!
NOW, SOLDIERS, MARCH AWAY! AND HOW THOU PLEASEST, GOD, DISPOSE THE DAY!

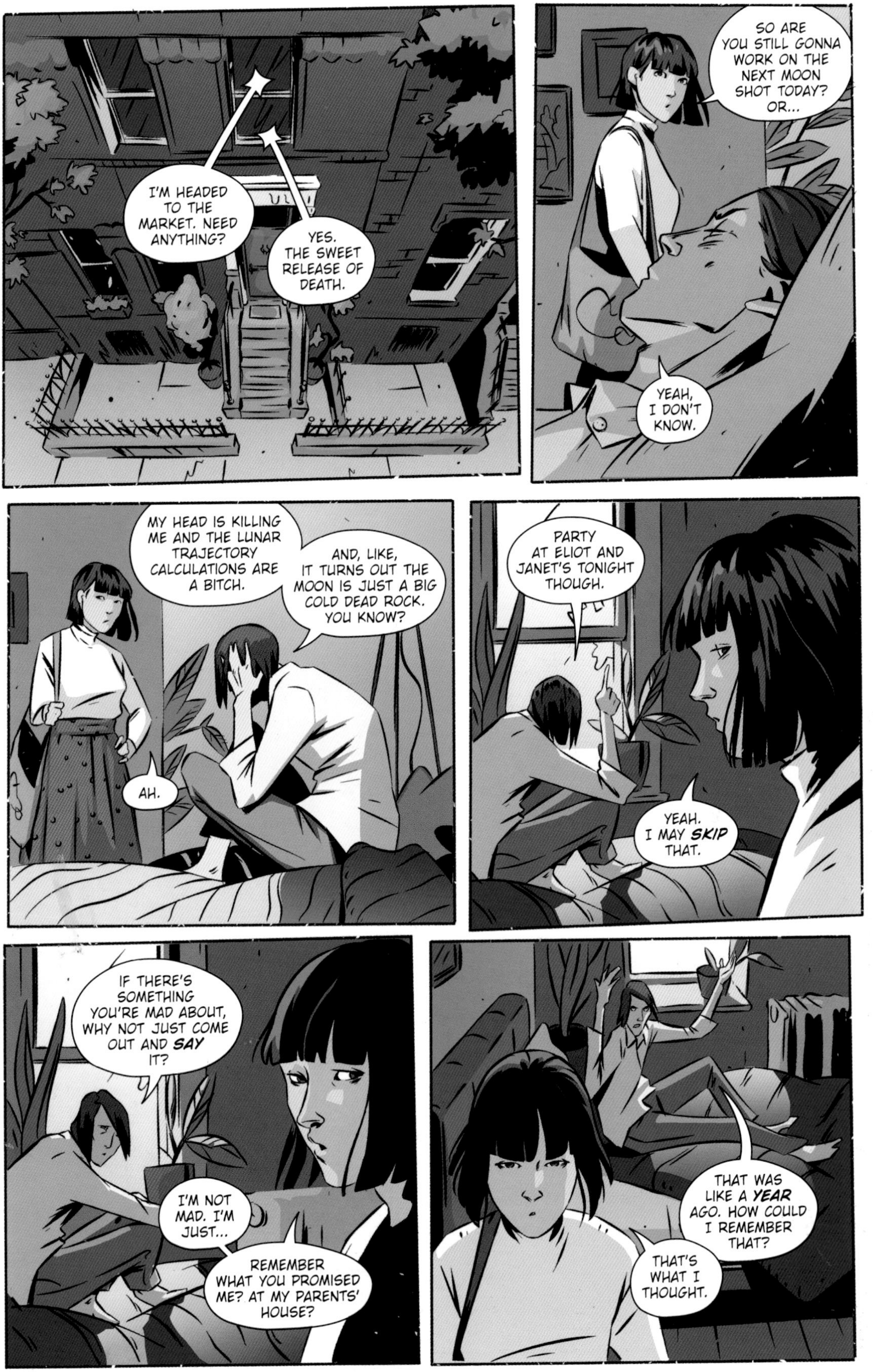
I'M HEADED TO THE MARKET. NEED ANYTHING?
YES. THE SWEET RELEASE OF DEATH.
SO ARE YOU STILL GONNA WORK ON THE NEXT MOON SHOT TODAY? OR...
YEAH, I DON'T KNOW.
MY HEAD IS KILLING ME AND THE LUNAR TRAJECTORY CALCULATIONS ARE A BITCH.
AND, LIKE, IT TURNS OUT THE MOON IS JUST A BIG COLD DEAD ROCK. YOU KNOW?
AH.
PARTY AT ELIOT AND JANET'S TONIGHT THOUGH.
YEAH. I MAY SKIP THAT.
IF THERE'S SOMETHING YOU'RE MAD ABOUT, WHY NOT JUST COME OUT AND SAY IT?
I'M NOT MAD. I'M JUST...
REMEMBER WHAT YOU PROMISED ME? AT MY PARENTS' HOUSE?
THAT WAS LIKE A YEAR AGO. HOW COULD I REMEMBER THAT?
THAT'S WHAT I THOUGHT.

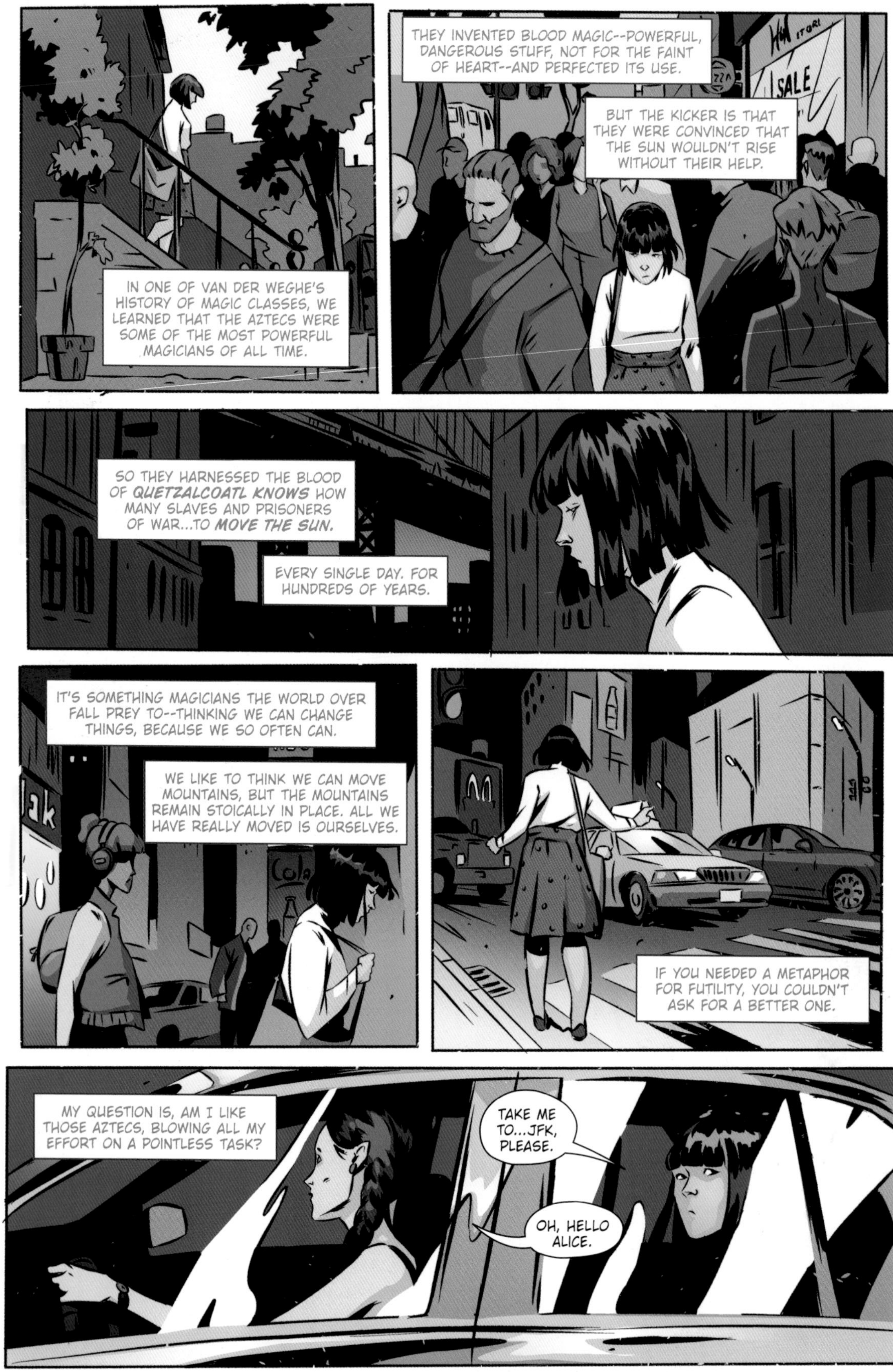
IN ONE OF VAN DER WEGHE'S HISTORY OF MAGIC CLASSES, WE LEARNED THAT THE AZTECS WERE SOME OF THE MOST POWERFUL MAGICIANS OF ALL TIME.
THEY INVENTED BLOOD MAGIC--POWERFUL, DANGEROUS STUFF, NOT FOR THE FAINT OF HEART--AND PERFECTED ITS USE.
SALE
BUT THE KICKER IS THAT THEY WERE CONVINCED THAT THE SUN WOULDN'T RISE WITHOUT THEIR HELP.
SO THEY HARNESSED THE BLOOD OF ***QUETZALCOATL KNOWS*** HOW MANY SLAVES AND PRISONERS OF WAR...TO ***MOVE THE SUN.***
EVERY SINGLE DAY. FOR HUNDREDS OF YEARS.
IT'S SOMETHING MAGICIANS THE WORLD OVER FALL PREY TO--THINKING WE CAN CHANGE THINGS, BECAUSE WE SO OFTEN CAN.
WE LIKE TO THINK WE CAN MOVE MOUNTAINS, BUT THE MOUNTAINS REMAIN STOICALLY IN PLACE. ALL WE HAVE REALLY MOVED IS OURSELVES.
Cola
IF YOU NEEDED A METAPHOR FOR FUTILITY, YOU COULDN'T ASK FOR A BETTER ONE.
MY QUESTION IS, AM I LIKE THOSE AZTECS, BLOWING ALL MY EFFORT ON A POINTLESS TASK?
TAKE ME TO...JFK, PLEASE.
OH, HELLO ALICE.

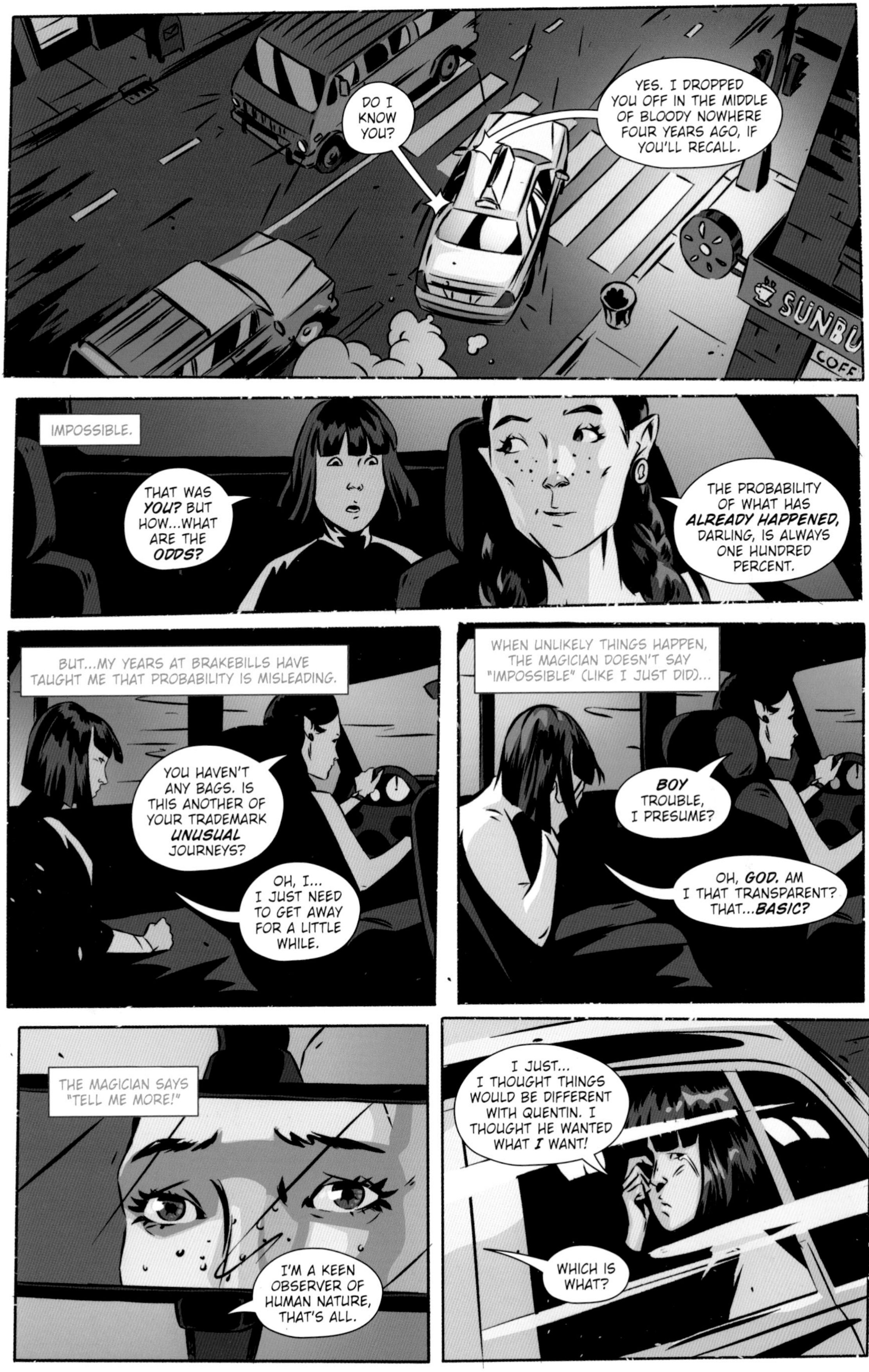
DO I KNOW YOU?
YES. I DROPPED YOU OFF IN THE MIDDLE OF BLOODY NOWHERE FOUR YEARS AGO, IF YOU'LL RECALL.
SUNBU
COFF
IMPOSSIBLE.
THAT WAS *YOU?* BUT HOW...WHAT ARE THE *ODDS?*
THE PROBABILITY OF WHAT HAS *ALREADY HAPPENED,* DARLING, IS ALWAYS ONE HUNDRED PERCENT.
BUT...MY YEARS AT BRAKEBILLS HAVE TAUGHT ME THAT PROBABILITY IS MISLEADING.
YOU HAVEN'T ANY BAGS. IS THIS ANOTHER OF YOUR TRADEMARK *UNUSUAL* JOURNEYS?
OH, I... I JUST NEED TO GET AWAY FOR A LITTLE WHILE.
WHEN UNLIKELY THINGS HAPPEN, THE MAGICIAN DOESN'T SAY "IMPOSSIBLE" (LIKE I JUST DID)...
BOY TROUBLE, I PRESUME?
OH, *GOD.* AM I THAT TRANSPARENT? THAT...*BASIC?*
THE MAGICIAN SAYS "TELL ME MORE!"
I'M A KEEN OBSERVER OF HUMAN NATURE, THAT'S ALL.
I JUST... I THOUGHT THINGS WOULD BE DIFFERENT WITH QUENTIN. I THOUGHT HE WANTED WHAT *I* WANT!
WHICH IS WHAT?

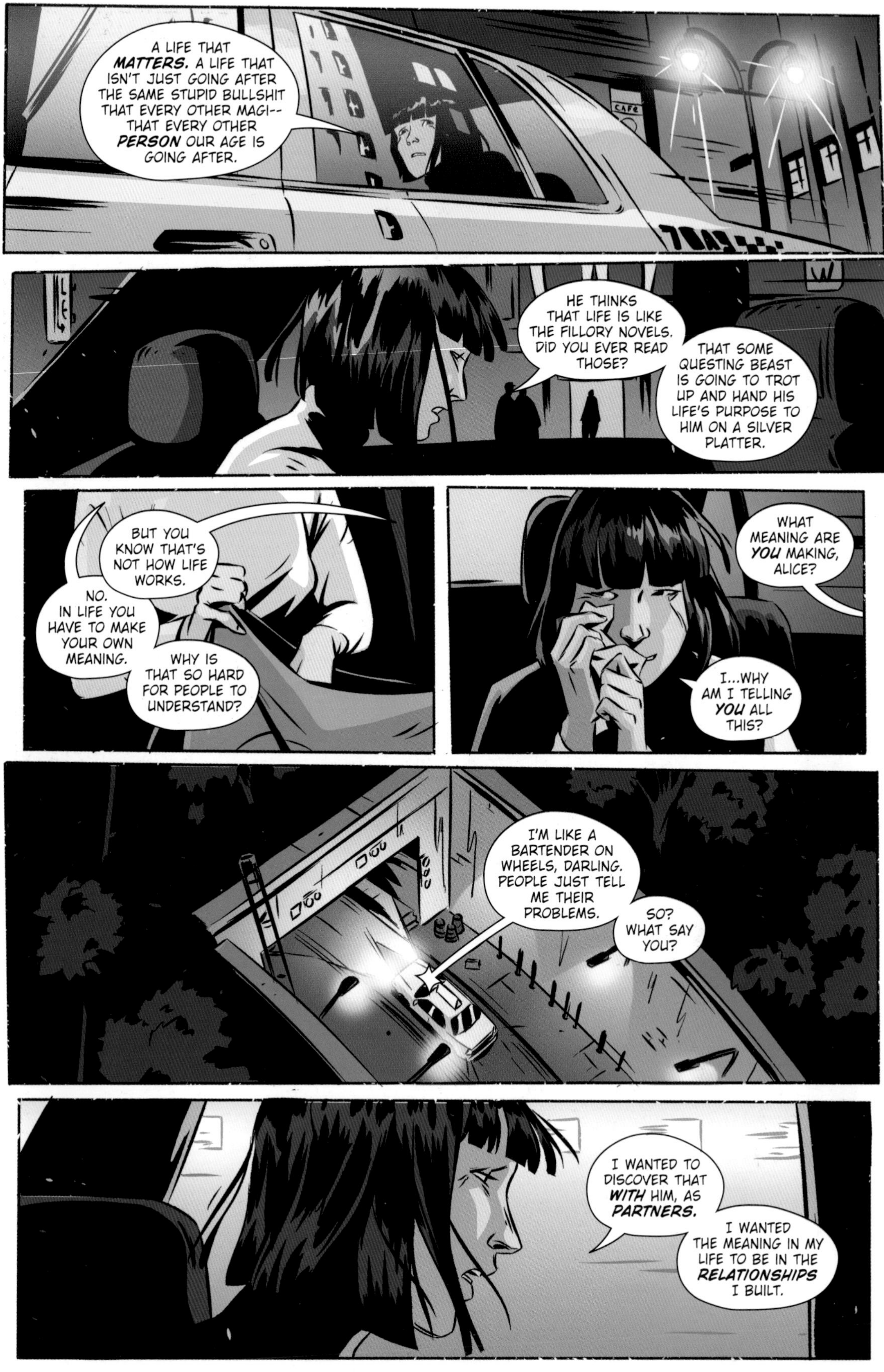
A LIFE THAT MATTERS. A LIFE THAT ISN'T JUST GOING AFTER THE SAME STUPID BULLSHIT THAT EVERY OTHER MAGI-- THAT EVERY OTHER PERSON OUR AGE IS GOING AFTER.
CAFE
HE THINKS THAT LIFE IS LIKE THE FILLORY NOVELS. DID YOU EVER READ THOSE?
THAT SOME QUESTING BEAST IS GOING TO TROT UP AND HAND HIS LIFE'S PURPOSE TO HIM ON A SILVER PLATTER.
BUT YOU KNOW THAT'S NOT HOW LIFE WORKS.
NO. IN LIFE YOU HAVE TO MAKE YOUR OWN MEANING.
WHY IS THAT SO HARD FOR PEOPLE TO UNDERSTAND?
WHAT MEANING ARE YOU MAKING, ALICE?
I...WHY AM I TELLING YOU ALL THIS?
I'M LIKE A BARTENDER ON WHEELS, DARLING. PEOPLE JUST TELL ME THEIR PROBLEMS.
SO? WHAT SAY YOU?
I WANTED TO DISCOVER THAT WITH HIM, AS PARTNERS.
I WANTED THE MEANING IN MY LIFE TO BE IN THE RELATIONSHIPS I BUILT.

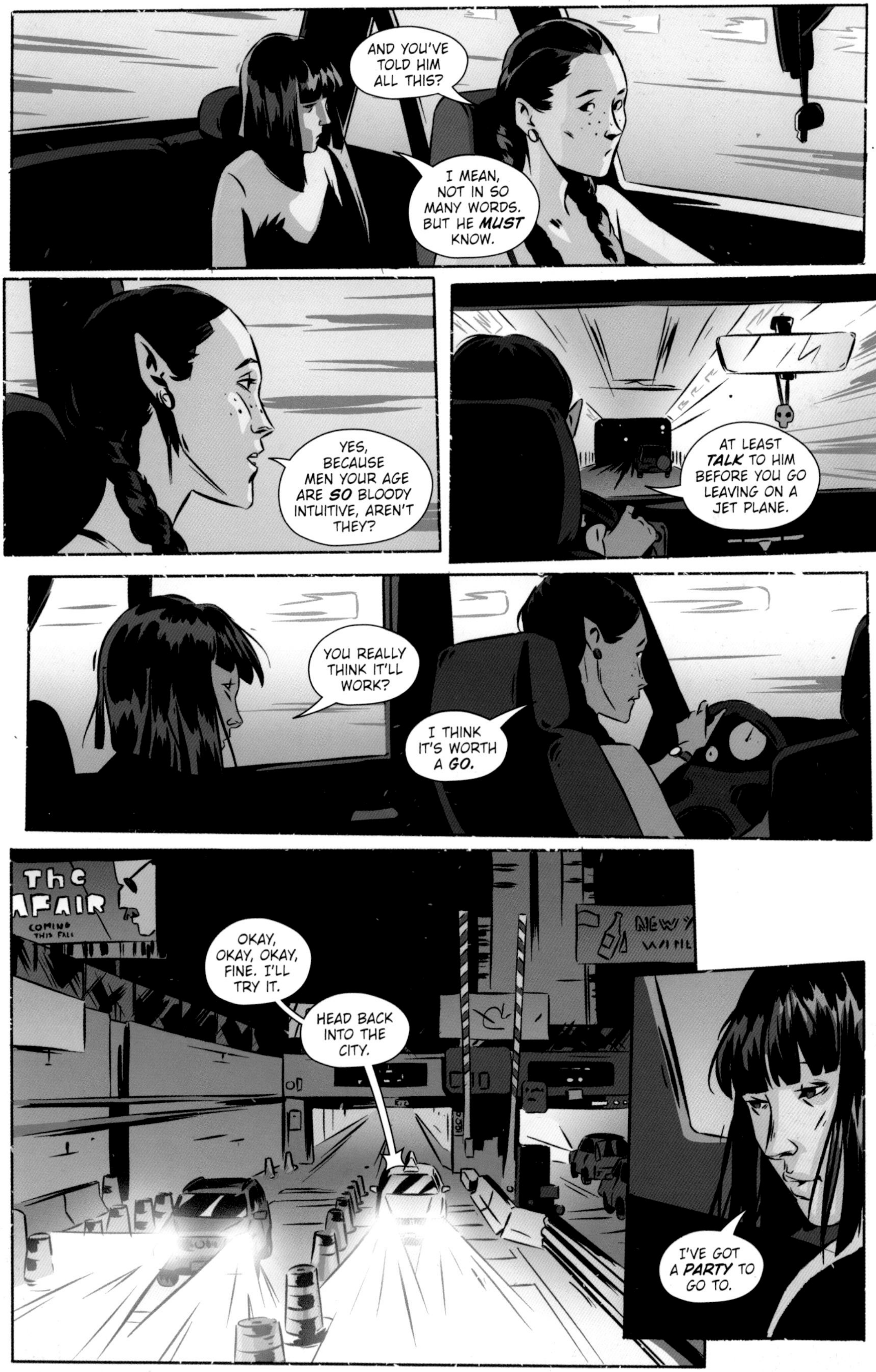
AND YOU'VE TOLD HIM ALL THIS?
I MEAN, NOT IN SO MANY WORDS. BUT HE **MUST** KNOW.
YES, BECAUSE MEN YOUR AGE ARE **SO** BLOODY INTUITIVE, AREN'T THEY?
AT LEAST **TALK** TO HIM BEFORE YOU GO LEAVING ON A JET PLANE.
YOU REALLY THINK IT'LL WORK?
I THINK IT'S WORTH A **GO.**
The
COMING THIS FALL
OKAY, OKAY, OKAY, FINE. I'LL TRY IT.
HEAD BACK INTO THE CITY.
I'VE GOT A **PARTY** TO GO TO.

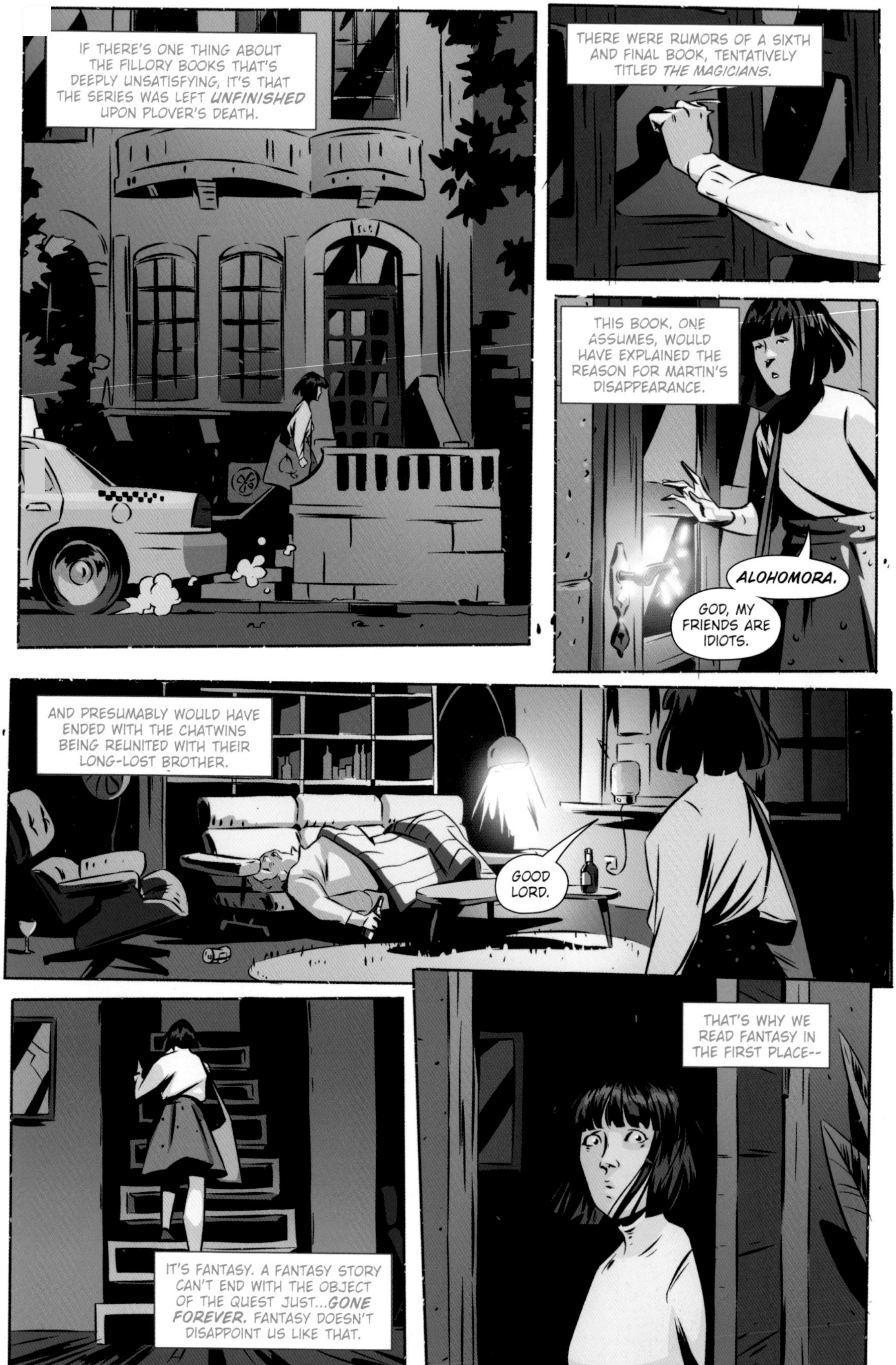
IF THERE'S ONE THING ABOUT THE FILLORY BOOKS THAT'S DEEPLY UNSATISFYING, IT'S THAT THE SERIES WAS LEFT *UNFINISHED* UPON PLOVER'S DEATH.
THERE WERE RUMORS OF A SIXTH AND FINAL BOOK, TENTATIVELY TITLED *THE MAGICIANS.*
THIS BOOK, ONE ASSUMES, WOULD HAVE EXPLAINED THE REASON FOR MARTIN'S DISAPPEARANCE.
ALOHOMORA.
GOD, MY FRIENDS ARE IDIOTS.
AND PRESUMABLY WOULD HAVE ENDED WITH THE CHATWINS BEING REUNITED WITH THEIR LONG-LOST BROTHER.
GOOD LORD.
IT'S FANTASY. A FANTASY STORY CAN'T END WITH THE OBJECT OF THE QUEST JUST...*GONE FOREVER.* FANTASY DOESN'T DISAPPOINT US LIKE THAT.
THAT'S WHY WE READ FANTASY IN THE FIRST PLACE--

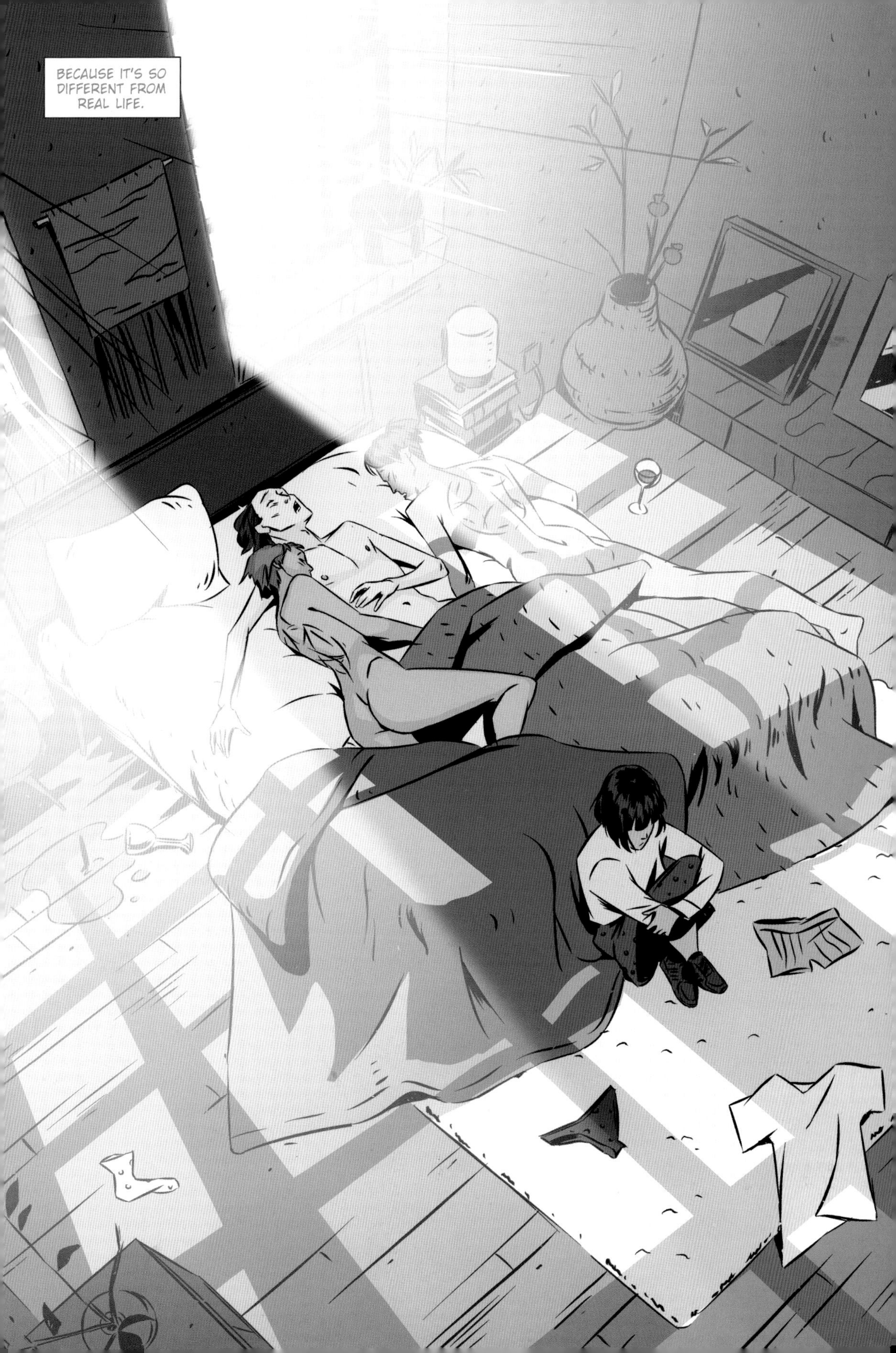
BECAUSE IT'S SO DIFFERENT FROM REAL LIFE.

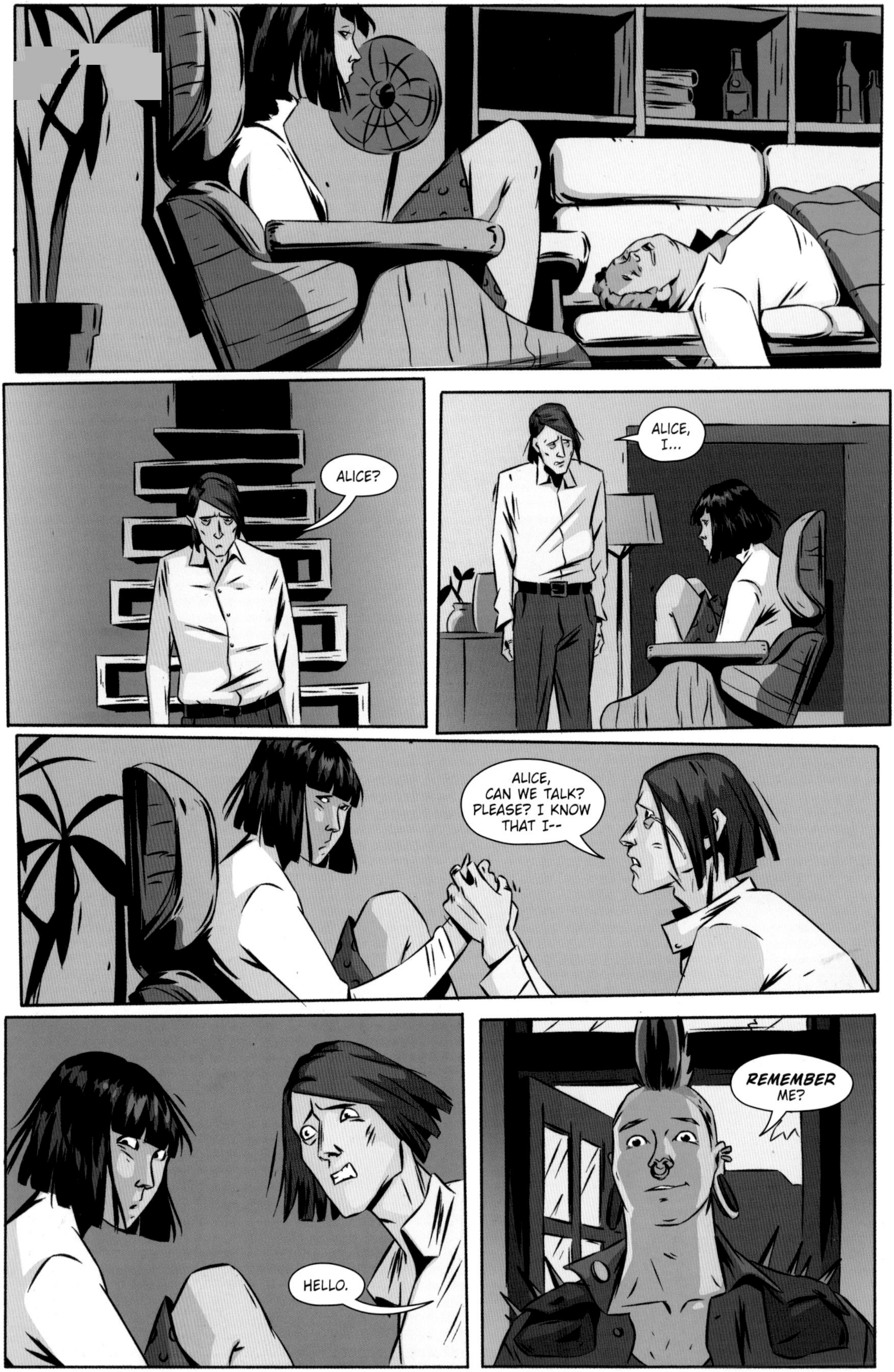
ALICE?
ALICE, I...
ALICE, CAN WE TALK? PLEASE? I KNOW THAT I--
HELLO.
REMEMBER ME?

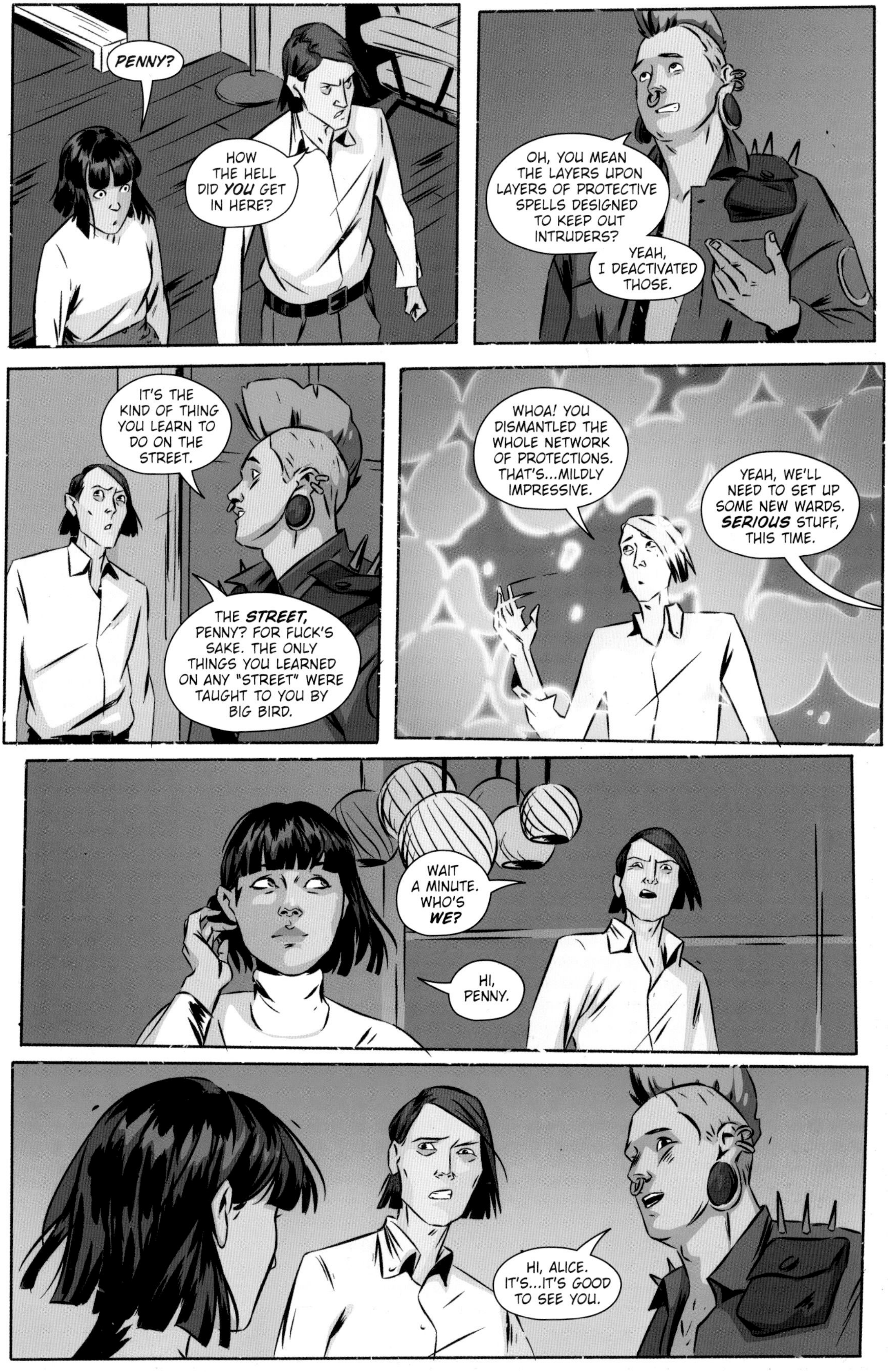
PENNY?
HOW THE HELL DID *YOU* GET IN HERE?
OH, YOU MEAN THE LAYERS UPON LAYERS OF PROTECTIVE SPELLS DESIGNED TO KEEP OUT INTRUDERS?
YEAH, I DEACTIVATED THOSE.
IT'S THE KIND OF THING YOU LEARN TO DO ON THE STREET.
THE *STREET,* PENNY? FOR FUCK'S SAKE. THE ONLY THINGS YOU LEARNED ON ANY "STREET" WERE TAUGHT TO YOU BY BIG BIRD.
WHOA! YOU DISMANTLED THE WHOLE NETWORK OF PROTECTIONS. THAT'S...MILDLY IMPRESSIVE.
YEAH, WE'LL NEED TO SET UP SOME NEW WARDS. *SERIOUS* STUFF, THIS TIME.
WAIT A MINUTE. WHO'S *WE?*
HI, PENNY.
HI, ALICE. IT'S...IT'S GOOD TO SEE YOU.

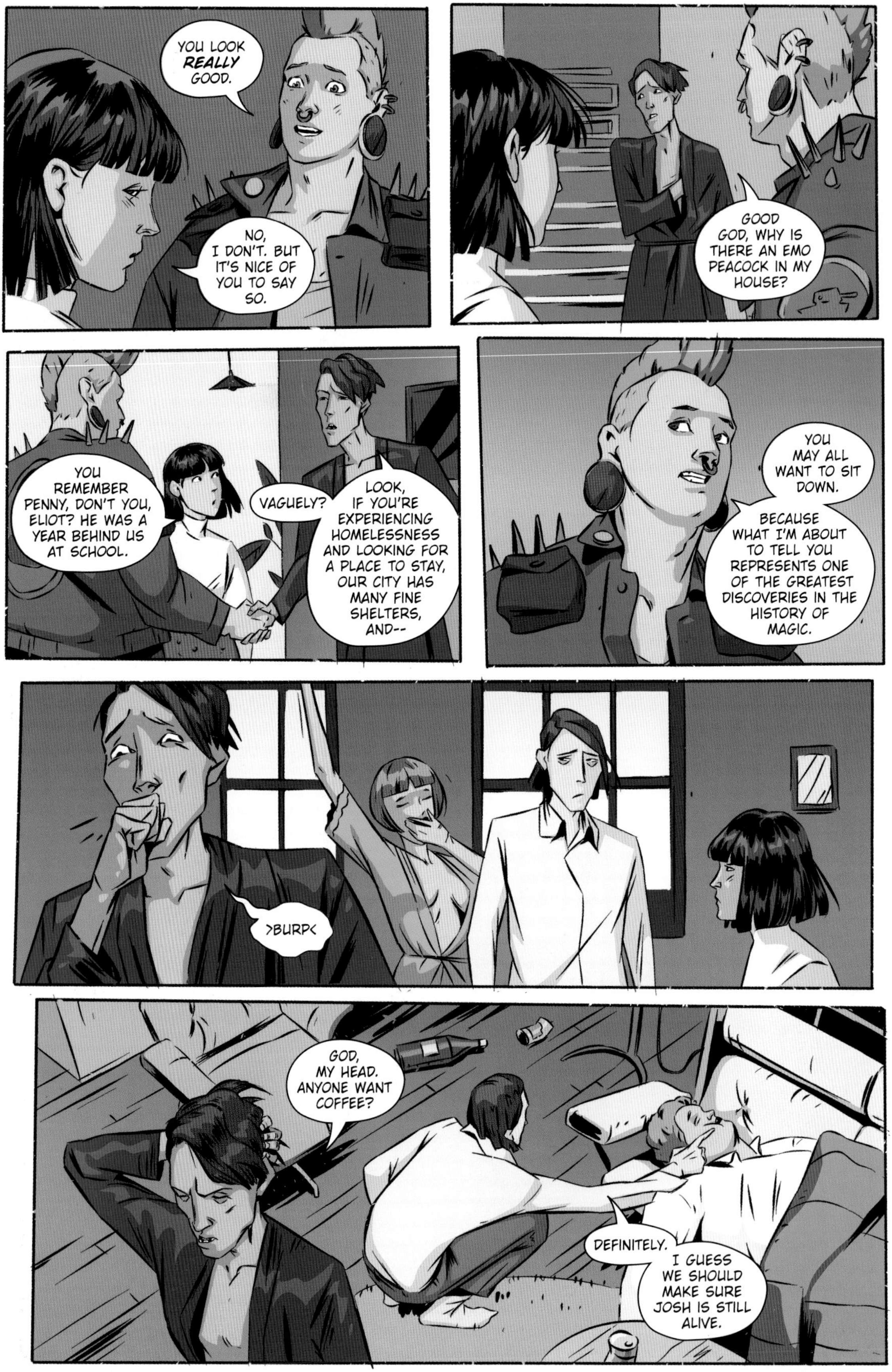
YOU LOOK **REALLY** GOOD.
NO, I DON'T. BUT IT'S NICE OF YOU TO SAY SO.
GOOD GOD, WHY IS THERE AN EMO PEACOCK IN MY HOUSE?
YOU REMEMBER PENNY, DON'T YOU, ELIOT? HE WAS A YEAR BEHIND US AT SCHOOL.
VAGUELY?
LOOK, IF YOU'RE EXPERIENCING HOMELESSNESS AND LOOKING FOR A PLACE TO STAY, OUR CITY HAS MANY FINE SHELTERS, AND--
YOU MAY ALL WANT TO SIT DOWN.
BECAUSE WHAT I'M ABOUT TO TELL YOU REPRESENTS ONE OF THE GREATEST DISCOVERIES IN THE HISTORY OF MAGIC.
>BURP<
GOD, MY HEAD. ANYONE WANT COFFEE?
DEFINITELY.
I GUESS WE SHOULD MAKE SURE JOSH IS STILL ALIVE.

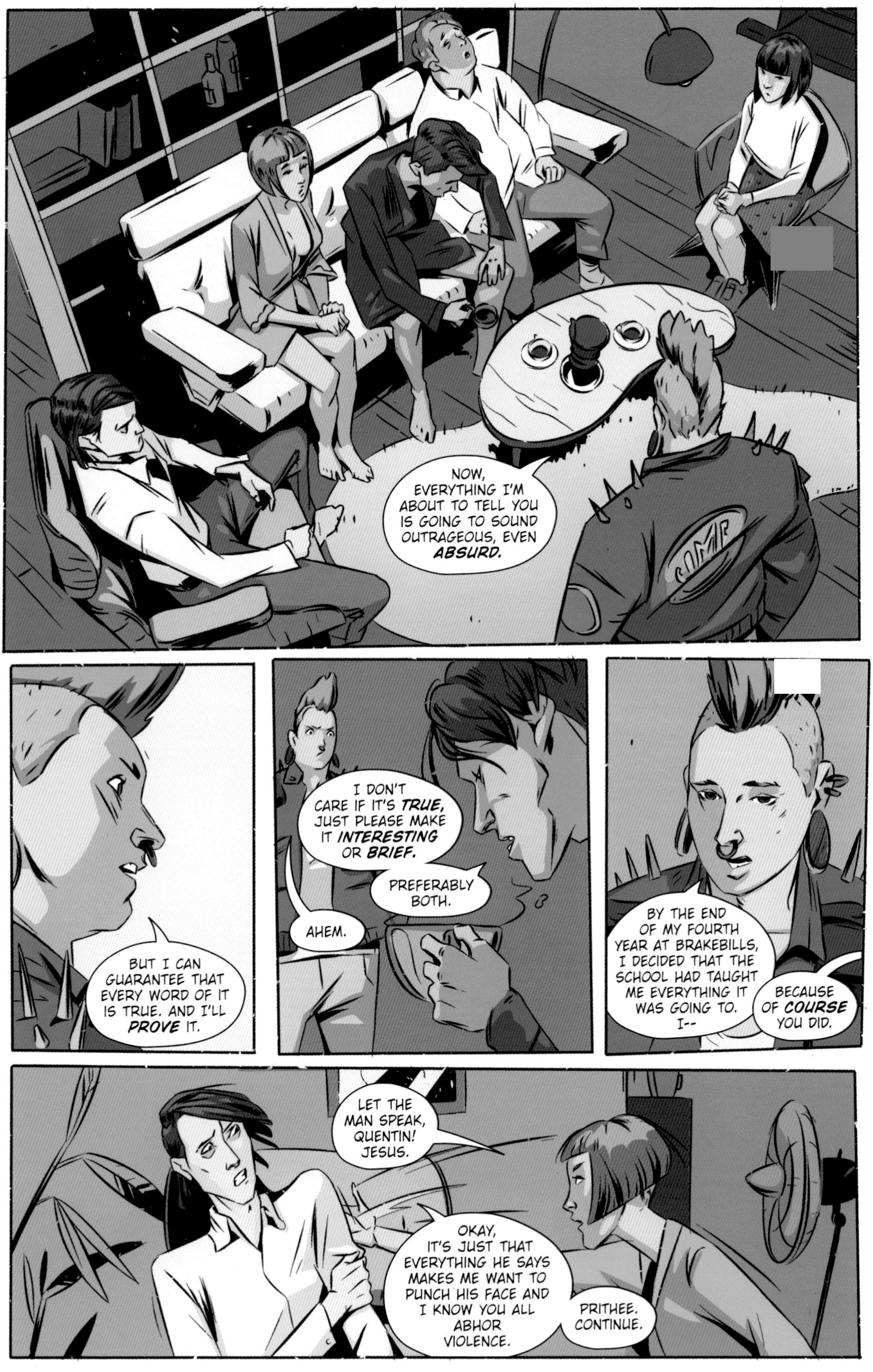
NOW, EVERYTHING I'M ABOUT TO TELL YOU IS GOING TO SOUND OUTRAGEOUS, EVEN ABSURD.
BUT I CAN GUARANTEE THAT EVERY WORD OF IT IS TRUE. AND I'LL PROVE IT.
I DON'T CARE IF IT'S TRUE, JUST PLEASE MAKE IT INTERESTING OR BRIEF.
PREFERABLY BOTH.
AHEM.
BY THE END OF MY FOURTH YEAR AT BRAKEBILLS, I DECIDED THAT THE SCHOOL HAD TAUGHT ME EVERYTHING IT WAS GOING TO. I--
BECAUSE OF COURSE YOU DID.
LET THE MAN SPEAK, QUENTIN! JESUS.
OKAY, IT'S JUST THAT EVERYTHING HE SAYS MAKES ME WANT TO PUNCH HIS FACE AND I KNOW YOU ALL ABHOR VIOLENCE.
PRITHEE. CONTINUE.

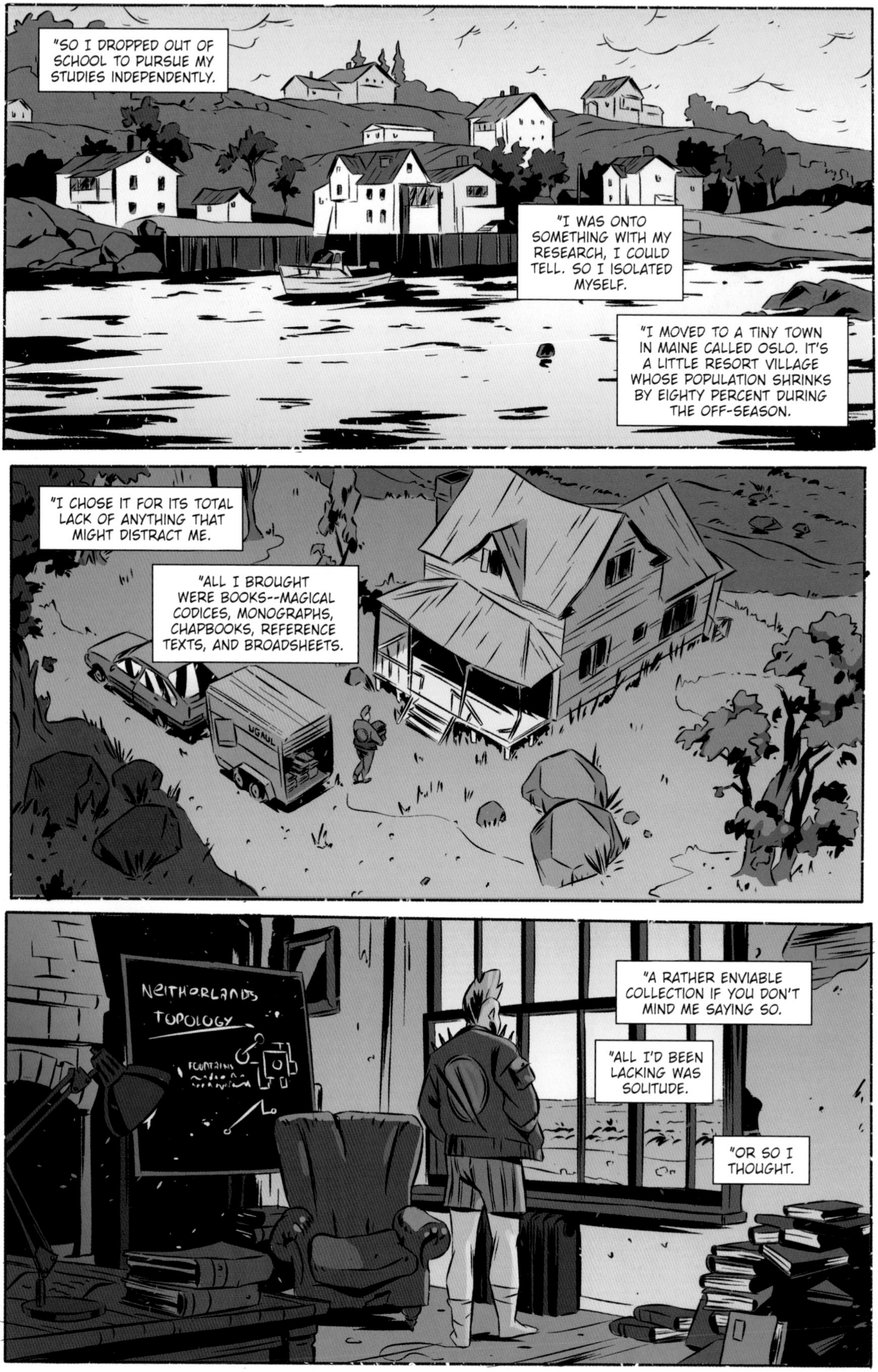
"SO I DROPPED OUT OF SCHOOL TO PURSUE MY STUDIES INDEPENDENTLY.
"I WAS ONTO SOMETHING WITH MY RESEARCH, I COULD TELL. SO I ISOLATED MYSELF.
"I MOVED TO A TINY TOWN IN MAINE CALLED OSLO. IT'S A LITTLE RESORT VILLAGE WHOSE POPULATION SHRINKS BY EIGHTY PERCENT DURING THE OFF-SEASON.
"I CHOSE IT FOR ITS TOTAL LACK OF ANYTHING THAT MIGHT DISTRACT ME.
"ALL I BROUGHT WERE BOOKS--MAGICAL CODICES, MONOGRAPHS, CHAPBOOKS, REFERENCE TEXTS, AND BROADSHEETS.
NEITHORLANDS
TOPOLOGY
"A RATHER ENVIABLE COLLECTION IF YOU DON'T MIND ME SAYING SO.
"ALL I'D BEEN LACKING WAS SOLITUDE.
"OR SO I THOUGHT.

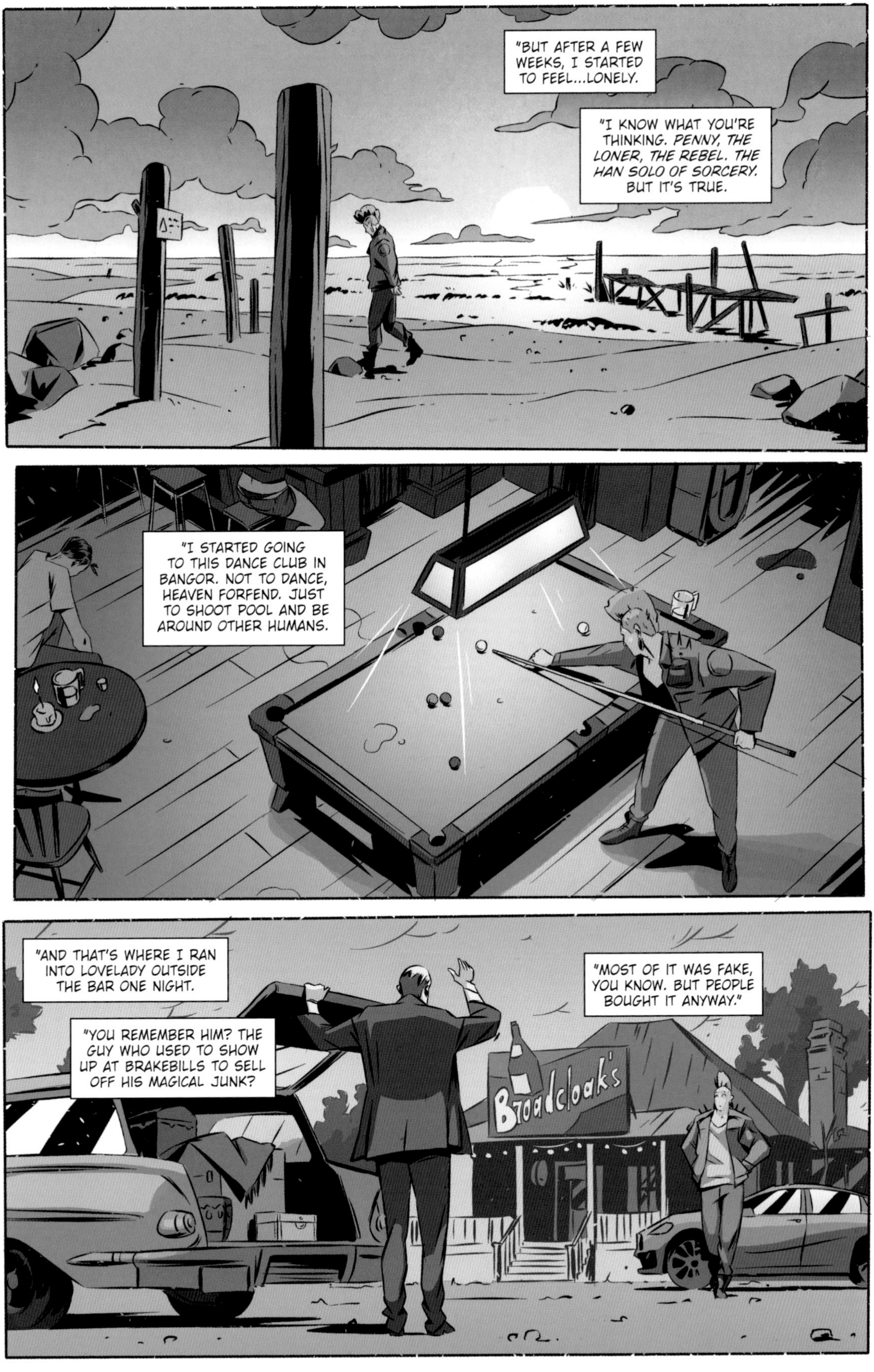
"BUT AFTER A FEW WEEKS, I STARTED TO FEEL...LONELY.
"I KNOW WHAT YOU'RE THINKING. PENNY, THE LONER, THE REBEL. THE HAN SOLO OF SORCERY. BUT IT'S TRUE.
"I STARTED GOING TO THIS DANCE CLUB IN BANGOR. NOT TO DANCE, HEAVEN FORFEND. JUST TO SHOOT POOL AND BE AROUND OTHER HUMANS.
"AND THAT'S WHERE I RAN INTO LOVELADY OUTSIDE THE BAR ONE NIGHT.
"YOU REMEMBER HIM? THE GUY WHO USED TO SHOW UP AT BRAKEBILLS TO SELL OFF HIS MAGICAL JUNK?
"MOST OF IT WAS FAKE, YOU KNOW. BUT PEOPLE BOUGHT IT ANYWAY."
Broadcloak's

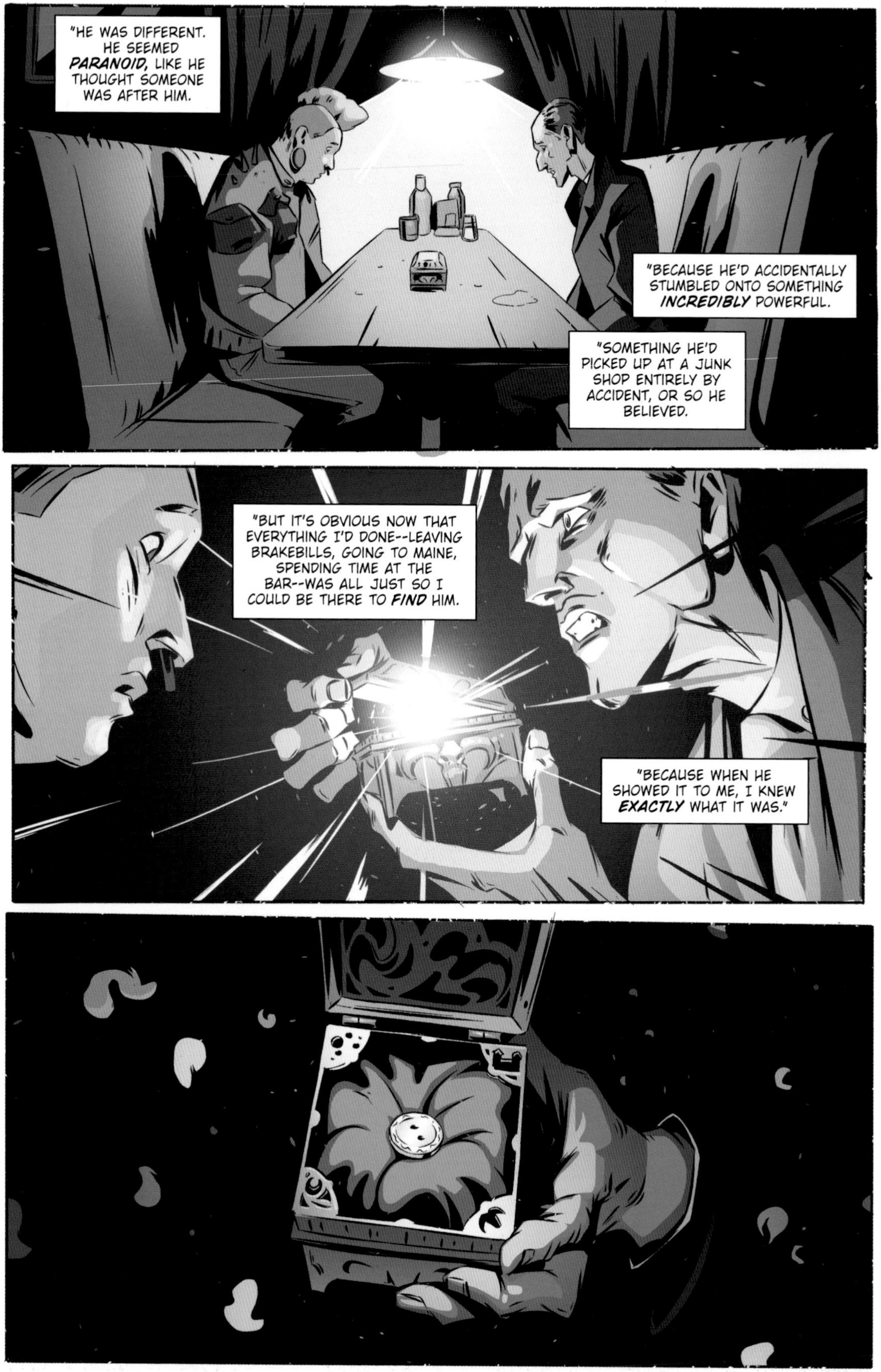
"HE WAS DIFFERENT. HE SEEMED PARANOID, LIKE HE THOUGHT SOMEONE WAS AFTER HIM.
"BECAUSE HE'D ACCIDENTALLY STUMBLED ONTO SOMETHING INCREDIBLY POWERFUL.
"SOMETHING HE'D PICKED UP AT A JUNK SHOP ENTIRELY BY ACCIDENT, OR SO HE BELIEVED.
"BUT IT'S OBVIOUS NOW THAT EVERYTHING I'D DONE--LEAVING BRAKEBILLS, GOING TO MAINE, SPENDING TIME AT THE BAR--WAS ALL JUST SO I COULD BE THERE TO FIND HIM.
"BECAUSE WHEN HE SHOWED IT TO ME, I KNEW EXACTLY WHAT IT WAS."

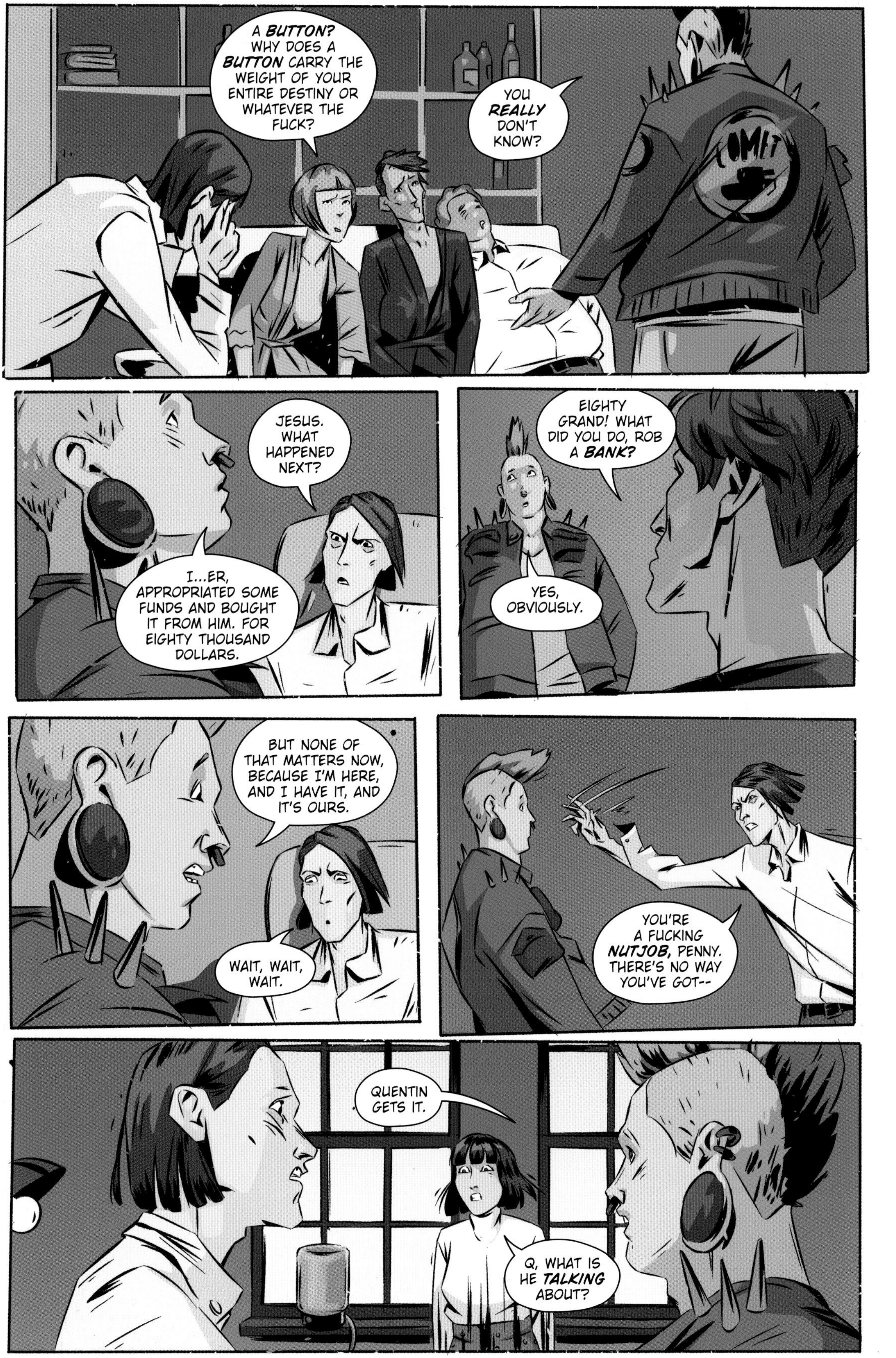
A BUTTON? WHY DOES A BUTTON CARRY THE WEIGHT OF YOUR ENTIRE DESTINY OR WHATEVER THE FUCK?
YOU REALLY DON'T KNOW?
COMIT
JESUS. WHAT HAPPENED NEXT?
I...ER, APPROPRIATED SOME FUNDS AND BOUGHT IT FROM HIM. FOR EIGHTY THOUSAND DOLLARS.
EIGHTY GRAND! WHAT DID YOU DO, ROB A BANK?
YES, OBVIOUSLY.
BUT NONE OF THAT MATTERS NOW, BECAUSE I'M HERE, AND I HAVE IT, AND IT'S OURS.
WAIT, WAIT, WAIT.
YOU'RE A FUCKING NUTJOB, PENNY. THERE'S NO WAY YOU'VE GOT--
QUENTIN GETS IT.
Q, WHAT IS HE TALKING ABOUT?

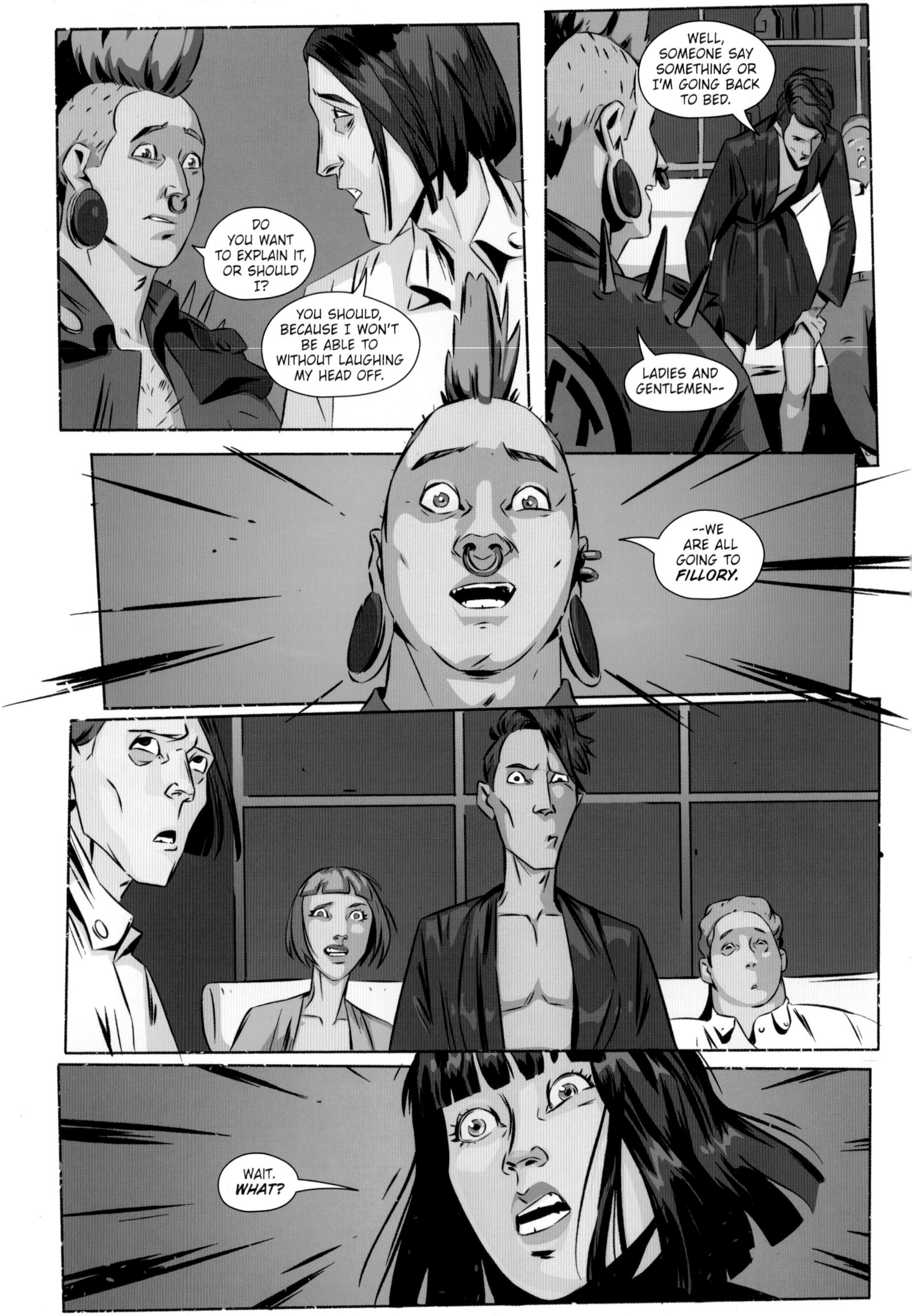
DO YOU WANT TO EXPLAIN IT, OR SHOULD I?
YOU SHOULD, BECAUSE I WON'T BE ABLE TO WITHOUT LAUGHING MY HEAD OFF.
WELL, SOMEONE SAY SOMETHING OR I'M GOING BACK TO BED.
LADIES AND GENTLEMEN--
--WE ARE ALL GOING TO *FILLORY.*
WAIT. *WHAT?*

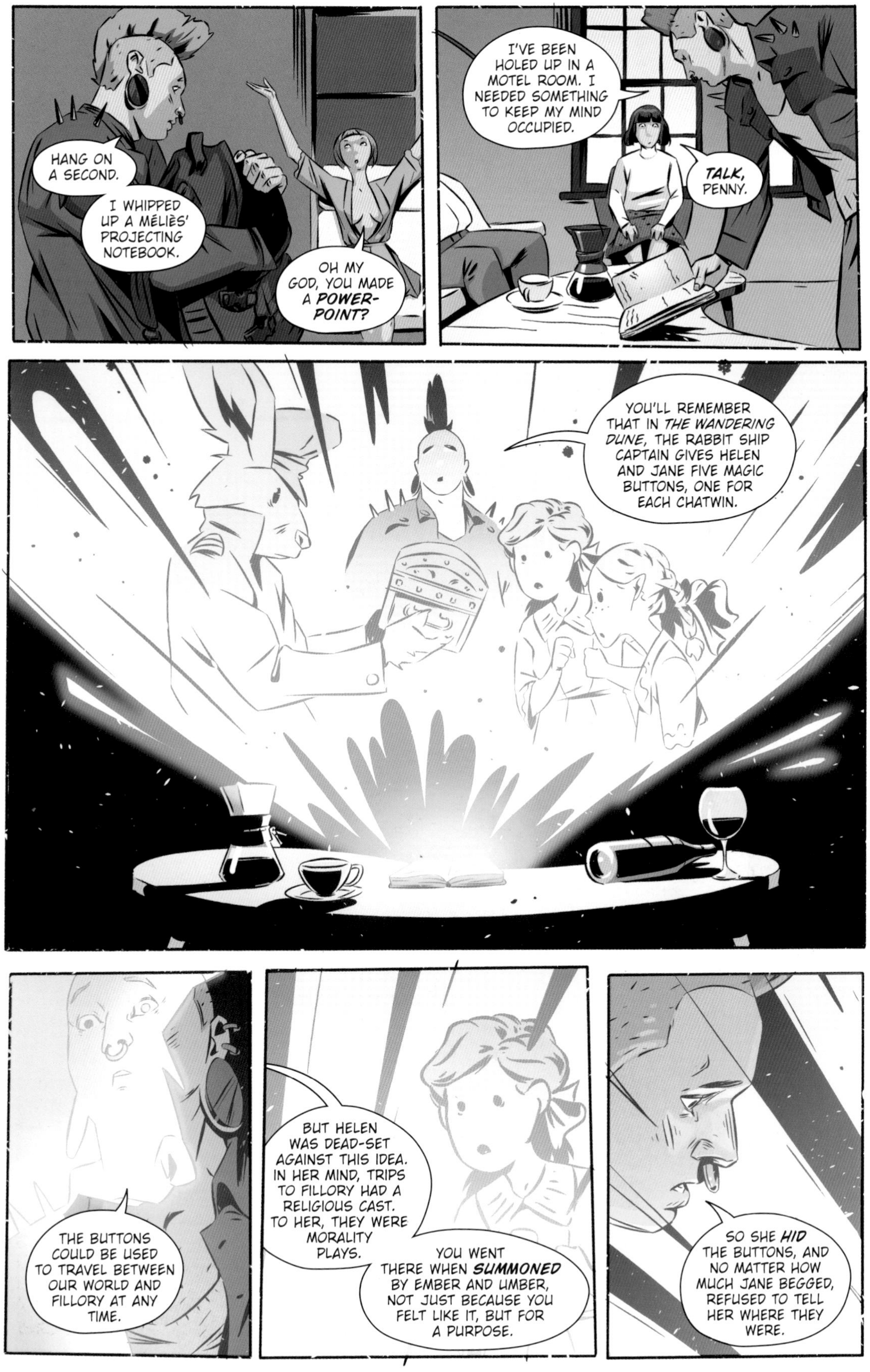
HANG ON A SECOND.
I WHIPPED UP A MÉLIÈS' PROJECTING NOTEBOOK.
OH MY GOD, YOU MADE A *POWER-POINT?*
I'VE BEEN HOLED UP IN A MOTEL ROOM. I NEEDED SOMETHING TO KEEP MY MIND OCCUPIED.
TALK, PENNY.
YOU'LL REMEMBER THAT IN *THE WANDERING DUNE*, THE RABBIT SHIP CAPTAIN GIVES HELEN AND JANE FIVE MAGIC BUTTONS, ONE FOR EACH CHATWIN.
THE BUTTONS COULD BE USED TO TRAVEL BETWEEN OUR WORLD AND FILLORY AT ANY TIME.
BUT HELEN WAS DEAD-SET AGAINST THIS IDEA. IN HER MIND, TRIPS TO FILLORY HAD A RELIGIOUS CAST. TO HER, THEY WERE MORALITY PLAYS.
YOU WENT THERE WHEN ***SUMMONED*** BY EMBER AND UMBER, NOT JUST BECAUSE YOU FELT LIKE IT, BUT FOR A PURPOSE.
SO SHE *HID* THE BUTTONS, AND NO MATTER HOW MUCH JANE BEGGED, REFUSED TO TELL HER WHERE THEY WERE.

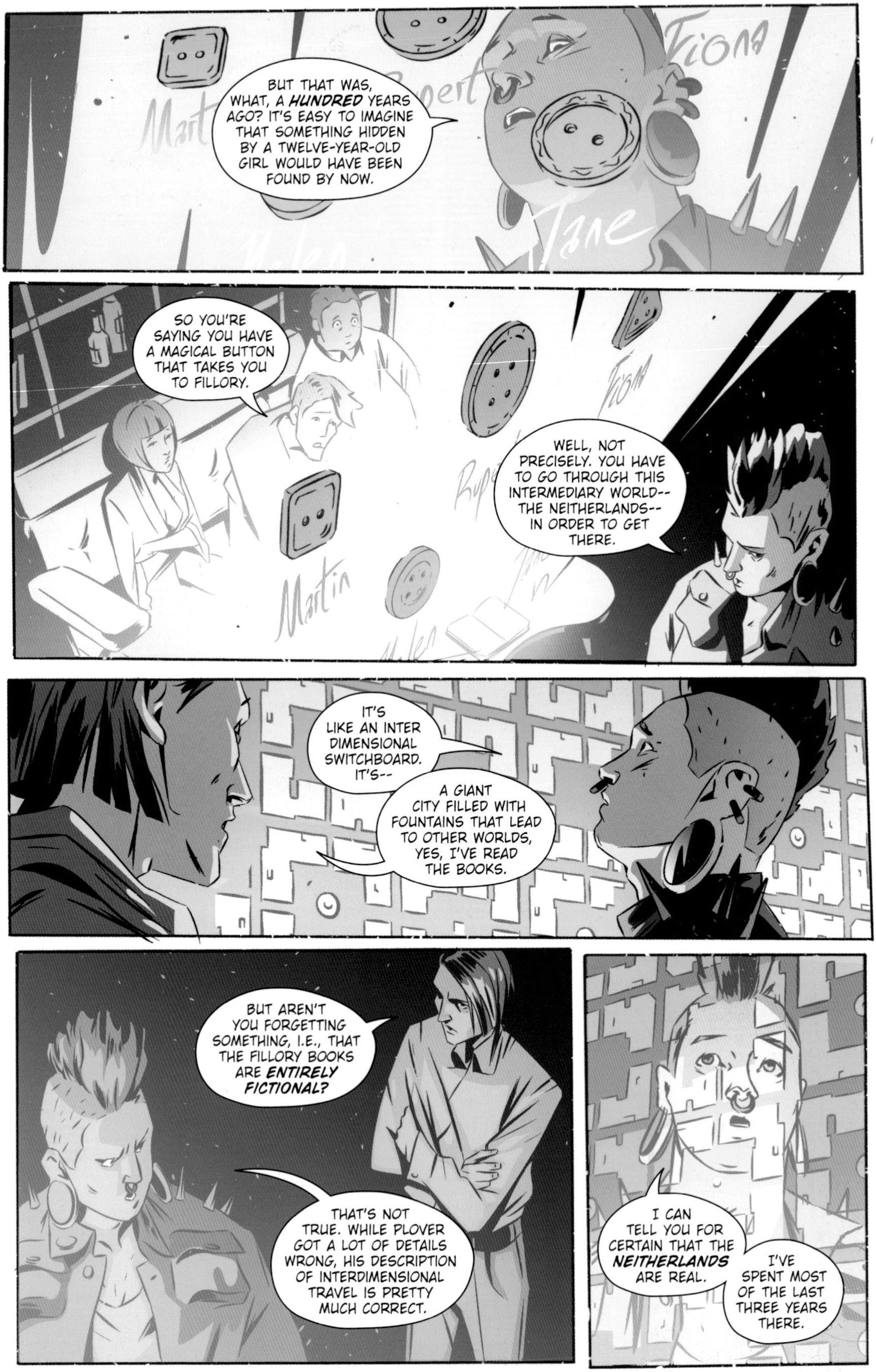

Martin
Rupert
Fiona
Jane
Helen
BUT THAT WAS, WHAT, A ***HUNDRED*** YEARS AGO? IT'S EASY TO IMAGINE THAT SOMETHING HIDDEN BY A TWELVE-YEAR-OLD GIRL WOULD HAVE BEEN FOUND BY NOW.
SO YOU'RE SAYING YOU HAVE A MAGICAL BUTTON THAT TAKES YOU TO FILLORY.
WELL, NOT PRECISELY. YOU HAVE TO GO THROUGH THIS INTERMEDIARY WORLD-- THE NEITHERLANDS-- IN ORDER TO GET THERE.
IT'S LIKE AN INTER DIMENSIONAL SWITCHBOARD. IT'S--
A GIANT CITY FILLED WITH FOUNTAINS THAT LEAD TO OTHER WORLDS, YES, I'VE READ THE BOOKS.
BUT AREN'T YOU FORGETTING SOMETHING, I.E., THAT THE FILLORY BOOKS ARE ***ENTIRELY FICTIONAL?***
THAT'S NOT TRUE. WHILE PLOVER GOT A LOT OF DETAILS WRONG, HIS DESCRIPTION OF INTERDIMENSIONAL TRAVEL IS PRETTY MUCH CORRECT.
I CAN TELL YOU FOR CERTAIN THAT THE ***NEITHERLANDS*** ARE REAL.
I'VE SPENT MOST OF THE LAST THREE YEARS THERE.

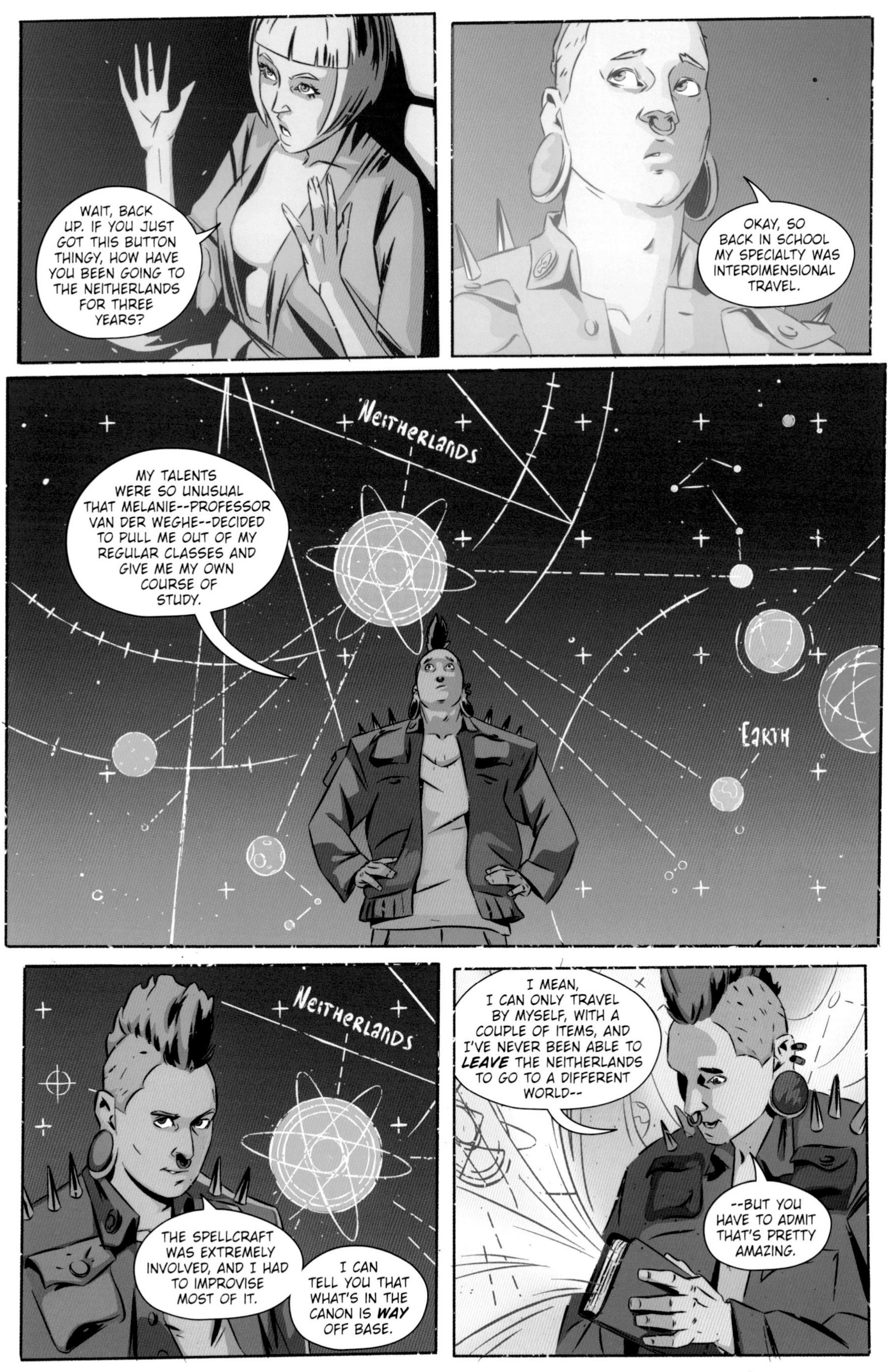
WAIT, BACK UP. IF YOU JUST GOT THIS BUTTON THINGY, HOW HAVE YOU BEEN GOING TO THE NEITHERLANDS FOR THREE YEARS?
OKAY, SO BACK IN SCHOOL MY SPECIALTY WAS INTERDIMENSIONAL TRAVEL.
NEITHERLANDS
MY TALENTS WERE SO UNUSUAL THAT MELANIE--PROFESSOR VAN DER WEGHE--DECIDED TO PULL ME OUT OF MY REGULAR CLASSES AND GIVE ME MY OWN COURSE OF STUDY.
EARTH
NEITHERLANDS
THE SPELLCRAFT WAS EXTREMELY INVOLVED, AND I HAD TO IMPROVISE MOST OF IT.
I CAN TELL YOU THAT WHAT'S IN THE CANON IS ***WAY*** OFF BASE.
I MEAN, I CAN ONLY TRAVEL BY MYSELF, WITH A COUPLE OF ITEMS, AND I'VE NEVER BEEN ABLE TO ***LEAVE*** THE NEITHERLANDS TO GO TO A DIFFERENT WORLD--
--BUT YOU HAVE TO ADMIT THAT'S PRETTY AMAZING.

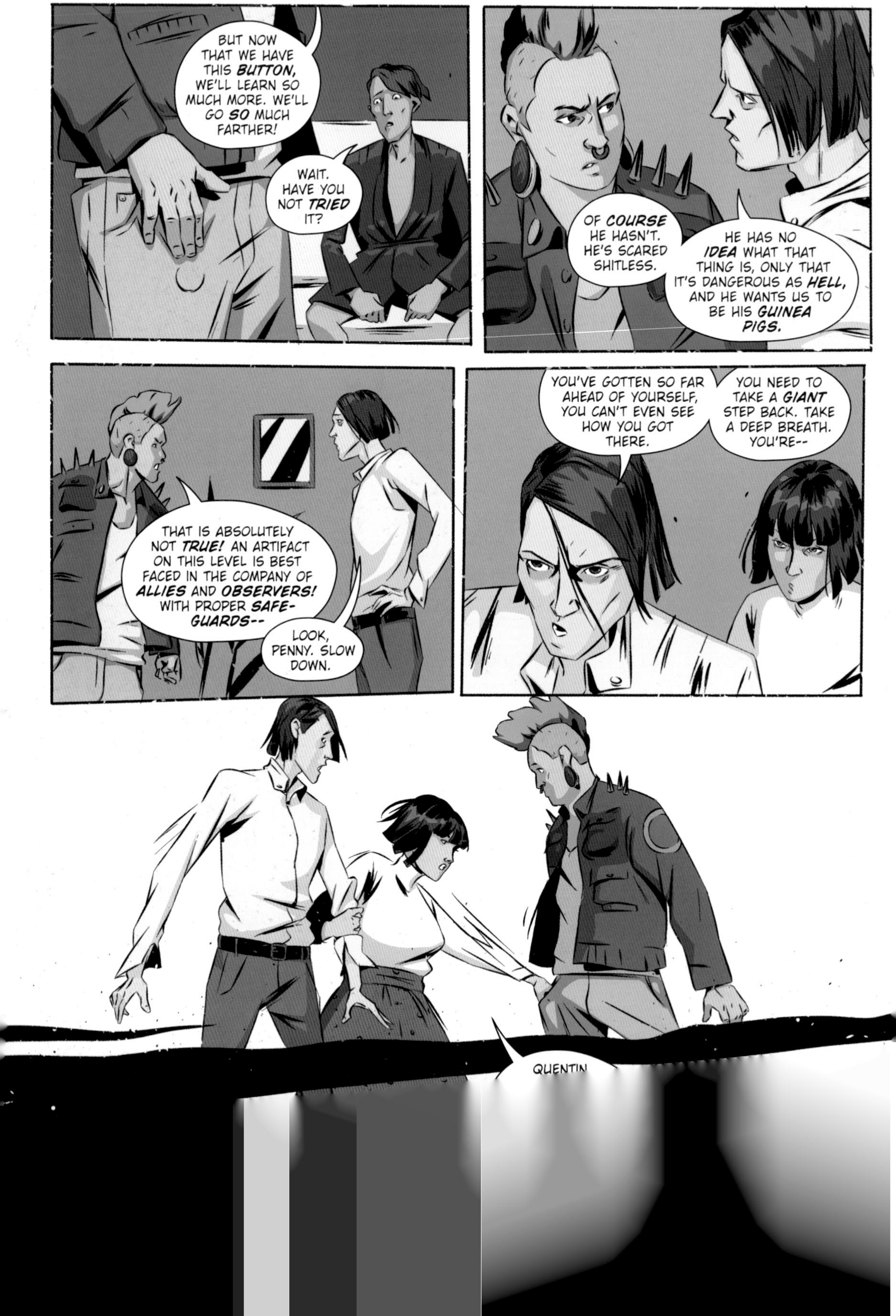
BUT NOW THAT WE HAVE THIS BUTTON, WE'LL LEARN SO MUCH MORE. WE'LL GO SO MUCH FARTHER!
WAIT. HAVE YOU NOT TRIED IT?
OF COURSE HE HASN'T. HE'S SCARED SHITLESS.
HE HAS NO IDEA WHAT THAT THING IS, ONLY THAT IT'S DANGEROUS AS HELL, AND HE WANTS US TO BE HIS GUINEA PIGS.
THAT IS ABSOLUTELY NOT TRUE! AN ARTIFACT ON THIS LEVEL IS BEST FACED IN THE COMPANY OF ALLIES AND OBSERVERS! WITH PROPER SAFE-GUARDS--
LOOK, PENNY. SLOW DOWN.
YOU'VE GOTTEN SO FAR AHEAD OF YOURSELF, YOU CAN'T EVEN SEE HOW YOU GOT THERE.
YOU NEED TO TAKE A GIANT STEP BACK. TAKE A DEEP BREATH. YOU'RE--
QUENTIN

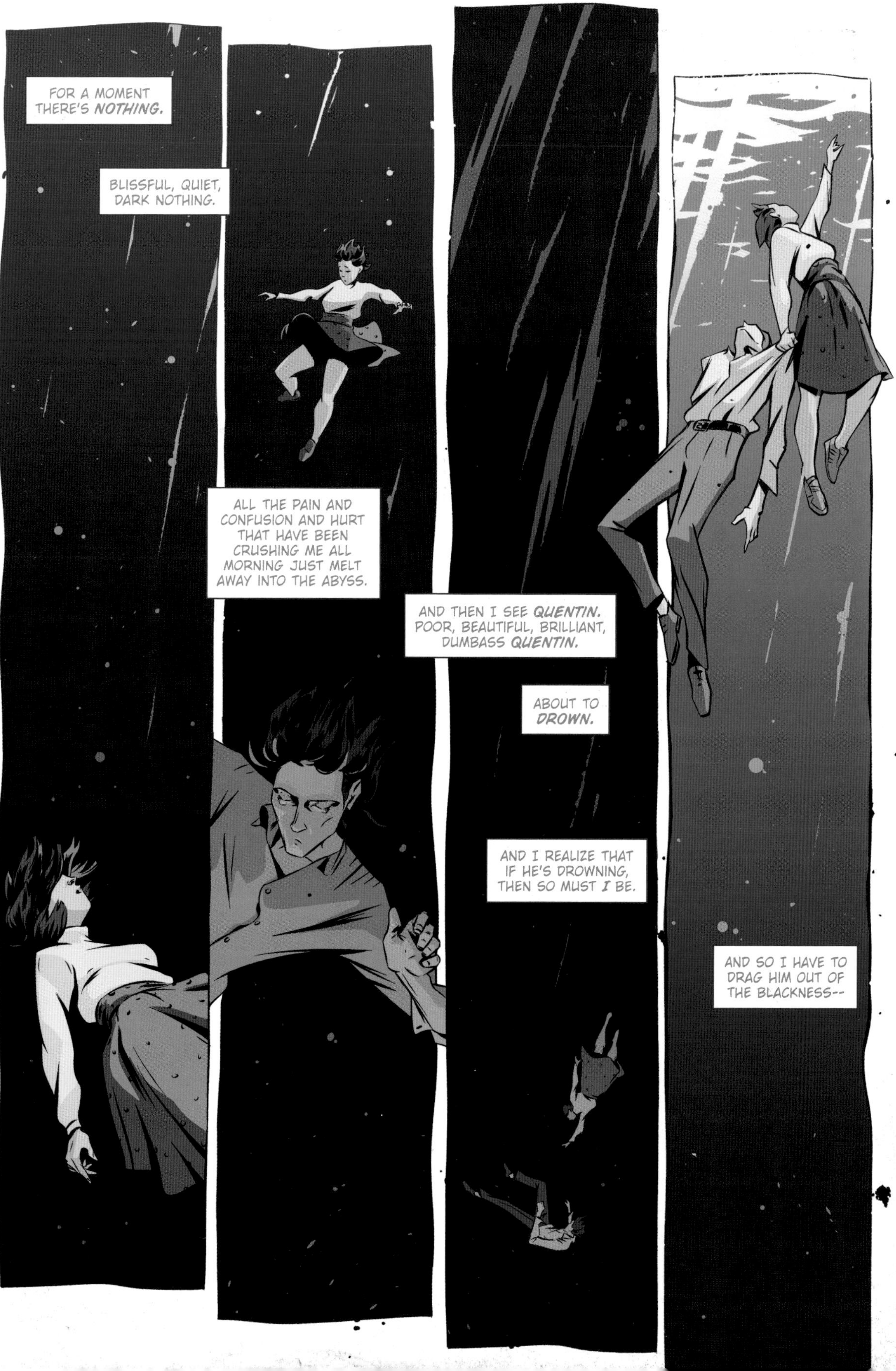
FOR A MOMENT THERE'S *NOTHING.*
BLISSFUL, QUIET, DARK NOTHING.
ALL THE PAIN AND CONFUSION AND HURT THAT HAVE BEEN CRUSHING ME ALL MORNING JUST MELT AWAY INTO THE ABYSS.
AND THEN I SEE *QUENTIN.* POOR, BEAUTIFUL, BRILLIANT, DUMBASS *QUENTIN.*
ABOUT TO *DROWN.*
AND I REALIZE THAT IF HE'S DROWNING, THEN SO MUST *I* BE.
AND SO I HAVE TO DRAG HIM OUT OF THE BLACKNESS--

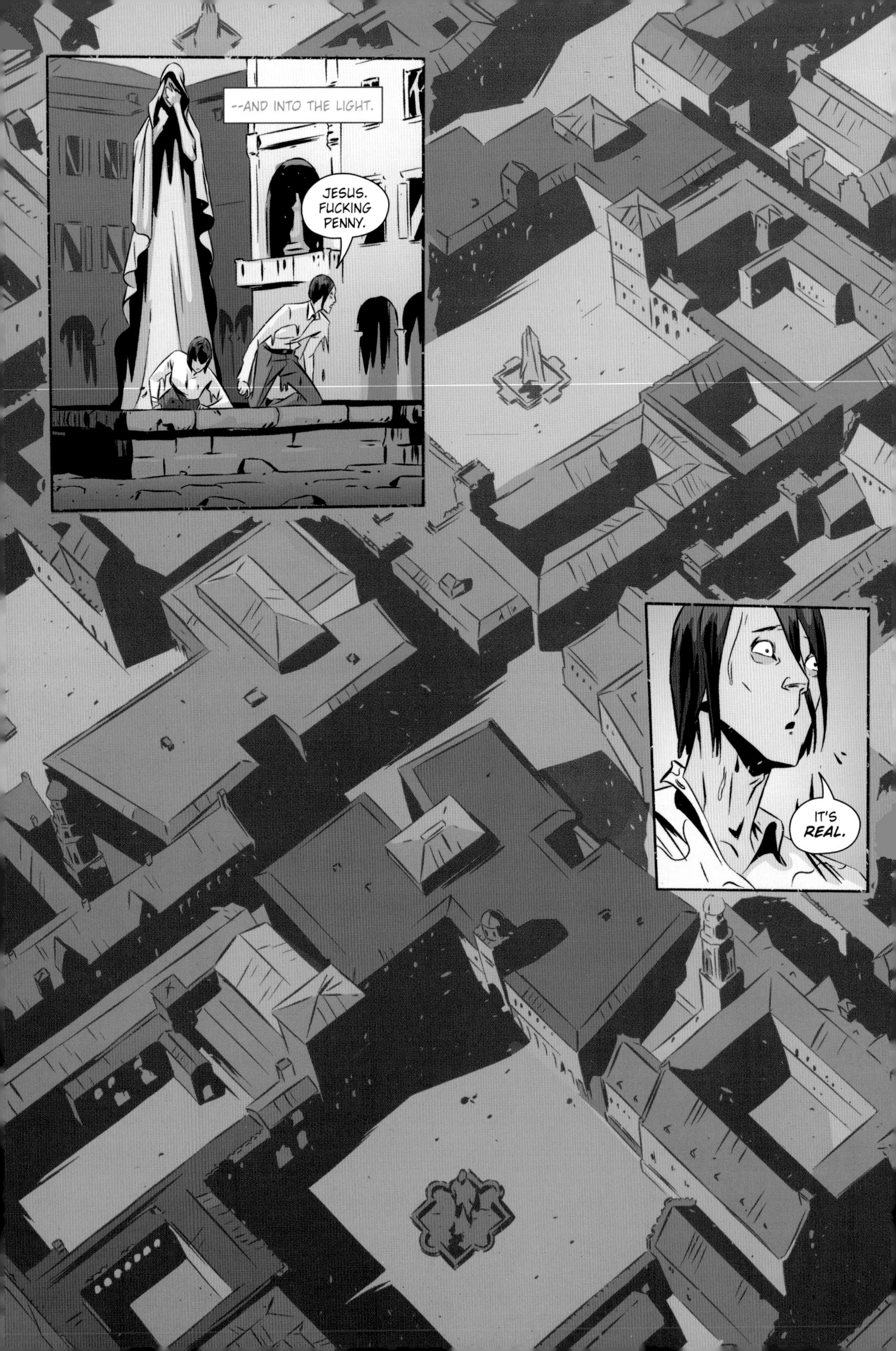
--AND INTO THE LIGHT.
JESUS. FUCKING PENNY.
IT'S REAL.

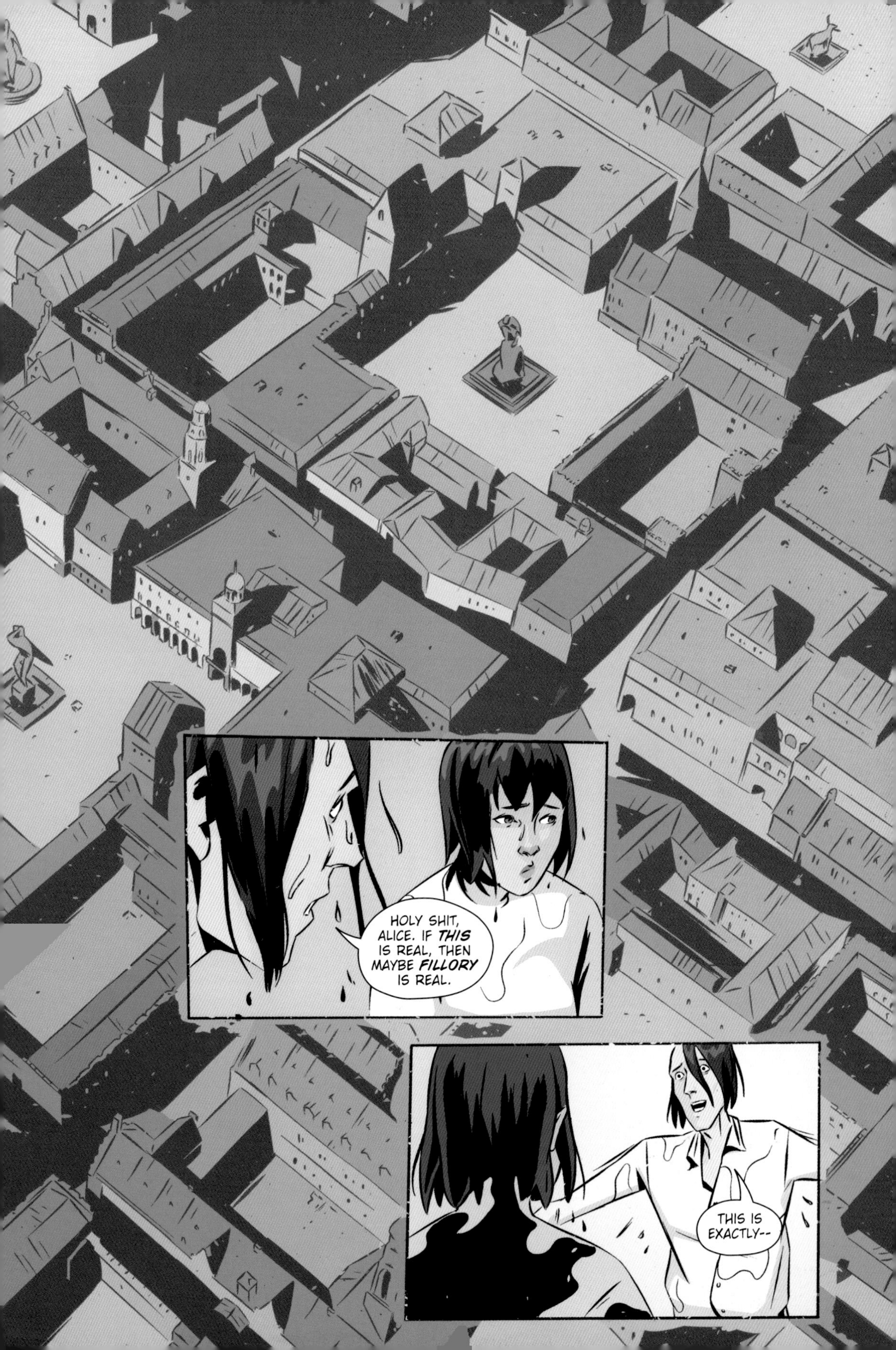
HOLY SHIT, ALICE. IF THIS IS REAL, THEN MAYBE FILLORY IS REAL.
THIS IS EXACTLY--

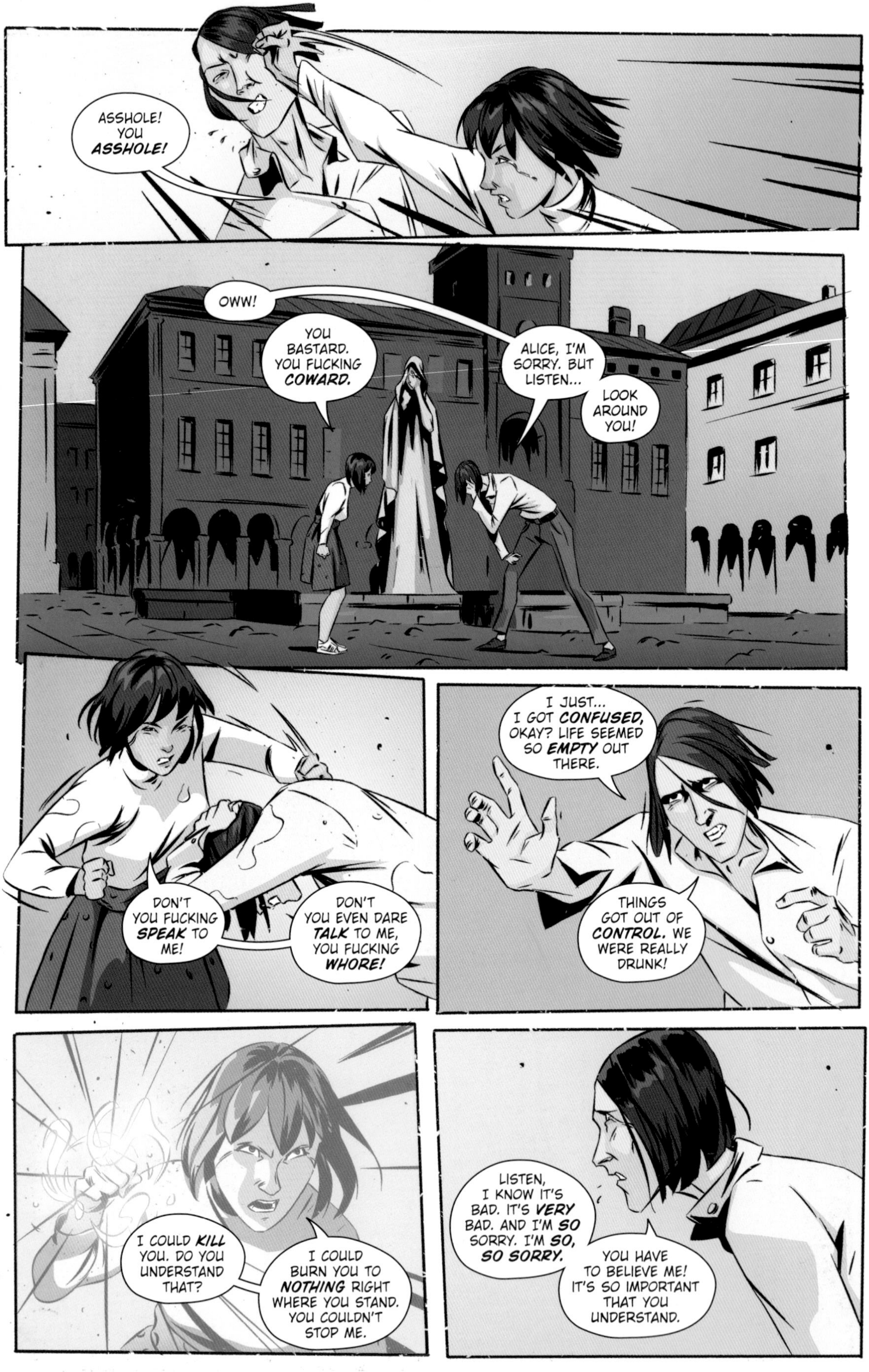
ASSHOLE! YOU **ASSHOLE!**
OWW!
YOU BASTARD. YOU FUCKING **COWARD.**
ALICE, I'M SORRY. BUT LISTEN...
LOOK AROUND YOU!
DON'T YOU FUCKING **SPEAK** TO ME!
DON'T YOU EVEN DARE **TALK** TO ME, YOU FUCKING **WHORE!**
I JUST... I GOT **CONFUSED,** OKAY? LIFE SEEMED SO **EMPTY** OUT THERE.
THINGS GOT OUT OF **CONTROL.** WE WERE REALLY DRUNK!
I COULD **KILL** YOU. DO YOU UNDERSTAND THAT?
I COULD BURN YOU TO **NOTHING** RIGHT WHERE YOU STAND. YOU COULDN'T STOP ME.
LISTEN, I KNOW IT'S BAD. IT'S **VERY** BAD. AND I'M **SO** SORRY. I'M **SO, SO SORRY.**
YOU HAVE TO BELIEVE ME! IT'S SO IMPORTANT THAT YOU UNDERSTAND.

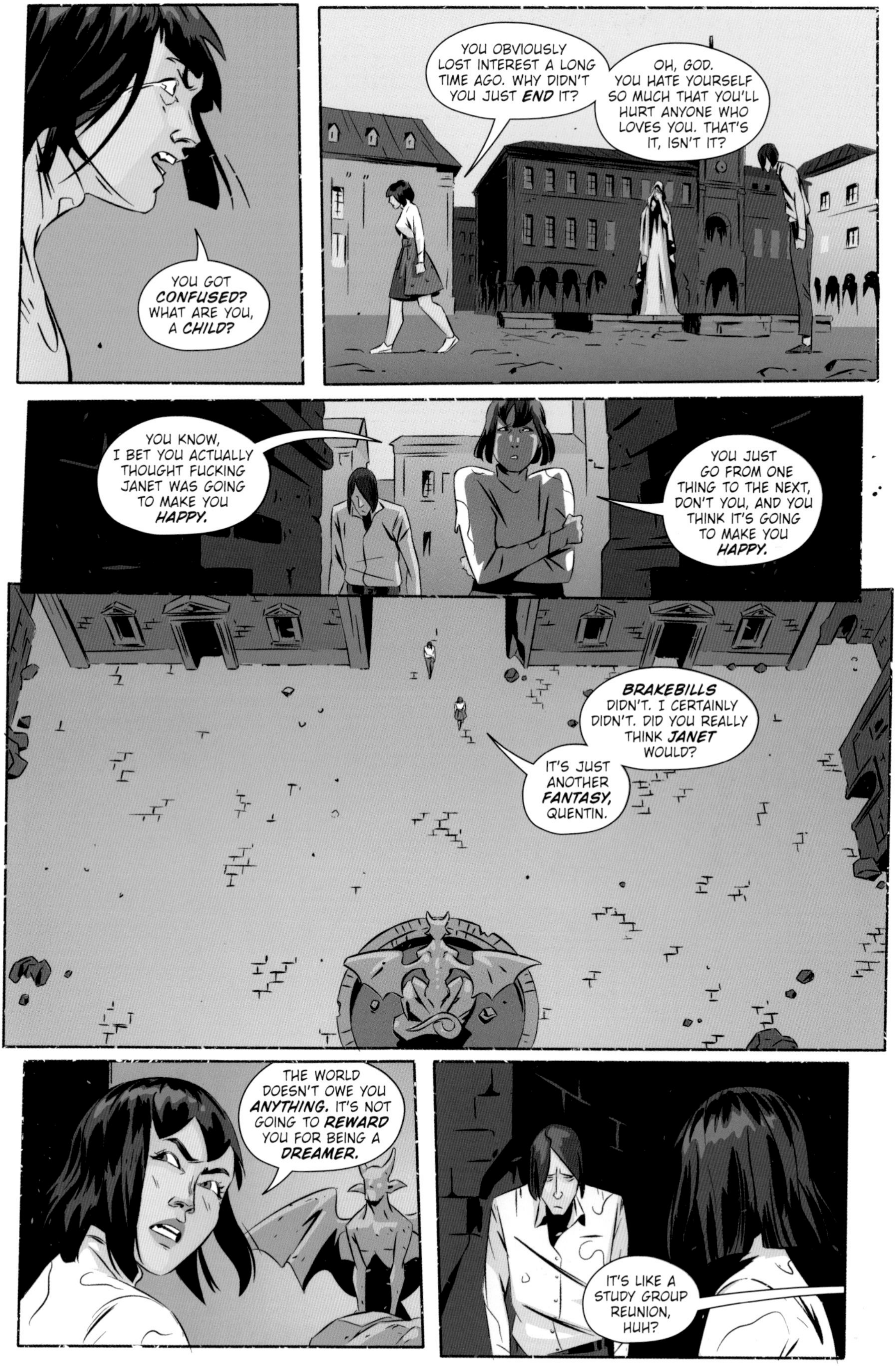
YOU GOT CONFUSED? WHAT ARE YOU, A CHILD?
YOU OBVIOUSLY LOST INTEREST A LONG TIME AGO. WHY DIDN'T YOU JUST END IT?
OH, GOD. YOU HATE YOURSELF SO MUCH THAT YOU'LL HURT ANYONE WHO LOVES YOU. THAT'S IT, ISN'T IT?
YOU KNOW, I BET YOU ACTUALLY THOUGHT FUCKING JANET WAS GOING TO MAKE YOU HAPPY.
YOU JUST GO FROM ONE THING TO THE NEXT, DON'T YOU, AND YOU THINK IT'S GOING TO MAKE YOU HAPPY.
BRAKEBILLS DIDN'T. I CERTAINLY DIDN'T. DID YOU REALLY THINK JANET WOULD?
IT'S JUST ANOTHER FANTASY, QUENTIN.
THE WORLD DOESN'T OWE YOU ANYTHING. IT'S NOT GOING TO REWARD YOU FOR BEING A DREAMER.
IT'S LIKE A STUDY GROUP REUNION, HUH?

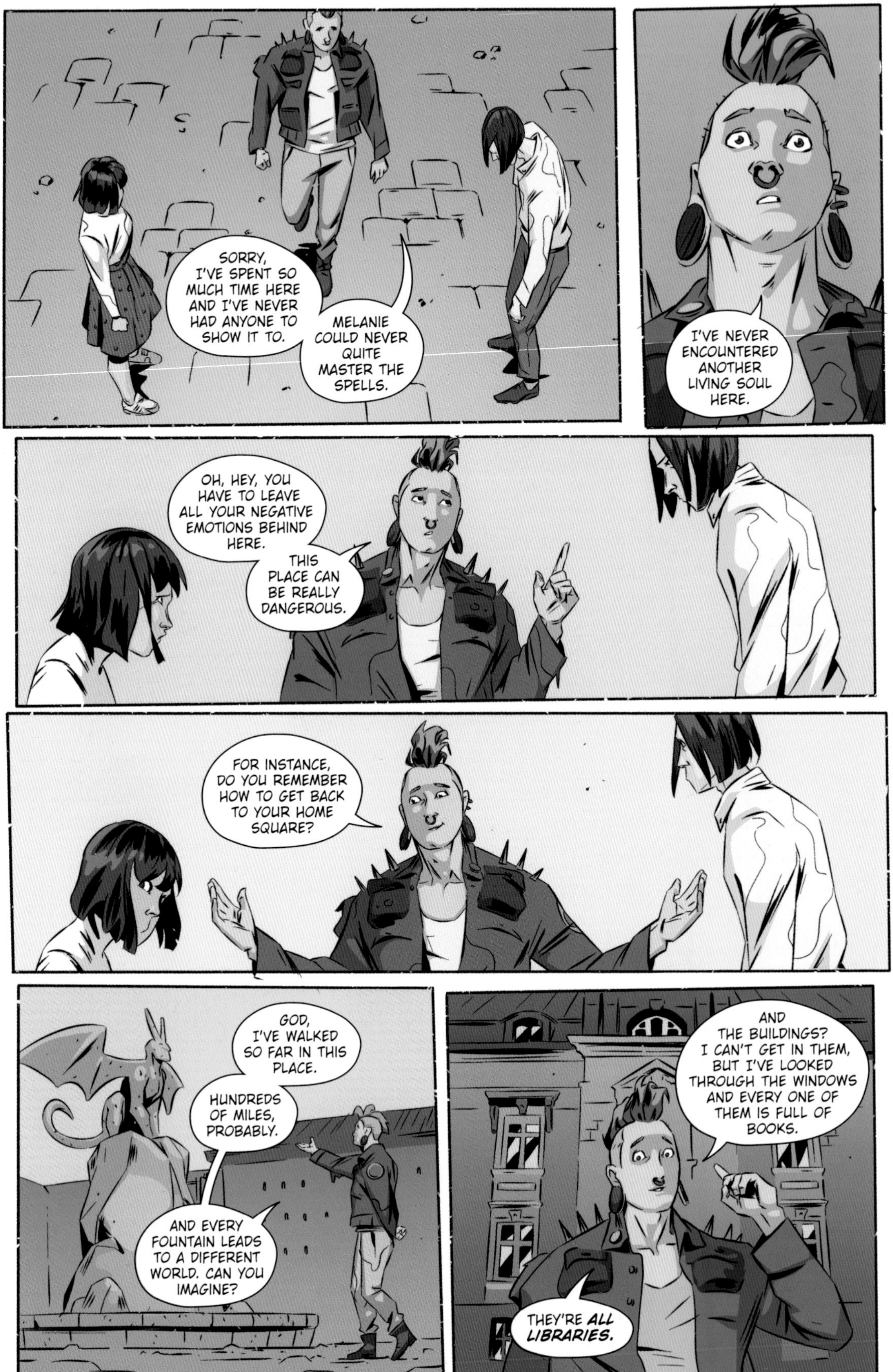
SORRY, I'VE SPENT SO MUCH TIME HERE AND I'VE NEVER HAD ANYONE TO SHOW IT TO.
MELANIE COULD NEVER QUITE MASTER THE SPELLS.
I'VE NEVER ENCOUNTERED ANOTHER LIVING SOUL HERE.
OH, HEY, YOU HAVE TO LEAVE ALL YOUR NEGATIVE EMOTIONS BEHIND HERE.
THIS PLACE CAN BE REALLY DANGEROUS.
FOR INSTANCE, DO YOU REMEMBER HOW TO GET BACK TO YOUR HOME SQUARE?
GOD, I'VE WALKED SO FAR IN THIS PLACE.
HUNDREDS OF MILES, PROBABLY.
AND EVERY FOUNTAIN LEADS TO A DIFFERENT WORLD. CAN YOU IMAGINE?
AND THE BUILDINGS? I CAN'T GET IN THEM, BUT I'VE LOOKED THROUGH THE WINDOWS AND EVERY ONE OF THEM IS FULL OF BOOKS.
THEY'RE ***ALL LIBRARIES.***

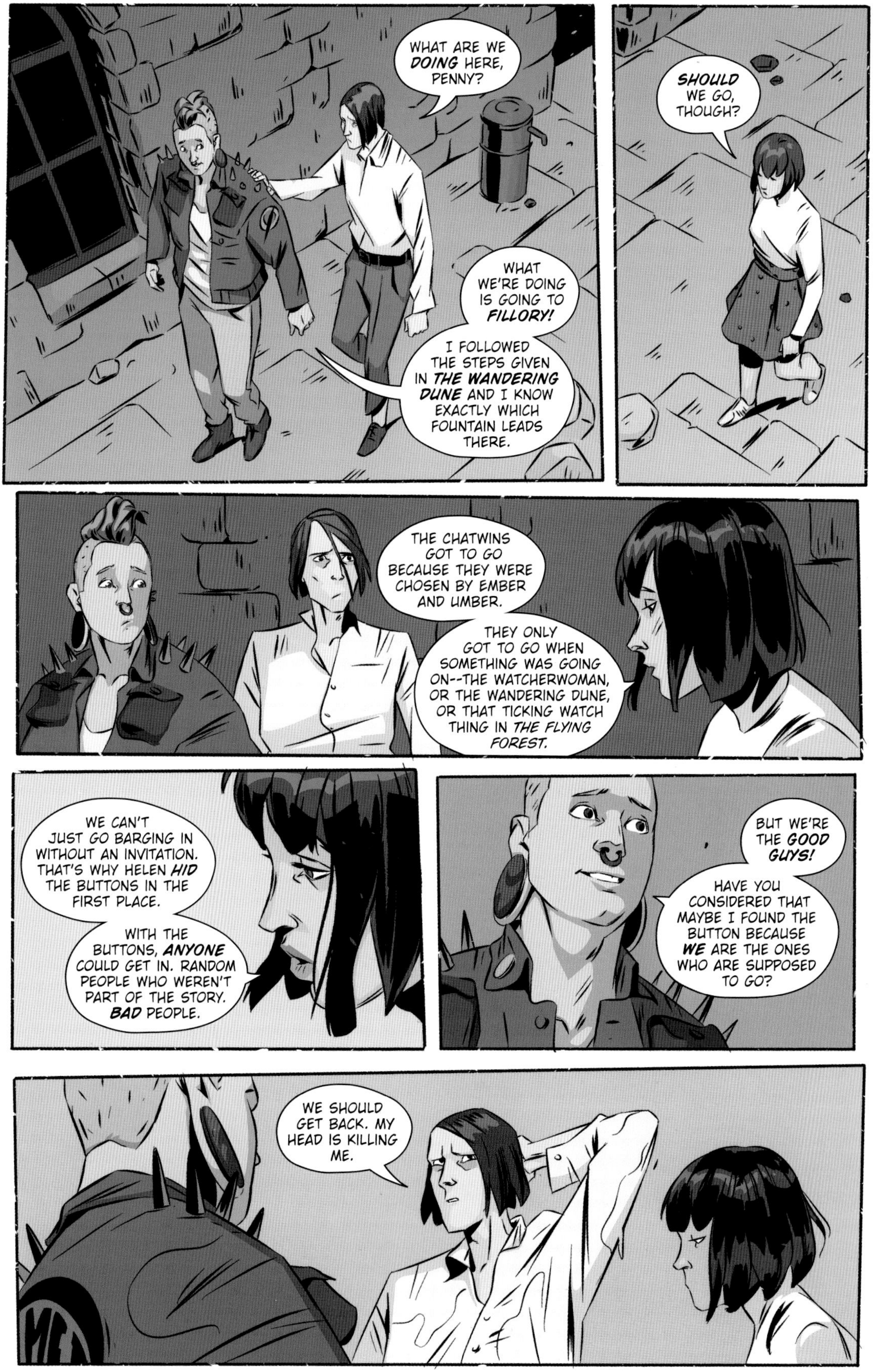
WHAT ARE WE DOING HERE, PENNY?
WHAT WE'RE DOING IS GOING TO FILLORY!
I FOLLOWED THE STEPS GIVEN IN THE WANDERING DUNE AND I KNOW EXACTLY WHICH FOUNTAIN LEADS THERE.
SHOULD WE GO, THOUGH?
THE CHATWINS GOT TO GO BECAUSE THEY WERE CHOSEN BY EMBER AND UMBER.
THEY ONLY GOT TO GO WHEN SOMETHING WAS GOING ON--THE WATCHERWOMAN, OR THE WANDERING DUNE, OR THAT TICKING WATCH THING IN THE FLYING FOREST.
WE CAN'T JUST GO BARGING IN WITHOUT AN INVITATION. THAT'S WHY HELEN HID THE BUTTONS IN THE FIRST PLACE.
WITH THE BUTTONS, ANYONE COULD GET IN. RANDOM PEOPLE WHO WEREN'T PART OF THE STORY. BAD PEOPLE.
BUT WE'RE THE GOOD GUYS!
HAVE YOU CONSIDERED THAT MAYBE I FOUND THE BUTTON BECAUSE WE ARE THE ONES WHO ARE SUPPOSED TO GO?
WE SHOULD GET BACK. MY HEAD IS KILLING ME.

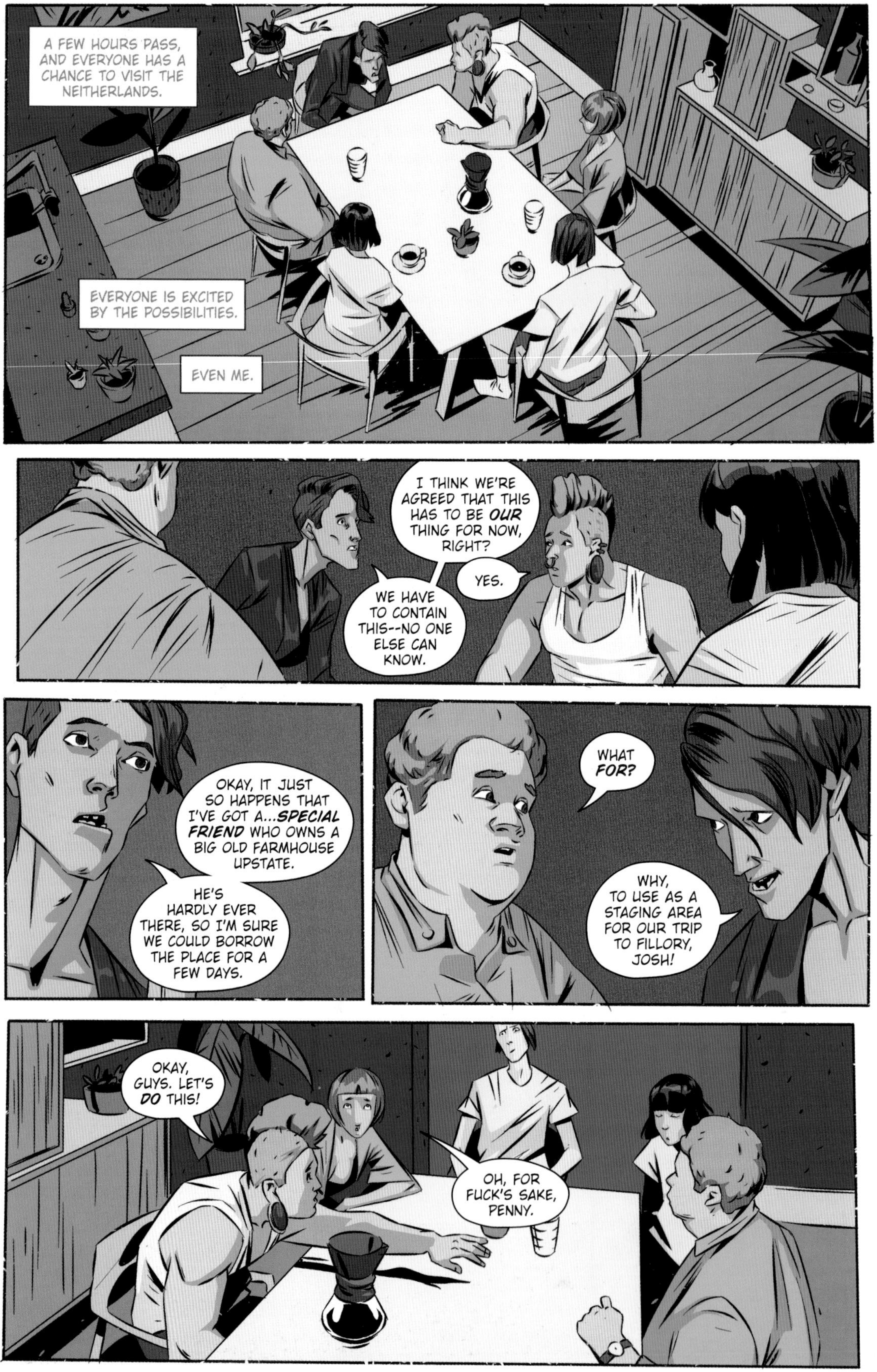
A FEW HOURS PASS, AND EVERYONE HAS A CHANCE TO VISIT THE NEITHERLANDS.
EVERYONE IS EXCITED BY THE POSSIBILITIES.
EVEN ME.
I THINK WE'RE AGREED THAT THIS HAS TO BE *OUR* THING FOR NOW, RIGHT?
WE HAVE TO CONTAIN THIS--NO ONE ELSE CAN KNOW.
YES.
OKAY, IT JUST SO HAPPENS THAT I'VE GOT A...***SPECIAL FRIEND*** WHO OWNS A BIG OLD FARMHOUSE UPSTATE.
HE'S HARDLY EVER THERE, SO I'M SURE WE COULD BORROW THE PLACE FOR A FEW DAYS.
WHAT ***FOR?***
WHY, TO USE AS A STAGING AREA FOR OUR TRIP TO FILLORY, JOSH!
OKAY, GUYS. LET'S ***DO*** THIS!
OH, FOR FUCK'S SAKE, PENNY.

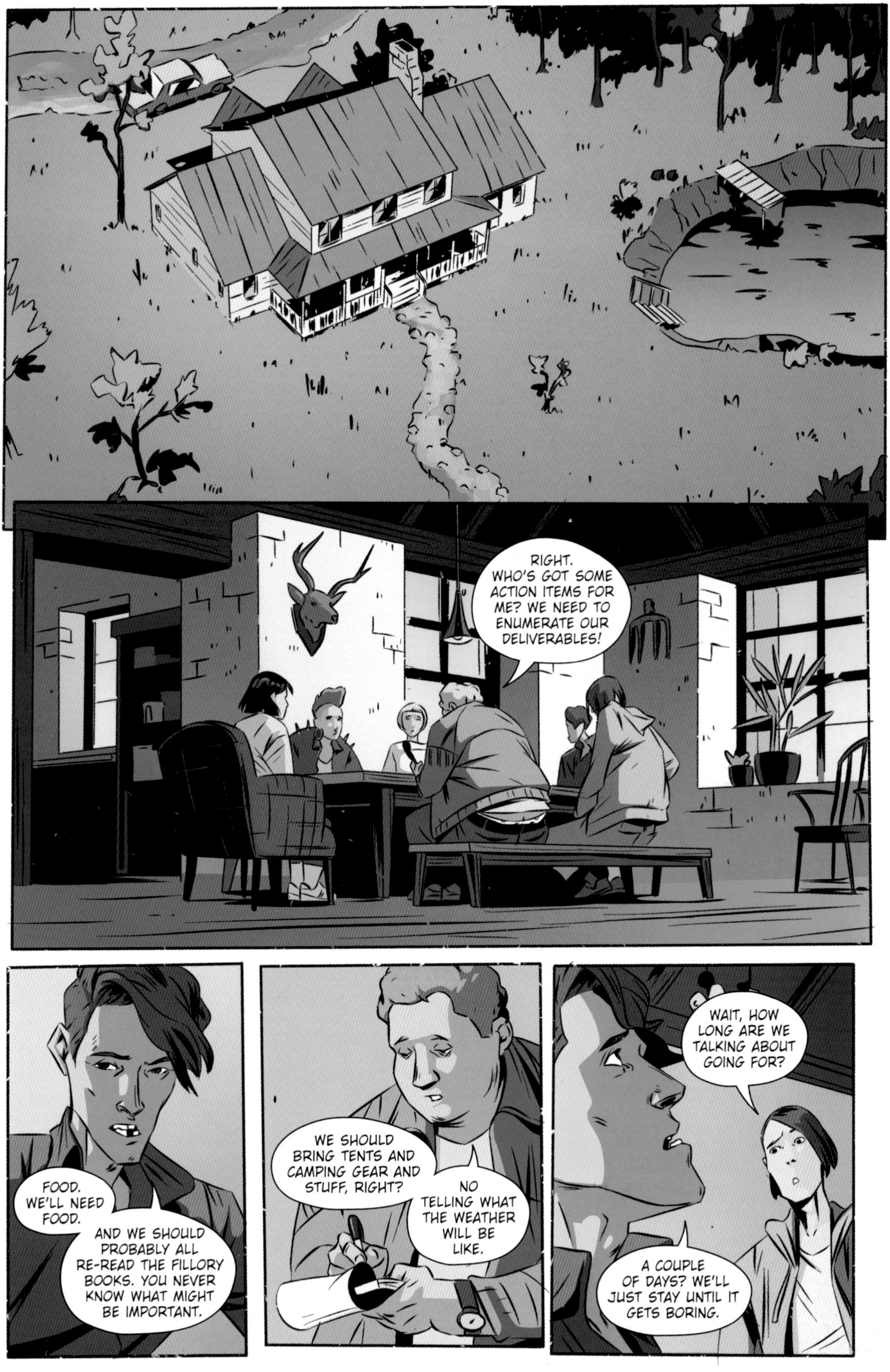
RIGHT. WHO'S GOT SOME ACTION ITEMS FOR ME? WE NEED TO ENUMERATE OUR DELIVERABLES!
FOOD. WE'LL NEED FOOD.
AND WE SHOULD PROBABLY ALL RE-READ THE FILLORY BOOKS. YOU NEVER KNOW WHAT MIGHT BE IMPORTANT.
WE SHOULD BRING TENTS AND CAMPING GEAR AND STUFF, RIGHT?
NO TELLING WHAT THE WEATHER WILL BE LIKE.
WAIT, HOW LONG ARE WE TALKING ABOUT GOING FOR?
A COUPLE OF DAYS? WE'LL JUST STAY UNTIL IT GETS BORING.

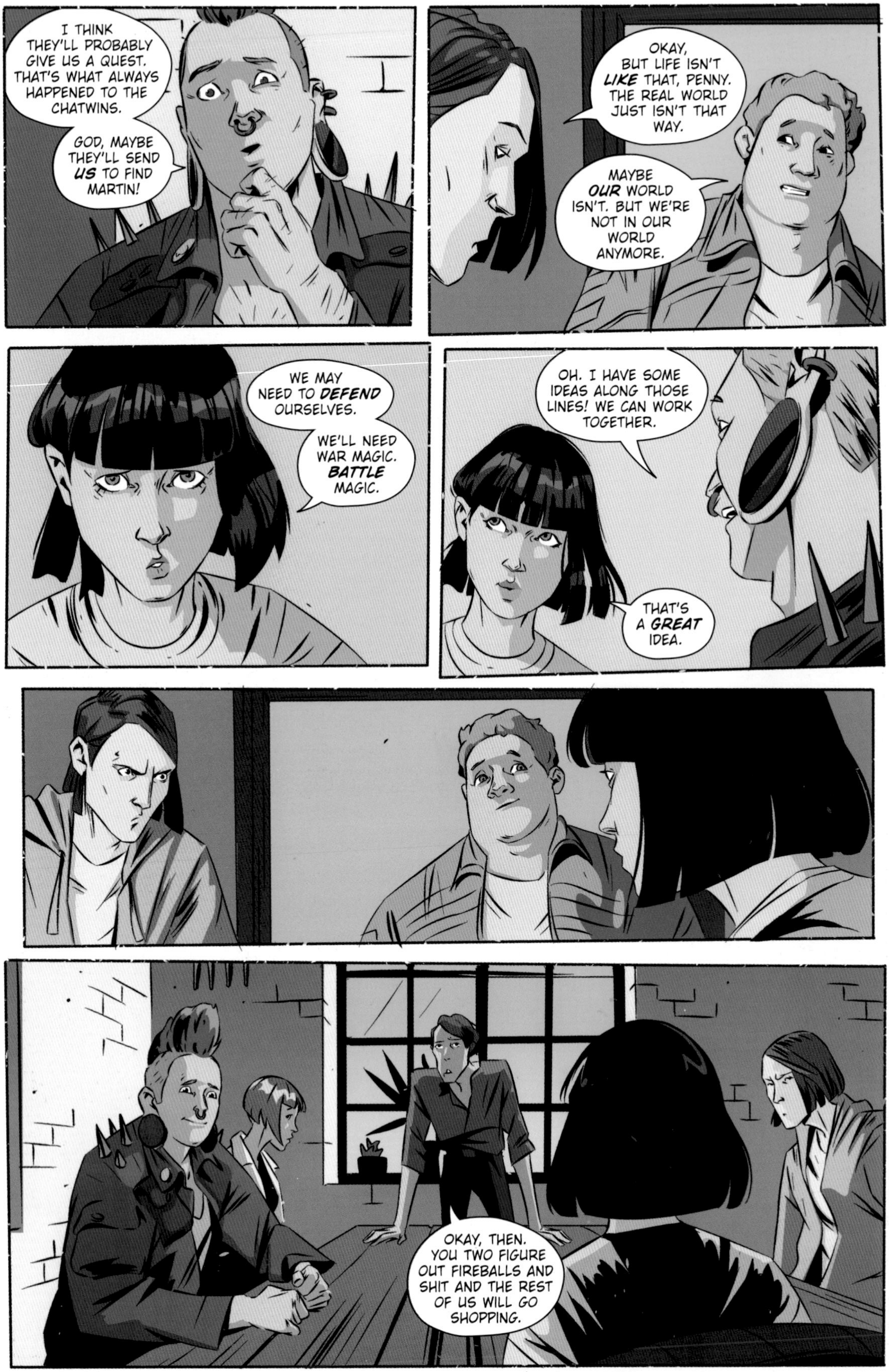
I THINK THEY'LL PROBABLY GIVE US A QUEST. THAT'S WHAT ALWAYS HAPPENED TO THE CHATWINS.
GOD, MAYBE THEY'LL SEND US TO FIND MARTIN!
OKAY, BUT LIFE ISN'T LIKE THAT, PENNY. THE REAL WORLD JUST ISN'T THAT WAY.
MAYBE OUR WORLD ISN'T. BUT WE'RE NOT IN OUR WORLD ANYMORE.
WE MAY NEED TO DEFEND OURSELVES.
WE'LL NEED WAR MAGIC. BATTLE MAGIC.
OH. I HAVE SOME IDEAS ALONG THOSE LINES! WE CAN WORK TOGETHER.
THAT'S A GREAT IDEA.
OKAY, THEN. YOU TWO FIGURE OUT FIREBALLS AND SHIT AND THE REST OF US WILL GO SHOPPING.

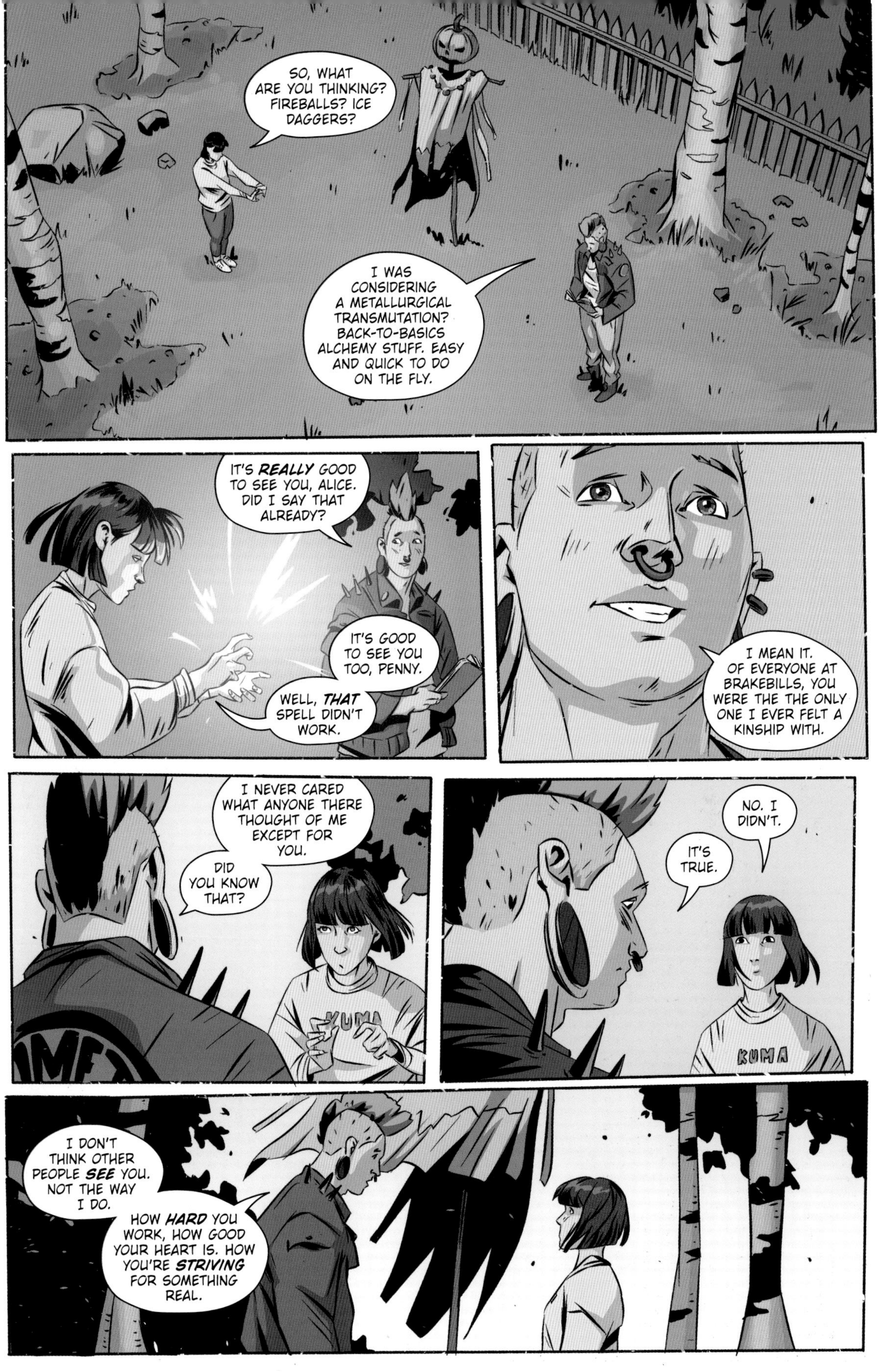
SO, WHAT ARE YOU THINKING? FIREBALLS? ICE DAGGERS?
I WAS CONSIDERING A METALLURGICAL TRANSMUTATION? BACK-TO-BASICS ALCHEMY STUFF. EASY AND QUICK TO DO ON THE FLY.
IT'S **REALLY** GOOD TO SEE YOU, ALICE. DID I SAY THAT ALREADY?
IT'S GOOD TO SEE YOU TOO, PENNY.
WELL, **THAT** SPELL DIDN'T WORK.
I MEAN IT. OF EVERYONE AT BRAKEBILLS, YOU WERE THE THE ONLY ONE I EVER FELT A KINSHIP WITH.
I NEVER CARED WHAT ANYONE THERE THOUGHT OF ME EXCEPT FOR YOU.
DID YOU KNOW THAT?
KUMA
NO. I DIDN'T.
IT'S TRUE.
KUMA
I DON'T THINK OTHER PEOPLE **SEE** YOU. NOT THE WAY I DO.
HOW **HARD** YOU WORK, HOW GOOD YOUR HEART IS. HOW YOU'RE **STRIVING** FOR SOMETHING REAL.

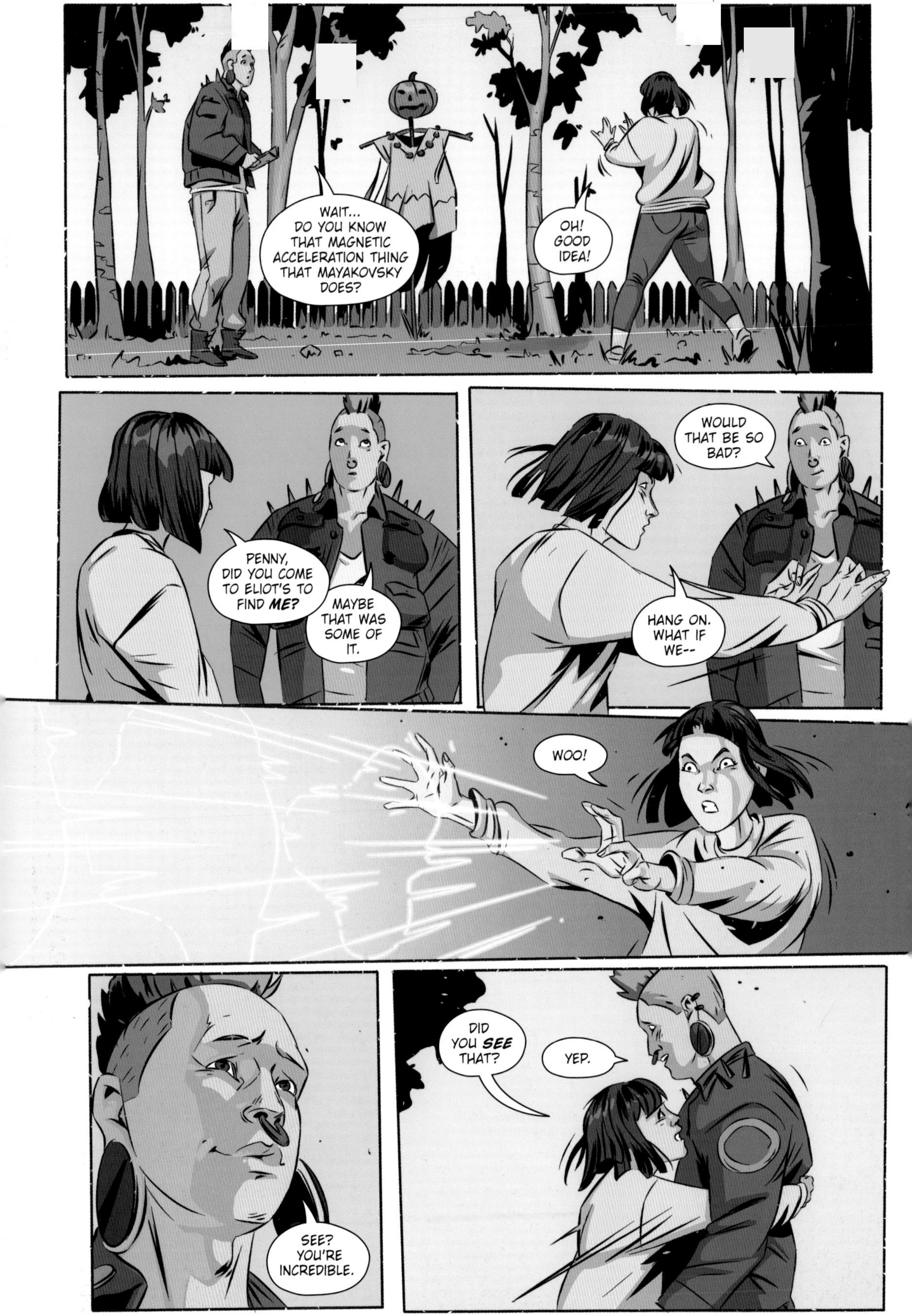
WAIT... DO YOU KNOW THAT MAGNETIC ACCELERATION THING THAT MAYAKOVSKY DOES?
OH! GOOD IDEA!
PENNY, DID YOU COME TO ELIOT'S TO FIND *ME?*
MAYBE THAT WAS SOME OF IT.
WOULD THAT BE SO BAD?
HANG ON. WHAT IF WE--
WOO!
SEE? YOU'RE INCREDIBLE.
DID YOU *SEE* THAT?
YEP.

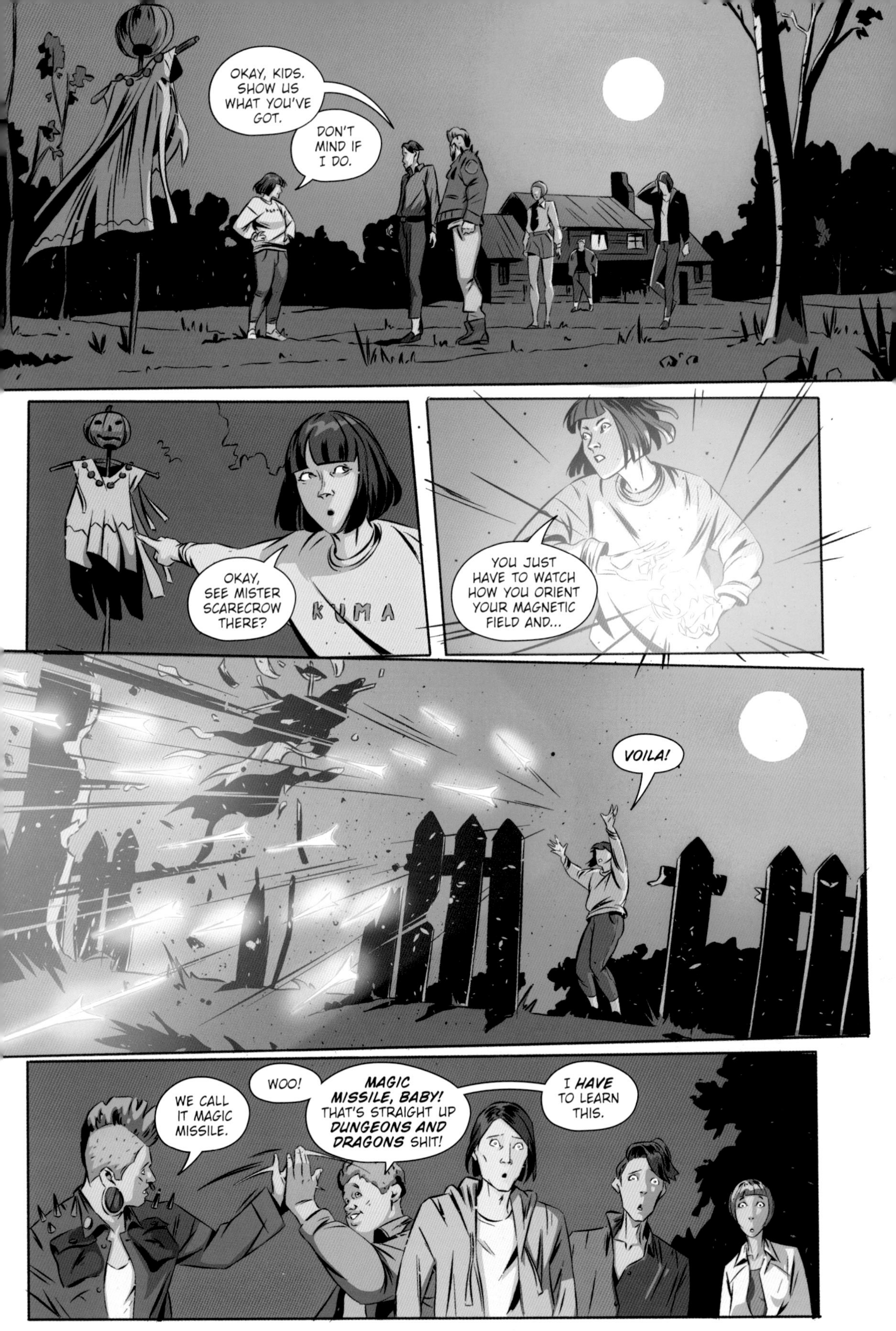
OKAY, KIDS. SHOW US WHAT YOU'VE GOT.
DON'T MIND IF I DO.
OKAY, SEE MISTER SCARECROW THERE?
KUMA
YOU JUST HAVE TO WATCH HOW YOU ORIENT YOUR MAGNETIC FIELD AND...
VOILA!
WE CALL IT MAGIC MISSILE.
WOO!
MAGIC MISSILE, BABY! THAT'S STRAIGHT UP DUNGEONS AND DRAGONS SHIT!
I HAVE TO LEARN THIS.

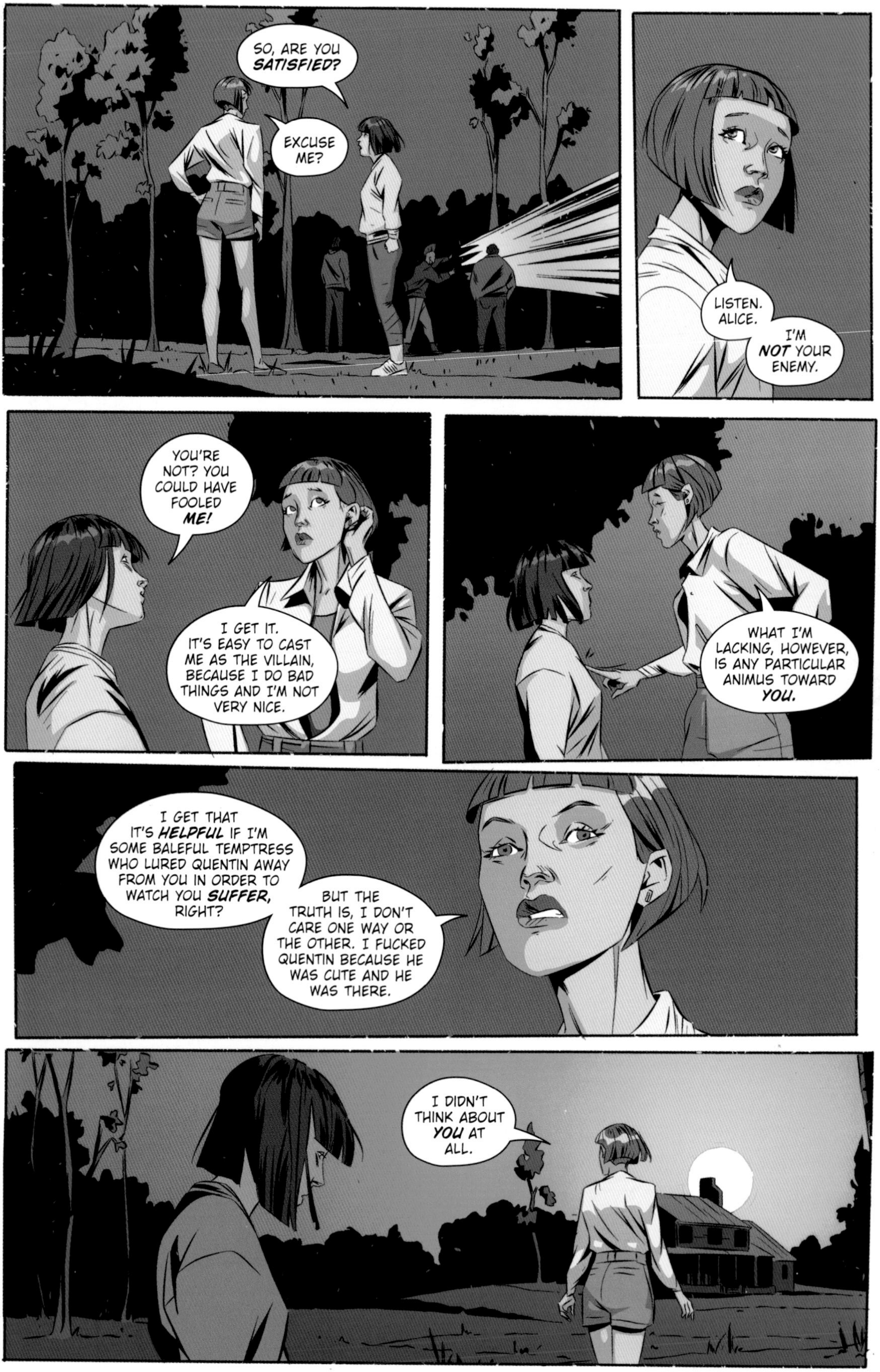
SO, ARE YOU SATISFIED?
EXCUSE ME?
LISTEN. ALICE.
I'M NOT YOUR ENEMY.
YOU'RE NOT? YOU COULD HAVE FOOLED ME!
I GET IT. IT'S EASY TO CAST ME AS THE VILLAIN, BECAUSE I DO BAD THINGS AND I'M NOT VERY NICE.
WHAT I'M LACKING, HOWEVER, IS ANY PARTICULAR ANIMUS TOWARD YOU.
I GET THAT IT'S HELPFUL IF I'M SOME BALEFUL TEMPTRESS WHO LURED QUENTIN AWAY FROM YOU IN ORDER TO WATCH YOU SUFFER, RIGHT?
BUT THE TRUTH IS, I DON'T CARE ONE WAY OR THE OTHER. I FUCKED QUENTIN BECAUSE HE WAS CUTE AND HE WAS THERE.
I DIDN'T THINK ABOUT YOU AT ALL.

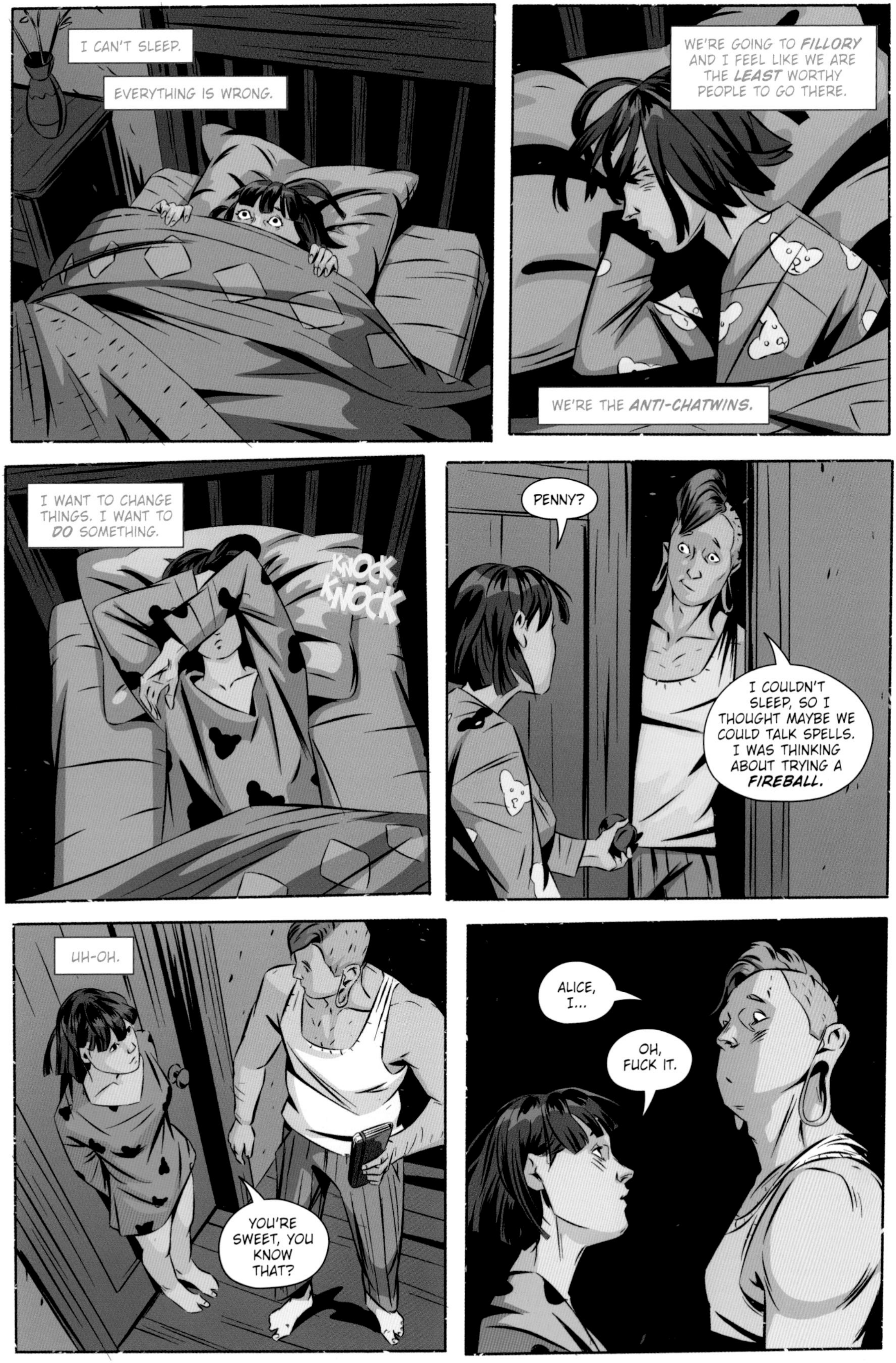

I CAN'T SLEEP.
EVERYTHING IS WRONG.
WE'RE GOING TO FILLORY AND I FEEL LIKE WE ARE THE LEAST WORTHY PEOPLE TO GO THERE.
WE'RE THE ANTI-CHATWINS.
I WANT TO CHANGE THINGS. I WANT TO DO SOMETHING.
KNOCK KNOCK
PENNY?
I COULDN'T SLEEP, SO I THOUGHT MAYBE WE COULD TALK SPELLS. I WAS THINKING ABOUT TRYING A FIREBALL.
UH-OH.
YOU'RE SWEET, YOU KNOW THAT?
ALICE, I...
OH, FUCK IT.

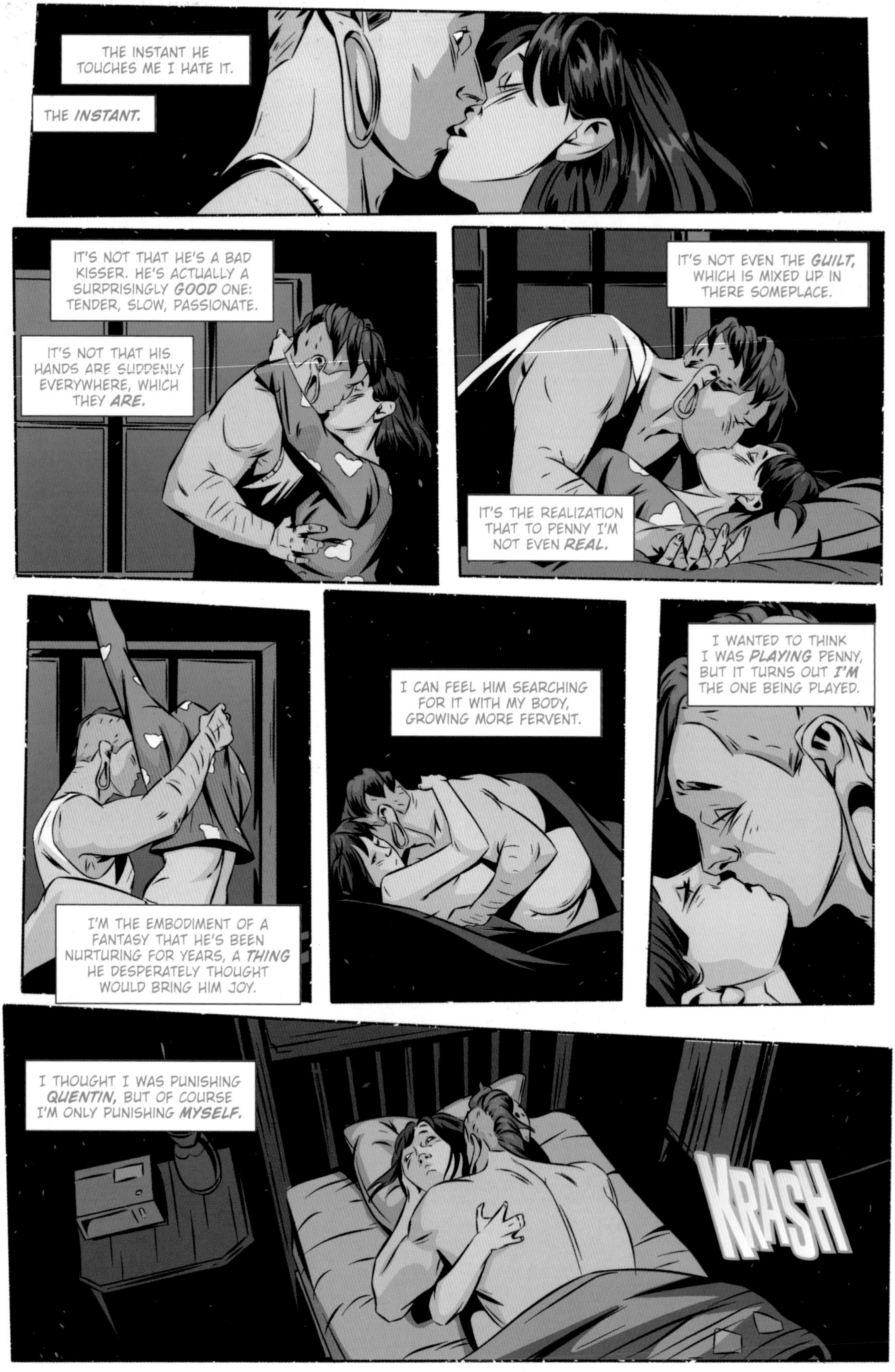
THE INSTANT HE TOUCHES ME I HATE IT.
THE *INSTANT.*
IT'S NOT THAT HE'S A BAD KISSER. HE'S ACTUALLY A SURPRISINGLY *GOOD* ONE: TENDER, SLOW, PASSIONATE.
IT'S NOT THAT HIS HANDS ARE SUDDENLY EVERYWHERE, WHICH THEY *ARE.*
IT'S NOT EVEN THE *GUILT,* WHICH IS MIXED UP IN THERE SOMEPLACE.
IT'S THE REALIZATION THAT TO PENNY I'M NOT EVEN *REAL.*
I'M THE EMBODIMENT OF A FANTASY THAT HE'S BEEN NURTURING FOR YEARS, A *THING* HE DESPERATELY THOUGHT WOULD BRING HIM JOY.
I CAN FEEL HIM SEARCHING FOR IT WITH MY BODY, GROWING MORE FERVENT.
I WANTED TO THINK I WAS *PLAYING* PENNY, BUT IT TURNS OUT *I'M* THE ONE BEING PLAYED.
I THOUGHT I WAS PUNISHING *QUENTIN,* BUT OF COURSE I'M ONLY PUNISHING *MYSELF.*
KRASH

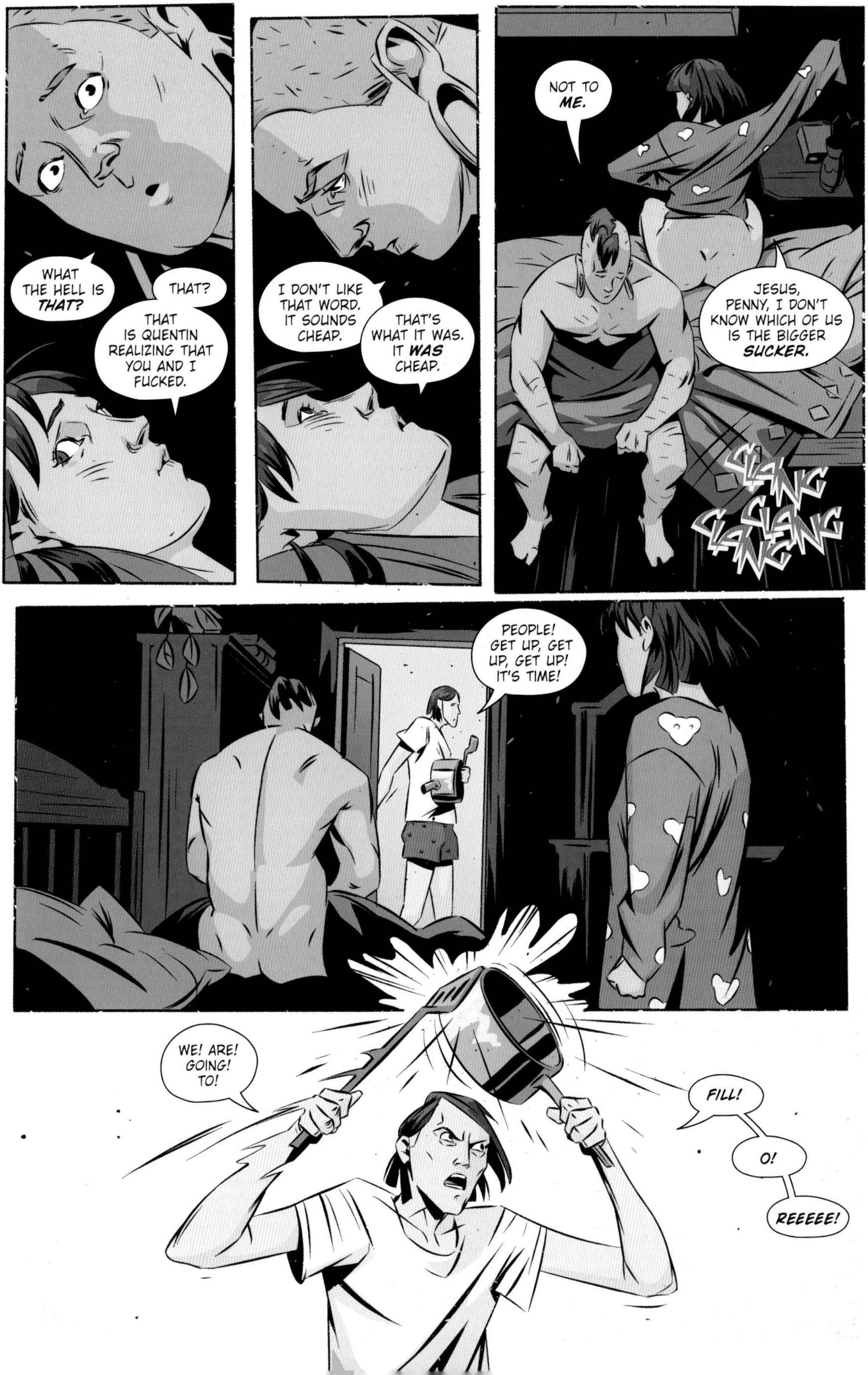
WHAT THE HELL IS ***THAT?***
THAT?
THAT IS QUENTIN REALIZING THAT YOU AND I FUCKED.
I DON'T LIKE THAT WORD. IT SOUNDS CHEAP.
THAT'S WHAT IT WAS. IT ***WAS*** CHEAP.
NOT TO ***ME.***
JESUS, PENNY, I DON'T KNOW WHICH OF US IS THE BIGGER ***SUCKER.***
CLANG CLANG CLANGANG
PEOPLE! GET UP, GET UP, GET UP! IT'S TIME!
WE! ARE! GOING! TO!
FILL!
O!
REEEEE!

"The merfolk will be forever grateful to you, Queen Fiona and Queen Helen," Ember proclaimed...

"The Sea of Tears shall be secret no longer, and henceforth it shall be known as the Sea of Laughter!"

The mermen and and mermaids let out a great cry of joy and then, after a further bit of celebration, slid back beneath the waves. The children watched them go with a mixture of joy and sadness. Fiona could taste the salt in the air and she thought it better than the seaside at home. More pure and more full of hope.

"The merfolk will be forever grateful to you, Queen Fiona and Queen Helen," Ember proclaimed, his voice soft and large like distant thunder. "As shall we."

"You're not cross with us?" asked Helen. "We didn't do as you asked." The children had never defied the twin rams before, and Helen was as nervous as she could remember being.

"You wished to find your missing brother," boomed Umber. "This we understand. Were I to lose Ember, my tears would create a sea of their own."

"Oh, thank goodness!" cried Fiona. She threw her arms around Ember's neck and breathed in the smells of sunlight and fresh hay.

"But now you must return to your own world, children," said Ember. "As you know well, Fillory is not your home and you mustn't grow old here."

"Will we return?" asked Helen.

"One of you shall, one of you shall not. That is all I can say," intoned Umber.

"Which one?" cried Fiona, but her voice was lost in the wind between worlds that whipped past her, carrying away her hat and sword.

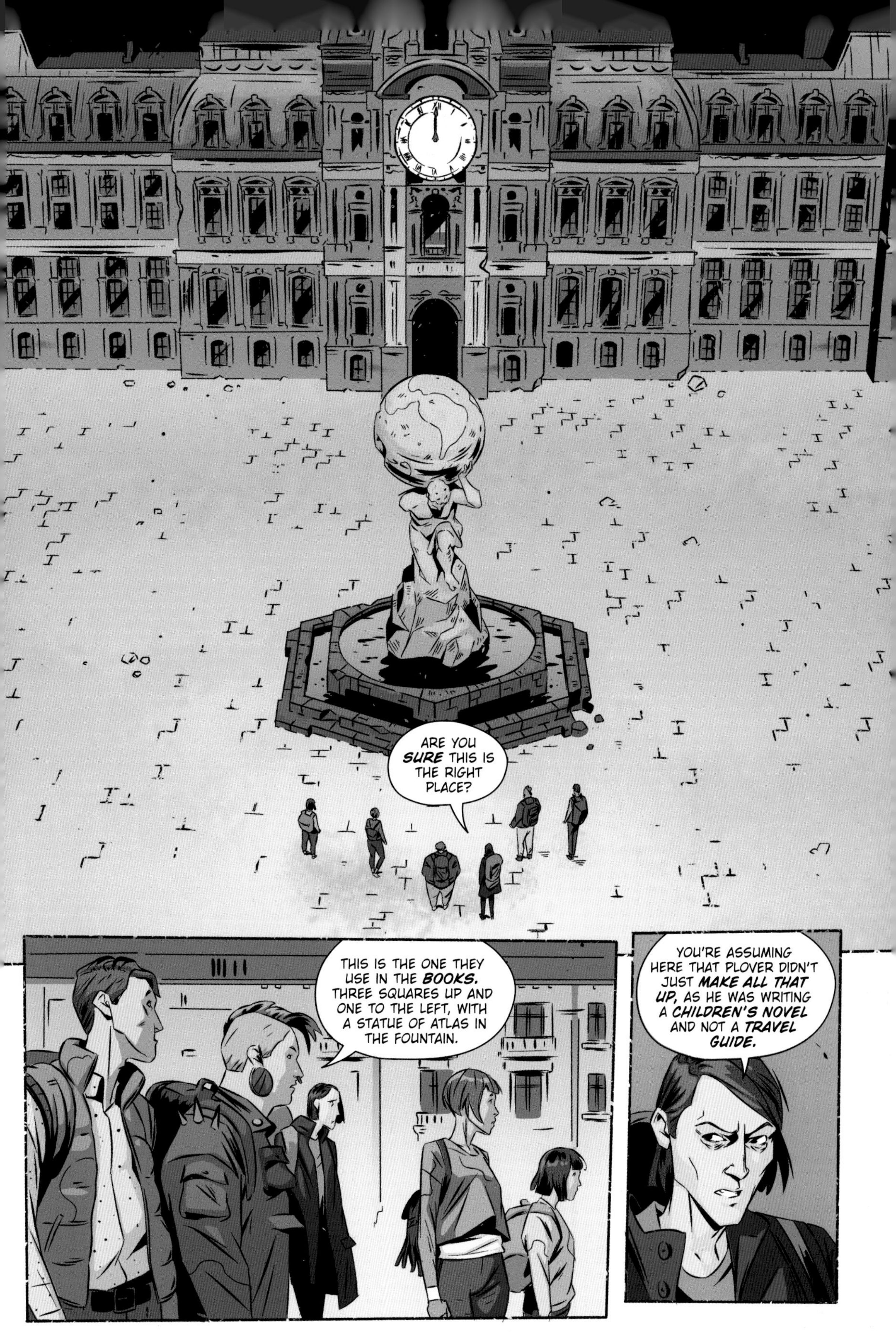

ARE YOU SURE THIS IS THE RIGHT PLACE?
THIS IS THE ONE THEY USE IN THE BOOKS. THREE SQUARES UP AND ONE TO THE LEFT, WITH A STATUE OF ATLAS IN THE FOUNTAIN.
YOU'RE ASSUMING HERE THAT PLOVER DIDN'T JUST MAKE ALL THAT UP, AS HE WAS WRITING A CHILDREN'S NOVEL AND NOT A TRAVEL GUIDE.

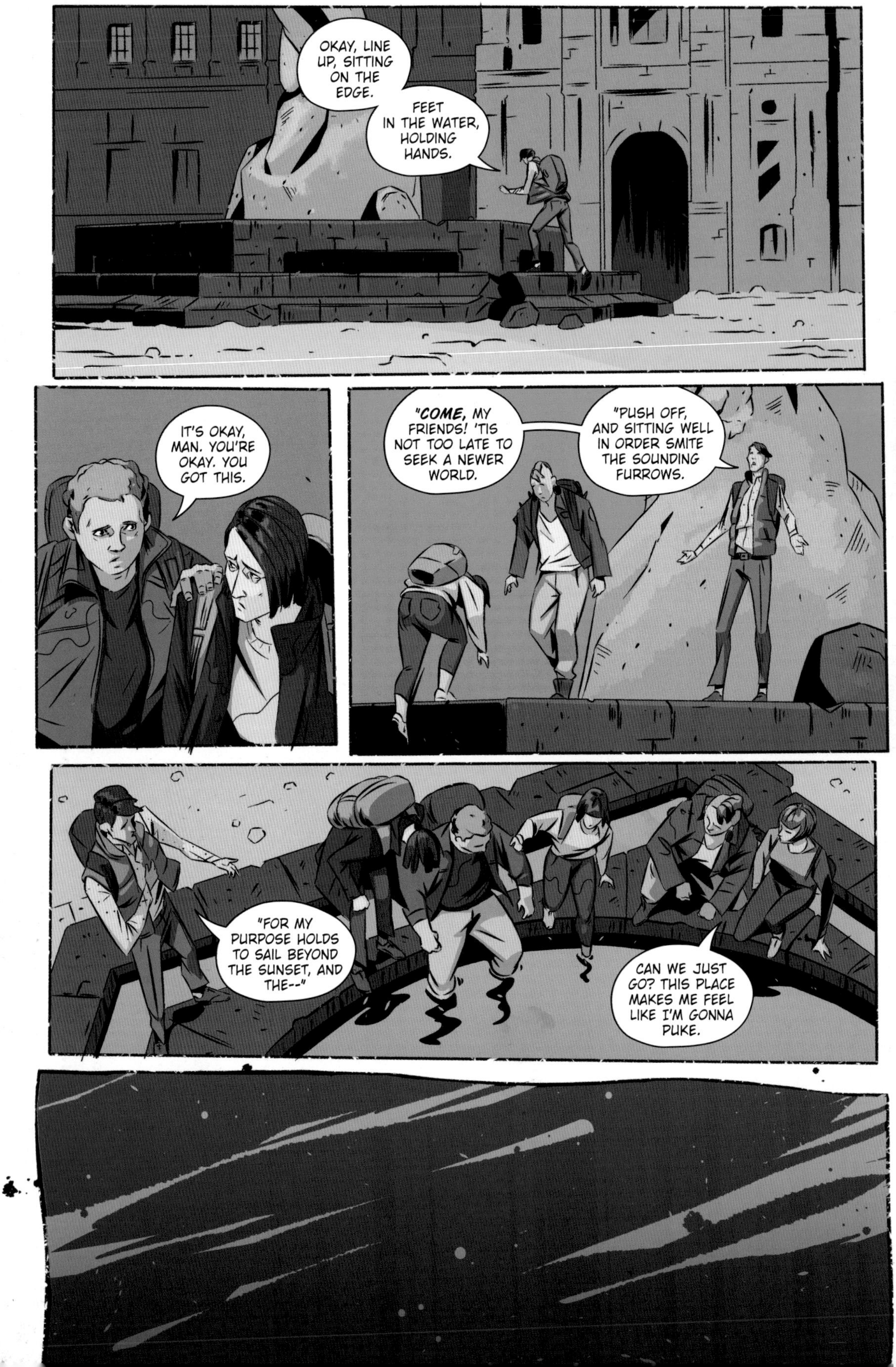
OKAY, LINE UP, SITTING ON THE EDGE.
FEET IN THE WATER, HOLDING HANDS.
IT'S OKAY, MAN. YOU'RE OKAY. YOU GOT THIS.
"COME, MY FRIENDS! 'TIS NOT TOO LATE TO SEEK A NEWER WORLD.
"PUSH OFF, AND SITTING WELL IN ORDER SMITE THE SOUNDING FURROWS.
"FOR MY PURPOSE HOLDS TO SAIL BEYOND THE SUNSET, AND THE--"
CAN WE JUST GO? THIS PLACE MAKES ME FEEL LIKE I'M GONNA PUKE.

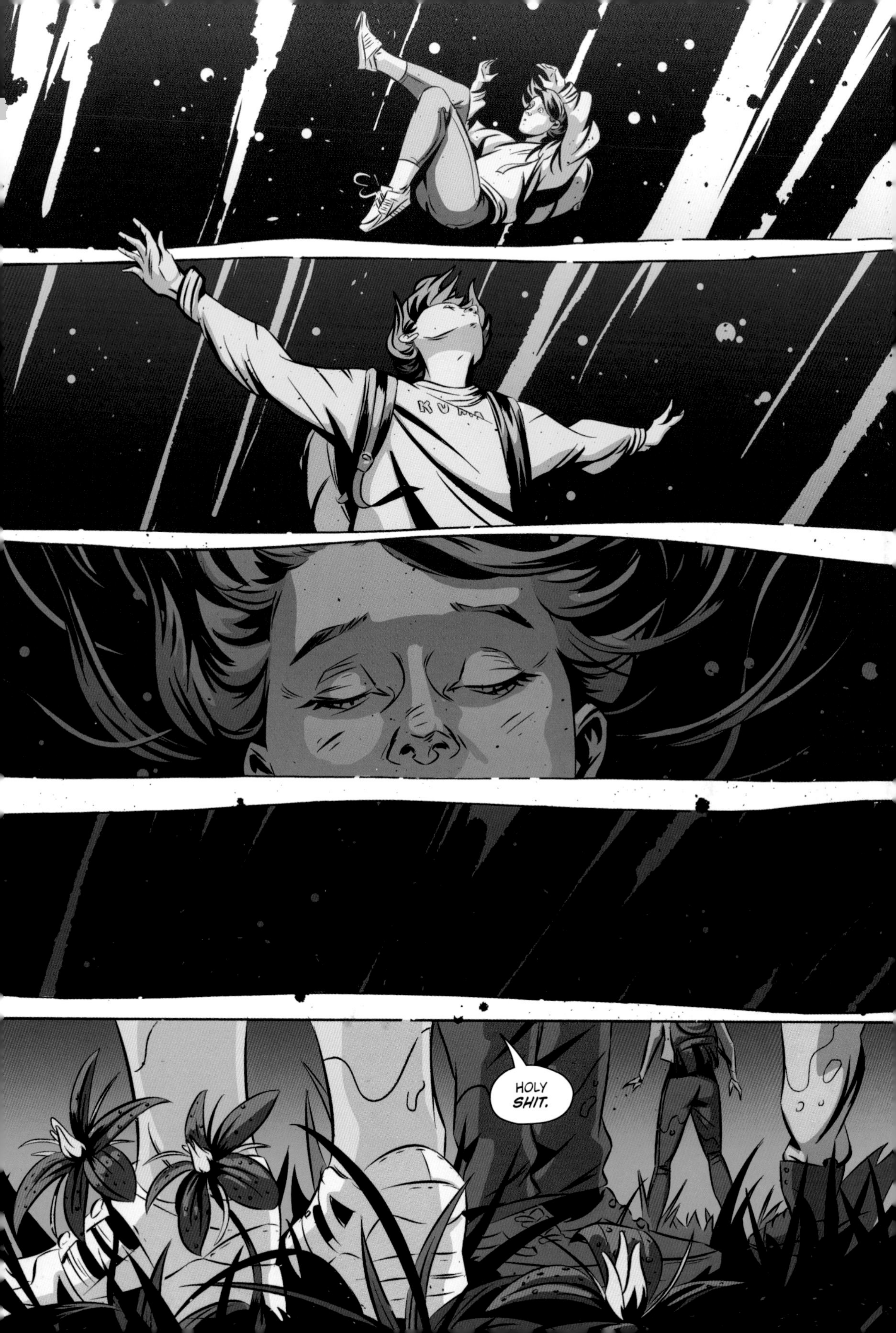
HOLY
SHIT.

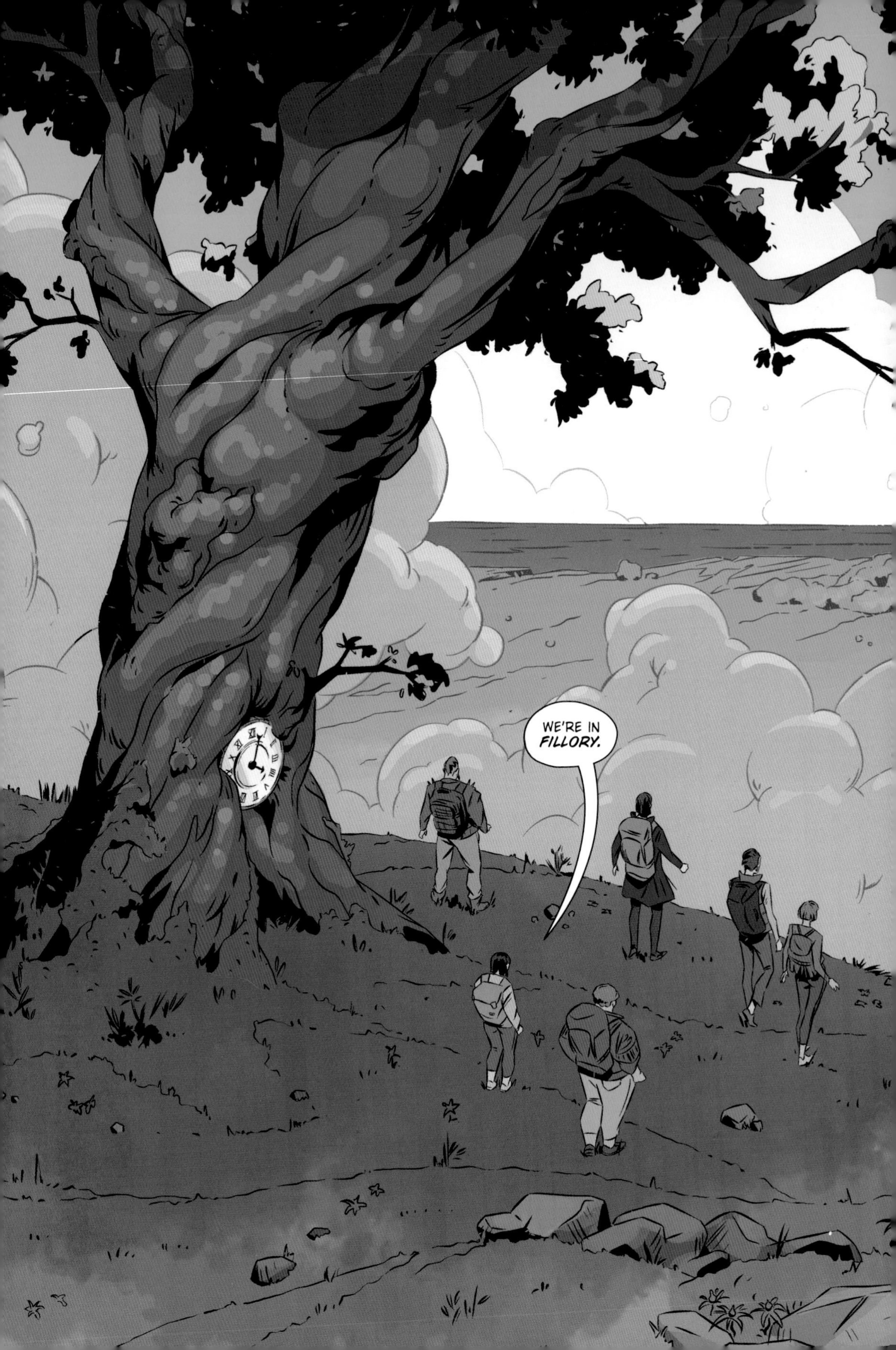
WE'RE IN FILLORY.

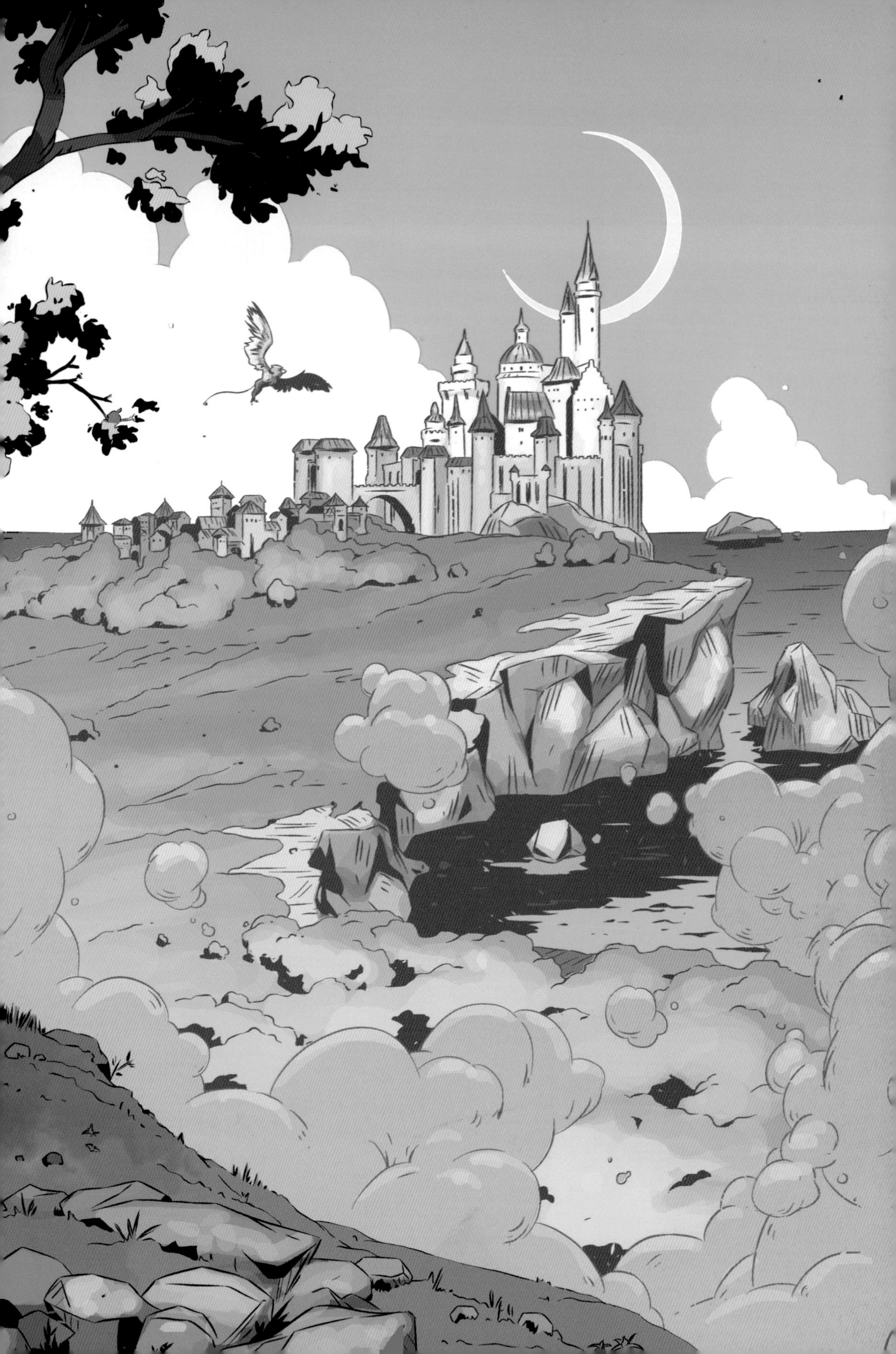

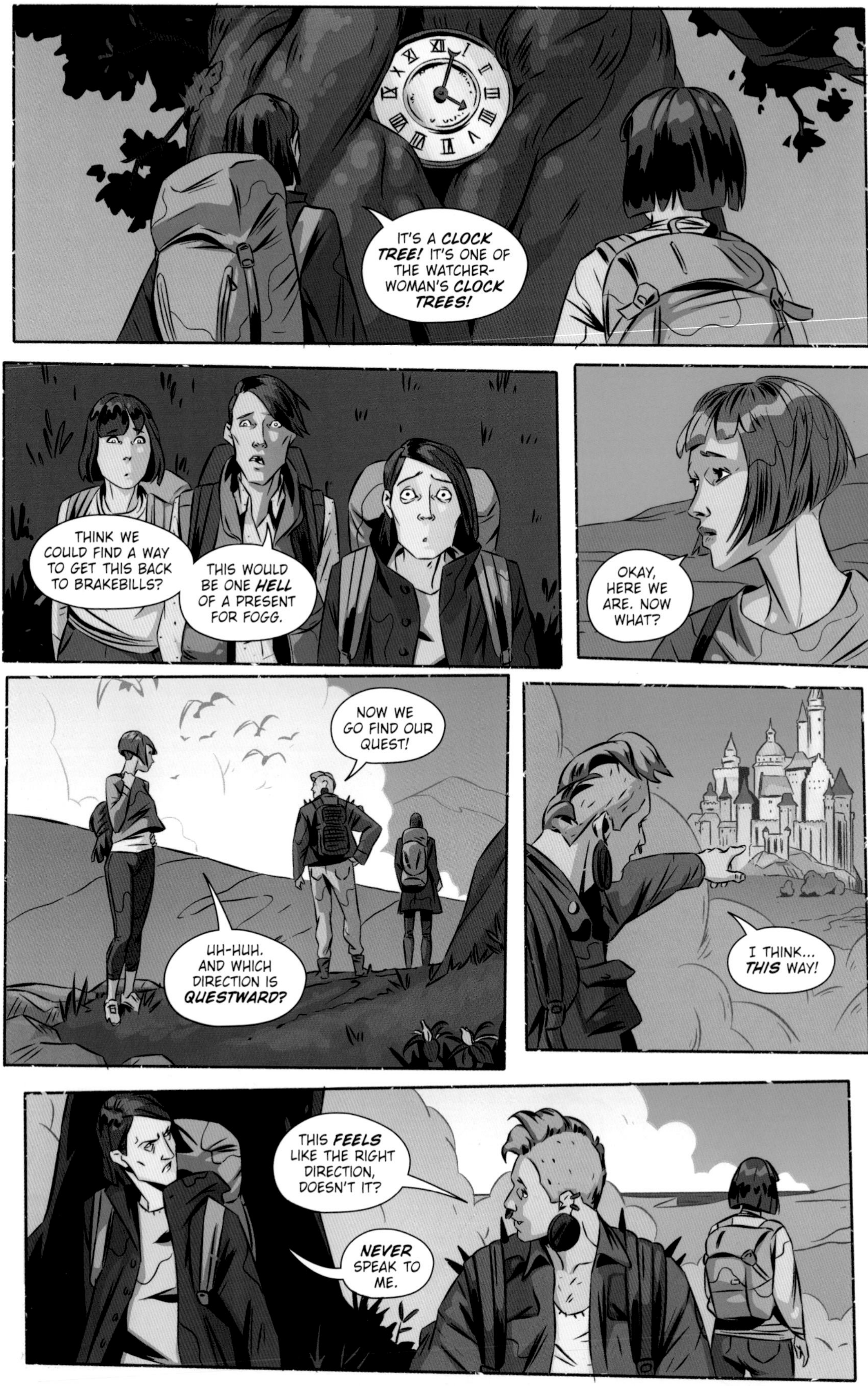
IT'S A CLOCK TREE! IT'S ONE OF THE WATCHER-WOMAN'S CLOCK TREES!
THINK WE COULD FIND A WAY TO GET THIS BACK TO BRAKEBILLS?
THIS WOULD BE ONE HELL OF A PRESENT FOR FOGG.
OKAY, HERE WE ARE. NOW WHAT?
NOW WE GO FIND OUR QUEST!
UH-HUH. AND WHICH DIRECTION IS QUESTWARD?
I THINK... THIS WAY!
THIS FEELS LIKE THE RIGHT DIRECTION, DOESN'T IT?
NEVER SPEAK TO ME.

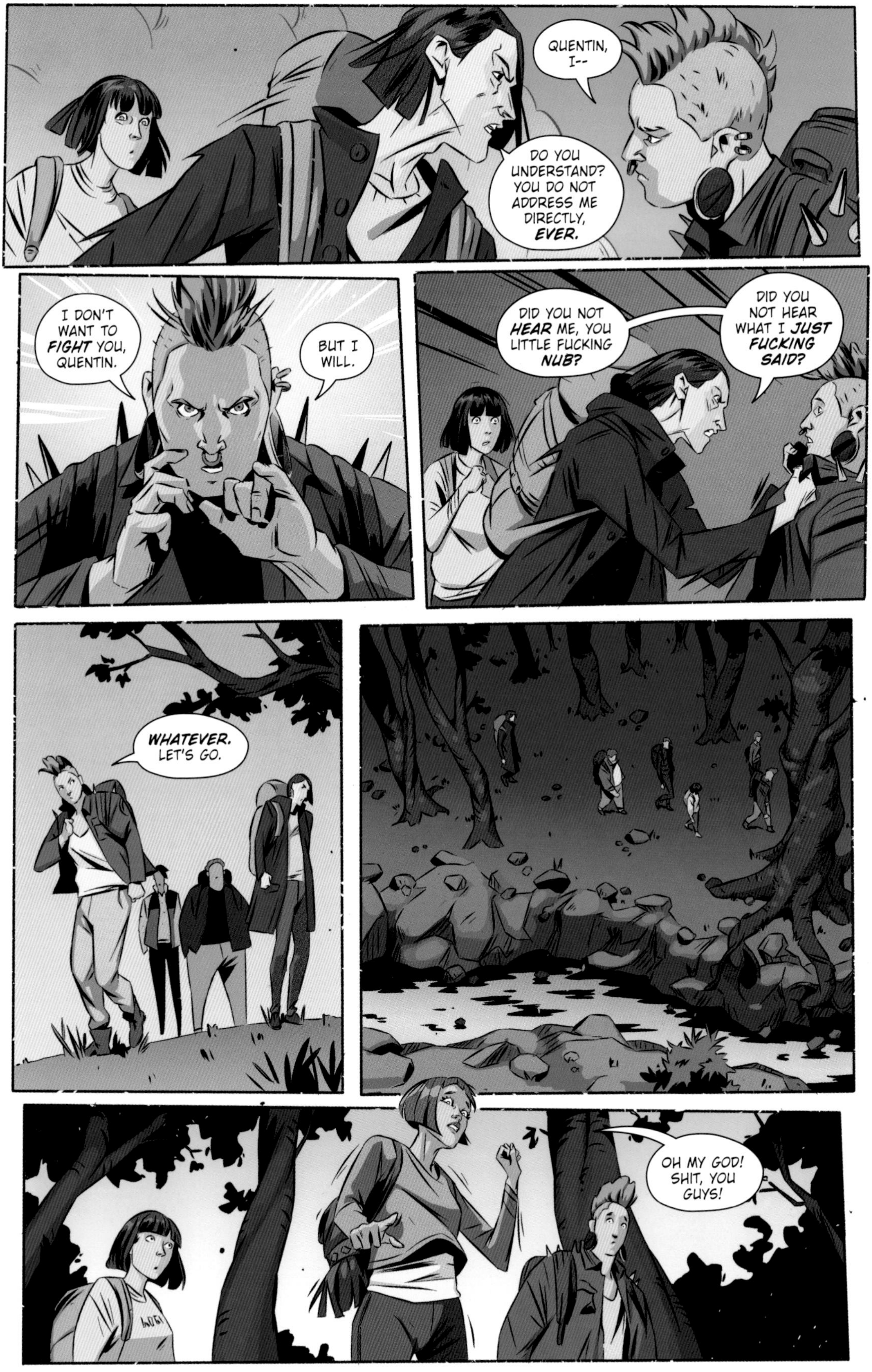
QUENTIN, I--
DO YOU UNDERSTAND? YOU DO NOT ADDRESS ME DIRECTLY, **EVER.**
I DON'T WANT TO **FIGHT** YOU, QUENTIN.
BUT I WILL.
DID YOU NOT **HEAR** ME, YOU LITTLE FUCKING **NUB?**
DID YOU NOT HEAR WHAT I **JUST FUCKING SAID?**
WHATEVER. LET'S GO.
OH MY GOD! SHIT, YOU GUYS!

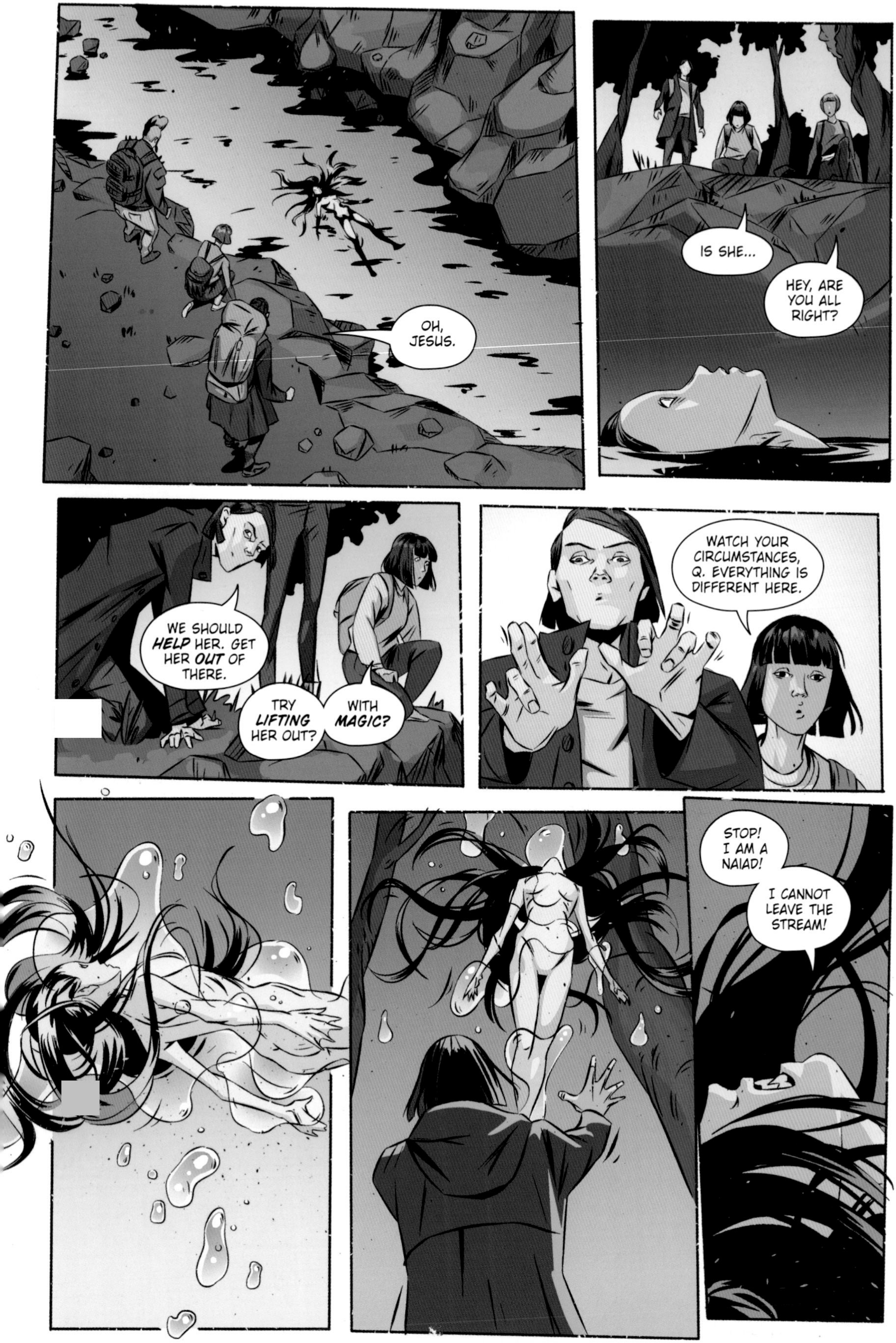
OH, JESUS.
IS SHE...
HEY, ARE YOU ALL RIGHT?
WE SHOULD HELP HER. GET HER OUT OF THERE.
TRY LIFTING HER OUT?
WITH MAGIC?
WATCH YOUR CIRCUMSTANCES, Q. EVERYTHING IS DIFFERENT HERE.
STOP! I AM A NAIAD!
I CANNOT LEAVE THE STREAM!

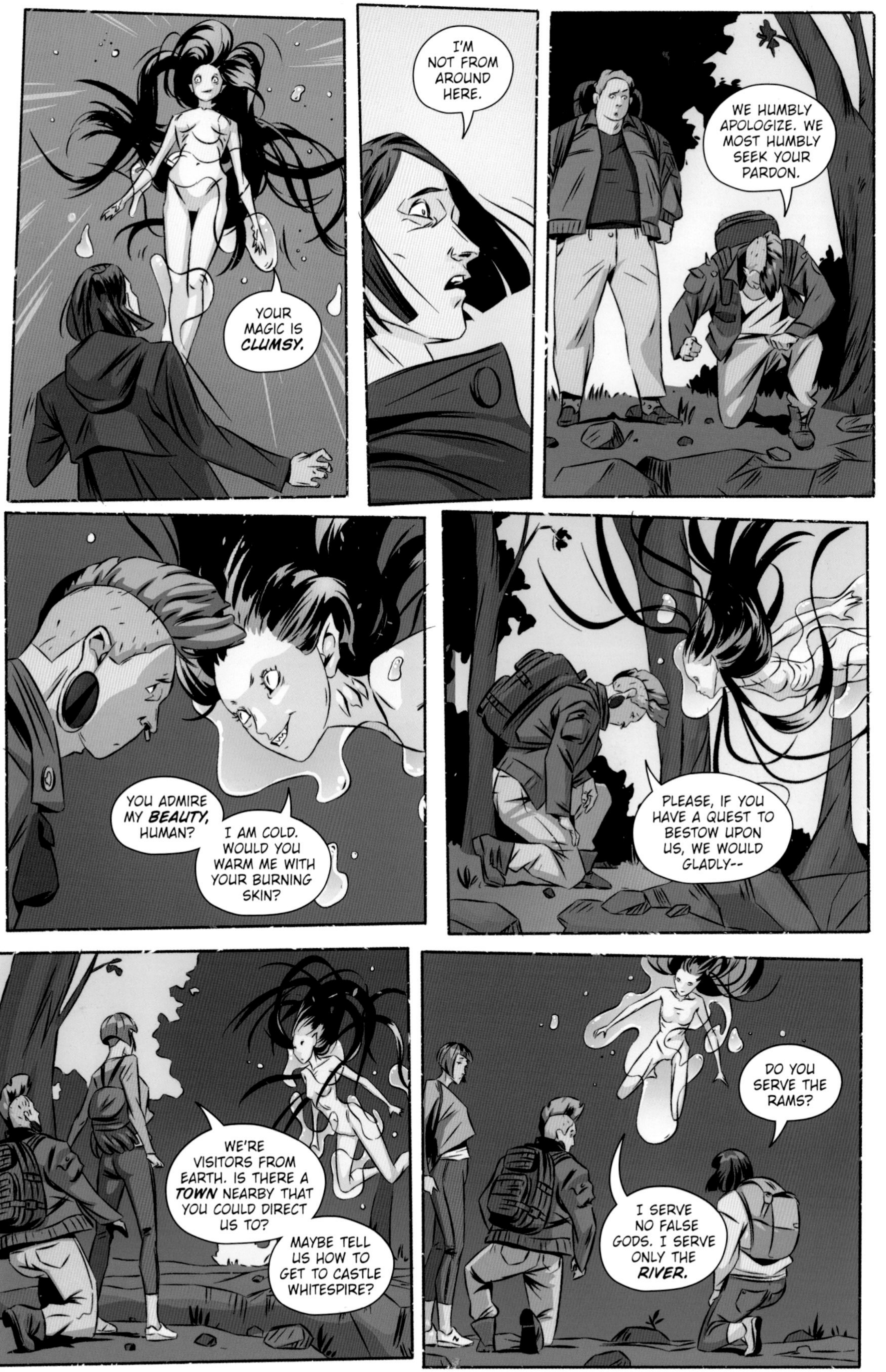
YOUR MAGIC IS CLUMSY.
I'M NOT FROM AROUND HERE.
WE HUMBLY APOLOGIZE. WE MOST HUMBLY SEEK YOUR PARDON.
YOU ADMIRE MY BEAUTY, HUMAN?
I AM COLD. WOULD YOU WARM ME WITH YOUR BURNING SKIN?
PLEASE, IF YOU HAVE A QUEST TO BESTOW UPON US, WE WOULD GLADLY--
WE'RE VISITORS FROM EARTH. IS THERE A TOWN NEARBY THAT YOU COULD DIRECT US TO?
MAYBE TELL US HOW TO GET TO CASTLE WHITESPIRE?
DO YOU SERVE THE RAMS?
I SERVE NO FALSE GODS. I SERVE ONLY THE RIVER.

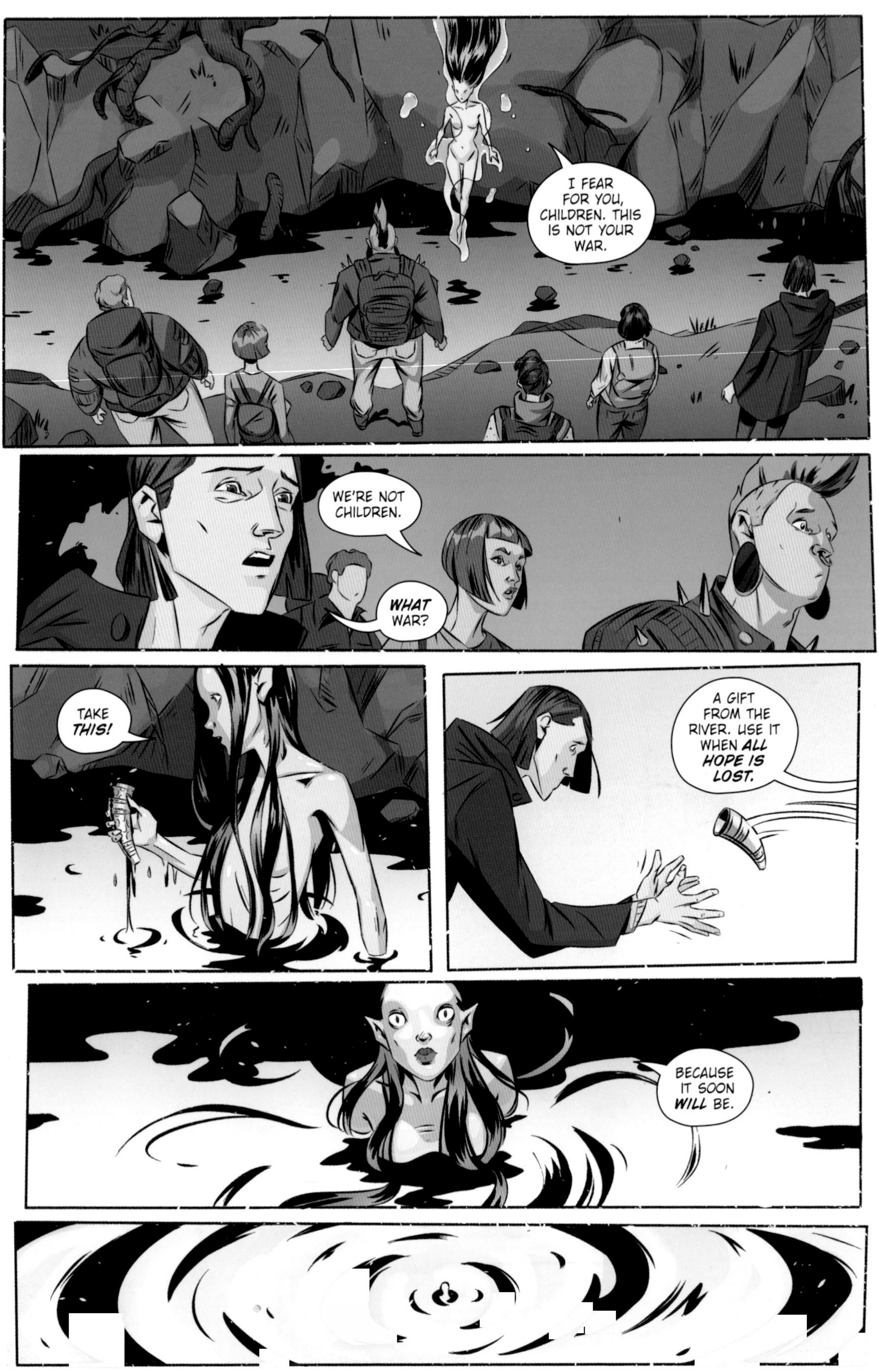
I FEAR FOR YOU, CHILDREN. THIS IS NOT YOUR WAR.
WE'RE NOT CHILDREN.
WHAT WAR?
TAKE THIS!
A GIFT FROM THE RIVER. USE IT WHEN ALL HOPE IS LOST.
BECAUSE IT SOON WILL BE.

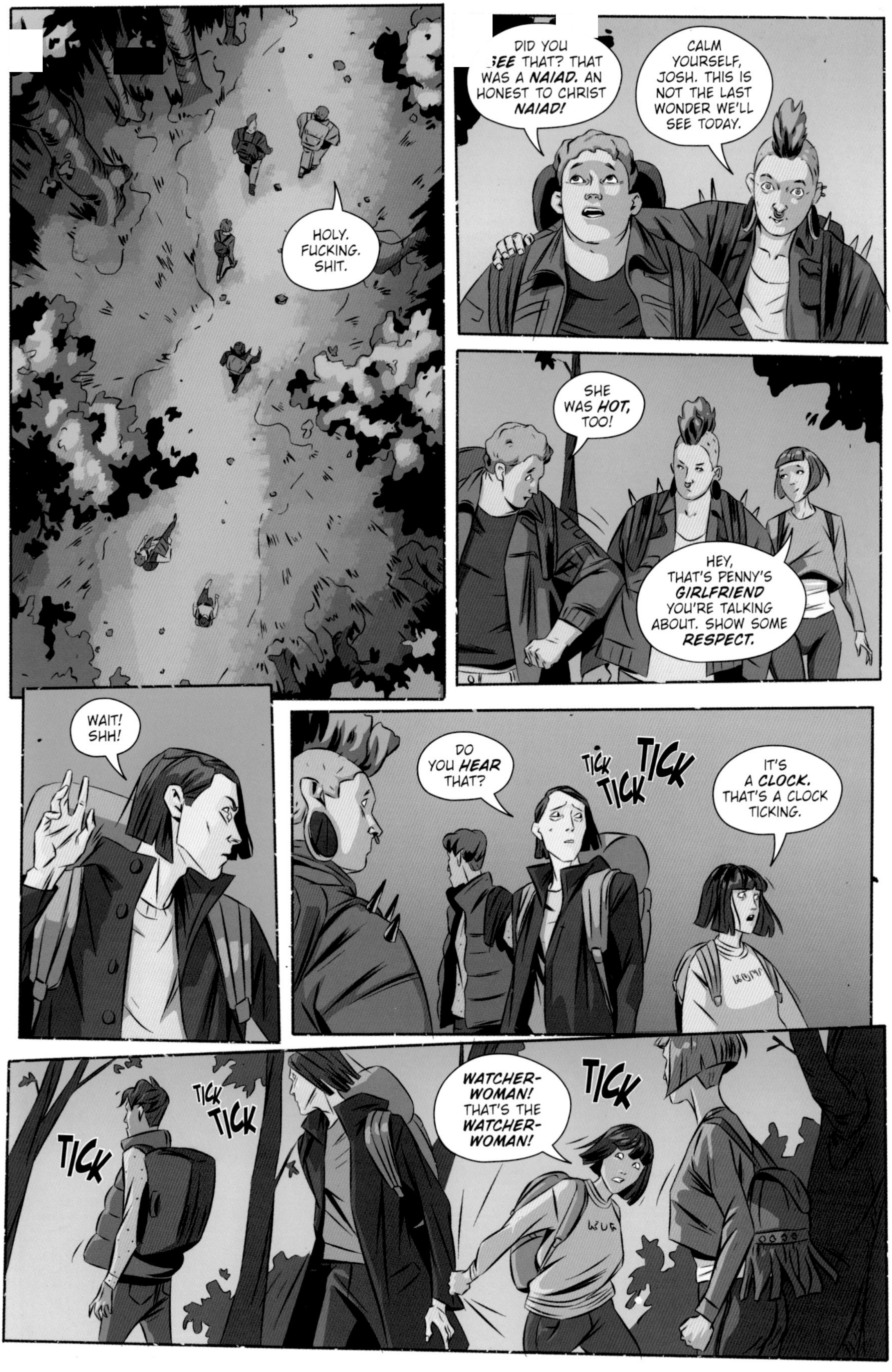
HOLY. FUCKING. SHIT.
DID YOU SEE THAT? THAT WAS A NAIAD. AN HONEST TO CHRIST NAIAD!
CALM YOURSELF, JOSH. THIS IS NOT THE LAST WONDER WE'LL SEE TODAY.
SHE WAS HOT, TOO!
HEY, THAT'S PENNY'S GIRLFRIEND YOU'RE TALKING ABOUT. SHOW SOME RESPECT.
WAIT! SHH!
DO YOU HEAR THAT?
TICK TICK TICK
IT'S A CLOCK. THAT'S A CLOCK TICKING.
TICK TICK TICK
WATCHER-WOMAN! THAT'S THE WATCHER-WOMAN!
TICK

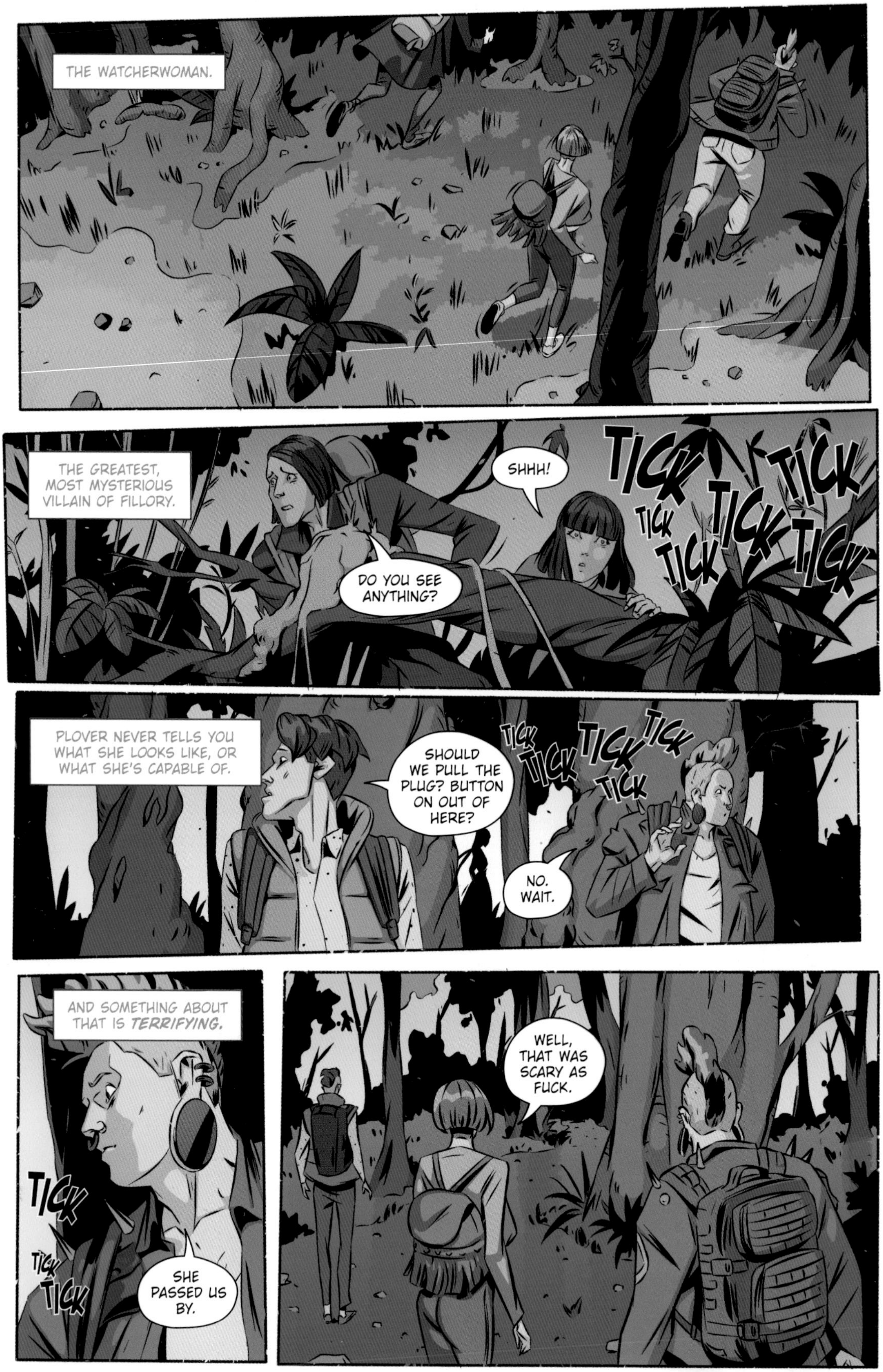
THE WATCHERWOMAN.
THE GREATEST, MOST MYSTERIOUS VILLAIN OF FILLORY.
SHHH!
DO YOU SEE ANYTHING?
TICK TICK TICK TICK TICK TICK
PLOVER NEVER TELLS YOU WHAT SHE LOOKS LIKE, OR WHAT SHE'S CAPABLE OF.
SHOULD WE PULL THE PLUG? BUTTON ON OUT OF HERE?
TICK TICK TICK TICK TICK
NO. WAIT.
AND SOMETHING ABOUT THAT IS *TERRIFYING.*
TICK TICK TICK
SHE PASSED US BY.
WELL, THAT WAS SCARY AS FUCK.

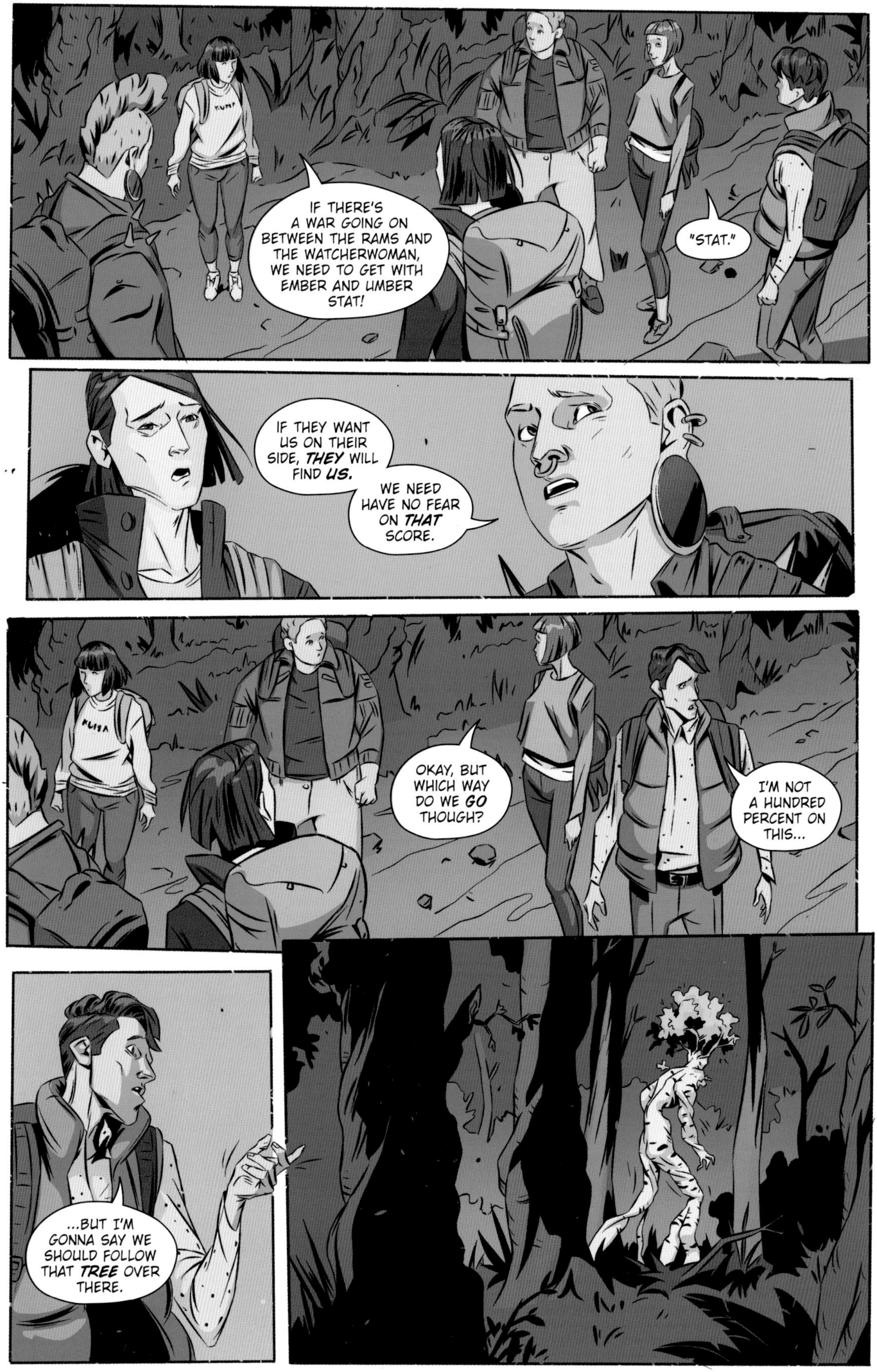
IF THERE'S A WAR GOING ON BETWEEN THE RAMS AND THE WATCHERWOMAN, WE NEED TO GET WITH EMBER AND UMBER STAT!
"STAT."
IF THEY WANT US ON THEIR SIDE, *THEY* WILL FIND *US.*
WE NEED HAVE NO FEAR ON *THAT* SCORE.
OKAY, BUT WHICH WAY DO WE *GO* THOUGH?
I'M NOT A HUNDRED PERCENT ON THIS...
...BUT I'M GONNA SAY WE SHOULD FOLLOW THAT *TREE* OVER THERE.

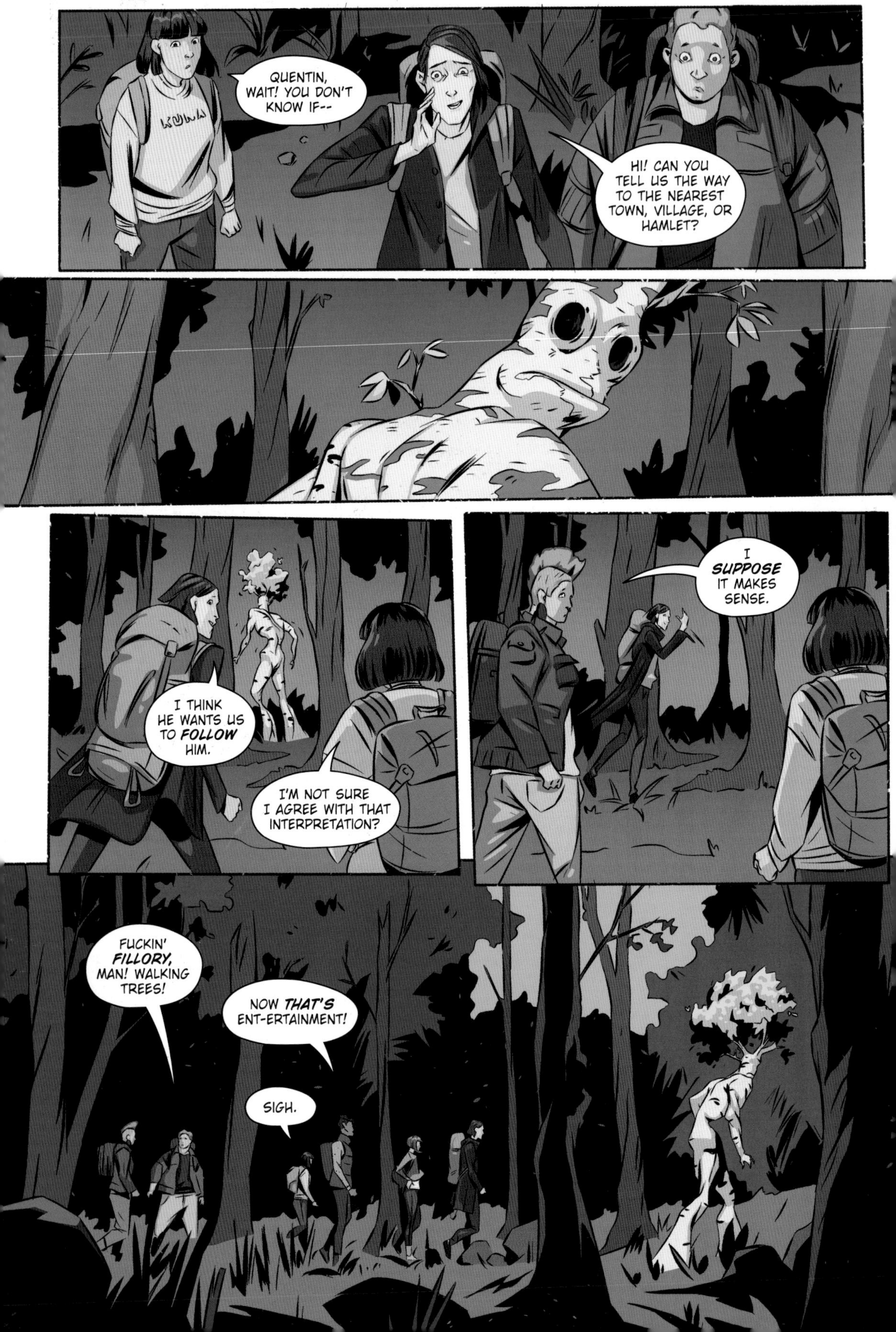
QUENTIN, WAIT! YOU DON'T KNOW IF--
HI! CAN YOU TELL US THE WAY TO THE NEAREST TOWN, VILLAGE, OR HAMLET?
I THINK HE WANTS US TO *FOLLOW* HIM.
I'M NOT SURE I AGREE WITH THAT INTERPRETATION?
I *SUPPOSE* IT MAKES SENSE.
FUCKIN' *FILLORY,* MAN! WALKING TREES!
NOW *THAT'S* ENT-ERTAINMENT!
SIGH.

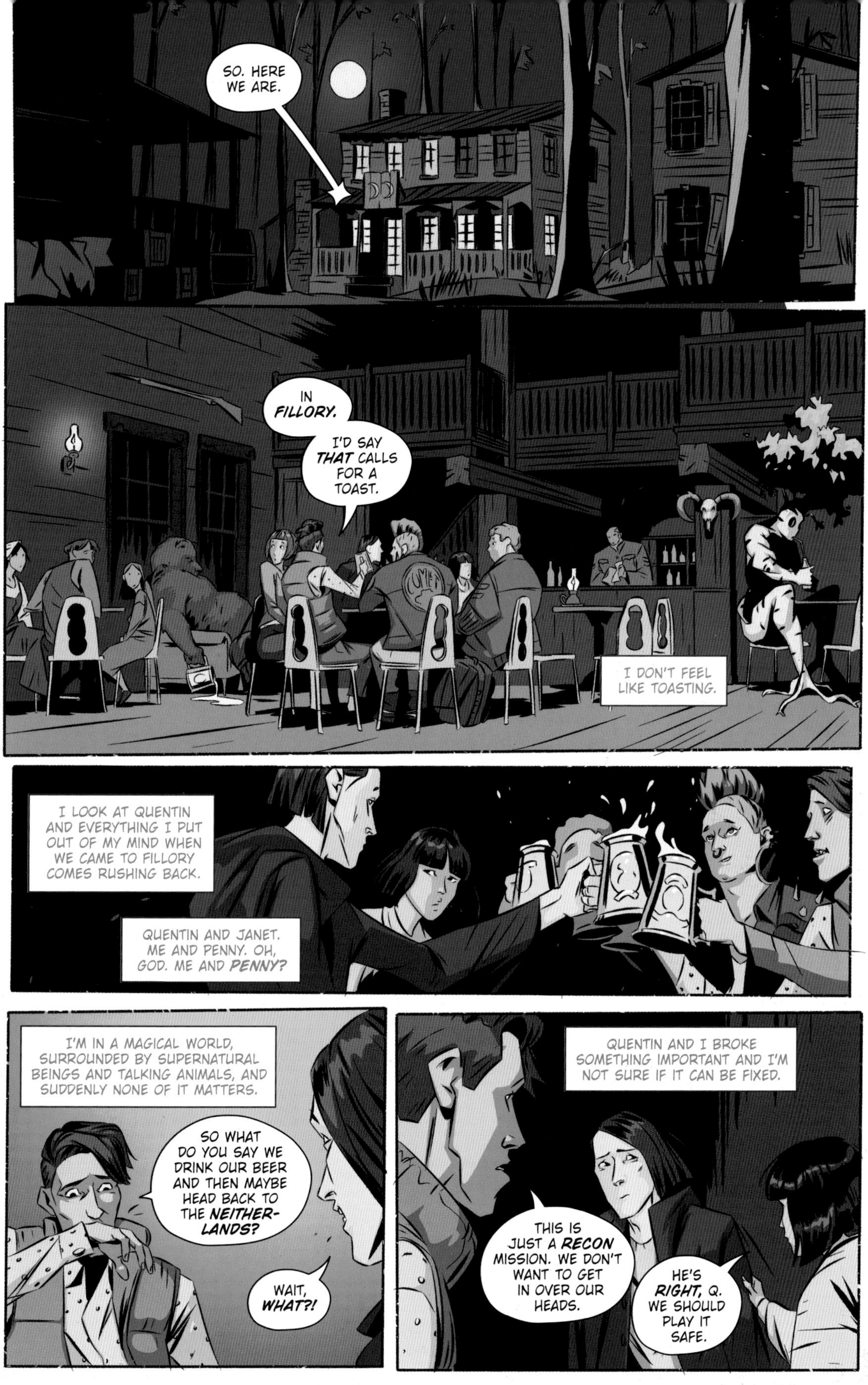
SO. HERE WE ARE.
IN FILLORY.
I'D SAY THAT CALLS FOR A TOAST.
I DON'T FEEL LIKE TOASTING.
I LOOK AT QUENTIN AND EVERYTHING I PUT OUT OF MY MIND WHEN WE CAME TO FILLORY COMES RUSHING BACK.
QUENTIN AND JANET. ME AND PENNY. OH, GOD. ME AND PENNY?
I'M IN A MAGICAL WORLD, SURROUNDED BY SUPERNATURAL BEINGS AND TALKING ANIMALS, AND SUDDENLY NONE OF IT MATTERS.
SO WHAT DO YOU SAY WE DRINK OUR BEER AND THEN MAYBE HEAD BACK TO THE NEITHER-LANDS?
WAIT, WHAT?!
QUENTIN AND I BROKE SOMETHING IMPORTANT AND I'M NOT SURE IF IT CAN BE FIXED.
THIS IS JUST A RECON MISSION. WE DON'T WANT TO GET IN OVER OUR HEADS.
HE'S RIGHT, Q. WE SHOULD PLAY IT SAFE.

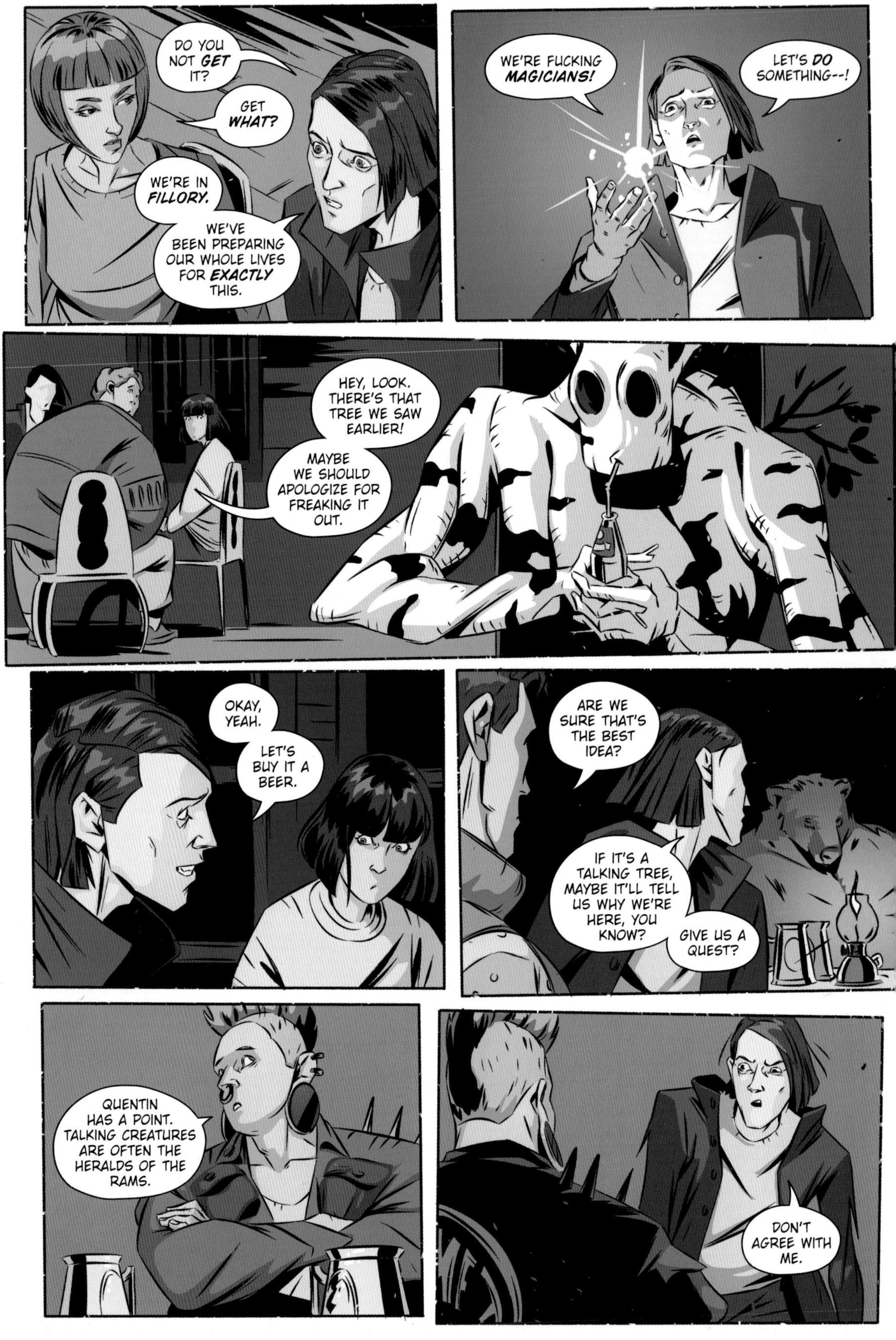
DO YOU NOT GET IT?
GET WHAT?
WE'RE IN FILLORY.
WE'VE BEEN PREPARING OUR WHOLE LIVES FOR EXACTLY THIS.
WE'RE FUCKING MAGICIANS!
LET'S DO SOMETHING--!
HEY, LOOK. THERE'S THAT TREE WE SAW EARLIER!
MAYBE WE SHOULD APOLOGIZE FOR FREAKING IT OUT.
OKAY, YEAH.
LET'S BUY IT A BEER.
ARE WE SURE THAT'S THE BEST IDEA?
IF IT'S A TALKING TREE, MAYBE IT'LL TELL US WHY WE'RE HERE, YOU KNOW?
GIVE US A QUEST?
QUENTIN HAS A POINT. TALKING CREATURES ARE OFTEN THE HERALDS OF THE RAMS.
DON'T AGREE WITH ME.

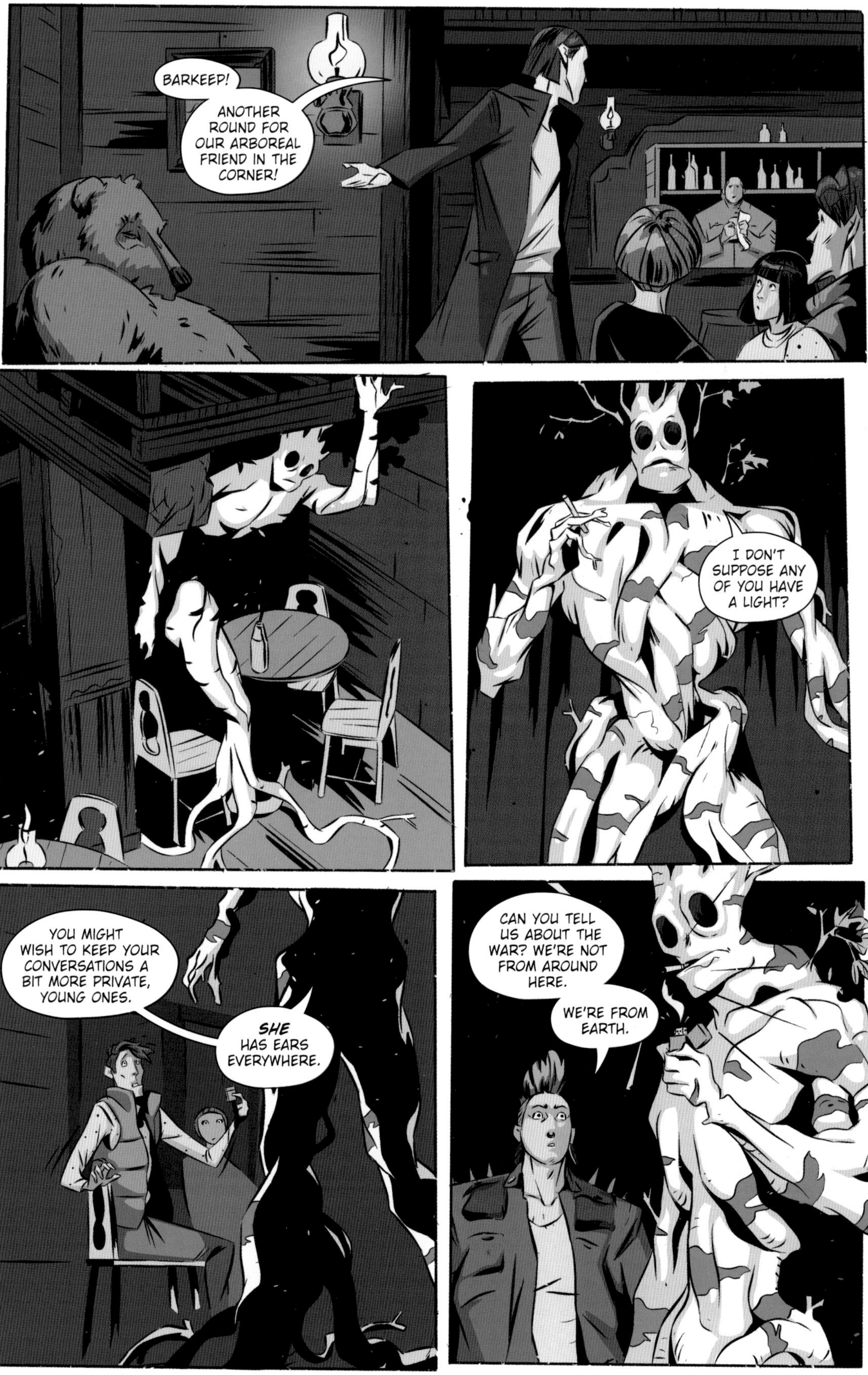
BARKEEP!
ANOTHER ROUND FOR OUR ARBOREAL FRIEND IN THE CORNER!
I DON'T SUPPOSE ANY OF YOU HAVE A LIGHT?
YOU MIGHT WISH TO KEEP YOUR CONVERSATIONS A BIT MORE PRIVATE, YOUNG ONES.
SHE HAS EARS EVERYWHERE.
CAN YOU TELL US ABOUT THE WAR? WE'RE NOT FROM AROUND HERE.
WE'RE FROM EARTH.

IT'S AS I HOPED! WHY, I NEVER THOUGHT I'D LIVE TO SEE THIS DAY!

DO YOU THINK IT'S WISE FOR YOU TO SMOKE? GIVEN THAT YOU'RE LITERALLY MADE ENTIRELY OF WOOD?

I AM FARVEL, SONS AND DAUGHTERS OF EARTH, AND I AM AT YOUR SERVICE.

NOW THAT'S MORE LIKE IT!

PERHAPS THERE IS HOPE AFTER ALL!

WHAT THIS WAR-RAVAGED COUNTRY NEEDS IS *KINGS AND QUEENS!*

THE THRONES IN CASTLE WHITESPIRE HAVE BEEN EMPTY TOO LONG, AND THEY CAN ONLY BE FILLED BY THE SONS AND DAUGHTERS OF EARTH.

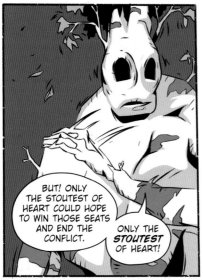

BUT! ONLY THE STOUTEST OF HEART COULD HOPE TO WIN THOSE SEATS AND END THE CONFLICT.

ONLY THE *STOUTEST* OF HEART!

AND WHAT WOULD THAT *INVOLVE,* FARVEL MY MAN?

WHY, YOU WOULD HAVE TO BRAVE EMBER'S TOMB AND RETRIEVE KING MARTIN'S CROWN.

BRING THE CROWN TO CASTLE WHITESPIRE AND YOU MAY OCCUPY THE THRONES YOURSELVES.

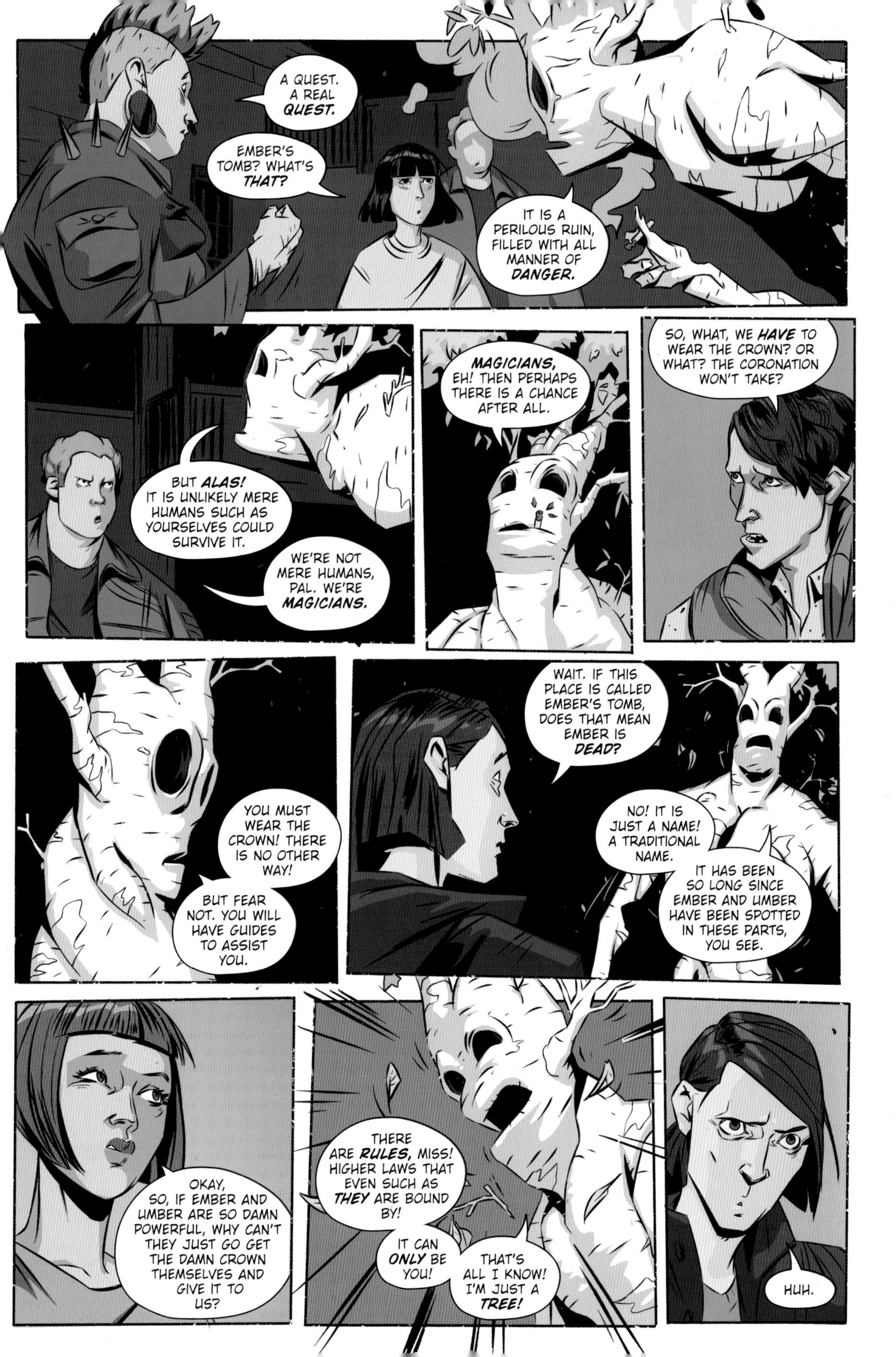
A QUEST. A REAL QUEST.
EMBER'S TOMB? WHAT'S THAT?
IT IS A PERILOUS RUIN, FILLED WITH ALL MANNER OF DANGER.
BUT ALAS! IT IS UNLIKELY MERE HUMANS SUCH AS YOURSELVES COULD SURVIVE IT.
WE'RE NOT MERE HUMANS, PAL. WE'RE MAGICIANS.
MAGICIANS, EH! THEN PERHAPS THERE IS A CHANCE AFTER ALL.
SO, WHAT, WE HAVE TO WEAR THE CROWN? OR WHAT? THE CORONATION WON'T TAKE?
YOU MUST WEAR THE CROWN! THERE IS NO OTHER WAY!
BUT FEAR NOT. YOU WILL HAVE GUIDES TO ASSIST YOU.
WAIT. IF THIS PLACE IS CALLED EMBER'S TOMB, DOES THAT MEAN EMBER IS DEAD?
NO! IT IS JUST A NAME! A TRADITIONAL NAME.
IT HAS BEEN SO LONG SINCE EMBER AND UMBER HAVE BEEN SPOTTED IN THESE PARTS, YOU SEE.
OKAY, SO, IF EMBER AND UMBER ARE SO DAMN POWERFUL, WHY CAN'T THEY JUST GO GET THE DAMN CROWN THEMSELVES AND GIVE IT TO US?
THERE ARE RULES, MISS! HIGHER LAWS THAT EVEN SUCH AS THEY ARE BOUND BY!
IT CAN ONLY BE YOU!
THAT'S ALL I KNOW! I'M JUST A TREE!
HUH.

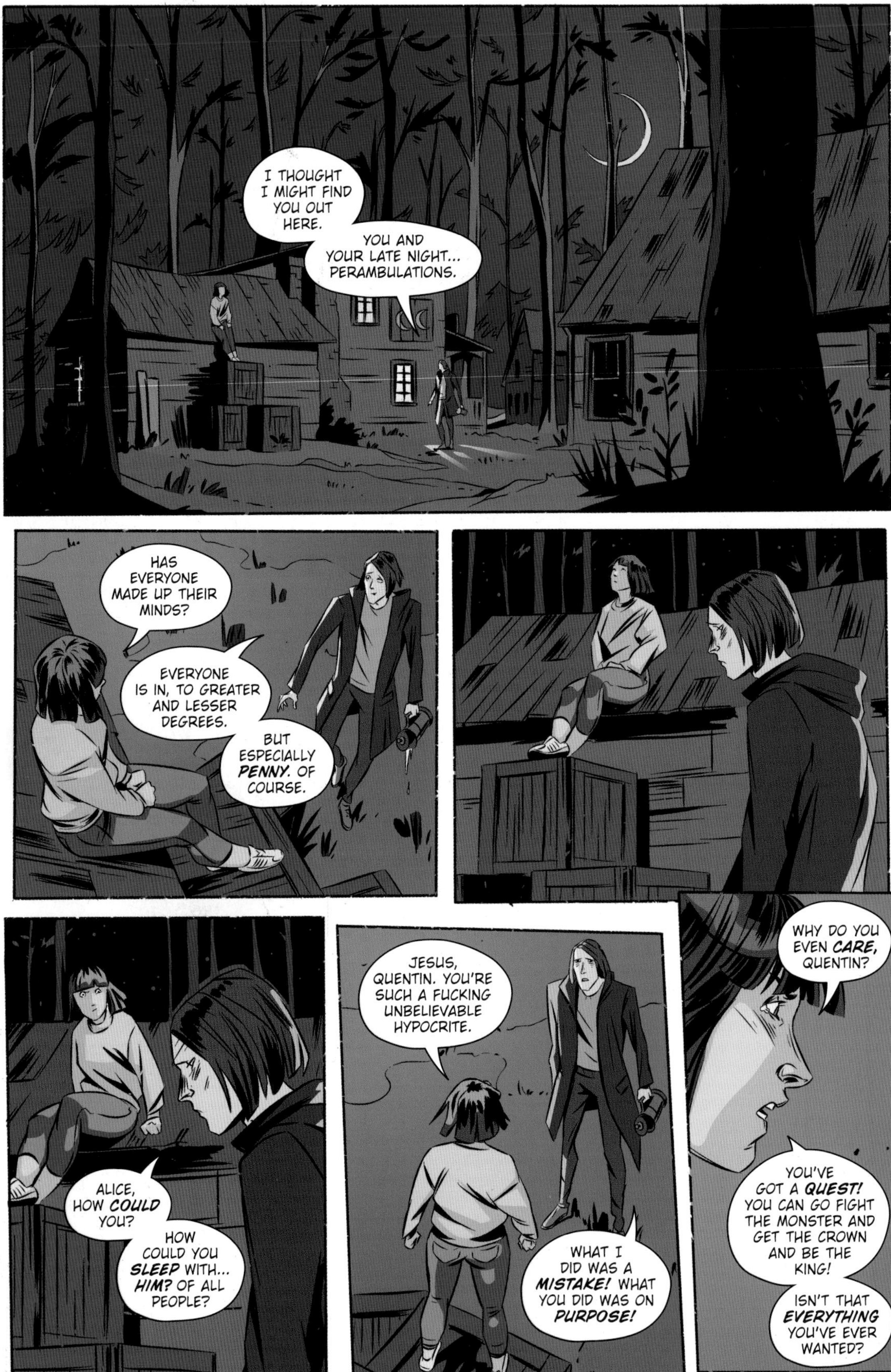
I THOUGHT I MIGHT FIND YOU OUT HERE.
YOU AND YOUR LATE NIGHT... PERAMBULATIONS.
HAS EVERYONE MADE UP THEIR MINDS?
EVERYONE IS IN, TO GREATER AND LESSER DEGREES.
BUT ESPECIALLY *PENNY*. OF COURSE.
ALICE, HOW *COULD* YOU?
HOW COULD YOU *SLEEP* WITH... *HIM?* OF ALL PEOPLE?
JESUS, QUENTIN. YOU'RE SUCH A FUCKING UNBELIEVABLE HYPOCRITE.
WHAT I DID WAS A *MISTAKE!* WHAT YOU DID WAS ON *PURPOSE!*
WHY DO YOU EVEN *CARE,* QUENTIN?
YOU'VE GOT A *QUEST!* YOU CAN GO FIGHT THE MONSTER AND GET THE CROWN AND BE THE KING!
ISN'T THAT *EVERYTHING* YOU'VE EVER WANTED?

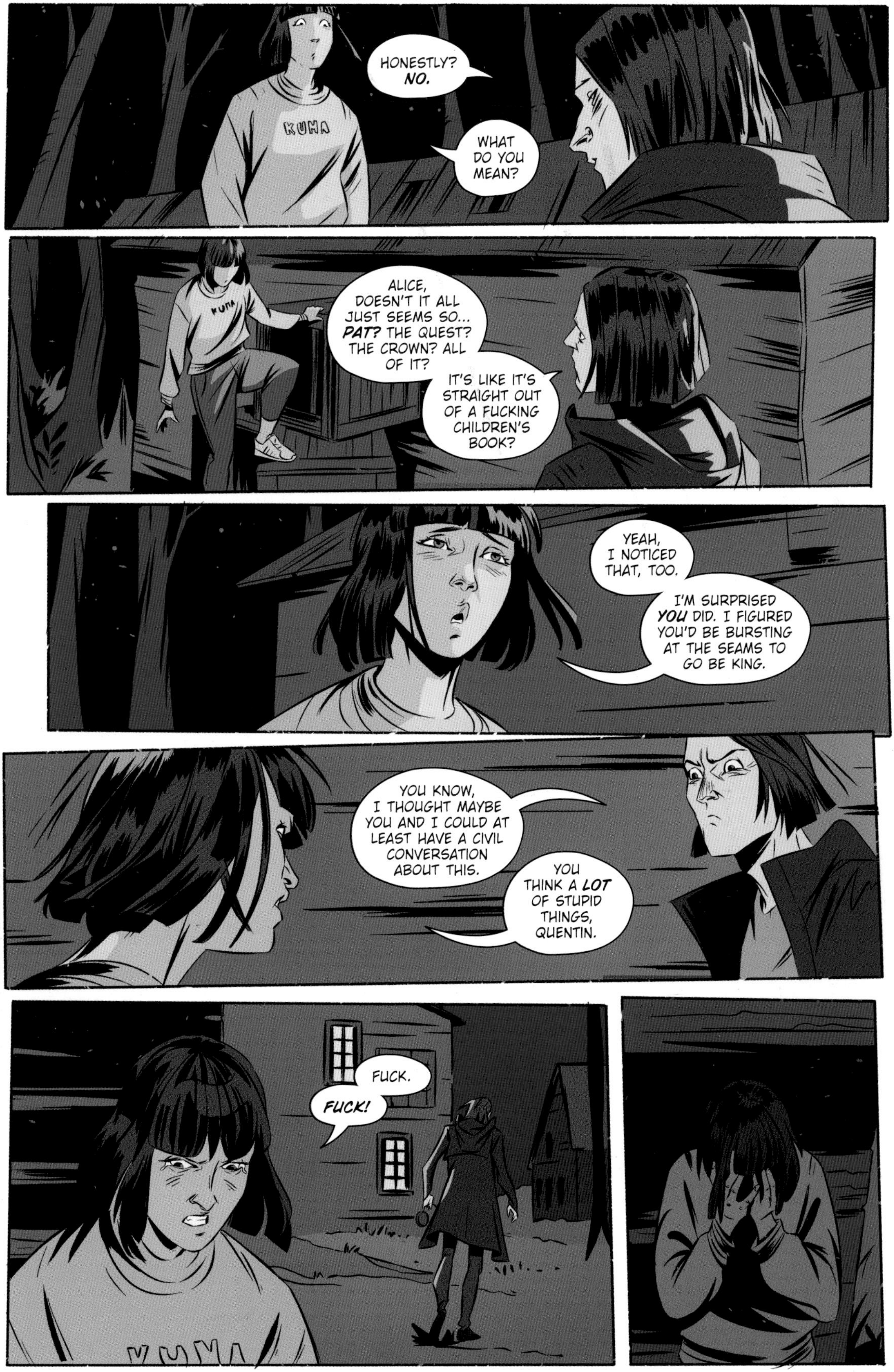

HONESTLY? *NO.*
WHAT DO YOU MEAN?
ALICE, DOESN'T IT ALL JUST SEEMS SO... *PAT?* THE QUEST? THE CROWN? ALL OF IT?
IT'S LIKE IT'S STRAIGHT OUT OF A FUCKING CHILDREN'S BOOK?
YEAH, I NOTICED THAT, TOO.
I'M SURPRISED *YOU* DID. I FIGURED YOU'D BE BURSTING AT THE SEAMS TO GO BE KING.
YOU KNOW, I THOUGHT MAYBE YOU AND I COULD AT LEAST HAVE A CIVIL CONVERSATION ABOUT THIS.
YOU THINK A *LOT* OF STUPID THINGS, QUENTIN.
FUCK.
FUCK!

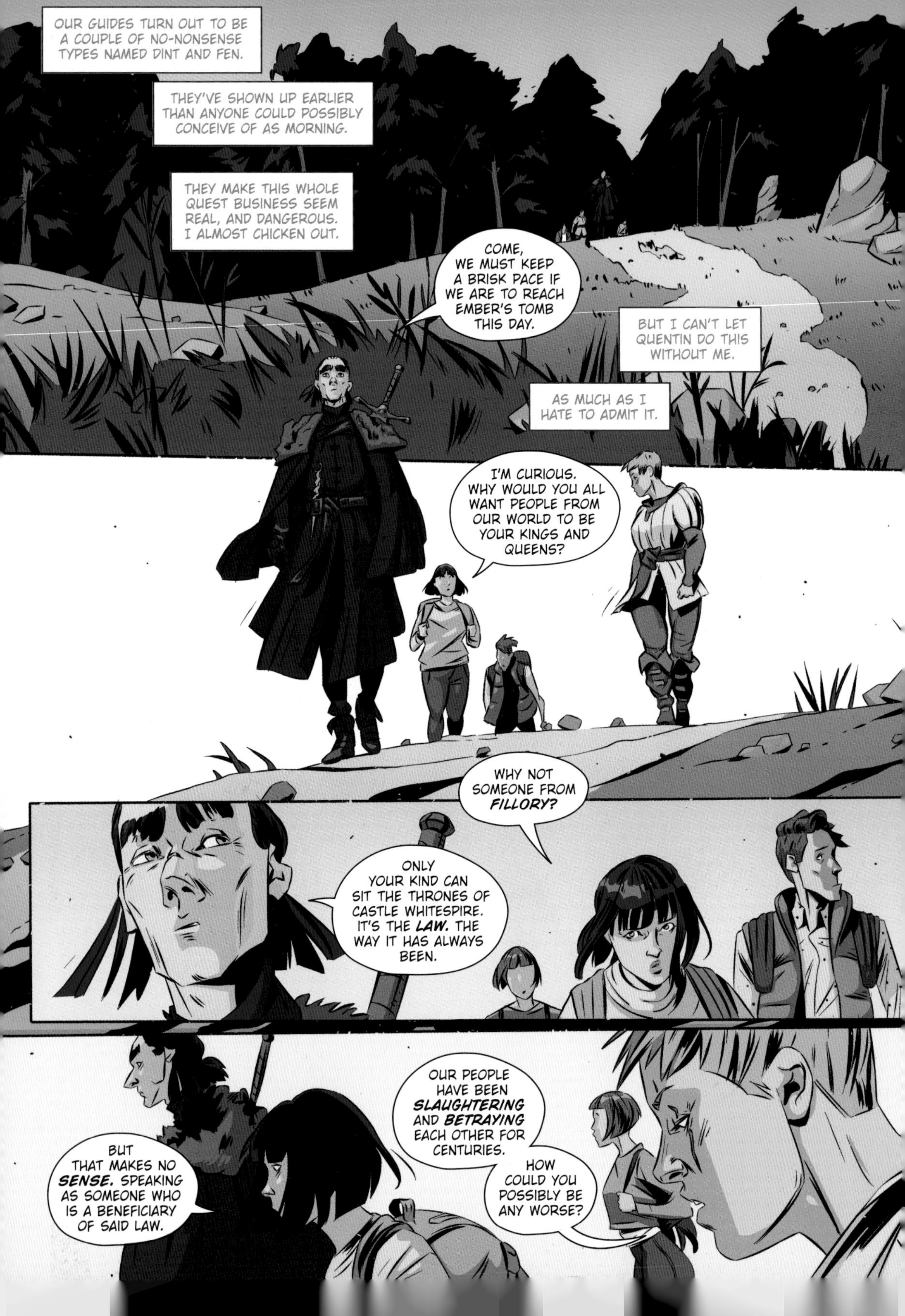

OUR GUIDES TURN OUT TO BE A COUPLE OF NO-NONSENSE TYPES NAMED DINT AND FEN.
THEY'VE SHOWN UP EARLIER THAN ANYONE COULD POSSIBLY CONCEIVE OF AS MORNING.
THEY MAKE THIS WHOLE QUEST BUSINESS SEEM REAL, AND DANGEROUS. I ALMOST CHICKEN OUT.
COME, WE MUST KEEP A BRISK PACE IF WE ARE TO REACH EMBER'S TOMB THIS DAY.
BUT I CAN'T LET QUENTIN DO THIS WITHOUT ME.
AS MUCH AS I HATE TO ADMIT IT.
I'M CURIOUS. WHY WOULD YOU ALL WANT PEOPLE FROM OUR WORLD TO BE YOUR KINGS AND QUEENS?
WHY NOT SOMEONE FROM ***FILLORY?***
ONLY YOUR KIND CAN SIT THE THRONES OF CASTLE WHITESPIRE. IT'S THE ***LAW.*** THE WAY IT HAS ALWAYS BEEN.
BUT THAT MAKES NO ***SENSE.*** SPEAKING AS SOMEONE WHO IS A BENEFICIARY OF SAID LAW.
OUR PEOPLE HAVE BEEN ***SLAUGHTERING*** AND ***BETRAYING*** EACH OTHER FOR CENTURIES.
HOW COULD YOU POSSIBLY BE ANY WORSE?

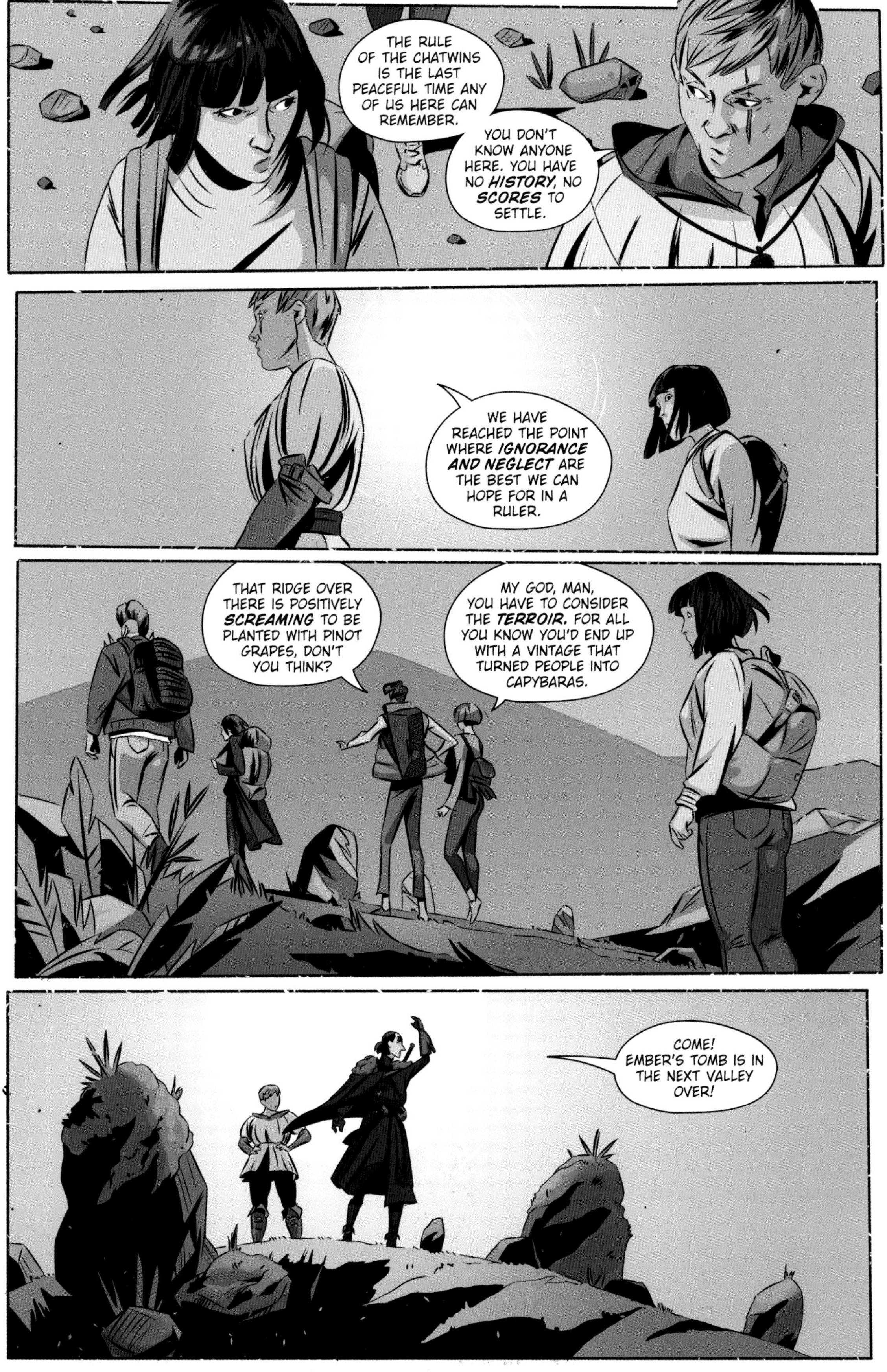
THE RULE OF THE CHATWINS IS THE LAST PEACEFUL TIME ANY OF US HERE CAN REMEMBER.
YOU DON'T KNOW ANYONE HERE. YOU HAVE NO *HISTORY*, NO *SCORES* TO SETTLE.
WE HAVE REACHED THE POINT WHERE *IGNORANCE AND NEGLECT* ARE THE BEST WE CAN HOPE FOR IN A RULER.
THAT RIDGE OVER THERE IS POSITIVELY *SCREAMING* TO BE PLANTED WITH PINOT GRAPES, DON'T YOU THINK?
MY GOD, MAN, YOU HAVE TO CONSIDER THE *TERROIR.* FOR ALL YOU KNOW YOU'D END UP WITH A VINTAGE THAT TURNED PEOPLE INTO CAPYBARAS.
COME! EMBER'S TOMB IS IN THE NEXT VALLEY OVER!

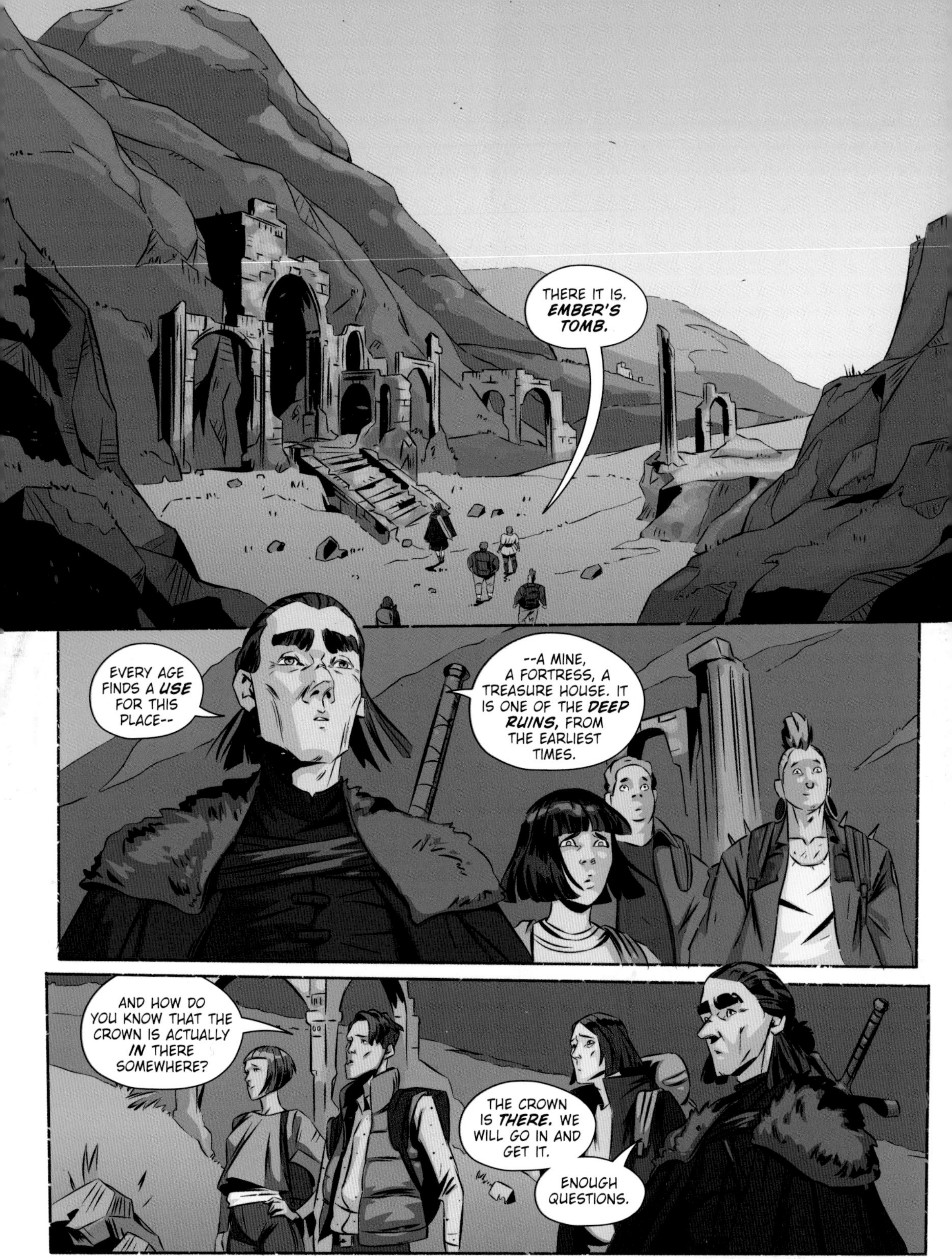
THERE IT IS. EMBER'S TOMB.
EVERY AGE FINDS A USE FOR THIS PLACE--
--A MINE, A FORTRESS, A TREASURE HOUSE. IT IS ONE OF THE DEEP RUINS, FROM THE EARLIEST TIMES.
AND HOW DO YOU KNOW THAT THE CROWN IS ACTUALLY IN THERE SOMEWHERE?
THE CROWN IS THERE. WE WILL GO IN AND GET IT.
ENOUGH QUESTIONS.

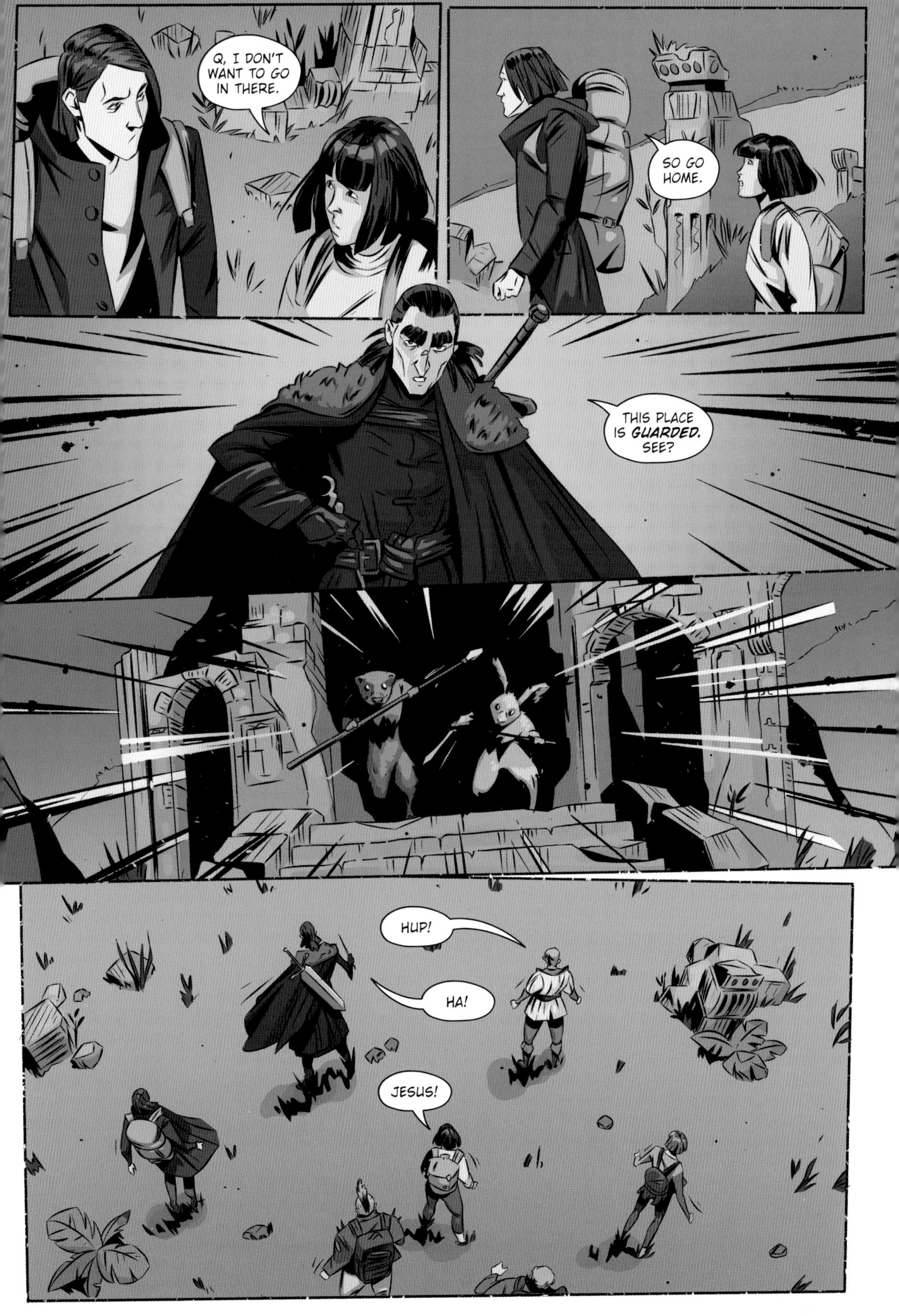
Q, I DON'T WANT TO GO IN THERE.
SO GO HOME.
THIS PLACE IS ***GUARDED.*** SEE?
HUP!
HA!
JESUS!

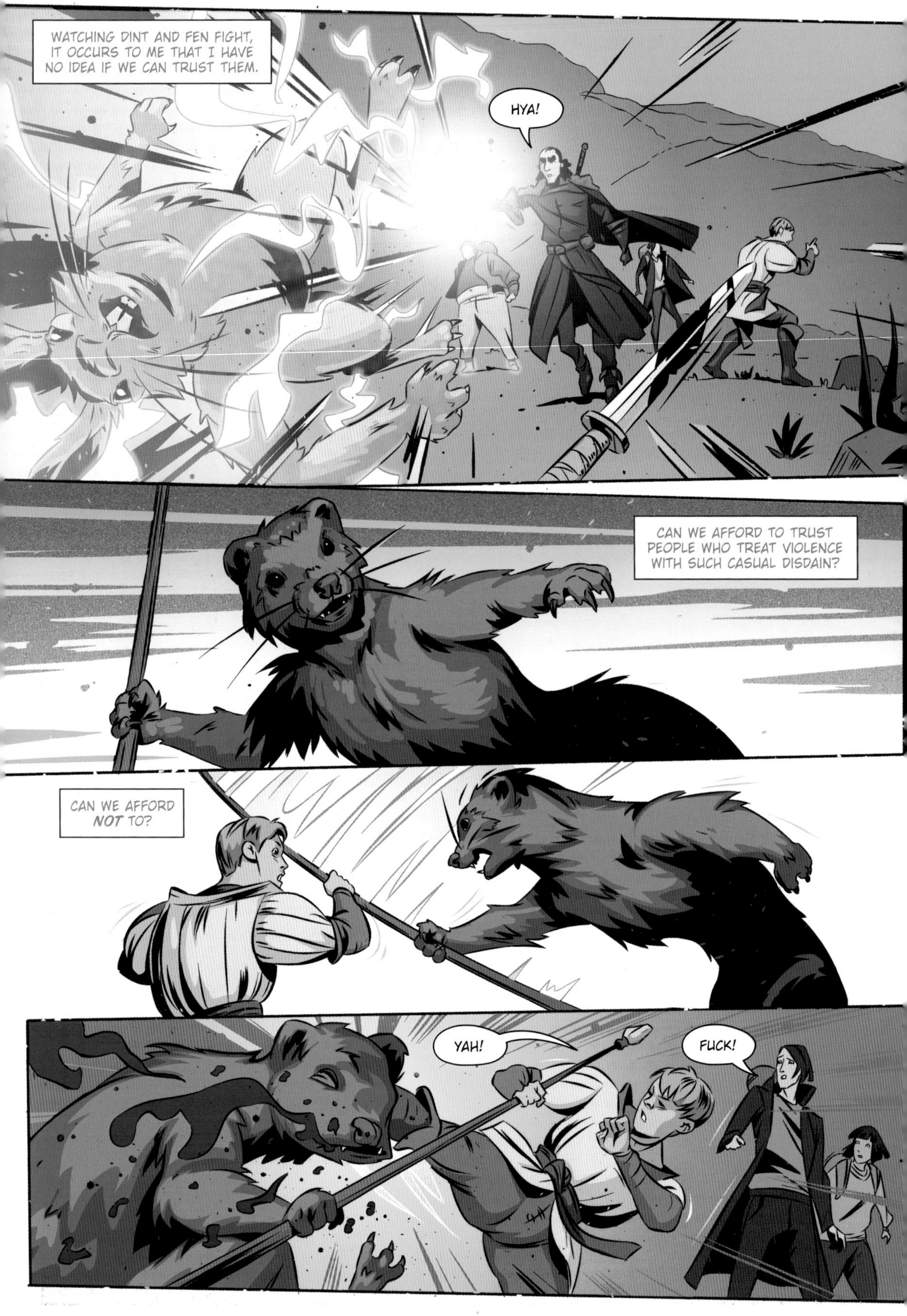
WATCHING DINT AND FEN FIGHT, IT OCCURS TO ME THAT I HAVE NO IDEA IF WE CAN TRUST THEM.
HYA!
CAN WE AFFORD TO TRUST PEOPLE WHO TREAT VIOLENCE WITH SUCH CASUAL DISDAIN?
CAN WE AFFORD *NOT* TO?
YAH!
FUCK!

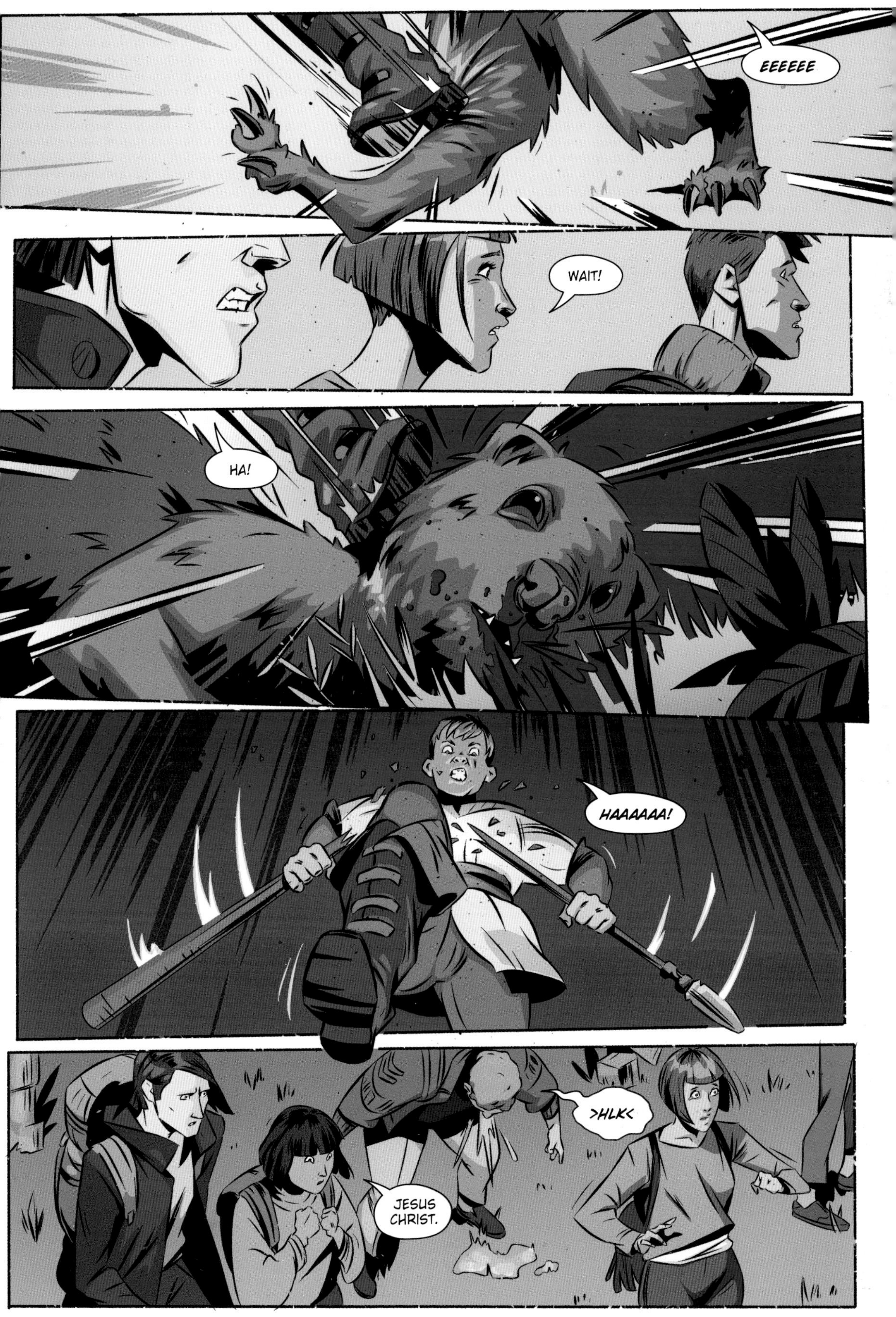
EEEEEE
WAIT!
HA!
HAAAAAA!
>HLK<
JESUS CHRIST.

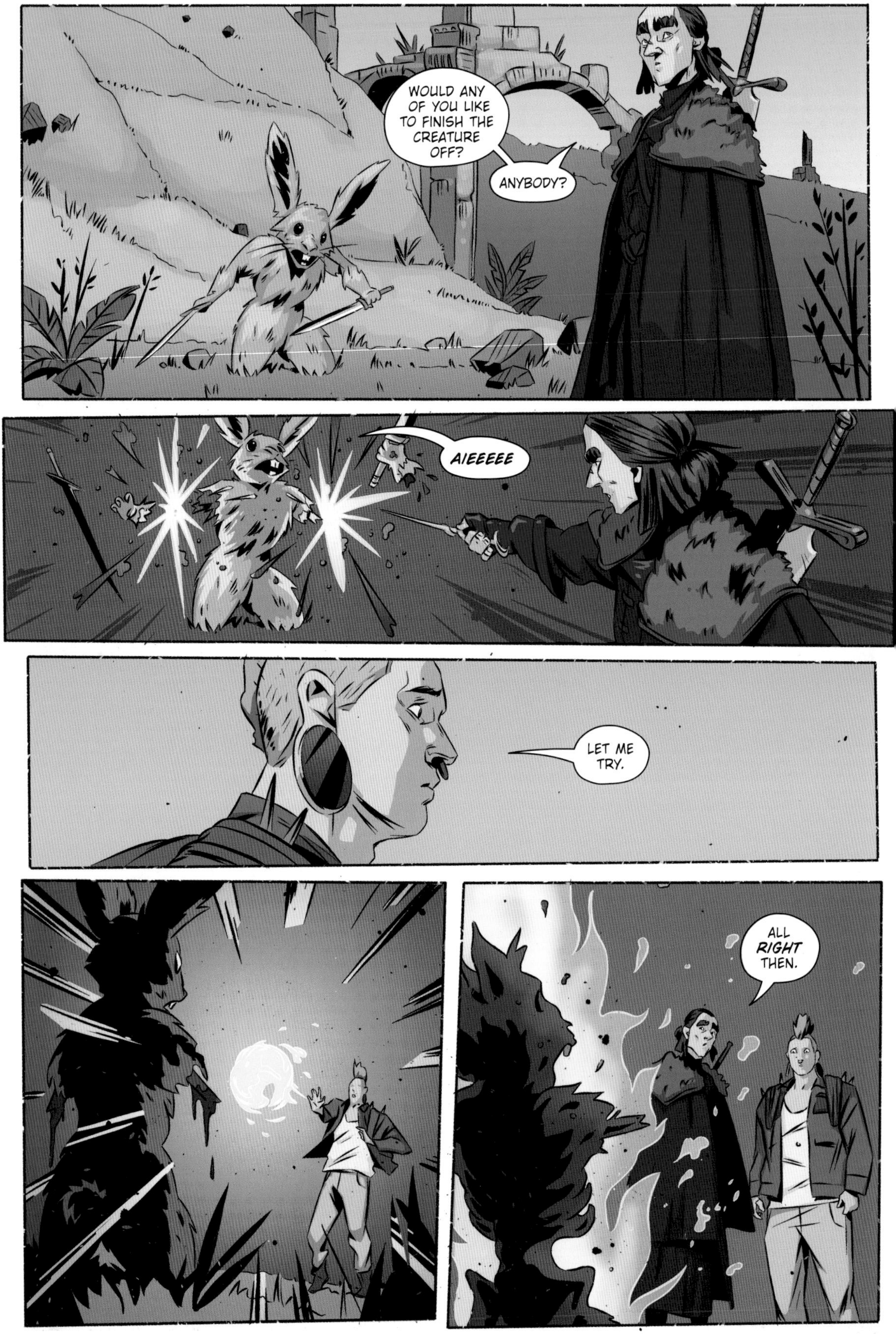

WOULD ANY OF YOU LIKE TO FINISH THE CREATURE OFF?
ANYBODY?
AIEEEEE
LET ME TRY.
ALL *RIGHT* THEN.

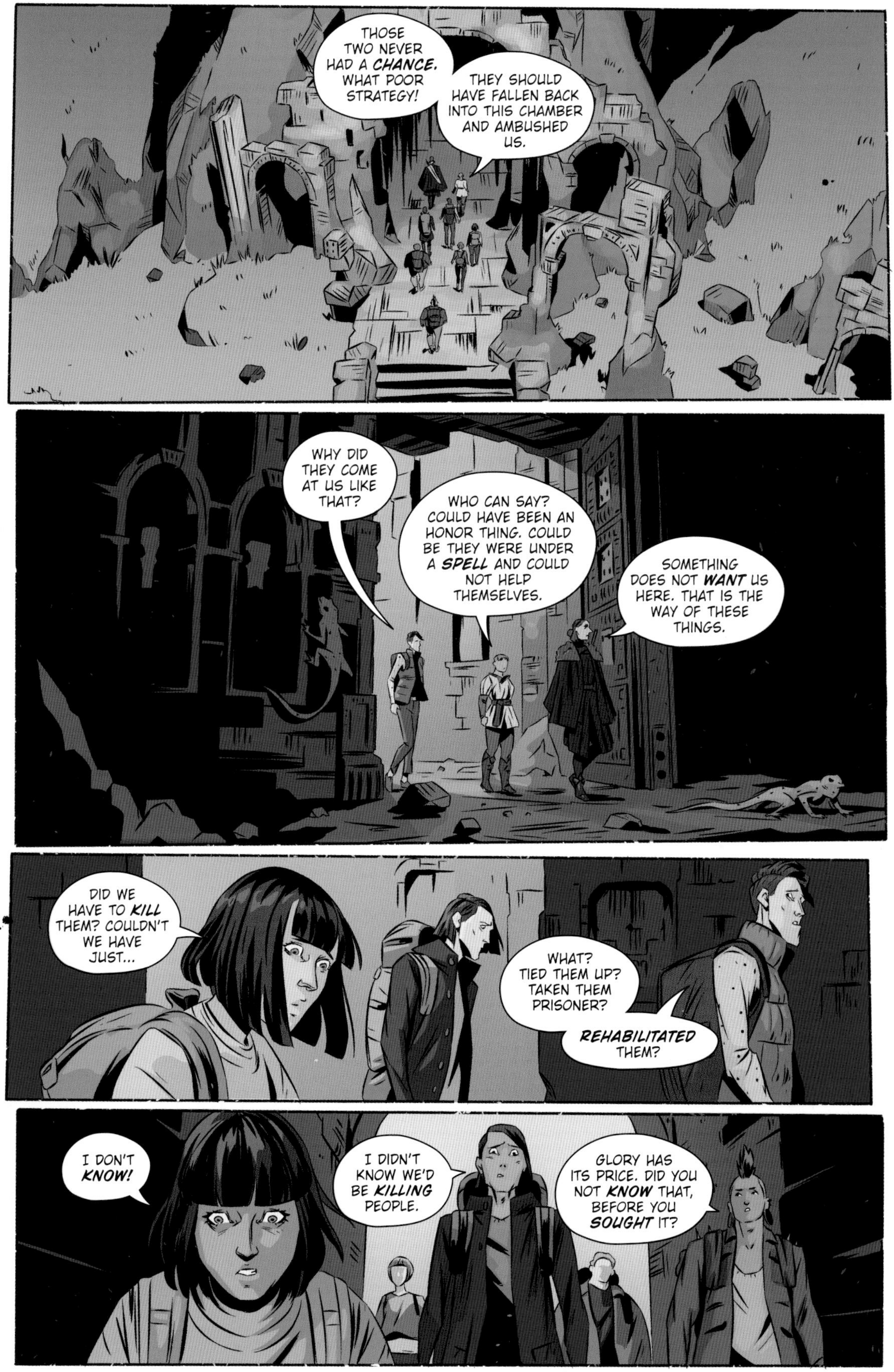
THOSE TWO NEVER HAD A CHANCE. WHAT POOR STRATEGY!
THEY SHOULD HAVE FALLEN BACK INTO THIS CHAMBER AND AMBUSHED US.
WHY DID THEY COME AT US LIKE THAT?
WHO CAN SAY? COULD HAVE BEEN AN HONOR THING. COULD BE THEY WERE UNDER A SPELL AND COULD NOT HELP THEMSELVES.
SOMETHING DOES NOT WANT US HERE. THAT IS THE WAY OF THESE THINGS.
DID WE HAVE TO KILL THEM? COULDN'T WE HAVE JUST...
WHAT? TIED THEM UP? TAKEN THEM PRISONER?
REHABILITATED THEM?
I DON'T KNOW!
I DIDN'T KNOW WE'D BE KILLING PEOPLE.
GLORY HAS ITS PRICE. DID YOU NOT KNOW THAT, BEFORE YOU SOUGHT IT?

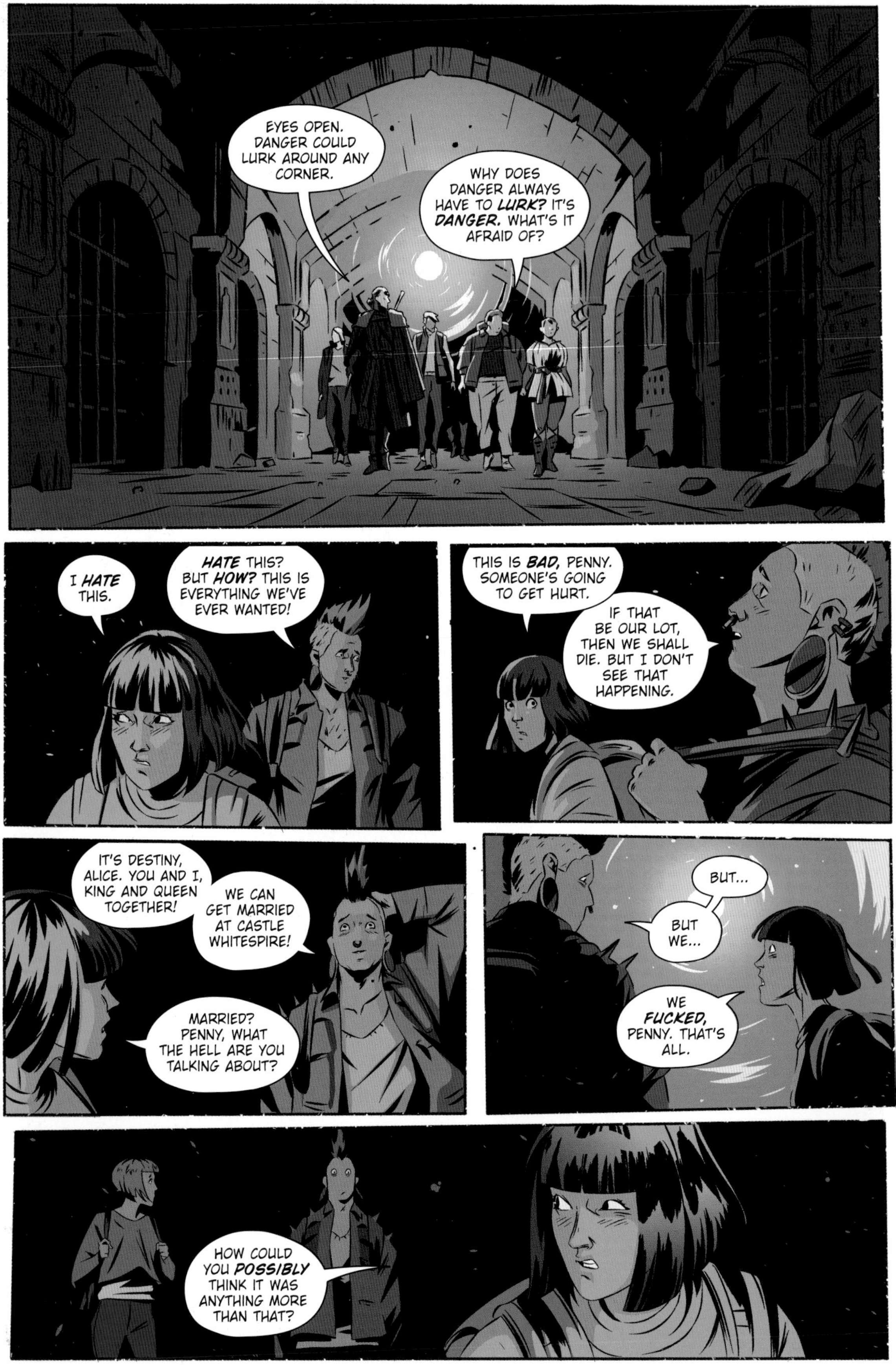
EYES OPEN. DANGER COULD LURK AROUND ANY CORNER.
WHY DOES DANGER ALWAYS HAVE TO **LURK?** IT'S **DANGER.** WHAT'S IT AFRAID OF?
I **HATE** THIS.
HATE THIS? BUT **HOW?** THIS IS EVERYTHING WE'VE EVER WANTED!
THIS IS **BAD,** PENNY. SOMEONE'S GOING TO GET HURT.
IF THAT BE OUR LOT, THEN WE SHALL DIE. BUT I DON'T SEE THAT HAPPENING.
IT'S DESTINY, ALICE. YOU AND I, KING AND QUEEN TOGETHER!
WE CAN GET MARRIED AT CASTLE WHITESPIRE!
MARRIED? PENNY, WHAT THE HELL ARE YOU TALKING ABOUT?
BUT...
BUT WE...
WE **FUCKED,** PENNY. THAT'S ALL.
HOW COULD YOU **POSSIBLY** THINK IT WAS ANYTHING MORE THAN THAT?

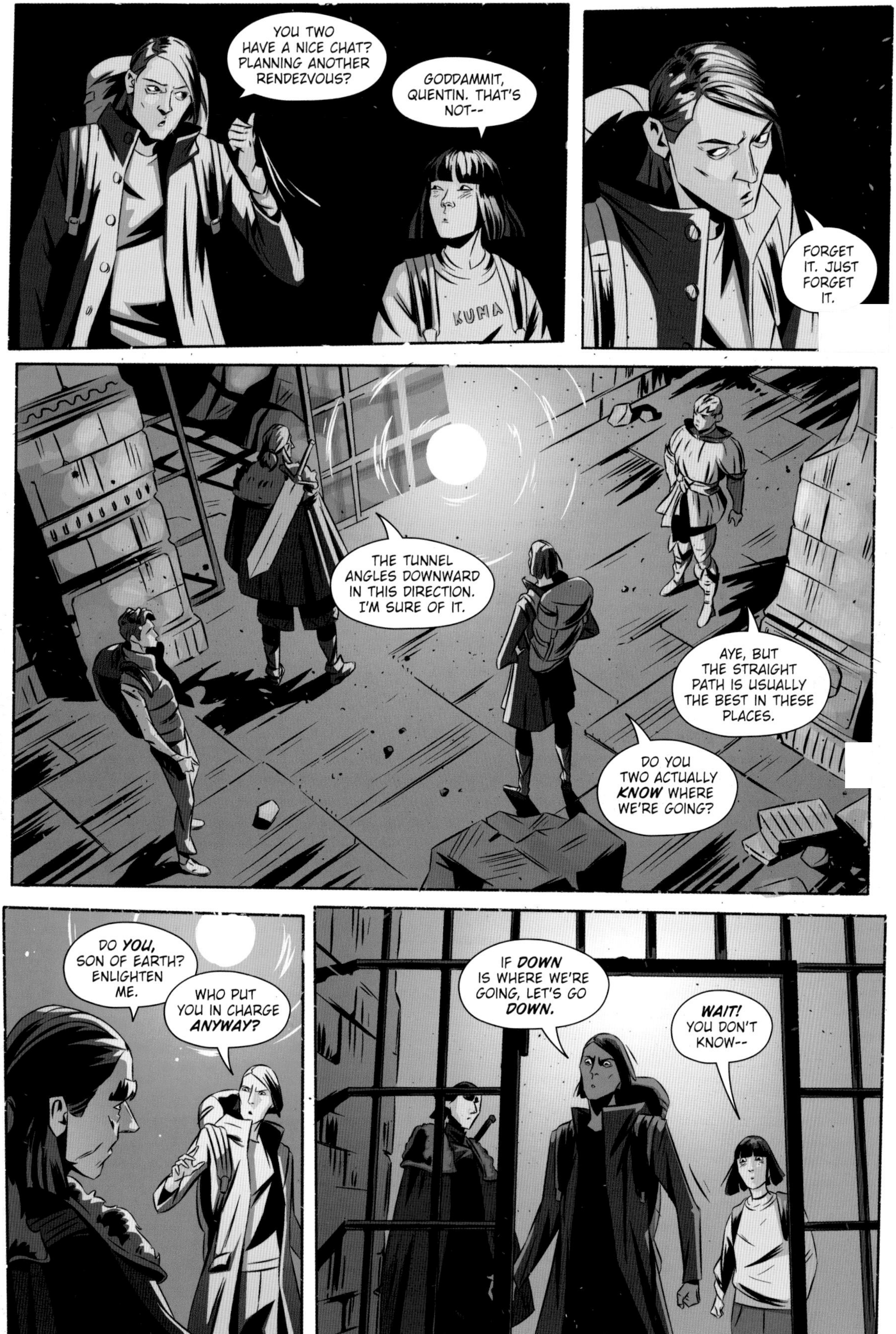
YOU TWO HAVE A NICE CHAT? PLANNING ANOTHER RENDEZVOUS?
GODDAMMIT, QUENTIN. THAT'S NOT--
FORGET IT. JUST FORGET IT.
KUMA
THE TUNNEL ANGLES DOWNWARD IN THIS DIRECTION. I'M SURE OF IT.
AYE, BUT THE STRAIGHT PATH IS USUALLY THE BEST IN THESE PLACES.
DO YOU TWO ACTUALLY KNOW WHERE WE'RE GOING?
DO YOU, SON OF EARTH? ENLIGHTEN ME.
WHO PUT YOU IN CHARGE ANYWAY?
IF DOWN IS WHERE WE'RE GOING, LET'S GO DOWN.
WAIT! YOU DON'T KNOW--

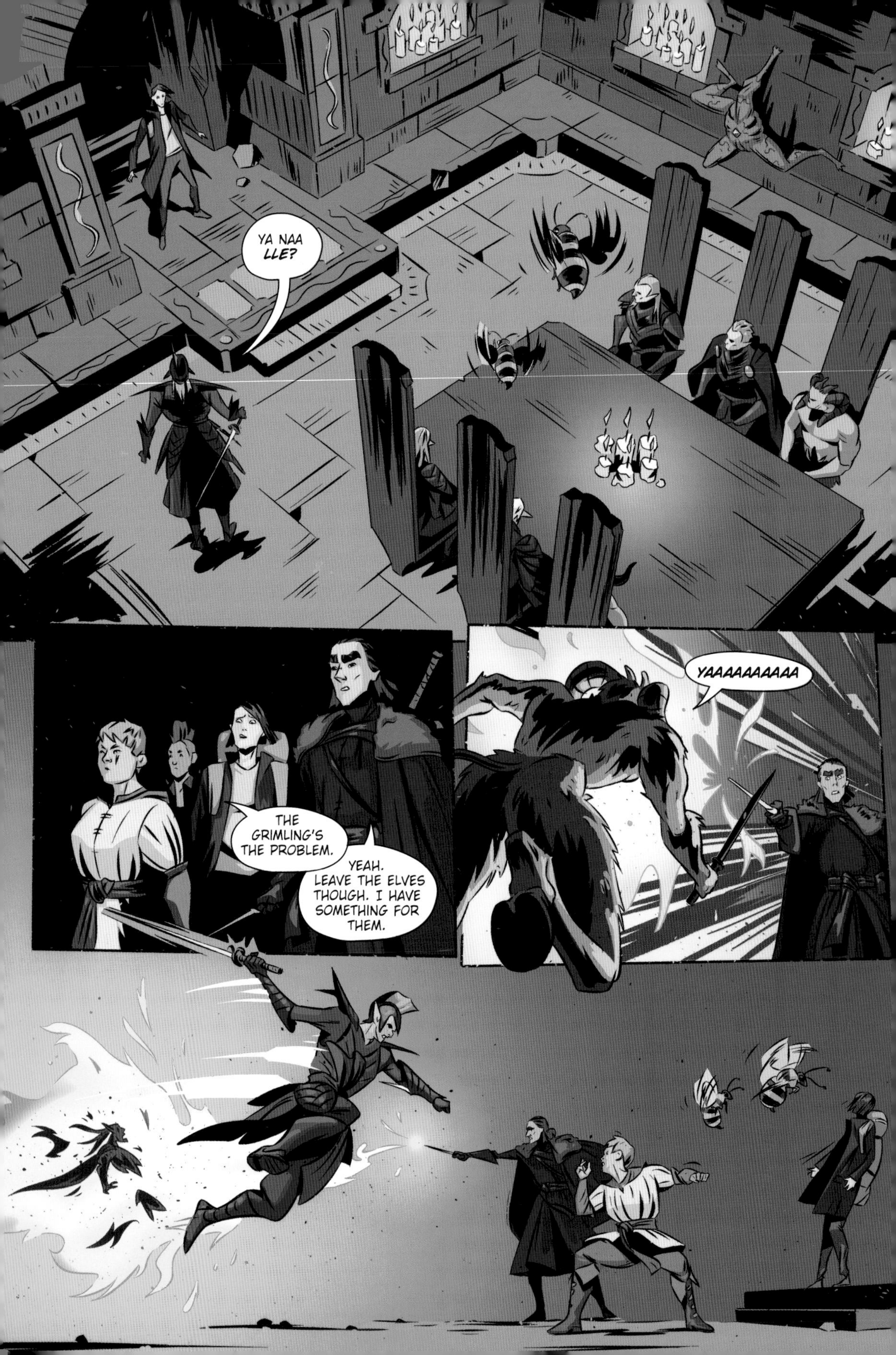
YA NAA LLE?
THE GRIMLING'S THE PROBLEM.
YEAH. LEAVE THE ELVES THOUGH. I HAVE SOMETHING FOR THEM.
YAAAAAAAAAA

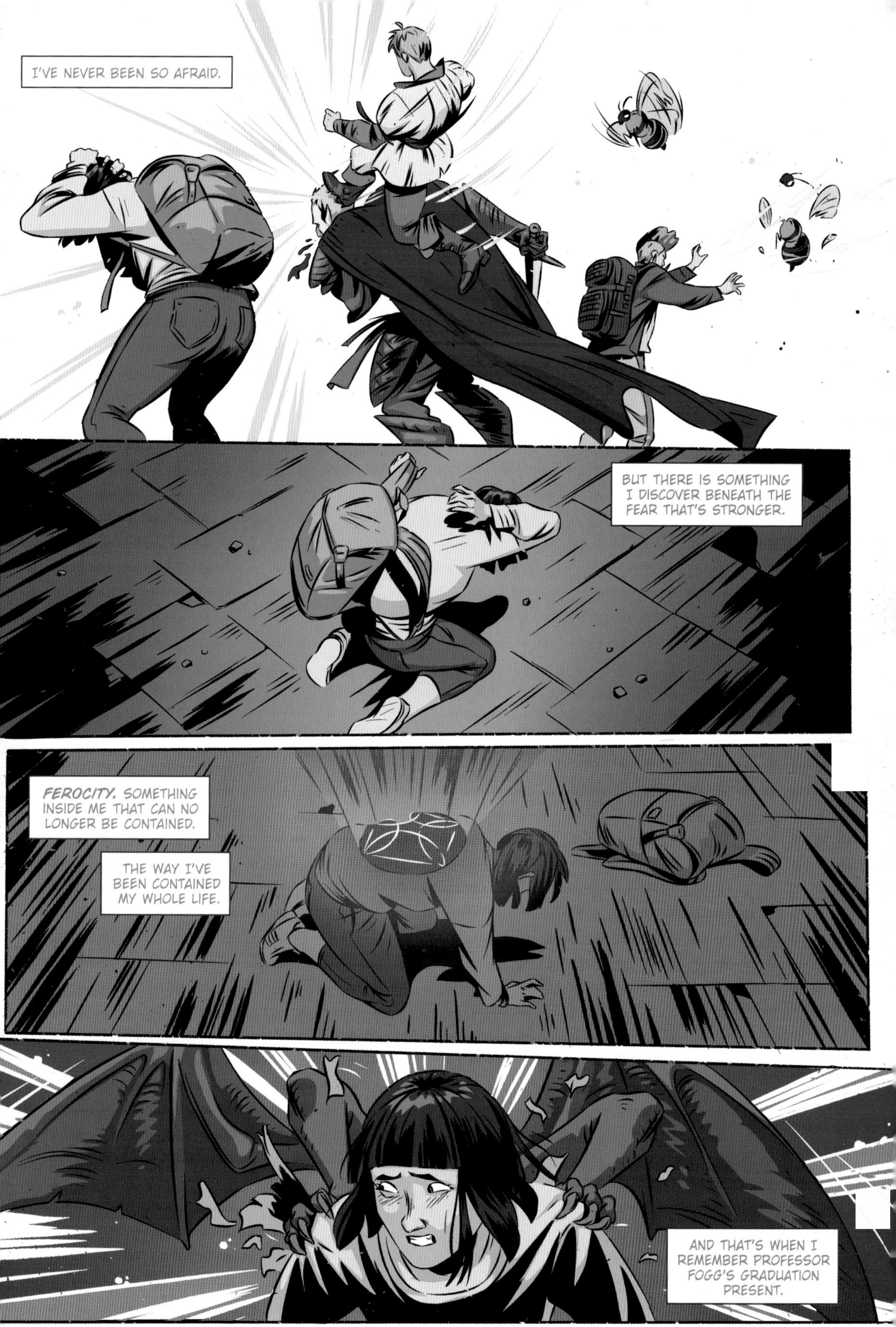
I'VE NEVER BEEN SO AFRAID.
BUT THERE IS SOMETHING I DISCOVER BENEATH THE FEAR THAT'S STRONGER.
FEROCITY. SOMETHING INSIDE ME THAT CAN NO LONGER BE CONTAINED.
THE WAY I'VE BEEN CONTAINED MY WHOLE LIFE.
AND THAT'S WHEN I REMEMBER PROFESSOR FOGG'S GRADUATION PRESENT.

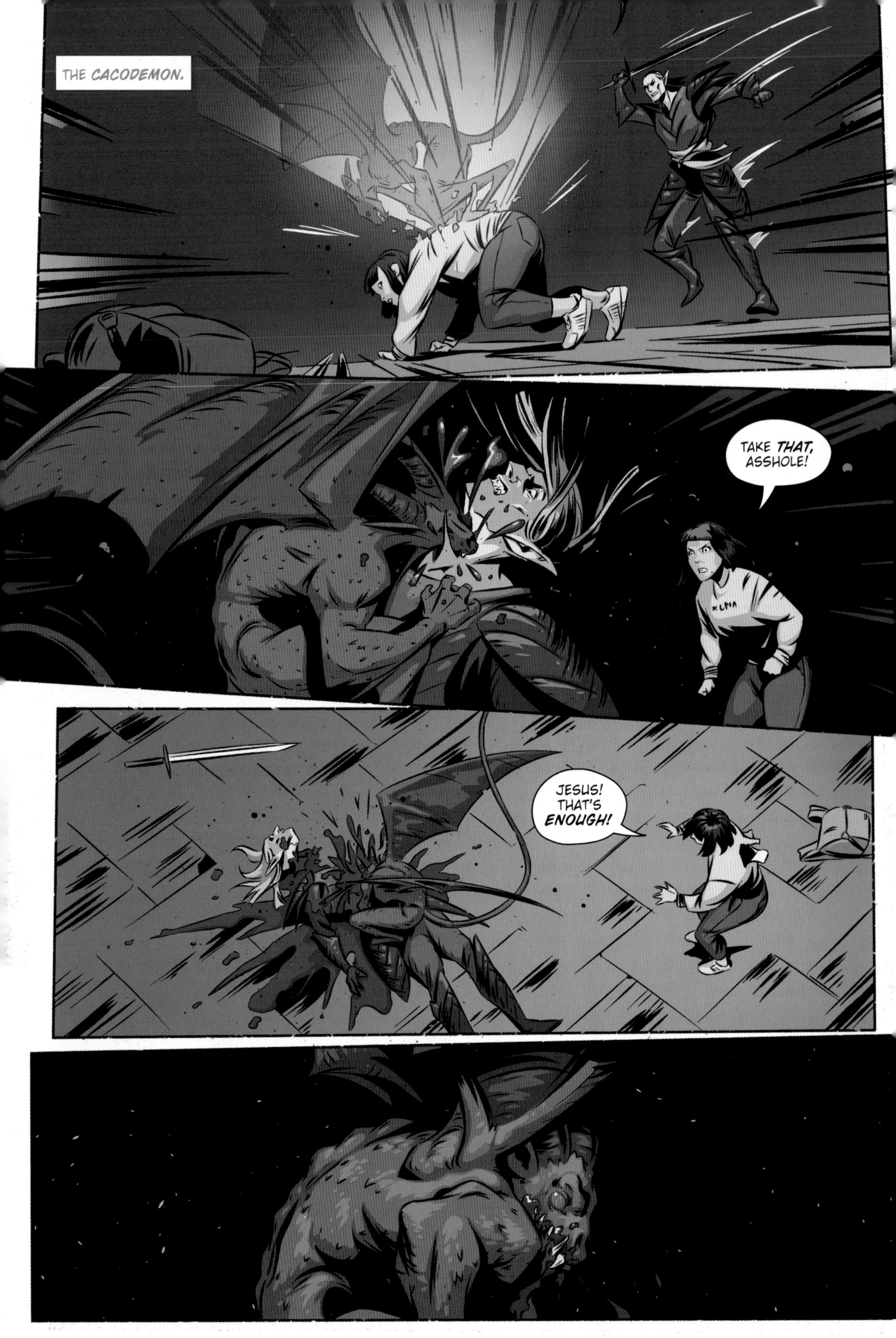
THE *CACODEMON.*
TAKE **THAT,** ASSHOLE!
JESUS! THAT'S **ENOUGH!**

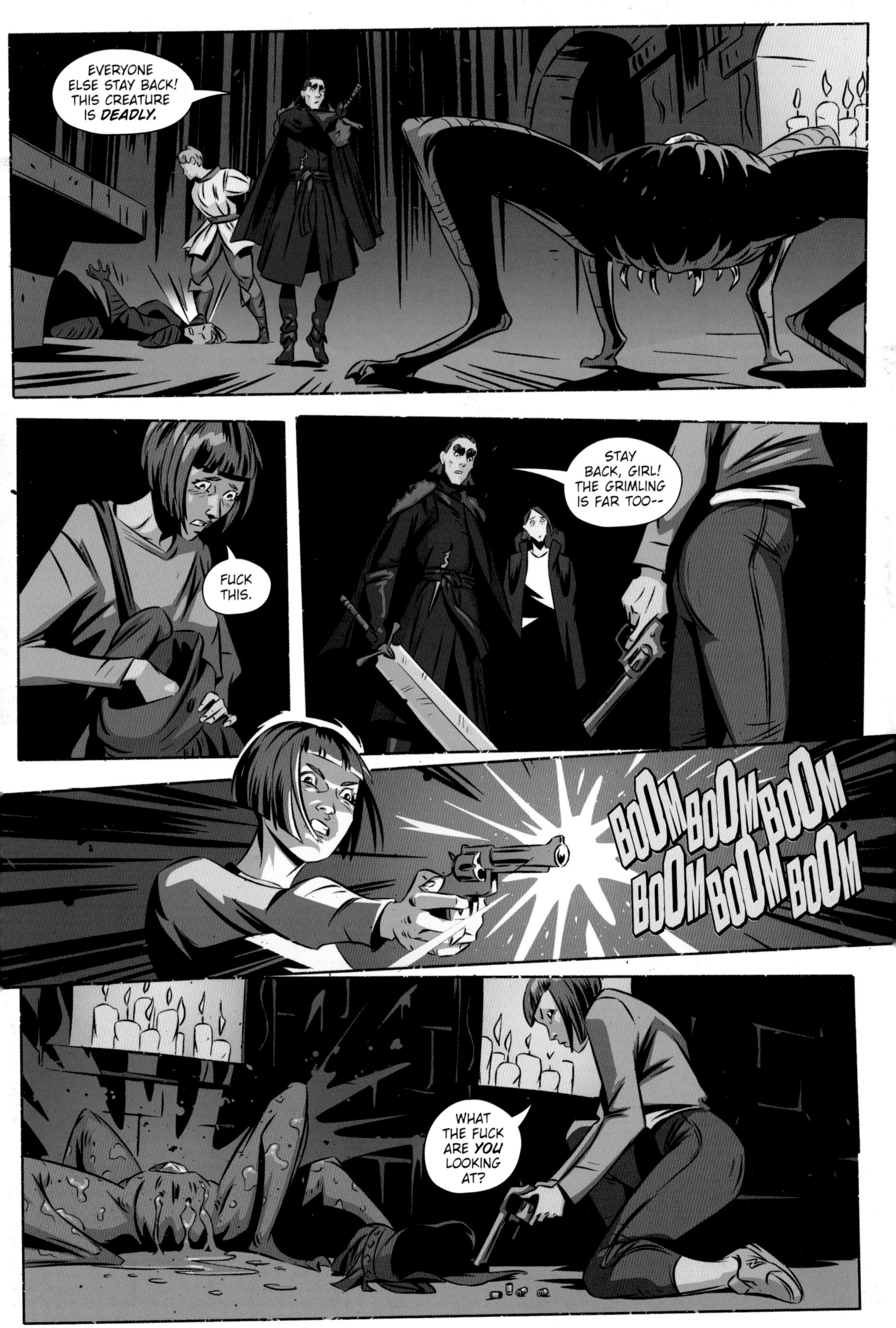
EVERYONE ELSE STAY BACK! THIS CREATURE IS *DEADLY.*
FUCK THIS.
STAY BACK, GIRL! THE GRIMLING IS FAR TOO--
BOOM BOOM BOOM BOOM BOOM BOOM
WHAT THE FUCK ARE *YOU* LOOKING AT?

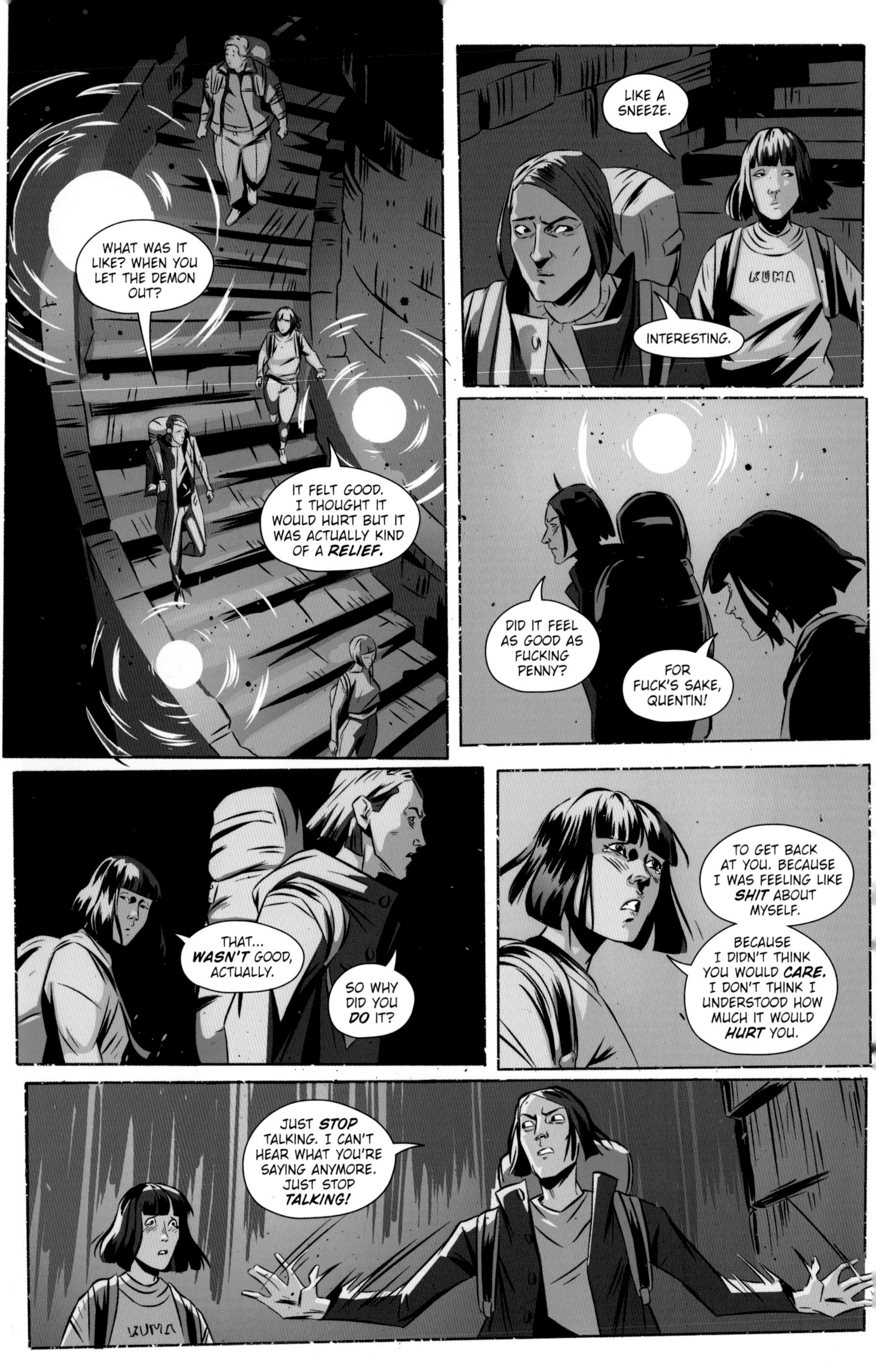
WHAT WAS IT LIKE? WHEN YOU LET THE DEMON OUT?
IT FELT GOOD. I THOUGHT IT WOULD HURT BUT IT WAS ACTUALLY KIND OF A RELIEF.
LIKE A SNEEZE.
INTERESTING.
DID IT FEEL AS GOOD AS FUCKING PENNY?
FOR FUCK'S SAKE, QUENTIN!
THAT... WASN'T GOOD, ACTUALLY.
SO WHY DID YOU DO IT?
TO GET BACK AT YOU. BECAUSE I WAS FEELING LIKE SHIT ABOUT MYSELF.
BECAUSE I DIDN'T THINK YOU WOULD CARE. I DON'T THINK I UNDERSTOOD HOW MUCH IT WOULD HURT YOU.
JUST STOP TALKING. I CAN'T HEAR WHAT YOU'RE SAYING ANYMORE. JUST STOP TALKING!

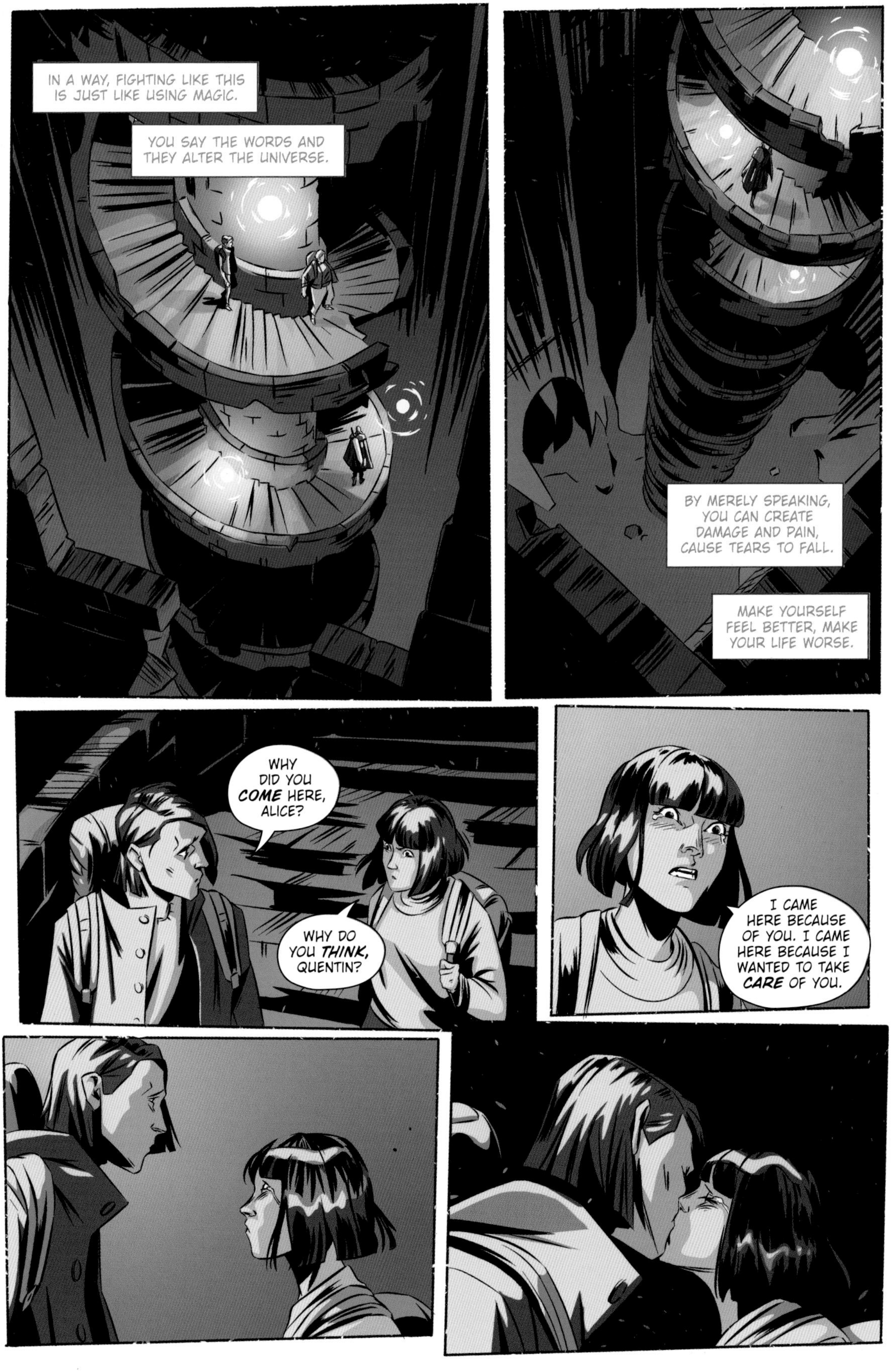
IN A WAY, FIGHTING LIKE THIS IS JUST LIKE USING MAGIC.
YOU SAY THE WORDS AND THEY ALTER THE UNIVERSE.
BY MERELY SPEAKING, YOU CAN CREATE DAMAGE AND PAIN, CAUSE TEARS TO FALL.
MAKE YOURSELF FEEL BETTER, MAKE YOUR LIFE WORSE.
WHY DID YOU COME HERE, ALICE?
WHY DO YOU THINK, QUENTIN?
I CAME HERE BECAUSE OF YOU. I CAME HERE BECAUSE I WANTED TO TAKE CARE OF YOU.

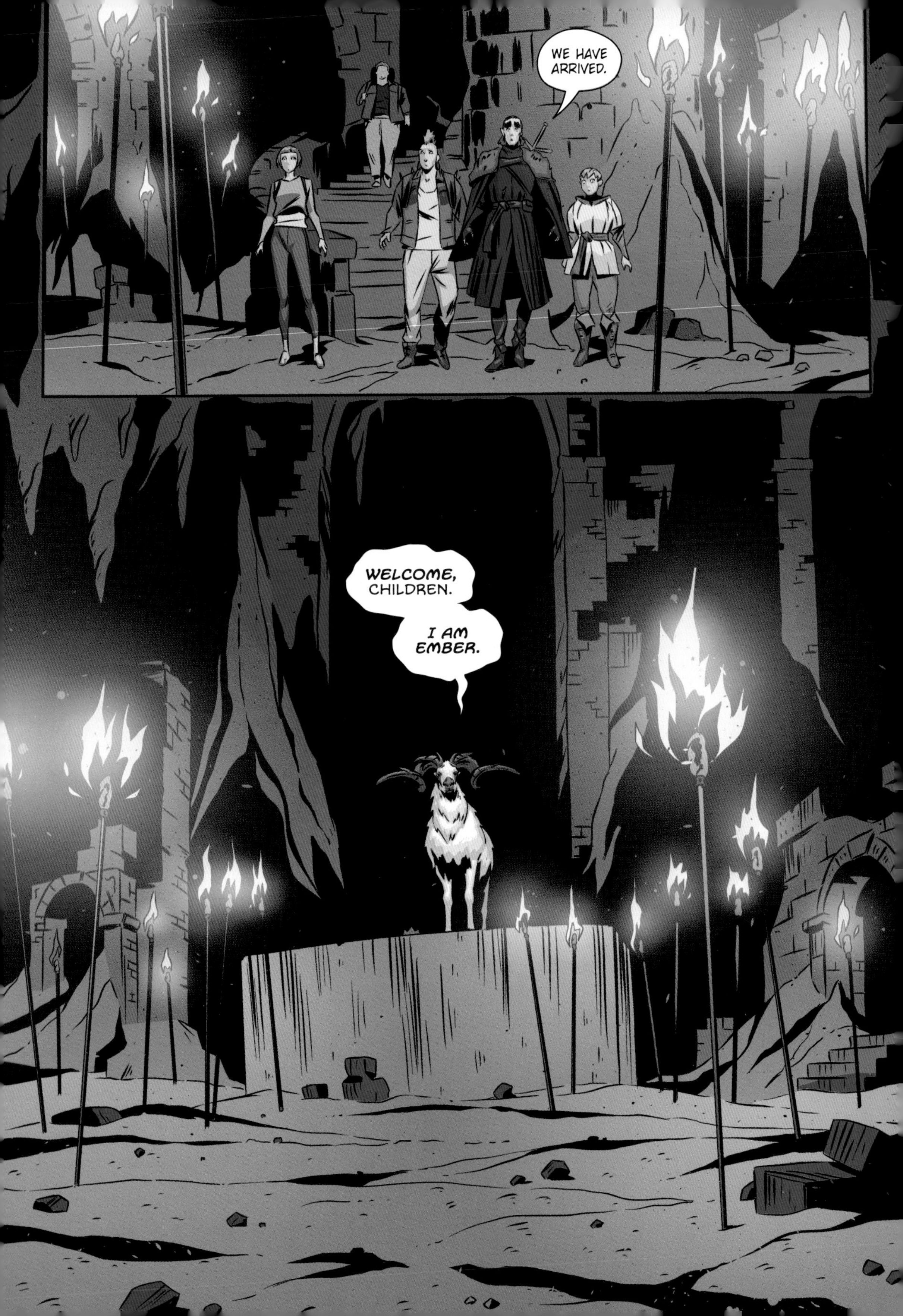
WE HAVE ARRIVED.
WELCOME, CHILDREN.
I AM EMBER.

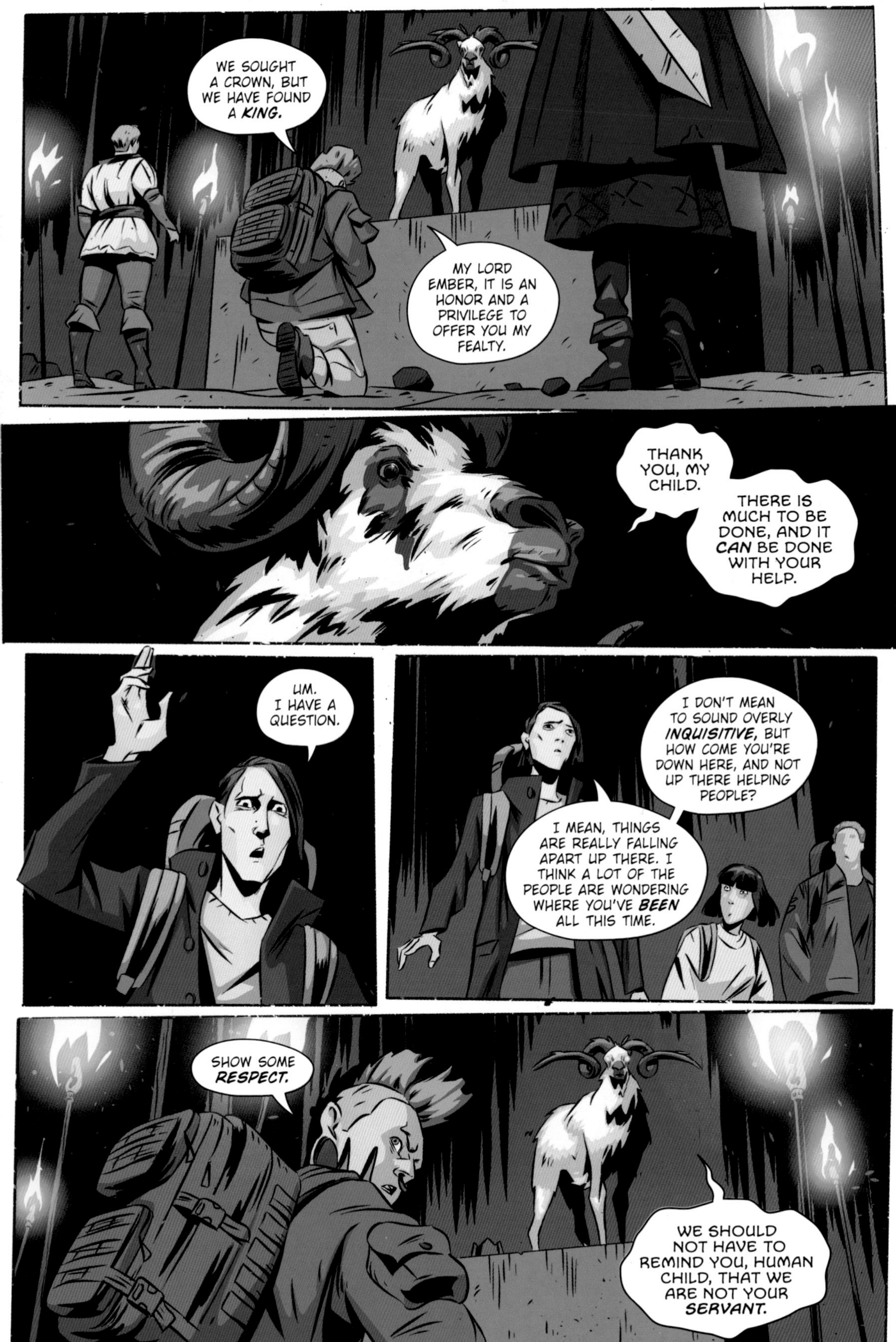

WE SOUGHT A CROWN, BUT WE HAVE FOUND A ***KING.***
MY LORD EMBER, IT IS AN HONOR AND A PRIVILEGE TO OFFER YOU MY FEALTY.
THANK YOU, MY CHILD.
THERE IS MUCH TO BE DONE, AND IT **CAN** BE DONE WITH YOUR HELP.
UM. I HAVE A QUESTION.
I DON'T MEAN TO SOUND OVERLY ***INQUISITIVE,*** BUT HOW COME YOU'RE DOWN HERE, AND NOT UP THERE HELPING PEOPLE?
I MEAN, THINGS ARE REALLY FALLING APART UP THERE. I THINK A LOT OF THE PEOPLE ARE WONDERING WHERE YOU'VE ***BEEN*** ALL THIS TIME.
SHOW SOME ***RESPECT.***
WE SHOULD NOT HAVE TO REMIND YOU, HUMAN CHILD, THAT WE ARE NOT YOUR ***SERVANT.***

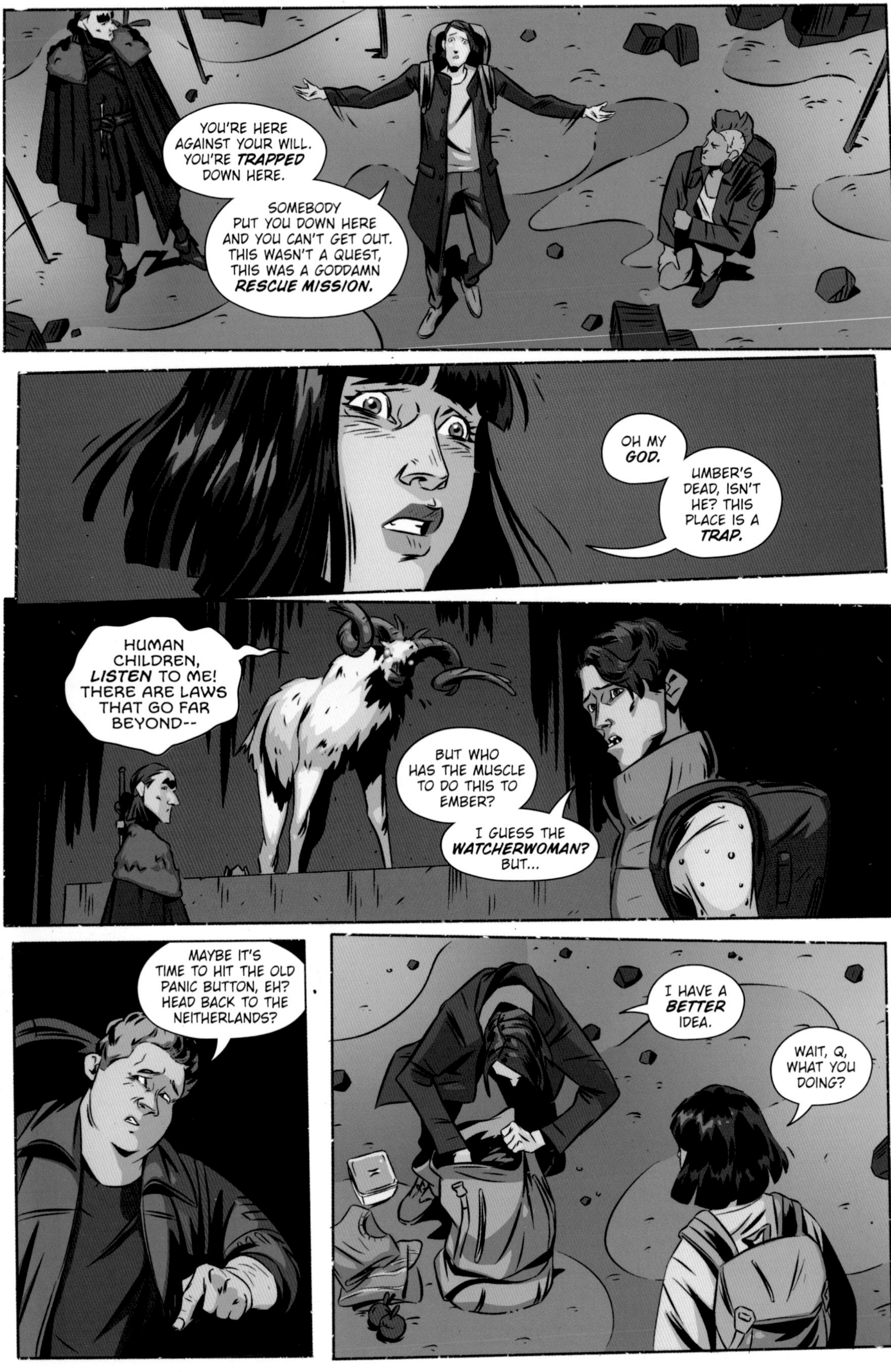
YOU'RE HERE AGAINST YOUR WILL. YOU'RE TRAPPED DOWN HERE.
SOMEBODY PUT YOU DOWN HERE AND YOU CAN'T GET OUT. THIS WASN'T A QUEST, THIS WAS A GODDAMN RESCUE MISSION.
OH MY GOD.
UMBER'S DEAD, ISN'T HE? THIS PLACE IS A TRAP.
HUMAN CHILDREN, LISTEN TO ME! THERE ARE LAWS THAT GO FAR BEYOND--
BUT WHO HAS THE MUSCLE TO DO THIS TO EMBER?
I GUESS THE WATCHERWOMAN? BUT...
MAYBE IT'S TIME TO HIT THE OLD PANIC BUTTON, EH? HEAD BACK TO THE NEITHERLANDS?
I HAVE A BETTER IDEA.
WAIT, Q, WHAT YOU DOING?

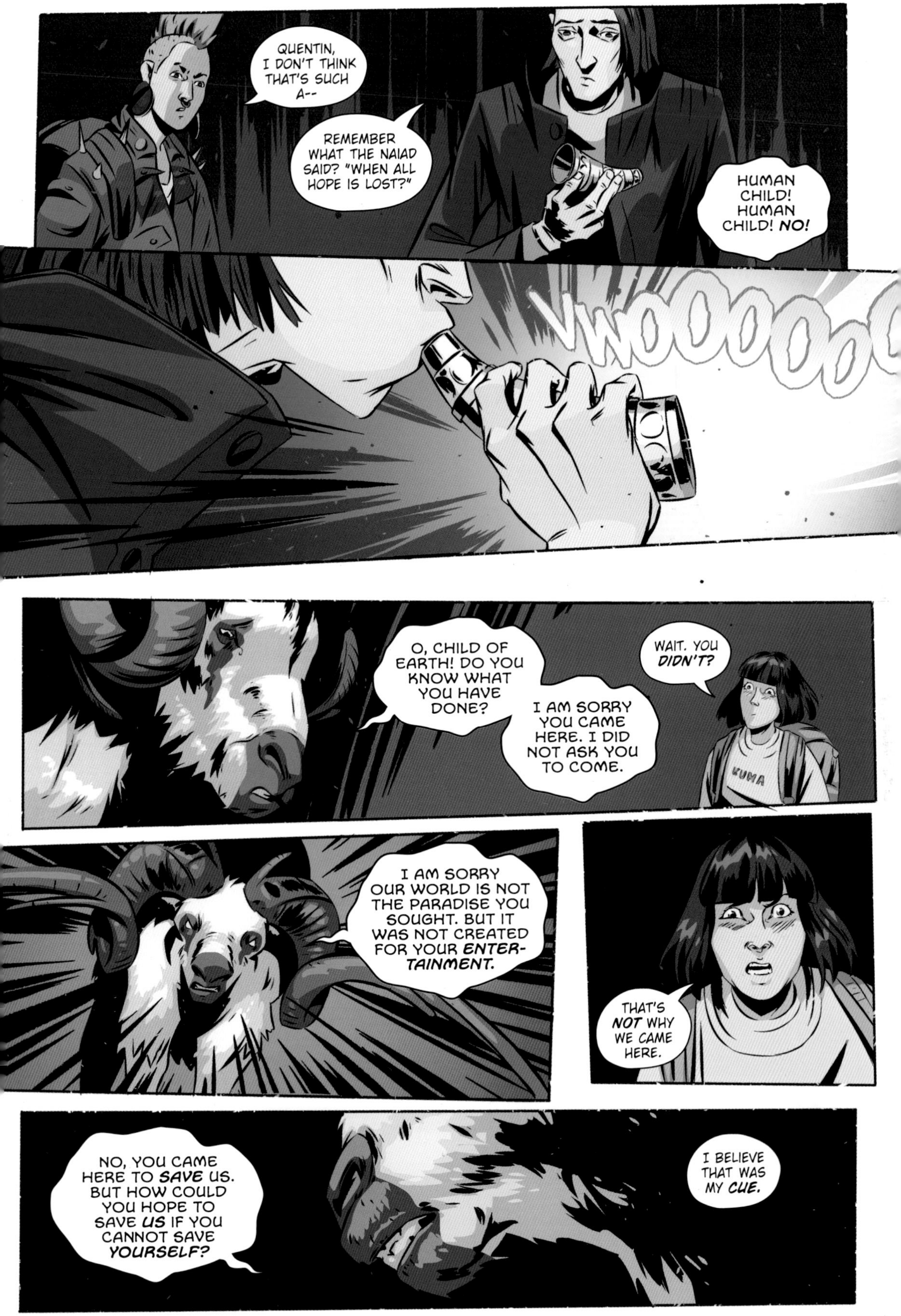
QUENTIN, I DON'T THINK THAT'S SUCH A--
REMEMBER WHAT THE NAIAD SAID? "WHEN ALL HOPE IS LOST?"
HUMAN CHILD! HUMAN CHILD! **NO!**
VWOOOOOO
O, CHILD OF EARTH! DO YOU KNOW WHAT YOU HAVE DONE?
I AM SORRY YOU CAME HERE. I DID NOT ASK YOU TO COME.
WAIT. YOU ***DIDN'T?***
KUMA
I AM SORRY OUR WORLD IS NOT THE PARADISE YOU SOUGHT. BUT IT WAS NOT CREATED FOR YOUR ***ENTERTAINMENT.***
THAT'S ***NOT*** WHY WE CAME HERE.
NO, YOU CAME HERE TO ***SAVE*** US. BUT HOW COULD YOU HOPE TO SAVE ***US*** IF YOU CANNOT SAVE ***YOURSELF?***
I BELIEVE THAT WAS MY ***CUE.***

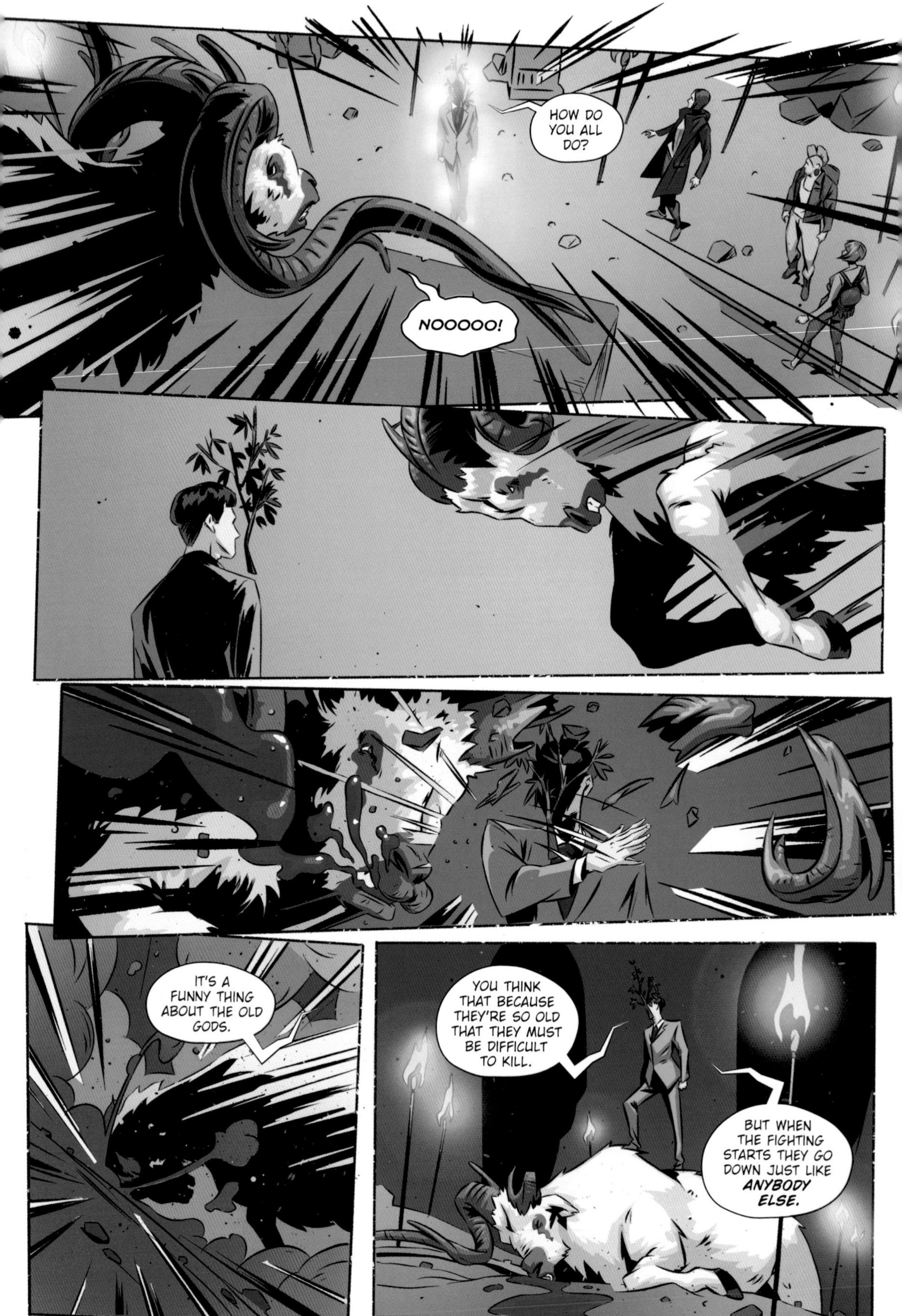
HOW DO YOU ALL DO?
NOOOOO!
IT'S A FUNNY THING ABOUT THE OLD GODS.
YOU THINK THAT BECAUSE THEY'RE SO OLD THAT THEY MUST BE DIFFICULT TO KILL.
BUT WHEN THE FIGHTING STARTS THEY GO DOWN JUST LIKE ANYBODY ELSE.

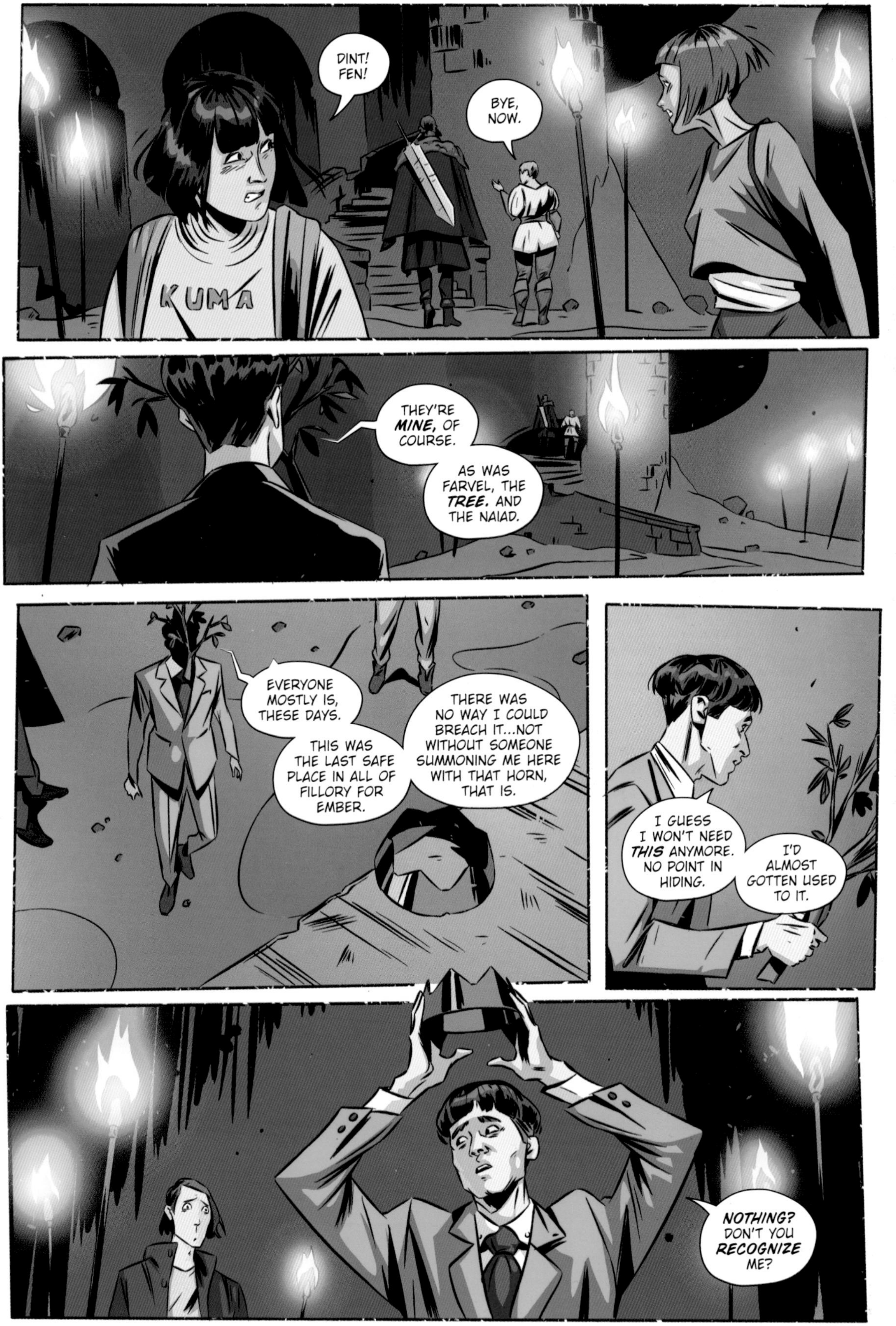
DINT! FEN!
BYE, NOW.
THEY'RE MINE, OF COURSE.
AS WAS FARVEL, THE TREE. AND THE NAIAD.
EVERYONE MOSTLY IS, THESE DAYS.
THIS WAS THE LAST SAFE PLACE IN ALL OF FILLORY FOR EMBER.
THERE WAS NO WAY I COULD BREACH IT...NOT WITHOUT SOMEONE SUMMONING ME HERE WITH THAT HORN, THAT IS.
I GUESS I WON'T NEED THIS ANYMORE. NO POINT IN HIDING.
I'D ALMOST GOTTEN USED TO IT.
NOTHING? DON'T YOU RECOGNIZE ME?

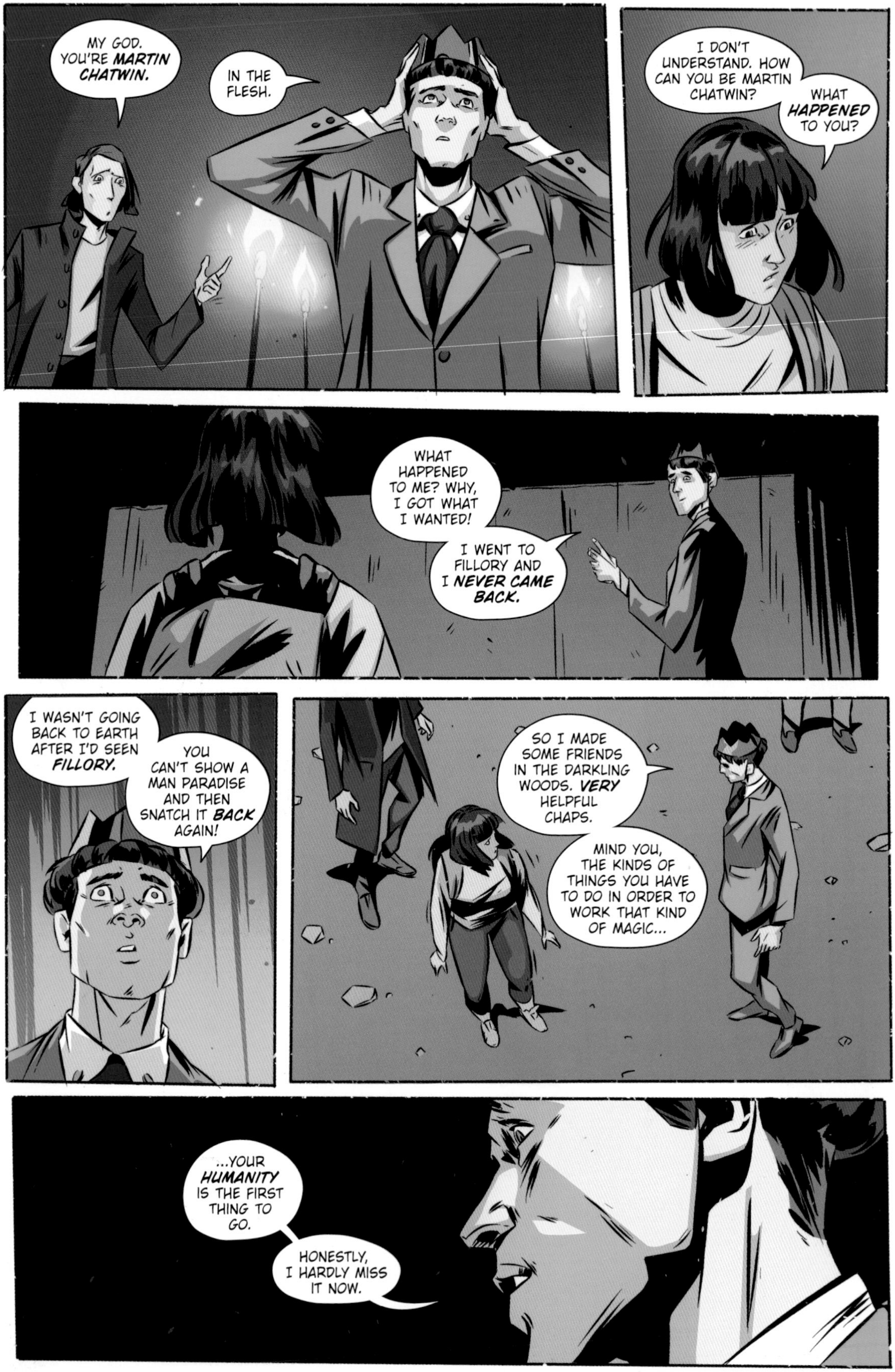
MY GOD. YOU'RE **MARTIN CHATWIN.**
IN THE FLESH.
I DON'T UNDERSTAND. HOW CAN YOU BE MARTIN CHATWIN?
WHAT **HAPPENED** TO YOU?
WHAT HAPPENED TO ME? WHY, I GOT WHAT I WANTED!
I WENT TO FILLORY AND I **NEVER CAME BACK.**
I WASN'T GOING BACK TO EARTH AFTER I'D SEEN **FILLORY.**
YOU CAN'T SHOW A MAN PARADISE AND THEN SNATCH IT **BACK** AGAIN!
SO I MADE SOME FRIENDS IN THE DARKLING WOODS. **VERY** HELPFUL CHAPS.
MIND YOU, THE KINDS OF THINGS YOU HAVE TO DO IN ORDER TO WORK THAT KIND OF MAGIC...
...YOUR **HUMANITY** IS THE FIRST THING TO GO.
HONESTLY, I HARDLY MISS IT NOW.

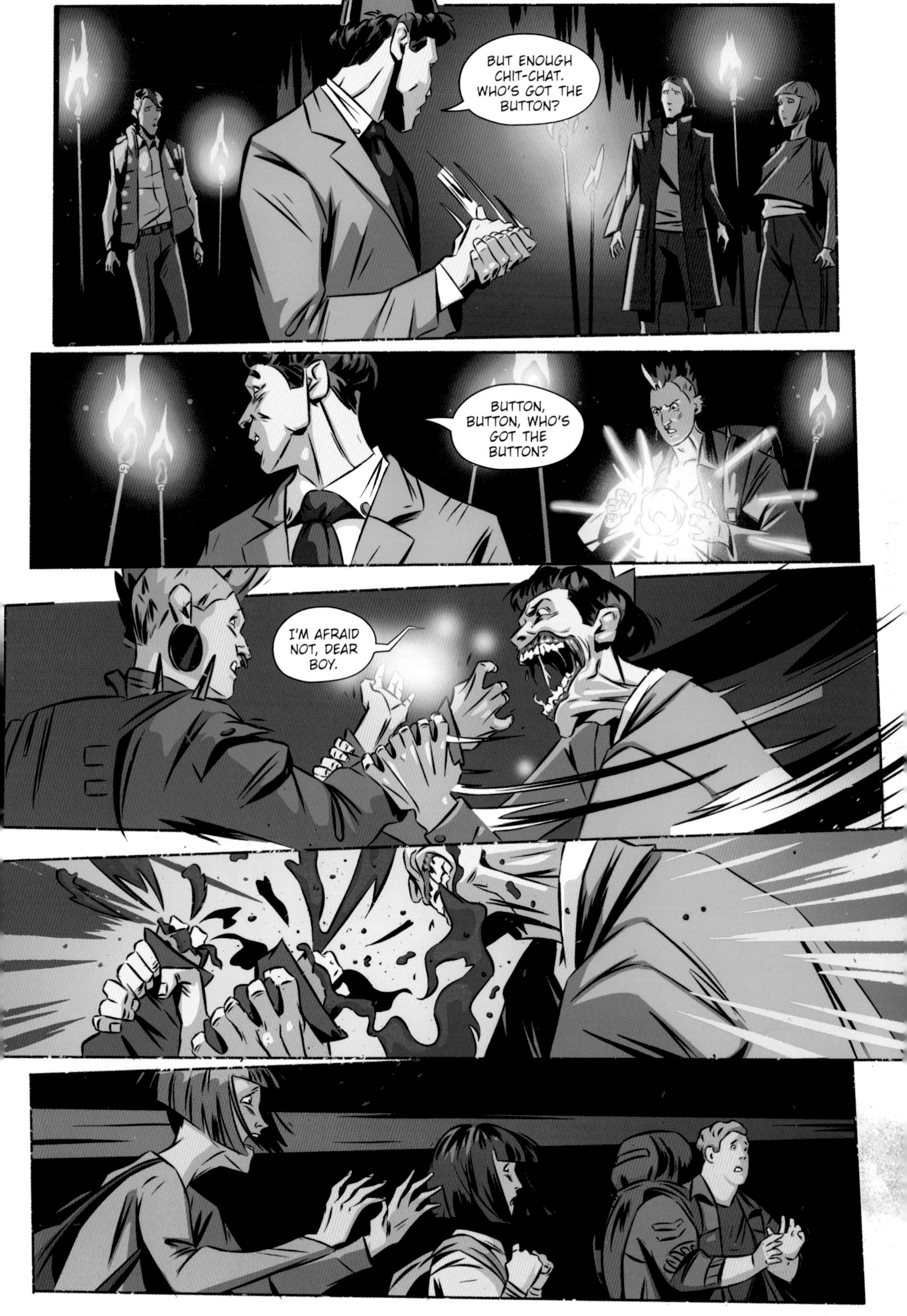
BUT ENOUGH CHIT-CHAT. WHO'S GOT THE BUTTON?
BUTTON, BUTTON, WHO'S GOT THE BUTTON?
I'M AFRAID NOT, DEAR BOY.

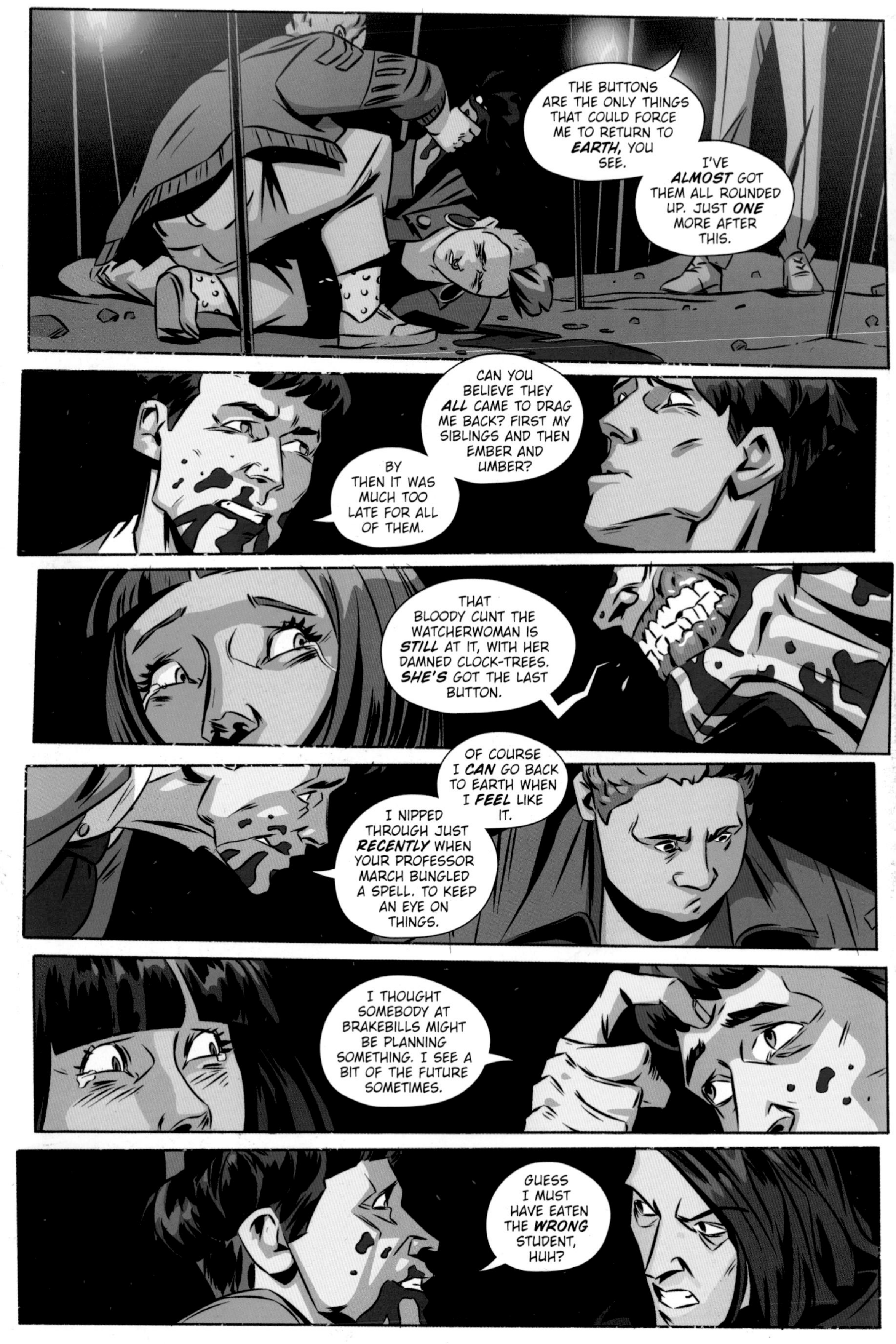
THE BUTTONS ARE THE ONLY THINGS THAT COULD FORCE ME TO RETURN TO EARTH, YOU SEE.
I'VE ALMOST GOT THEM ALL ROUNDED UP. JUST ONE MORE AFTER THIS.
CAN YOU BELIEVE THEY ALL CAME TO DRAG ME BACK? FIRST MY SIBLINGS AND THEN EMBER AND UMBER?
BY THEN IT WAS MUCH TOO LATE FOR ALL OF THEM.
THAT BLOODY CUNT THE WATCHERWOMAN IS STILL AT IT, WITH HER DAMNED CLOCK-TREES. SHE'S GOT THE LAST BUTTON.
OF COURSE I CAN GO BACK TO EARTH WHEN I FEEL LIKE IT.
I NIPPED THROUGH JUST RECENTLY WHEN YOUR PROFESSOR MARCH BUNGLED A SPELL. TO KEEP AN EYE ON THINGS.
I THOUGHT SOMEBODY AT BRAKEBILLS MIGHT BE PLANNING SOMETHING. I SEE A BIT OF THE FUTURE SOMETIMES.
GUESS I MUST HAVE EATEN THE WRONG STUDENT, HUH?

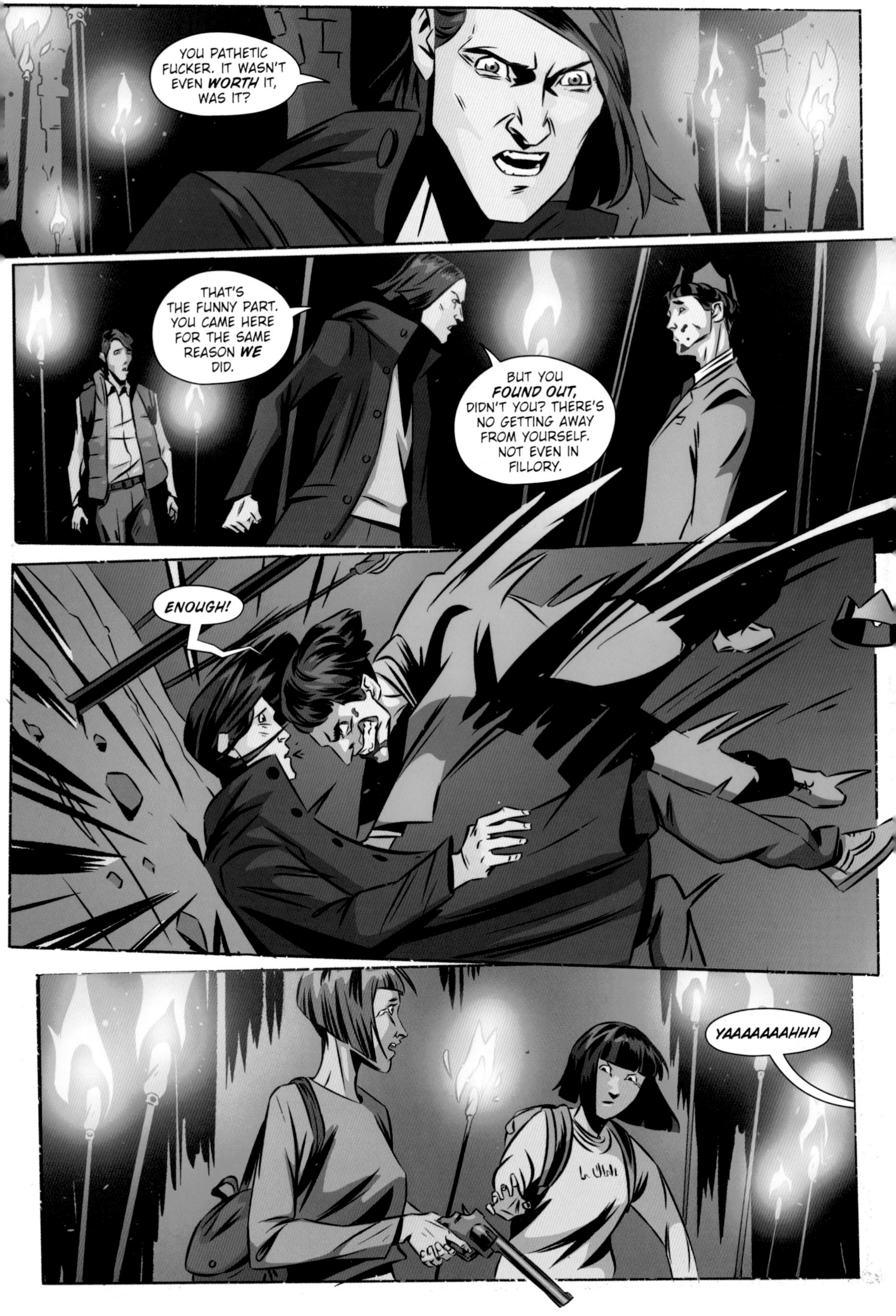
YOU PATHETIC FUCKER. IT WASN'T EVEN **WORTH** IT, WAS IT?
THAT'S THE FUNNY PART. YOU CAME HERE FOR THE SAME REASON **WE** DID.
BUT YOU **FOUND OUT,** DIDN'T YOU? THERE'S NO GETTING AWAY FROM YOURSELF. NOT EVEN IN FILLORY.
ENOUGH!
YAAAAAAAHHH

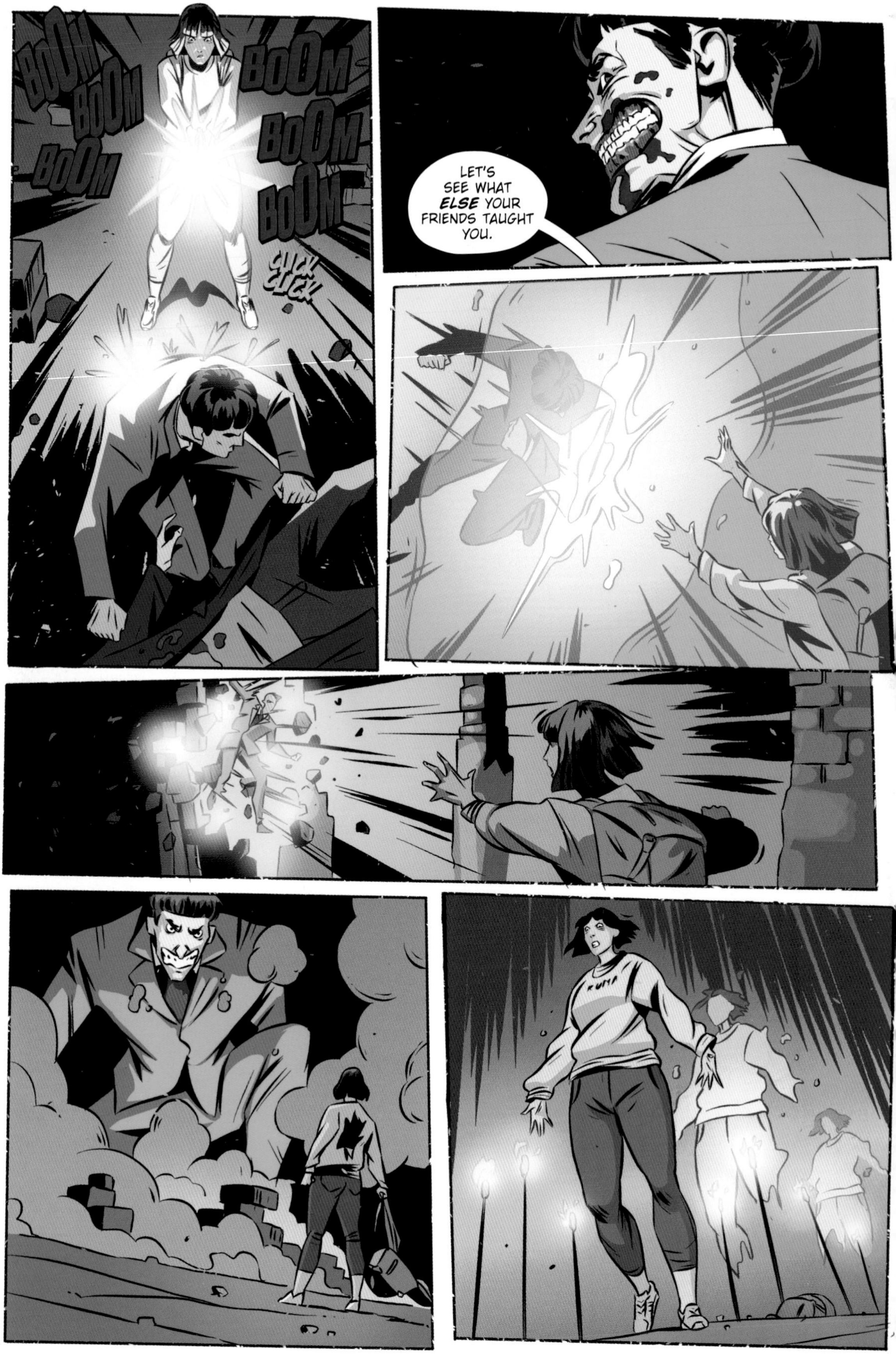
BOOM
BOOM
BOOM
BOOM
BOOM
BOOM
CLICK CLICK
LET'S SEE WHAT ELSE YOUR FRIENDS TAUGHT YOU.
RUMA

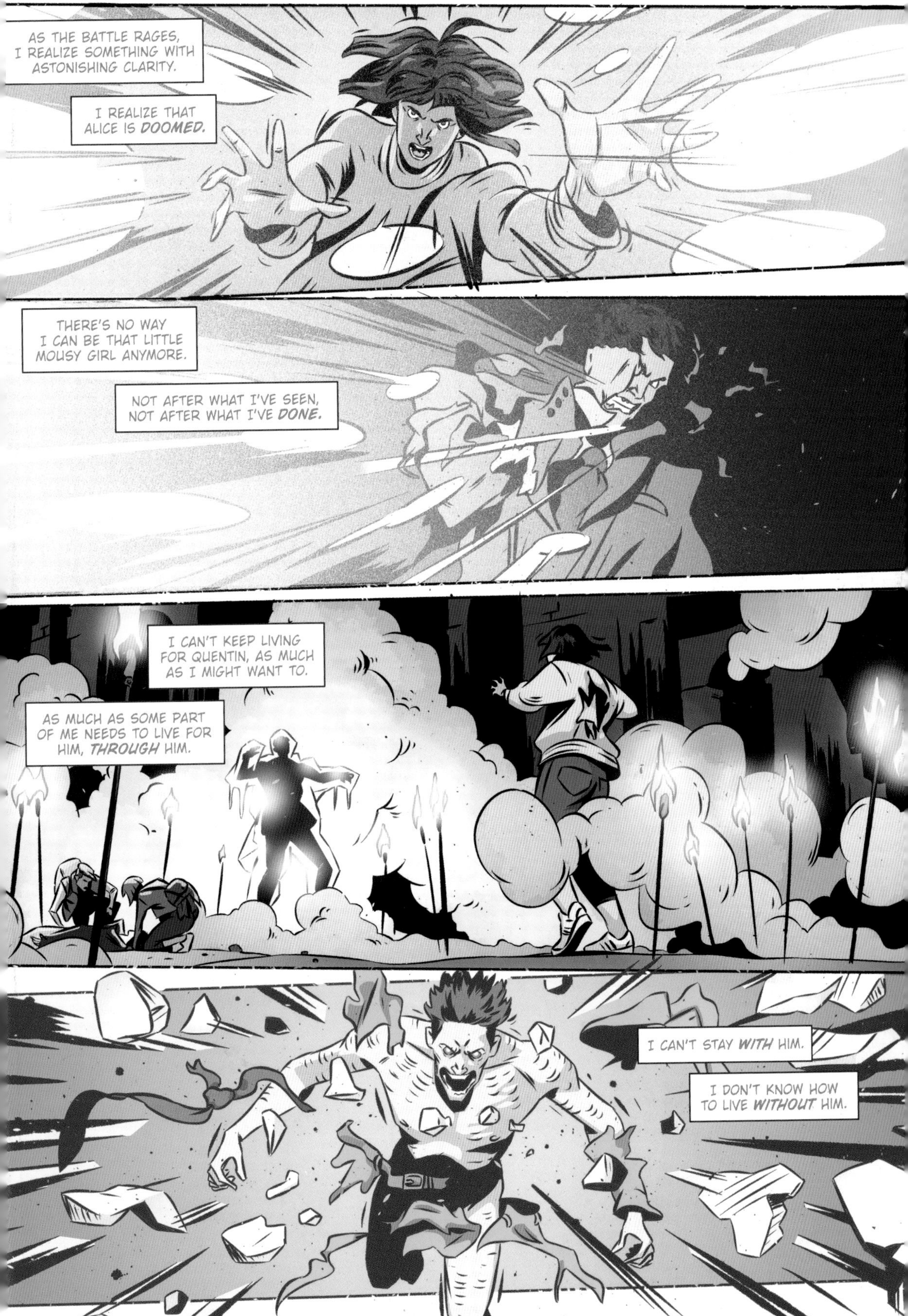
AS THE BATTLE RAGES, I REALIZE SOMETHING WITH ASTONISHING CLARITY.
I REALIZE THAT ALICE IS DOOMED.
THERE'S NO WAY I CAN BE THAT LITTLE MOUSY GIRL ANYMORE.
NOT AFTER WHAT I'VE SEEN, NOT AFTER WHAT I'VE DONE.
I CAN'T KEEP LIVING FOR QUENTIN, AS MUCH AS I MIGHT WANT TO.
AS MUCH AS SOME PART OF ME NEEDS TO LIVE FOR HIM, THROUGH HIM.
I CAN'T STAY WITH HIM.
I DON'T KNOW HOW TO LIVE WITHOUT HIM.

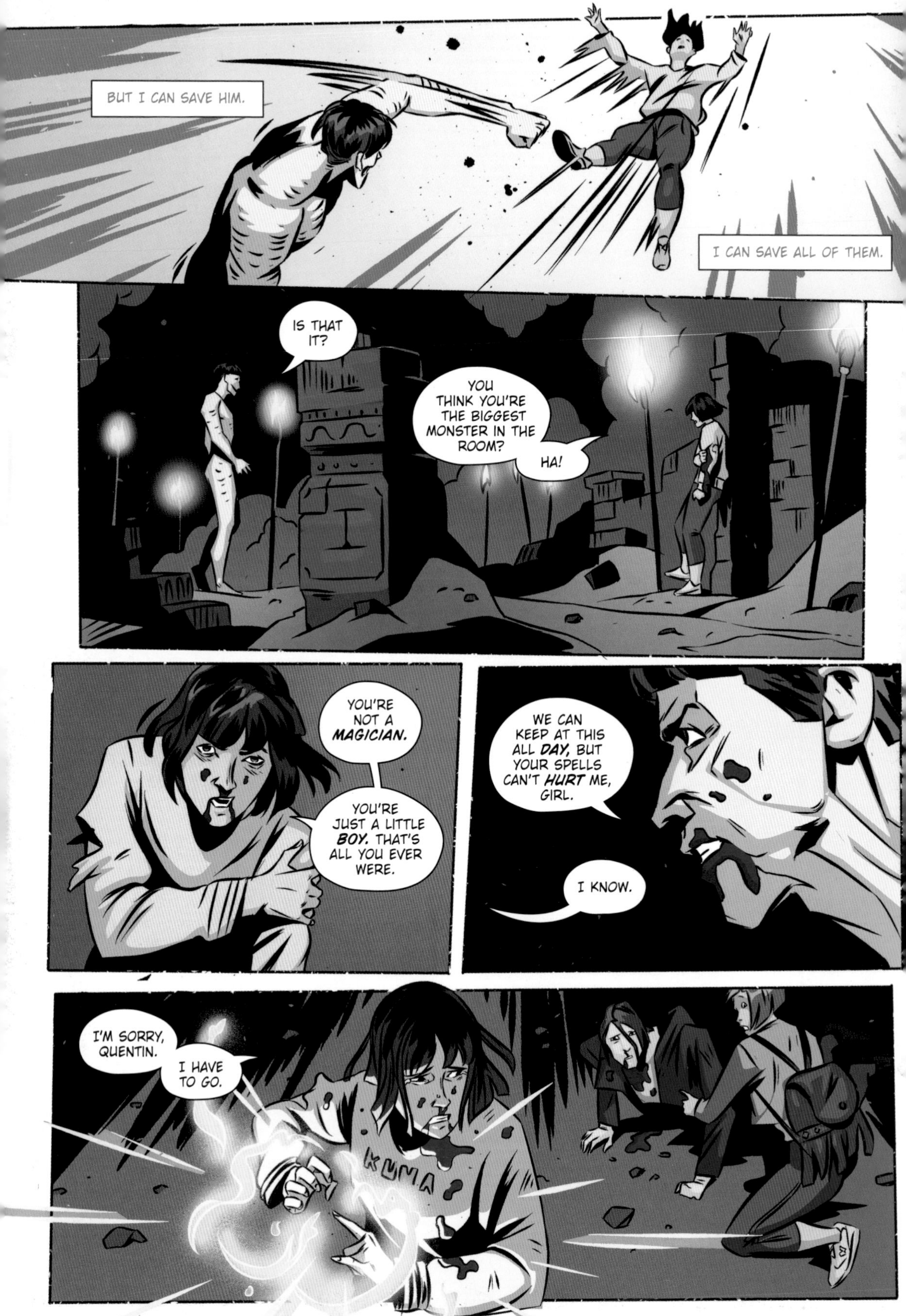
BUT I CAN SAVE HIM.
I CAN SAVE ALL OF THEM.
IS THAT IT?
YOU THINK YOU'RE THE BIGGEST MONSTER IN THE ROOM?
HA!
YOU'RE NOT A MAGICIAN.
YOU'RE JUST A LITTLE BOY. THAT'S ALL YOU EVER WERE.
WE CAN KEEP AT THIS ALL DAY, BUT YOUR SPELLS CAN'T HURT ME, GIRL.
I KNOW.
I'M SORRY, QUENTIN.
I HAVE TO GO.
KUMA

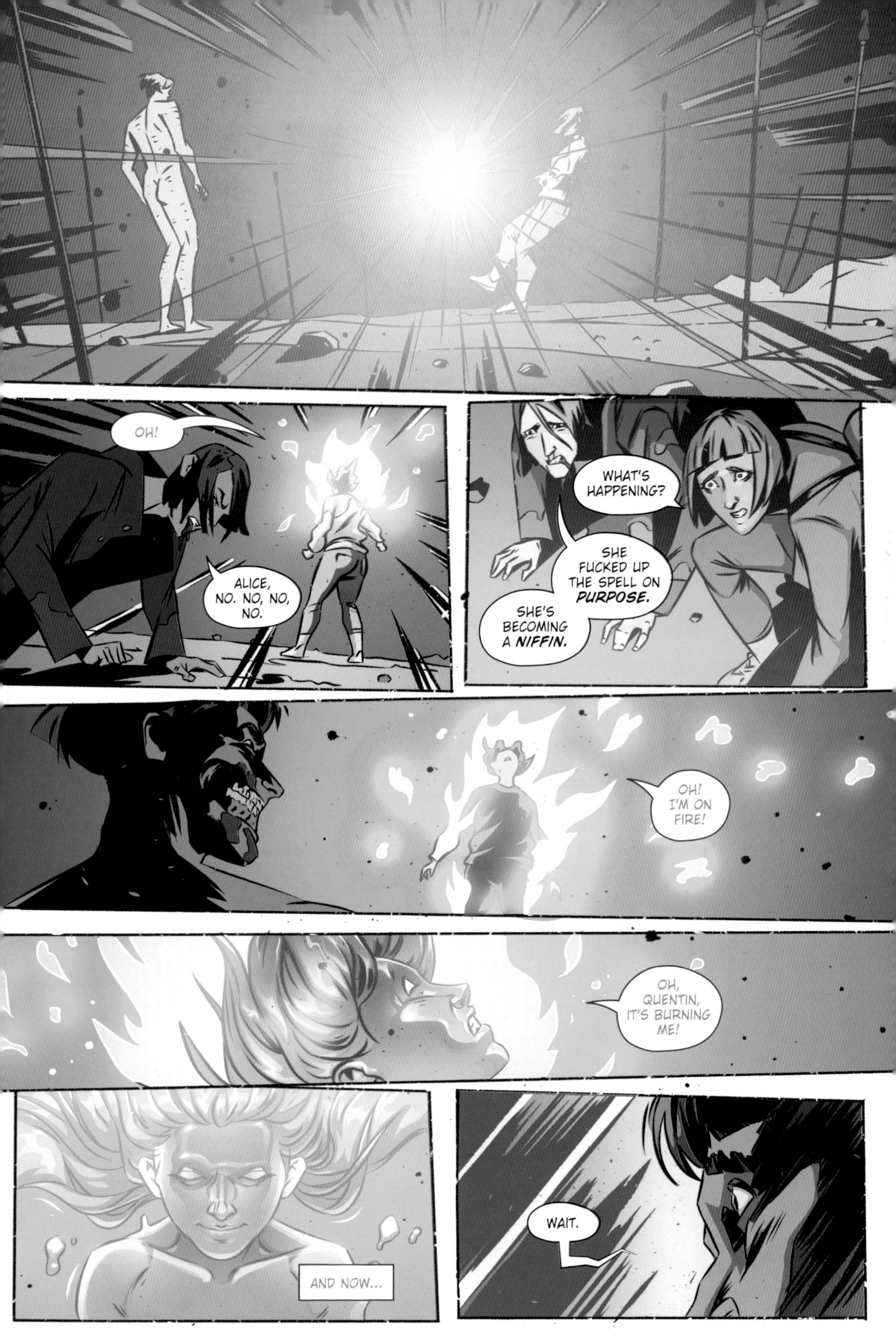

OH!
ALICE, NO. NO, NO, NO.
WHAT'S HAPPENING?
SHE FUCKED UP THE SPELL ON *PURPOSE.*
SHE'S BECOMING A *NIFFIN.*
OH! I'M ON FIRE!
OH, QUENTIN, IT'S BURNING ME!
AND NOW...
WAIT.

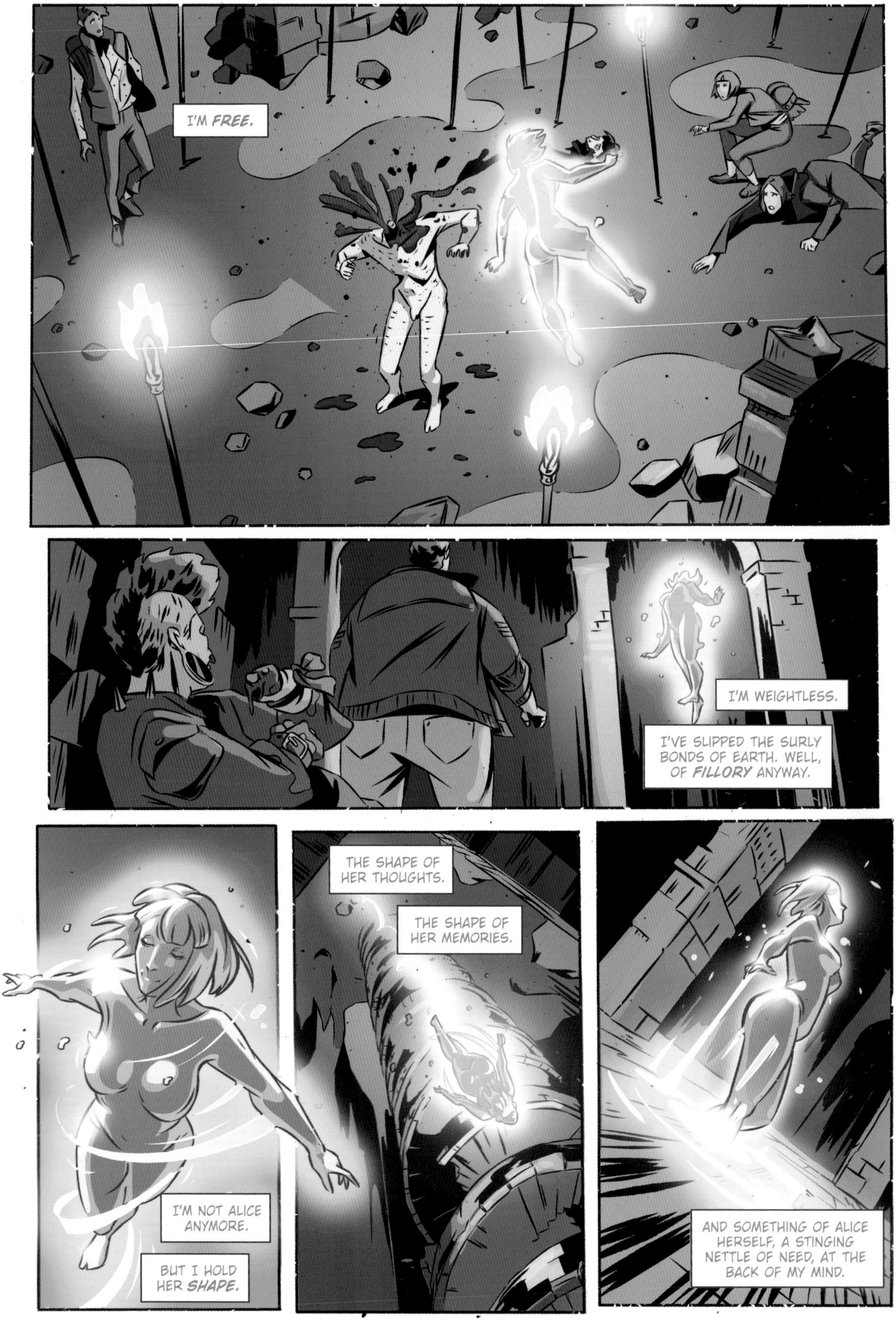
I'M FREE.
I'M WEIGHTLESS.
I'VE SLIPPED THE SURLY BONDS OF EARTH. WELL, OF FILLORY ANYWAY.
I'M NOT ALICE ANYMORE.
BUT I HOLD HER SHAPE.
THE SHAPE OF HER THOUGHTS.
THE SHAPE OF HER MEMORIES.
AND SOMETHING OF ALICE HERSELF, A STINGING NETTLE OF NEED, AT THE BACK OF MY MIND.

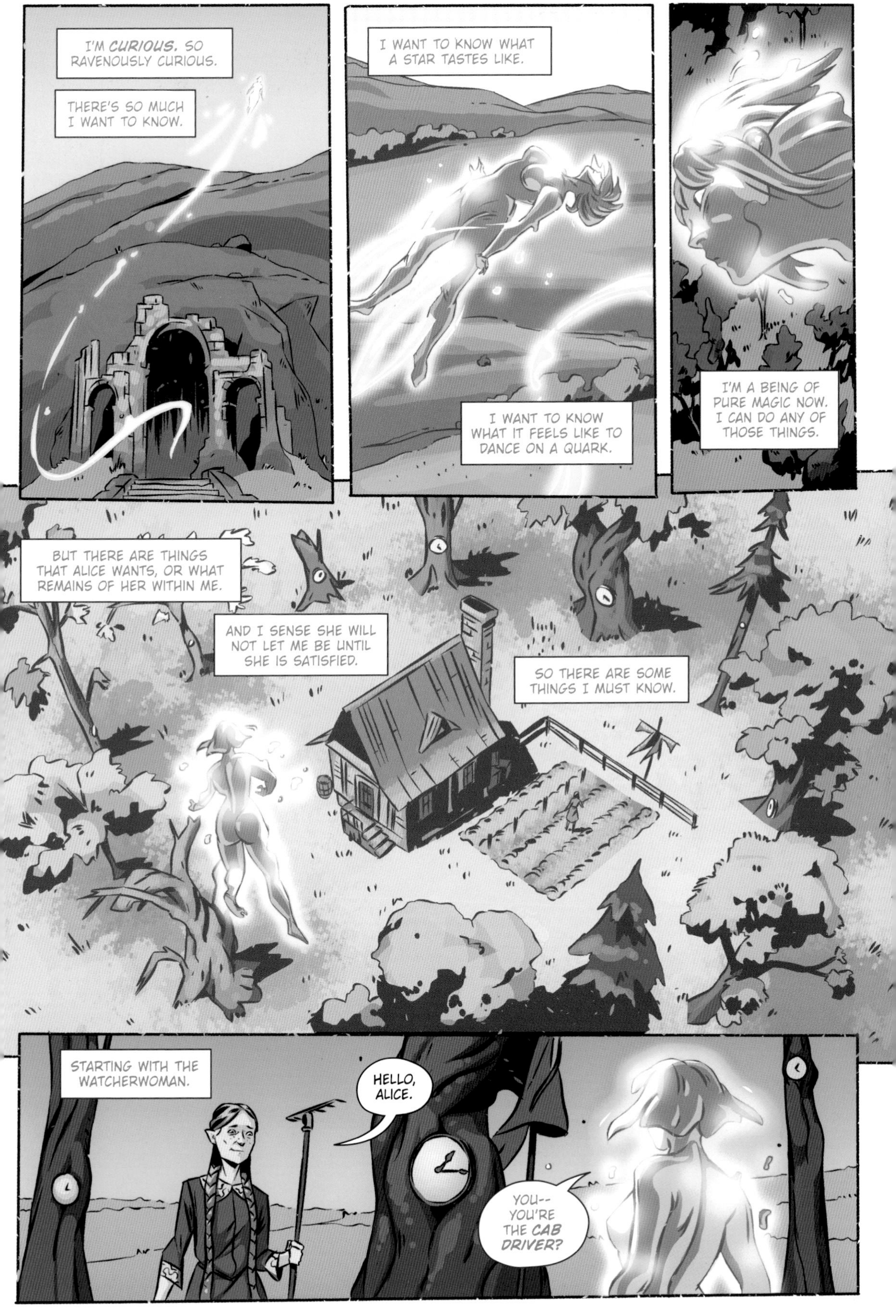
I'M *CURIOUS.* SO RAVENOUSLY CURIOUS.
THERE'S SO MUCH I WANT TO KNOW.
I WANT TO KNOW WHAT A STAR TASTES LIKE.
I WANT TO KNOW WHAT IT FEELS LIKE TO DANCE ON A QUARK.
I'M A BEING OF PURE MAGIC NOW. I CAN DO ANY OF THOSE THINGS.
BUT THERE ARE THINGS THAT ALICE WANTS, OR WHAT REMAINS OF HER WITHIN ME.
AND I SENSE SHE WILL NOT LET ME BE UNTIL SHE IS SATISFIED.
SO THERE ARE SOME THINGS I MUST KNOW.
STARTING WITH THE WATCHERWOMAN.
HELLO, ALICE.
YOU-- YOU'RE THE *CAB DRIVER?*

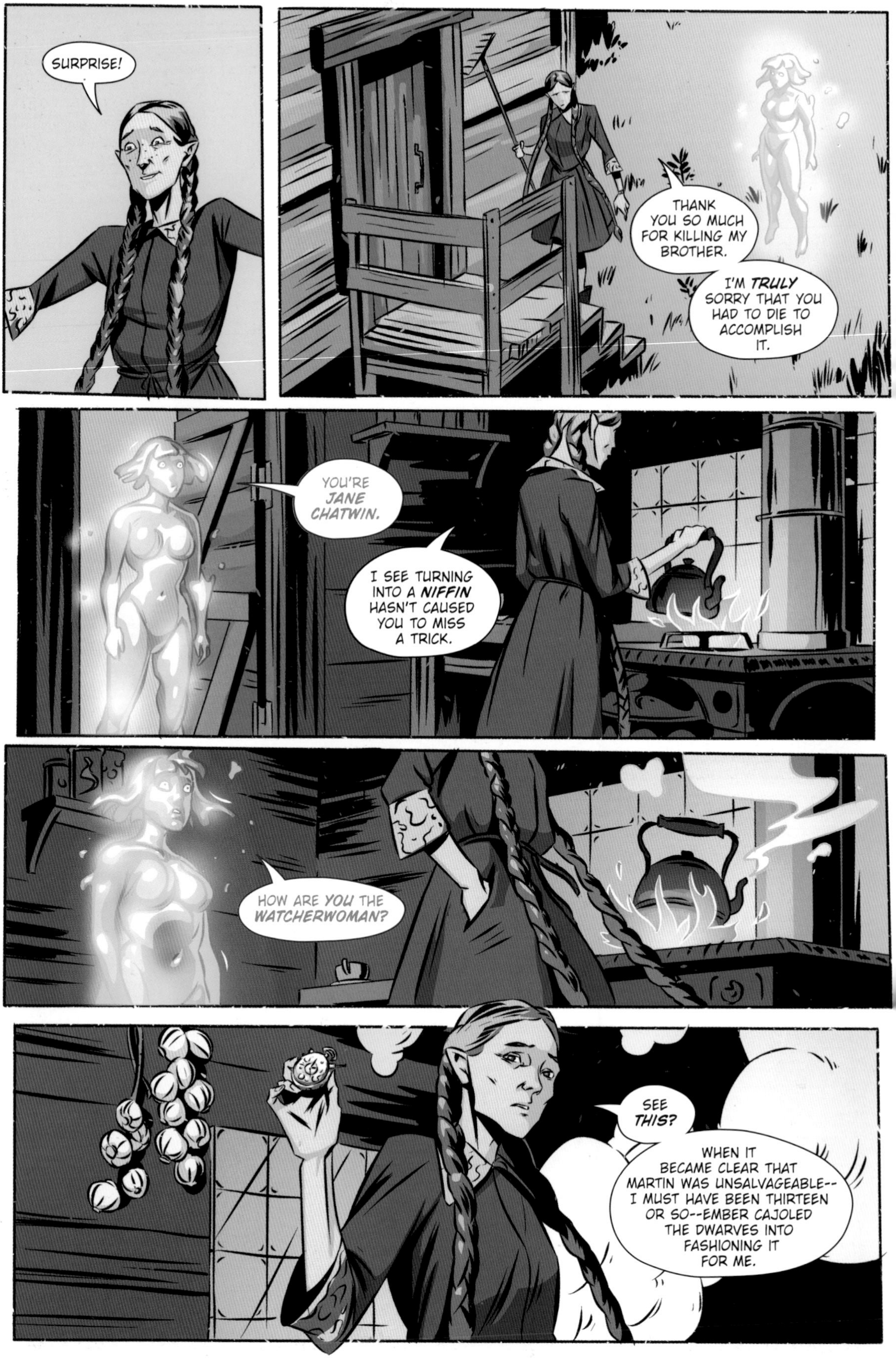

SURPRISE!
THANK YOU SO MUCH FOR KILLING MY BROTHER.
I'M **TRULY** SORRY THAT YOU HAD TO DIE TO ACCOMPLISH IT.
YOU'RE ***JANE CHATWIN.***
I SEE TURNING INTO A ***NIFFIN*** HASN'T CAUSED YOU TO MISS A TRICK.
HOW ARE *YOU* THE ***WATCHERWOMAN?***
SEE ***THIS?***
WHEN IT BECAME CLEAR THAT MARTIN WAS UNSALVAGEABLE--I MUST HAVE BEEN THIRTEEN OR SO--EMBER CAJOLED THE DWARVES INTO FASHIONING IT FOR ME.

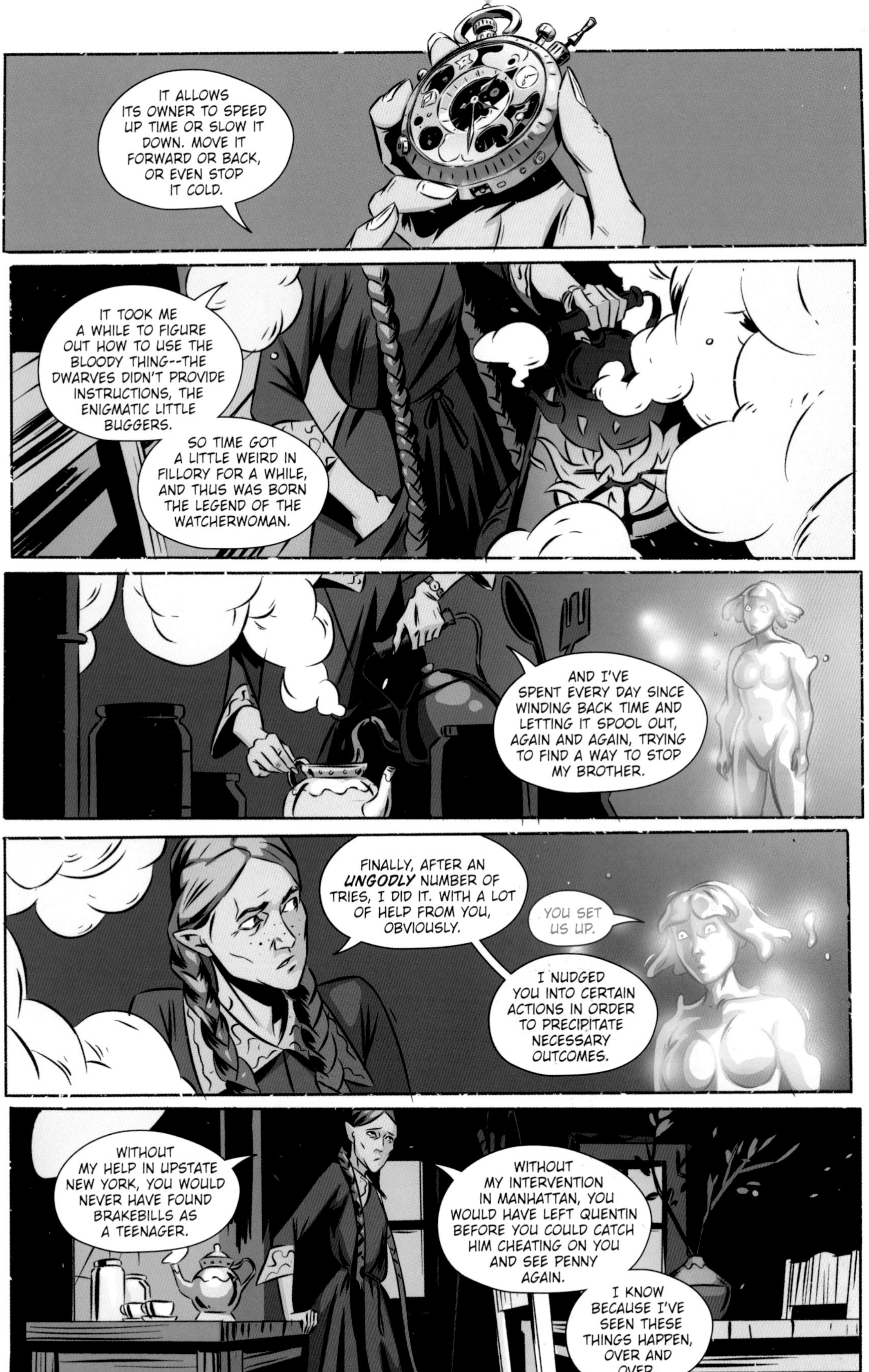
IT ALLOWS ITS OWNER TO SPEED UP TIME OR SLOW IT DOWN. MOVE IT FORWARD OR BACK, OR EVEN STOP IT COLD.
IT TOOK ME A WHILE TO FIGURE OUT HOW TO USE THE BLOODY THING--THE DWARVES DIDN'T PROVIDE INSTRUCTIONS, THE ENIGMATIC LITTLE BUGGERS.
SO TIME GOT A LITTLE WEIRD IN FILLORY FOR A WHILE, AND THUS WAS BORN THE LEGEND OF THE WATCHERWOMAN.
AND I'VE SPENT EVERY DAY SINCE WINDING BACK TIME AND LETTING IT SPOOL OUT, AGAIN AND AGAIN, TRYING TO FIND A WAY TO STOP MY BROTHER.
FINALLY, AFTER AN *UNGODLY* NUMBER OF TRIES, I DID IT. WITH A LOT OF HELP FROM YOU, OBVIOUSLY.
YOU SET US UP.
I NUDGED YOU INTO CERTAIN ACTIONS IN ORDER TO PRECIPITATE NECESSARY OUTCOMES.
WITHOUT MY HELP IN UPSTATE NEW YORK, YOU WOULD NEVER HAVE FOUND BRAKEBILLS AS A TEENAGER.
WITHOUT MY INTERVENTION IN MANHATTAN, YOU WOULD HAVE LEFT QUENTIN BEFORE YOU COULD CATCH HIM CHEATING ON YOU AND SEE PENNY AGAIN.
I KNOW BECAUSE I'VE SEEN THESE THINGS HAPPEN, OVER AND OVER.

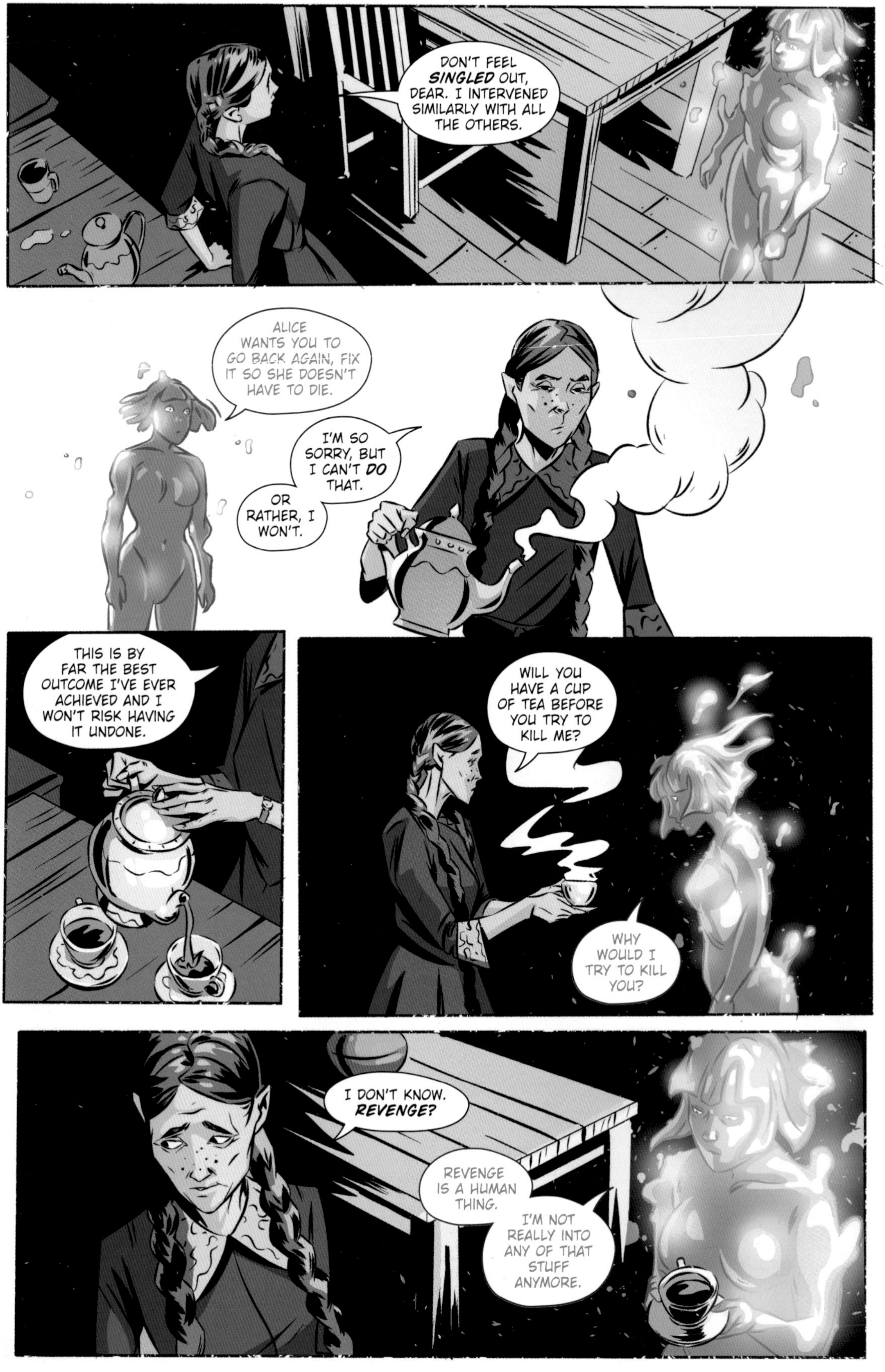

DON'T FEEL SINGLED OUT, DEAR. I INTERVENED SIMILARLY WITH ALL THE OTHERS.
ALICE WANTS YOU TO GO BACK AGAIN, FIX IT SO SHE DOESN'T HAVE TO DIE.
I'M SO SORRY, BUT I CAN'T DO THAT.
OR RATHER, I WON'T.
THIS IS BY FAR THE BEST OUTCOME I'VE EVER ACHIEVED AND I WON'T RISK HAVING IT UNDONE.
WILL YOU HAVE A CUP OF TEA BEFORE YOU TRY TO KILL ME?
WHY WOULD I TRY TO KILL YOU?
I DON'T KNOW. REVENGE?
REVENGE IS A HUMAN THING.
I'M NOT REALLY INTO ANY OF THAT STUFF ANYMORE.

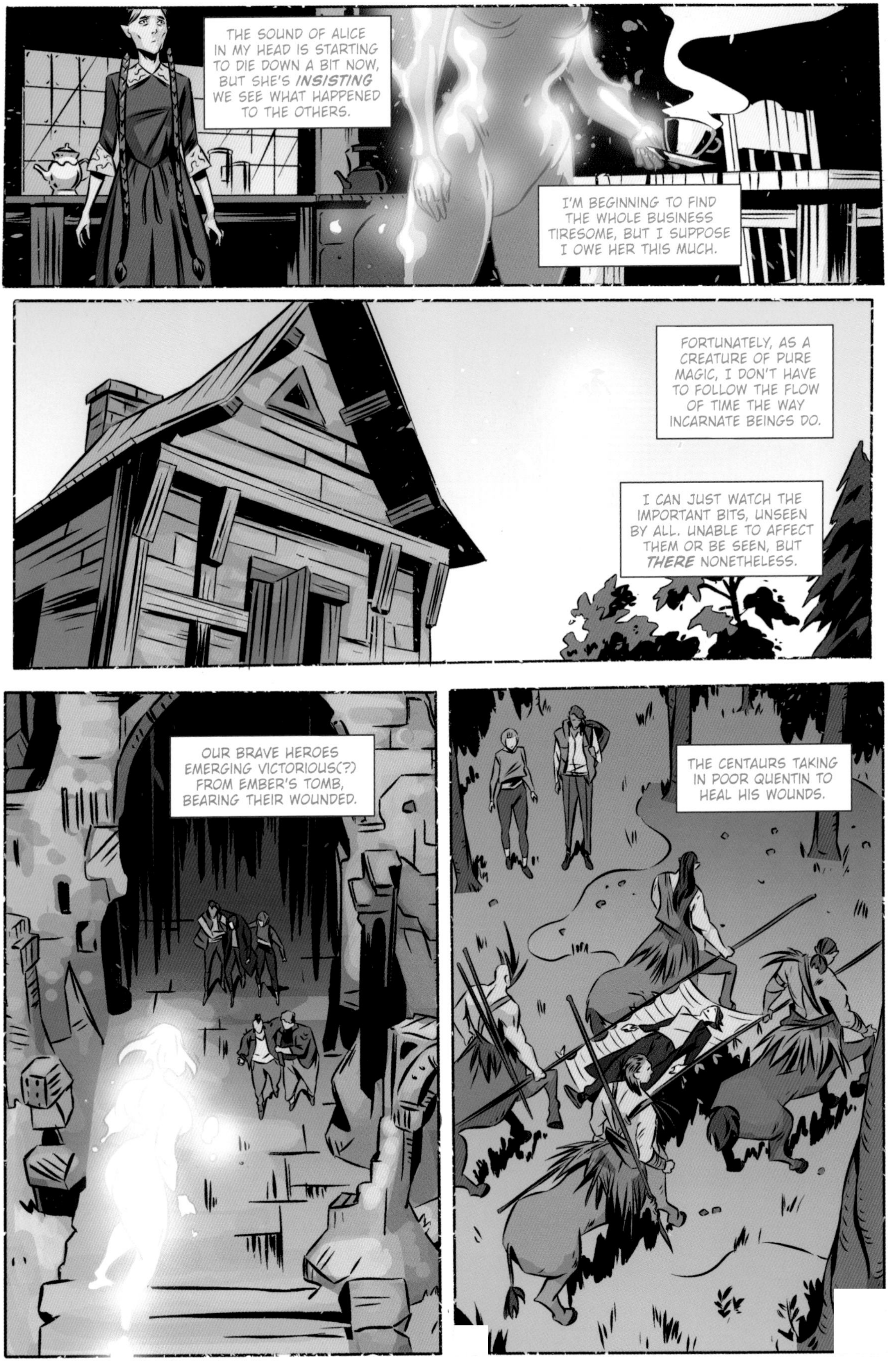
THE SOUND OF ALICE IN MY HEAD IS STARTING TO DIE DOWN A BIT NOW, BUT SHE'S *INSISTING* WE SEE WHAT HAPPENED TO THE OTHERS.
I'M BEGINNING TO FIND THE WHOLE BUSINESS TIRESOME, BUT I SUPPOSE I OWE HER THIS MUCH.
FORTUNATELY, AS A CREATURE OF PURE MAGIC, I DON'T HAVE TO FOLLOW THE FLOW OF TIME THE WAY INCARNATE BEINGS DO.
I CAN JUST WATCH THE IMPORTANT BITS, UNSEEN BY ALL. UNABLE TO AFFECT THEM OR BE SEEN, BUT *THERE* NONETHELESS.
OUR BRAVE HEROES EMERGING VICTORIOUS(?) FROM EMBER'S TOMB, BEARING THEIR WOUNDED.
THE CENTAURS TAKING IN POOR QUENTIN TO HEAL HIS WOUNDS.

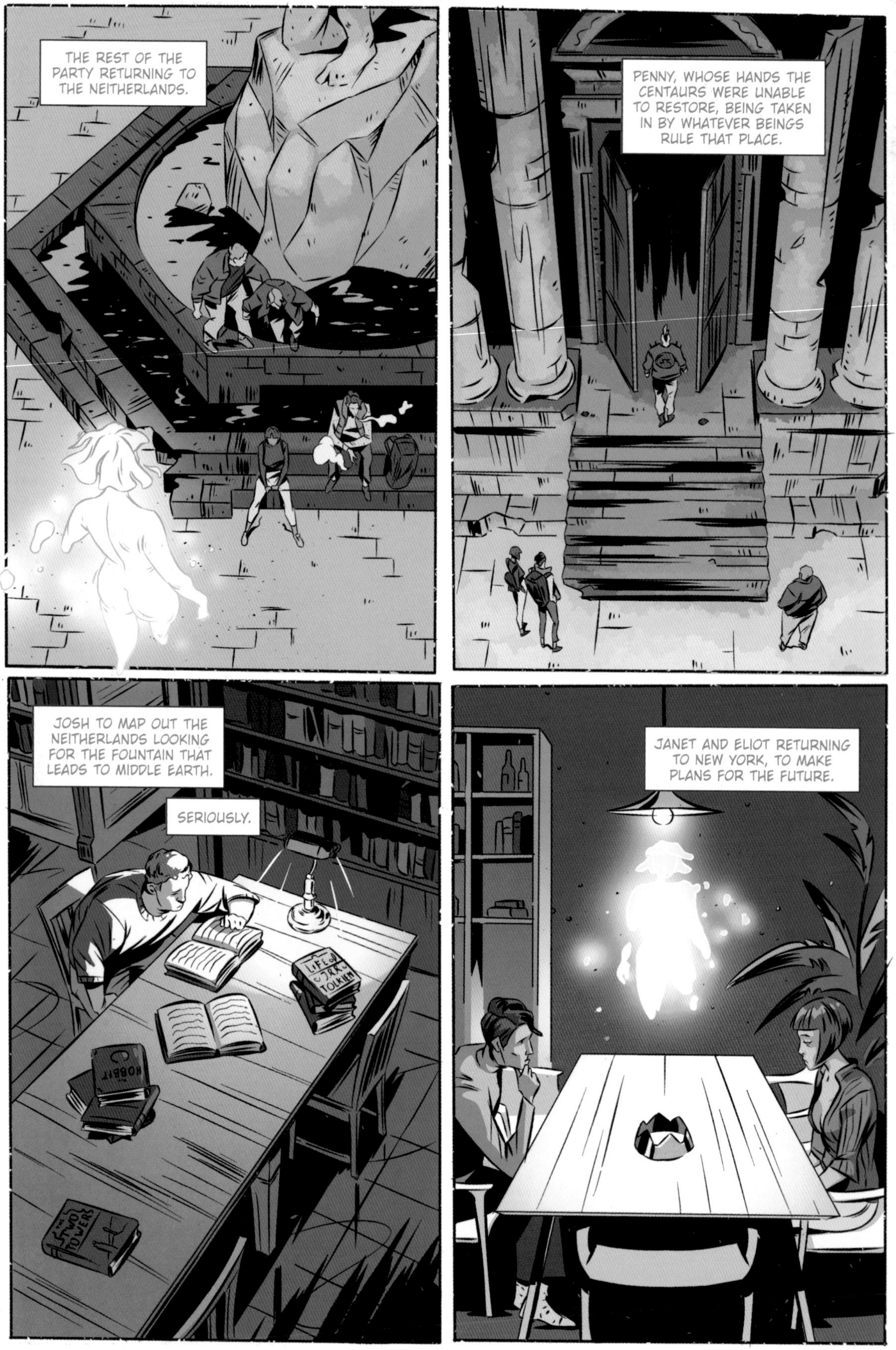
THE REST OF THE PARTY RETURNING TO THE NEITHERLANDS.
PENNY, WHOSE HANDS THE CENTAURS WERE UNABLE TO RESTORE, BEING TAKEN IN BY WHATEVER BEINGS RULE THAT PLACE.
JOSH TO MAP OUT THE NEITHERLANDS LOOKING FOR THE FOUNTAIN THAT LEADS TO MIDDLE EARTH.
SERIOUSLY.
LIFE OF JRR TOLKIEN
HOBBIT
TWO TOWERS
JANET AND ELIOT RETURNING TO NEW YORK, TO MAKE PLANS FOR THE FUTURE.

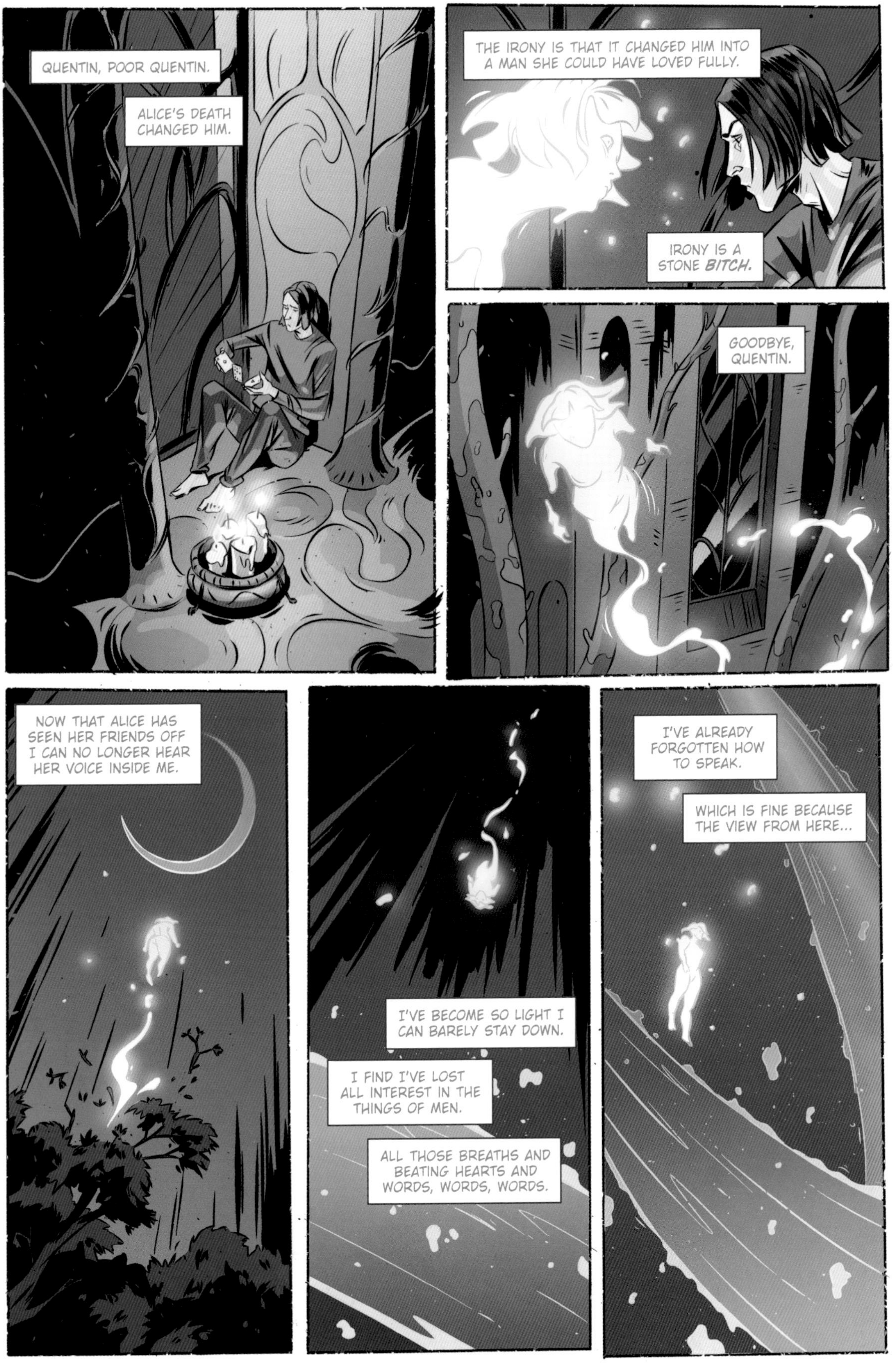
QUENTIN, POOR QUENTIN.
ALICE'S DEATH CHANGED HIM.
THE IRONY IS THAT IT CHANGED HIM INTO A MAN SHE COULD HAVE LOVED FULLY.
IRONY IS A STONE BITCH.
GOODBYE, QUENTIN.
NOW THAT ALICE HAS SEEN HER FRIENDS OFF I CAN NO LONGER HEAR HER VOICE INSIDE ME.
I'VE BECOME SO LIGHT I CAN BARELY STAY DOWN.
I FIND I'VE LOST ALL INTEREST IN THE THINGS OF MEN.
ALL THOSE BREATHS AND BEATING HEARTS AND WORDS, WORDS, WORDS.
I'VE ALREADY FORGOTTEN HOW TO SPEAK.
WHICH IS FINE BECAUSE THE VIEW FROM HERE...

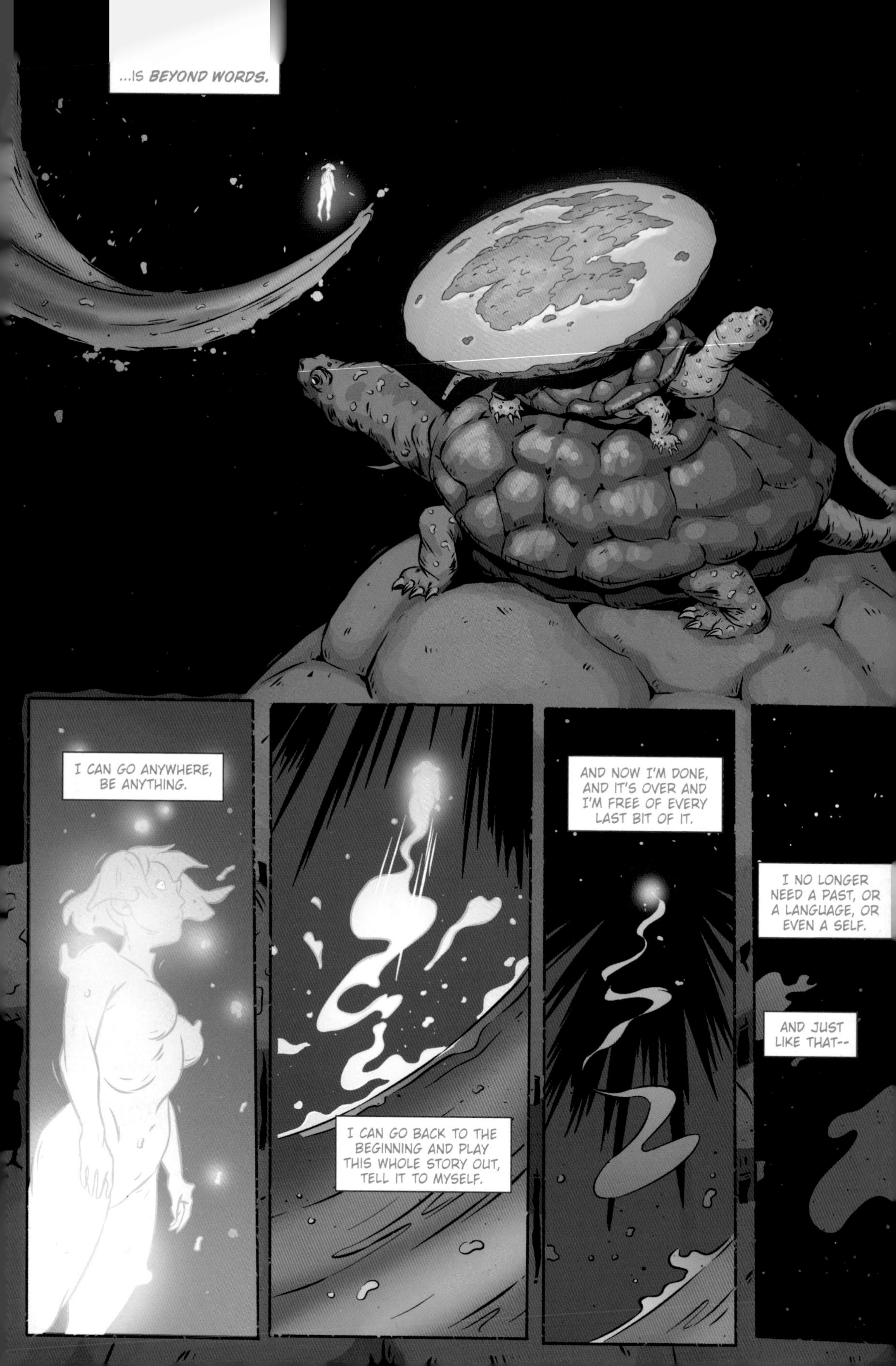
...IS BEYOND WORDS.
I CAN GO ANYWHERE, BE ANYTHING.
I CAN GO BACK TO THE BEGINNING AND PLAY THIS WHOLE STORY OUT, TELL IT TO MYSELF.
AND NOW I'M DONE, AND IT'S OVER AND I'M FREE OF EVERY LAST BIT OF IT.
I NO LONGER NEED A PAST, OR A LANGUAGE, OR EVEN A SELF.
AND JUST LIKE THAT--

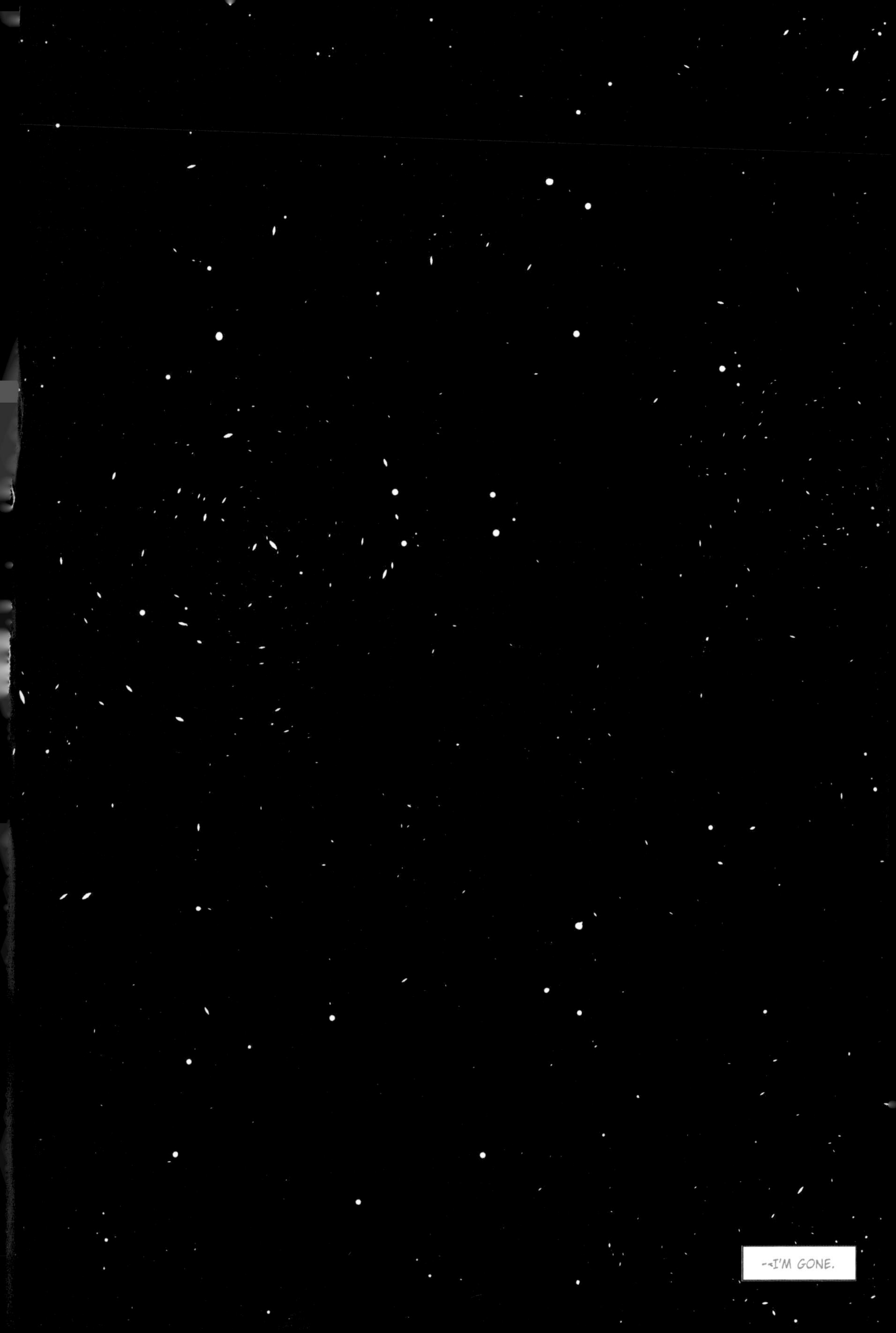
--I'M GONE.